THE PRESIDENTS ON
THE PRESIDENCY

THE
PRESIDENTS
ON THE
PRESIDENCY

ARTHUR BERNON TOURTELLOT

NEW YORK / RUSSELL & RUSSELL

ACKNOWLEDGMENTS

The author is indebted to Judge Samuel I. Rosenman and to Fred Friendly, for courtesies in the clearing of material for this book, to Judge Rosenman for the quotation, from his absorbing *Working with Roosevelt*, in the Introduction, to Dr. Allan Nevins for permission to use quotes from *Grover Cleveland: A Study in Courage*, and to the Columbia Broadcasting System, Inc. for CBS Reports' "Eisenhower on The Presidency."

Helen M. Brown was of great help in tracking down some of the source documents, as was Miss Lee Szilagyi of Senator Claiborne Pell's staff in the case of the letters of President Tyler. Nellie White Nelson was most helpful in preparing the manuscript.

Grateful acknowledgment is made to the following for permission to use copyrighted material:

Columbia University Press—*Our Chief Magistrate and His Powers* by William Howard Taft. Columbia University Press, 1925. Reprinted by permission of the publisher.

John Coolidge—*The Autobiography of Calvin Coolidge*. Cosmopolitan Book Corporation, 1929. Reprinted by permission of John Coolidge.

Harvard University Press—*The Letters of Theodore Roosevelt*, edited by Elting E. Morison. Copyright 1951, 1952, 1954 by The President and Fellows of Harvard College. Reprinted by permission of Harvard University Press.

The Macmillian Company—*The Memoirs of Herbert Hoover: The Cabinet and the Presidency, 1920–1933* by Herbert Hoover. Copyright 1951, 1952 by Herbert Hoover. Reprinted by permission of The Macmillan Company.

Charles Scribner's Sons—*The Autobiography of Theodore Roosevelt*. Copyright 1913 by Charles Scribner's Sons; renewal copyright 1941 by Edith K. Carow Roosevelt. Reprinted by permission of the publisher.

Time, Inc.—*Year of Decisions, Memoirs* by Harry S Truman—Volume 1. Copyright © 1955 by Time, Inc., and *Years of Trial and Hope, Memoirs* by Harry S Truman—Volume 2. Copyright © 1956 by Time, Inc. Published by Doubleday & Company, Inc., and reprinted by permission of Time, Inc.

A.B.T.

For
JONATHAN BERNON
and
CHRISTOPHER TRAYNE

FOREWORD

The American presidency has often been referred to as the most powerful democratic office on earth. The extent and nature of its powers and responsibilities have been the subject of much of our civil history. The role of the presidency has been the object of both judicial and legislative, and occasionally even of popular, attack. Presidential leadership has staked out the broad avenues of the national development of the United States and has been its most powerful and most articulate influence in world affairs. The public opinion forming force of the presidency is swift and vast. "That part of the government," wrote Woodrow Wilson, many years before he held public office, "which has the most direct access to opinion has the best chance of leadership and mastery; at present [Wilson was writing during Theodore Roosevelt's administration] that part is the President."

The bibliography of the presidency is constantly growing and at an accelerated pace. There are, nevertheless, some basic omissions. In an extensive inquiry into the interplay of the presidency and public opinion, which is still in progress, I have felt particularly the lack of a central source of the views of the office held by the Presidents themselves. This volume seeks to present those views as they were phrased by the Presidents either while holding office or in retrospect afterward. It does not include their appraisals of the presidency or comments on it before holding the office, because the value of the presidential estimates of the presidency attaches to their uniqueness as the expressions of men given the opportunity for special insight into the office and direct experience in carrying out its functions.

This stricture has led to some situations that may at first glance seem surprising. Madison and Wilson, for example, who wrote at length about the office before holding it, are represented by far fewer observations than Polk and Truman, both of whom wrote more about it, in the first case, during his tenure and, in the second, after holding office. From the time of Buchanan, whose whole postpresidential life was devoted to justifying his lack of action on the simmering rebellion that led to the Civil War, it has become a tradition for ex-Presidents to write explanatory works on their administrations. Few of these are as sparse as Coolidge's, few as exuberant as Theodore Roosevelt's or Truman's. Among the post-Civil War Presidents, surviving their terms, only four refrained from writing about the problems during their administrations: Johnson, Grant (who prudently limited his best-selling *Personal Memoirs* to his military years), Arthur, and Wilson, who never sufficiently recovered from the paralytic illness that struck him in his second term. Hoover, alone among the Presidents, wrote a biographical work on a predecessor after himself leaving office—the sympathetic but limited *The Ordeal of Woodrow Wilson.*

I have tried to omit presidential references to the office that were limited in their relevance to a single event; but I include comments on such events when there were implicit, in the comments, views of the office and its powers that went beyond the immediate occasion giving rise to the comments.

I have been somewhat arbitrary in classifying the excerpts in this book under eleven headings, some of which necessarily tend to overlap, and also in determining the order in which those classifications appear. However, the reader will detect some reason for the latter. Selections, as a rule, have been arranged chronologically within sections. Notes have been added, directly following excerpts, only when necessary for clarification. Most excerpts are self-explanatory.

There is, in addition to a general introduction on the writings of the Presidents, an introduction to each of the eleven sections, based to some extent on my discussion of various aspects of the presidency in *An Anatomy of American Politics.*

It will be noted that certain aspects of the office have been more commonly discussed than others by the Presidents, and that these have changed to some extent over the history of the presidency. Most conspicuous are the degrees to which Presidents have been concerned with the legislative role of the office and its relationship, frequently contentious, with the Congress, and with the appointive and removal powers. Until the Hayes reforms, the appointive function was the cause of bitter and justified complaints by nearly all the Presidents, while before then reform as such seems to have been regarded as an inherent duty of the office only by Jackson. Some Presidents commented little on the office and some at great length. Presidents who long survived their terms usually wrote at far greater length and frequency than those who had less time for second thoughts and reflection.

Broadly speaking, all presidential views of the office fall within either the Whig doctrine of a passive, custodial executive or the opposite view of active, creative leadership—but even the more passive Presidents took vigorous opposition, in many instances, to legislative or judicial moves to diminish the presidency. In all cases, the personality of the President as an individual, far more than party philosophies and often more than historic forces, has governed most clearly and directly both his concept and his use of the office.

Everyone is familiar with Charles Evans Hughes's comment on the Constitution, "We live under a Constitution, but the Constitution is what the judges say it is." It may be similarly said that we live under a presidency, but the presidency is what the President thinks it is. And what he thought of it has more often than not been the measure of a President's achievement in the office. Historically effective Presidents, those who tended to master the events of their time, have taken a strong and affirmative view of the presidency. The less effective Presidents, those who have tended to be controlled and limited by the events of their time, have taken a restrained and narrow view of the office.

The Presidents' views of the presidency incline toward any one of these four concepts: the two strong theories of vigorous, independent presidential leadership—one based on thoughtful conviction, as in the cases of Washington and Lincoln, and the other based on political improvisation, as exemplified by Jackson and

Franklin Roosevelt; and the two weak theories of a passive, limited presidential role—one based on Congressional supremacy and the other on states' rights.

The language of the Constitution was purposely general about the functions of the presidency. The founding fathers implied rather than stated its powers, partly because the delegates to the Constitutional Convention of 1787 were sure that Washington, who presided over its deliberations, would be the first President and they wanted to leave the specific nature of the office to his shaping, and partly because the bad example of the "cipher" governors of most of the colonial states made the delegates fearful of rendering the office too weak by restricting its powers and duties through the use of too specific language. Even the language of the prescribed presidential oath was vague, requiring only that the incoming President "will faithfully execute the office of President of the United States" and "to the best of my ability preserve, protect and defend the Constitution of the United States." There was not a word of what he should refrain from doing nor was there any literal pledge that he would even obey, much less enforce, the statutes. As a matter of fact, shortly after his first inauguration, Abraham Lincoln violated an article of the Constitution itself and said afterward that circumstances forced him to do so if he were to preserve the Constitution as a whole: ". . . would not the official oath be broken if the government should be overthrown, when it was believed that disregarding the single law would tend to preserve it?"

Indeed, on only three points was the language of the Constitution specific with regard to the presidency. It fixed the term definitely at four years; but it did not restrict the number of terms, and Jefferson could write to Adams of the office, "Their [the Constitution-makers'] President seems a bad edition of a Polish king. He may be elected from four years to four years to life." It empowered the President to grant pardons or reprieves for any federal offenses, excluding only cases of impeachment; but it put no qualification on the power, and any President so minded could empty every federal prison by a stroke of his pen. It made the President "Commander in Chief of the Army and

Navy of the United States," but did nothing to hinder him from going out to lead the Army in the field or the fleet at sea, however incompetent militarily he might be, or to help him have general officers solely of his own choosing—a failure that gave Madison some trouble during the War of 1812, and Polk much during the Mexican War.

At the same time, the drafters of the Constitution, after a good deal of discussion, were careful to plant in that document the seeds of the implied powers of the presidency, and it is from these that the strong Presidents nurtured the office along three major courses of development: as the nation's instrument for the conduct of foreign relations, as its central agency for the administration of domestic affairs, and as its leader in initiating legislative action. These great functions were all developed, however, from what appear on the surface to be minor provisions of the Constitution.

The nature of the American presidency was thus left open to its incumbent's appraisal of the office. In a very literal sense and to an extent true of no other office, therefore, a presidential election is a vote for or against the man who aspires to it, even when partisan philosophies of the role of the presidency are considered. Woodrow Wilson wrote long before he held the office: "The President is at liberty, both in law and in conscience, to be as big a man as he can. His capacity will set the limit. . . ." The variety of that capacity, including particularly a President's grasp of the potentialities of the office, is the substance of the history of the American presidency and has almost alone determined its real dimensions. (It is for this reason—the confrontation of personalities as much as of issues—that the presidential debates of 1960 may well turn out to be the most significant development in the election of Presidents since public opinion forced abandonment of the choice of presidential electors by state legislators in favor of direct popular choice.) A most revealing key to this variety of presidential concepts of the presidency is in the writings of the Presidents themselves.

I have sought out every likely source of comment on the presidency in presidential writings—messages to the Congress, speeches, letters, diaries, interviews when reported verbatim, autobiographies, essays, lectures, memoirs, other books, and occasional writings. Indirect quotations and paraphrasings have been omitted. I am sure that much material has escaped my attention and would hope to add any of significance to future editions. But my purpose has been to make the book comprehensive rather than inclusive.

Arthur Bernon Tourtellot

Wilton, Connecticut
July twenty-third, 1963.

POSTSCRIPT

After the type was set on this book, but before it was printed, President John F. Kennedy was assassinated. Although I had included observations on the presidency made by him before taking office, I had omitted consideration of his record, because it was incomplete, from the introductory essays. I have, therefore, added a note on Kennedy as President and writer; and any factual changes necessitated throughout the book by the accession of a thirty-fifth man to the office have been made.

A.B.T.

New York, N.Y.
December tenth, 1963

CONTENTS

INTRODUCTION: THE PRESIDENTS AS WRITERS   1

I   THE PRESIDENT AS NATIONAL LEADER   16

II   THE PRESIDENT AS ADMINISTRATOR   73

III   THE APPOINTIVE AND REMOVAL POWER   135

IV   THE PRESIDENCY AND THE CONGRESS   181

V   THE PRESIDENCY AND THE JUDICIARY   264

VI   THE PRESIDENCY AND FOREIGN RELATIONS   272

VII   THE PRESIDENT AS COMMANDER IN CHIEF   309

VIII   THE BURDENS AND PRIVILEGES OF THE PRESIDENCY   345

IX   THE PRESIDENT AND PARTY POLITICS   375

X   THE PRESIDENT AS REFORMER   395

XI   LIMITATIONS OF THE PRESIDENCY   406

A NOTE ON KENNEDY AS PRESIDENT AND WRITER   431

NOTES AND SOURCES   441

A BIBLIOGRAPHY OF PRESIDENTIAL WRITINGS   471

INDICES: BY AUTHOR   489

       BY SUBJECT   497

THE PRESIDENTS ON
THE PRESIDENCY

THE PRESIDENTS AS WRITERS

The great bulk of the writings of the Presidents are, of course, their public papers—inaugurals and other ceremonial speeches, messages to Congress, executive orders, campaign talks, proclamations. There has been soaring eloquence, as in the cases of Lincoln, easily the most gifted literary talent among the Presidents, and of the mystical homiletics of Wilson. But there have also been examples, in abundance, of the most routine drabness. They have all, however, borne the unmistakable imprint of their authors.

It is true, of course, that many Presidents have had literary assistance and that many more would have benefited from it. This in no way detracts from their responsibility for their papers. John Quincy Adams was, in the strictest sense, the author of the Monroe Doctrine, but it is nevertheless Monroe's instrument, and it was he who assumed responsibility for it, who adopted the language as his own and who, as an act of creative and foresighted statesmanship, saw its historic relevance and timeliness. It is impossible for any student of presidential writings to conclude that any man ever imposed the personality of his own writings upon a President. Both Madison and Hamilton wrote paragraphs for Washington's Farewell Address.[1] Madison furnished ten paragraphs as early as 1792, which were written for the end of Washington's first term, if he had seen fit to retire then, and which Washington told Hamilton four years later he would still like to use. Hamilton, in 1796, sent Washington two drafts, one in August and one in September. But Washington, like all Presidents who used writing aid, knew what he wanted and had his own standards of style: he wanted his own suggested version "curtailed, if too verbose; and relieved of all tautology, not necessary to enforce the ideas in the original or quoted part. My wish is that the whole may appear in a plain stile; and be handed to the public in an honest; unaffected; simple garb."[2] Washington had the allegiance of most eighteenth-century men to the written word, and he wrote voluminously though without great felicity or feeling, except when he was writing of nature. But his sharp and sure insight extended to communication, to style as well as to substance, and the speeches of Washington all reflect his character and his values.

The historic Nullification Proclamation of Jackson, also one of the great papers of American history, was the drafting work primarily of Edward Livingston, but it is charged throughout with the spirit and tenacity of Andrew Jackson. Daniel Webster assumed that it was his duty to compose the heavy utterances of Whig Presidents and took it amiss that the venerable Harrison did not wholly accept his prescribed text. The historian Bancroft wrote Andrew Johnson's first message to Congress, and Seward drafted many of his later papers. Cleveland had the literary assistance of Richard Olney, and McKinley that of John Hay. But none of these men delegated the content or the responsibility or even the style of their speeches, which in all cases bore clear evidence of the presidential personalities involved. Harry Truman has summarized very well the relationship of a President to his writings: "All presidential messages must begin with the President himself. He must decide what he wants to say and how he wants to say it. Many drafts are usually drawn up. . . . The final version, however, is the final word of the President himself, expressing his own convictions and his policy. These he cannot delegate to any man if he would be President in his own right."[3]

Judge Samuel I. Rosenman, who saw clearly the degree to which "what he said and wrote in his public life"[4] was the measure of a President, and who had the longest and probably the most productive literary relationship of any man to a President of the United States, has described Franklin Roosevelt's speechwriting method: "The speeches as finally delivered were his— and his alone—no matter who the collaborators were. He had gone over every point, every word, time and again. He had studied, reviewed, and read aloud each draft, and had changed it again and again, either in his own handwriting, by dictating inserts, or making deletions."[5] This is remarkably akin to a reconstruction of the writing of the Farewell Address as derived from the Washington, Hamilton, and Madison papers.

Some presidential state papers are notable sources for reflections of the Presidents on such specific constitutional aspects of the presidency as the veto power and the powers of appointment and removal. Franklin Pierce's veto messages, for example, constitute a thoughtful rationale of his position that illumines the whole history of the period of Congressional dominance; and even the interminable inaugural of William Henry Harrison is a valuable and able exposition of the Whig theory of the presidency. James Monroe's papers reveal him as an admirable reporter. Jefferson's philosophic bent, Tyler's solitary integrity, Lincoln's vast perspective, Johnson's angry temperament, Grant's earnest incompetence, Theodore Roosevelt's political evangelism, Wilson's Calvinist straining, Franklin Roosevelt's buoyant improvising—all such essential traits of the men and their administrations show through their presidential writings. Harding's limitations and the uneasy groping of his short administration were fully apparent in his confused and at times completely incoherent inaugural address: of the League of Nations, "There was ample discussion, and there is a public mandate in manifest understanding";[6] of world trade, "We have not strengthened ours in accordance with our resources or genius, notably on our own continent, where a galaxy of Republics reflects the glory of New-World democracy, but in the new order of finance and trade we mean to promote enlarged activities and seek expanded confidence";[7] of world peace and industrial peace, "We have mistaken unpreparedness to embrace it to be a challenge of the reality, and due concern for making all citizens fit for participation will give added strength of citizenship and magnify our achievement."[8] There is no need to linger over the vacuous, intricate illiteracies of Harding, the only professional journalist to occupy the presidential office, any longer than to note that among the other thirty-four men who became President, there is not a single example of comparable meaninglessness.

This is not to say that literary competence or profound thought stands out in all presidential writings. But the quality of the latter is surprisingly high over an extraordinary range of writing. Many of the Presidents were "literary" men long before entering the office, in the sense that they had turned naturally to the written word to express themselves. All the first six—Washington, John Adams, Jefferson, Madison, Monroe, and John Quincy Adams— were thoroughly at home with the pen. Washington's published writings, including his diaries, occupy over forty large volumes, and there are still considerable unpublished pieces. In his youth, Washington wrote poetry, as one concerned with words if not gifted with talent:

> And with gladness never to wake
> In deluded sleepings let my eyelids close
> That in an enraptured dream I may
> In a soft lulling sleep and gentle repose
> Possess those joys denied by day.[9]

From his youth Washington also revealed, in his letters, and occasionally in a diary that he began at sixteen and did not end until the day before he died, the same care for the graceful expression: "In silence I now express my joy [he wrote to Sally Fairfax in 1758]; silence, which in some cases—I wish the present —speaks more intelligently than the sweetest eloquence."[10] In his maturity Washington's writing was shaped by the events of his life. His diaries and notebooks became lean, Spartan, observant; his public papers formal, stately, carefully thought out.

Washington had, of course, none of the intellectual range of his first five successors, nor has the American presidency since had five such intellects in a row. John Adams wrote extensively, both in private and for public purposes, almost since childhood. His diaries and correspondence are, in substance and in style, excellent. His answers to Daniel Leonard, in his "Novanglus Papers" were the most thoughtful presentation of the revolutionary viewpoint. His interests—philosophic, artistic, historic—were broad and informed, and they showed through in his writings. He was the best autobiographer and the best letter writer of the Revolutionary period. He prized words: ". . . put down in writing every word with its meaning,"[11] he advised John Quincy Adams as a young lawyer. And years earlier, during his son's student days in Europe, he had written, "Suffer no careless scroll ever to go out of your hand. Take time to think, even upon the most trifling card. Turn your thoughts in your mind, and vary your phrases and the order of your words that taste and judgment may appear even in the most ordinary composition."[12]

Jefferson, the author of the Declaration of Independence and of the Virginia statute on religious freedom, was, of course, a master of the language, the strategic use of which was perhaps his greatest achievement. He valued the classics, he wrote, "as models of pure taste in writing. To these we are certainly indebted for the national [sic] and chaste style of modern composition which so much distinguishes the nations to whom these languages are familiar. Without these models we should probably have continued the inflated style of our northern ancestors, or the hypothetical and vague one of the east."[13] Jefferson's pen was prolific, practised and certain, as he ranged over all fields of human knowledge and experience. His contemporary, Madison, hardly less distinguished as a creative writer in statecraft, reversed presidential procedures that both preceded and followed him by ghostwriting for his first Secretary of State, the literarily inept Robert Smith. Monroe, who replaced Smith, and later became Madison's successor, turned to the writing of his autobiography after leaving the presidency, and also wrote The People, the Sovereigns, the first tract on American political institutions by an ex-President, revealing an educated curiosity about their classical counterparts. Though neither a brilliant intellect nor a powerful author, Monroe wrote well, uncluteredly and factually.

The last of the products of the age of reason to hold the office, John Quincy Adams, was perhaps the most versatile writer of all the Presidents. And except when his writings, as was also the case occasionally with his father's, were overcrowded with gloomy and consistently premature predictions of his own early death (John Adams lived to be ninety and John Quincy Adams to eighty), his writings were spirited, gossipy, bristling with character and conviction. With his father and Polk, he was the outstanding diarist among the Presidents, but like his father and unlike Polk, whose very full diary was limited to the presidential years, John Quincy Adams kept his diary very casually and only intermittently during his presidency. "I wrote very little this evening," he complained, halfway through his administration, "and my diary now runs again in arrear day after day. . . ."[14] The next year, however, the President of the United States was writing—and completing—a sonnet before breakfast, an ode to a chanticleer he had chosen, characteristically, to adorn his signet ring:

> Minstrel of morn, whose eager ken decries
> The ray first beaming from night's region drear . . .
> Bird of the brave, whose valiant heart supplies
> The beak of eagles and the falcon's spear. . . .[15]

John Quincy Adams took his writing chores seriously. During his first term in the House after his presidency, he occupied himself on the way from Quincy to Washington by composing "twenty-three stanzas of versions of the Psalms—all bad but as good as I could make them."[16] He labored for months on his two-hour ceremonial orations, which he seemed to consider a duty, on such subjects as the Declaration of Independence, Lafayette, and Monroe. He also resumed his diary once he left the presidency, and it remains unexcelled for its wealth of detail on the events, personalities, and trends in the capital for seventeen years covering the administrations of five Presidents.

Jackson was the first of the modern Presidents, and a prolific writer of letters, nearly all of them dealing with the problems or the personalities of the members of his official and private families and many of them characterized by a curiously appealing tenderness—an almost soft apprehension of the sensitivity of others. This was, of course, not a conspicuous quality in his public papers, which are bold, cocky, sometimes verging on arrogance and ruthlessness in their positiveness. Nevertheless, they show a restoration of a harder concept of presidential leadership than any since Washington's; or perhaps more accurately they reveal the reaching of a new plateau in the evolution of the presidency —a level from which a century later other Presidents would still be taking off. The theory of the presidency did not interest Jackson—only its capacity for action, and on that he had no brooding doubts.

During the long interlude of passive Presidents between Jackson and Lincoln, only Polk was an exception, and only Polk took to the written word to record both the events of his highly active administration and his observations on the presidency. Polk wrote well—clearly, unemotionally, sensibly, primarily as a reporter for his own purposes and as a good one. For the rest, only Buchanan wrote at length, largely after he left office and to tell an unheeding generation deeply immersed in the blood of the Civil War why he had not and could not have done anything to prevent it. From all this, more than from the record of his hesitant administration, are seen the real dimensions of Buchanan's tragic performance as President—explanations "from the heart of an old public functionary,"[17] as he limply described himself in a message to Congress. The whole focus of Buchanan was on what he saw as the limitations of the presidency—its impotence—and he was as surely a victim of this view in his inability to cope with the drift to civil war as Hoover was of his limited concept of the office in attempting to cope with the Depression.

Lincoln, of course, towers over all the Presidents in his literary genius as he did in his clarity of purpose and in his confidence in the capacity of the office to do anything that it was necessary be done. The mythmakers have all but destroyed the exceptional intellectual powers of Lincoln, and the almost absolute self-assurance with which he used them. Well read in such diverse authors as Shakespeare, Voltaire, Volnay, Thomas Paine, and Burns, Lincoln not only knew the power of words but had extraordinary deftness in their use and fully realized his ability.

Edmund Wilson has discerningly pointed out, "He seems always to have had the conviction of his own superiority."[18] There is a witness to this, in Lincoln's law partner of twenty years, William Herndon, who told how Lincoln locked himself in a back room over a store in Springfield and, bringing with him only a copy of the Constitution, Jackson's Nullification Proclamation, and one speech each of Clay and Webster, wrote the first inaugural in solitude—getting no help, asking no help, wanting no help, though Nicolay and Hay said Seward later made suggestions. "No man ever asked less aid than he," Herndon continued; "his confidence in his own ability to meet the requirements of every hour was so marked that his friends never thought of tendering their aid, and therefore no one could share his responsibilities. I never wrote a line for him; he never asked me to . . . he often asked as to the use of a word or the turn of a sentence, but if I volunteered to recommend or even suggest a change of language which involved a change of sentiment I found him the most inflexible man I have ever seen."[19]

Lincoln used his mastery of the language both tactically and strategically. Literary devices were to him familiar tools, and he handled them with the touch of genius that is given to few men —even those who spend their lives as men of letters. The haunting, memorable constructions occur over and over. Lincoln wrote poetry well into his maturity, and the phrases of stanzas he wrote at thirty-five, when he passed his childhood home, were suggestible of the first inaugural: "O Memory, thou midway world/ 'Twixt earth and paradise"[20] of the poem and "the mystic chords of memory" of the first inaugural.[21] The sophisticated architecture of his phrasing was consistently skillful: "Him who can go with me and stay with you,"[22] of God, when he was saying farewell to his Springfield neighbors; "Fondly do we hope, fervently do we pray,"[23] in the second inaugural; "And thus there will be some black men who can remember that with silent tongue, and clenched teeth, and steady eye, and well-poised bayonet, they have helped mankind on to this great consummation, while I fear there will be some white ones unable to forget that with malignant heart and deceitful speech they strove to hinder it,"[24] from his letter to James Conkling. But there was fiber in Lincoln's writing, too, and sometimes curt directness. "Please do it,"[25] he frequently ended his communications to Stanton, and his hard practicality irked the fierier abolitionists constantly. One of the most hardheaded utterances in American political literature is Lincoln's sharp reply to Greeley: "If I could save the Union without freeing *any* slave, I would do it, and if I could save it by freeing *all* the slaves, I would do it; and if I could save it by freeing some and leaving others alone, I would also do that."[26]

Lincoln was forced both by history and by his own introspective nature to comment more on the presidency and its powers during his term that any of his predecessors. It was characteristic, however, that his observations all related to the strain that the Civil War and a giant insurrection put upon the office, for Lincoln was convinced that only the strength with which he used the presidential office could save the nation; and nothing—no legal consideration, no political advantage—could convince him to yield an iota of the extraconstitutional powers he boldly read into the office.

Closest to Lincoln's presidential writings in literary force were probably those of Woodrow Wilson, equally troubled as he was by the tides of history, and yet equally confident of an aroused people's capacity to deal with them. The only scholar, the only doctor of philosophy, among Presidents, Wilson often wrote without spirit or vitality when he was not writing words to be spoken. Although his prepresidential writings on political institutions were—and still are—of considerable importance, and his occasional essays, graceful and provocative, his historical writings were poor—flat, superficial, monotonous. But this world-minded Calvinist rose to great literary heights when his compositions were directed to an audience listening to him. Of the purpose of education, "You do not know the world until you know the men who have possessed it and tried its ways before ever you were given your brief run upon it."[27] Of immigrants to America, "They saw this star of the West rising over the peoples of the world, and they said, 'That is the star of hope and the star of salvation. We will set our footsteps towards the West and join that body of men whom God has blessed with the vision of liberty.' "[28] And of the failure of the United States to join the League of Nations (with a haunting, rhythmic use of the image of the night), "And the glory of the Armies and Navies of the United States is gone like a dream in the night, and there ensues upon it, in the suitable darkness of the night, the nightmare of dread which lay upon the nations before this war came; and there will come sometime, in the vengeful Providence of God, another struggle in which, not a few hundred thousand fine men from America will have to die, but as many millions as are necessary to accomplish the final freedom of the peoples of the world."[29]

In the cases of other Presidents, the most prolific were not necessarily the most extensive commentators on the presidency—as witness the comparatively lean comments of the Adamses, to whom, as Lyman Butterfield has pointed out, "toil at their writing desks was as natural . . . as eating and walking."[30] Others seemed to have little introspective interest in the office while they held it or retrospective thoughts afterward. For all his delight in the presidency, Franklin Roosevelt, for example, wrote and spoke comparatively little of the presidency as such. One is conscious over and over again in perusing his speeches and writings how much he merely used the office as a point of departure, with very little probing into its nature, its capacities or, certainly, its limitations. As dissimilar an incumbent as Calvin Coolidge was no more searching. At the end of six years' service in the office he was invited to discuss some aspect of the presidency in the centennial edition of the *St. Louis Post-Dispatch*, and he could think of nothing more important to dwell upon than the need to provide the President with suitable vacation quarters.[31]

Presidential autobiographies, apologia for administrations, appraisals of the powers and limitations of the office—all these became time-honored employment for ex-Presidents only after the Civil War. Altogether ten Presidents, more than a third of the twenty-seven who have survived their terms, wrote their own accounts of their administrations, and of these all but John

Quincy Adams and Buchanan came after the Civil War. All twentieth-century Presidents who survived their terms, except Wilson, have written such volumes.

These are not, on the whole, distinguished, but they furnish invaluable insight into what the Presidents conceived the office to be. Two activists in the office, Theodore Roosevelt and Truman, turned out to be the most spirited theorists and, for men diverse in almost all other respects, remarkably similar in their exuberant extraction of all the power the office held and in their unabashed explanation of it. Both of them had a fundamental and very real respect for the office—Truman almost a worshipful regard—and they shared a vigorous approach to its capacities— which communicated itself to both the style and the form of their autobiographies. Coolidge, by contrast, seemed as acutely distressed by recalling his incumbency in his autobiography as he seemed by serving it; he was absorbed by none of the duties and responsibilities of the office, though he was intrigued by the Secret Service, discussing its methods in protecting him at greater length than any problems or issues that confronted him. The autobiography of Coolidge reaches literary distinction only when he writes of the austere boyhood of the fragile child growing up in the unrelenting Vermont mountains. There is more than a touch of poetry in his recollection of his mother, who died when he was eleven: "It seemed as though the rich green tints of the foliage and the blossoms of the flowers came for her in the springtime, and in the autumn it was for her that the mountain sides were struck with crimson and with gold."[32]

Cleveland, Benjamin Harrison, and Taft wrote no narrative autobiographies, but each addressed himself to specific presidential problems or to specific aspects of the presidency. Harrison, in a series of articles for a national magazine, and Taft, in a series of university lectures that seemed intended to cast doubts on the prudence, if not the essential validity, of Theodore Roosevelt's doctrine of virtually unlimited presidential powers, wrote more extensively of the institutional characteristics of the presidency than any other President. Both men had a feeling for institutional politics and a taste for teaching, and their essays, published in book form, are calm, leisurely reviews of the office, its powers, and limitations. Both presided over the country in periods of quiet; both were interludes between reform administrations; and both were custodial Presidents, uncreative, unimaginative, upon whom no heavy or extraordinary demands were made. The Benjamin Harrison and Taft years were years seldom duplicated in the American presidency for their serenity, the Monroe and Coolidge administrations alone equaling them in untroubled general conditions. Their concepts of the office were, of course, shaped to some extent by such tranquillity, though Taft's feud with Theodore Roosevelt and also his irascible temperament under the jovial exterior, as compared to Harrison's imperturbable, level disposition, sharpened his wording on occasion.

Since diaries unintended for publication are usually the most revealing of all literature, it is unfortunate that more Presidents were not great diarists. But great diarists of any calling being rare in every field, the wonder is perhaps that four out of the thirty-five Presidents were acceptable diarists. The two Adamses, sure of themselves, of monumental rectitude, uninhibited judges of their fellow men, rather than coming to terms with life expecting life to come to terms with them, were outstanding diarists. The other two of special interest were Polk, the most thorough of the presidential diarists, and Rutherford B. Hayes, the effect of whom as a historic corrective after eight years of Grant and twelve of congressional rule is difficult to overestimate. The dedicated drive of Polk, his absolute devotion to his job, the incredible toil he carried on for four years—all most clearly revealed in his copious diaries—stemmed from a conscientious determination rare indeed not only among Presidents but among political administrators anywhere. All his limitations are there, too, the narrow if far vision, the lack of imaginative insight, the stubborn, inflexible attitude that made no allowances and envisioned no alternatives. His was probably the most dynamic concept of presidential leadership, nevertheless, and it was wholly affirmative in character; and he labored day and night at the job, seldom taking even a day off, as though he would not have enough time to finish his self-imposed purposes. All this is in the diaries, and one can see wholly how Polk viewed the presidency only by reading every word of them.

Hayes, more the reformer by nature than any other occupant of the office, kept a far slenderer and certainly less hectic diary. But the extraordinary purity and generosity of character of the man are apparent on every page, not only in the motives that impelled him during his own administration but in the qualities of fairness and sympathy that he brought to his appraisal of the four successors he lived to see inaugurated. Hayes, of a religious and philanthropic nature, had almost a pastor's idea of the office, and very little personal ambition to change it. He expected goodness in all public offices, not just passively, by way of example to the people of the republic—an aroma of sanctity about the White House was, with sufficient reason, a source of annoyance to many during his administration—but also actively in bringing about political reform, even if it meant, as it did to Hayes himself, the sacrifice of survival in office. But the want of a powerful and forceful personality, of long-range energy, of strong political leadership limited his influence and achievement as well as his career, and characterized his writings as well.

The age of great diarists is probably gone, and the age of many press conferences is just beginning. Except for some spontaneity, the press conference has little, of course, in common with a diary. The press conference is in fact a misnomer. There is little conferring, the occasion being limited in recent administrations to questions and answers. But there are political and strategic uses of the press conference that make it an increasingly important device of statecraft as well as an informational vehicle. Press conferences are called and canceled now at the pleasure of the President, whose pleasure is apt to be governed less by the amount of information at hand than by his judgment as to the best time to give it or to the desirability of withholding it. The fact that the press conference has grown greatly in size has little to do with its value, despite frequent protests to the contrary. The conferences of Franklin Roosevelt were small, compared to those in later administrations, but they were frequently consumed, after the President gave a talk on some public matter, by rather pointless banter.

Wilson, who introduced the regular, formal press conference, never understood either newspapers or newspapermen and his hostility to them severely inhibited his communicativeness at the conferences, which he finally abandoned altogether. Harding restored them and entered upon a series of friendly, agreeable sessions, far closer to conferences than any before or after his time. As in all presidential press conferences until Eisenhower's, Harding permitted no direct quotations. Coolidge continued Harding's conferences, required questions written and submitted in advance and laconically answered those he felt like answering and ignored the others. He revealed little of his views of the presidency in them and generally left the newsmen covering them cold. Hoover's press conferences were dominated by a mutual distrust of the President and the correspondents, and lacked any spontaneousness or confidences. They gradually degenerated as the working press turned more and more against Hoover, and declined from twenty-three during the first year to twelve in the last year of his unhappy administration.

Although Franklin Roosevelt enjoyed his press conferences, frequently lecturing the correspondents, they did not achieve the tight responsiveness of Truman at his best. Truman's answers, when he was not avoiding a question or, according to some correspondents, being blatantly deceptive, were without the circuitous complexities in which Kennedy occasionally lost his way and which, in Eisenhower's case, sometimes defied all attempts at decodification.

Thirty-five men have occupied the Presidency in a hundred and seventy-five years. At this writing there have been thirty-four views of the office—noted far more on the whole for their differences than for their similarities. But they have been the views, almost without exception, of upright men, though occasionally inadequate to the office, in some instances negligent, and often unimaginative and passive.

Sometimes presidential actions have spoken more persuasively than presidential words; but generally presidential actions have inhered in the presidential utterances. The level of those utterances is, with only very few exceptions, high—reflecting, in the words of the reformer President, Hayes, perhaps the most singular fact in the history of an office the occupants of which have been chosen at times in the most haphazard or cynical way: "Now, the wisdom of the fathers has given to the President a host of motives to be honest and patriotic. Presidents in the past have always been better than their adversaries have predicted . . . All were free from the least taint of personal corruption. All were honest men."[33] In the case of an office which at the outset John Adams said "has no equal in the world,"[34] this is, if nothing more, impressive evidence of the soundness of a people's instinct for self-government.

Chapter I

THE PRESIDENT AS NATIONAL LEADER

As far as national leadership goes, the Constitution does little more than present an opportunity to the President. His performance as the leader of the nation has depended entirely upon his own appraisal of the capacities of the office. Consequently, the growth of the presidency as the national leadership has not been a steady one, but subject to leaps and bounds. At times it has not grown at all. It has yielded to judicial supremacy, as in the early days of the Republic, and to congressional supremacy, as during the long years before Lincoln and the longer ones between Lincoln and Cleveland. Sometimes it has simply drifted, becoming almost empty and admittedly powerless, as it did between Woodrow Wilson and the second Roosevelt.

In nearly all cases, the limitations of the office and its periods of retrogression were not primarily the results of external pressures upon the incumbent, although congressional hostility has played a large role, but rather of the attitudes of the incumbents themselves—particularly of their concepts of presidential leadership. No overwhelming pressures were exerted on Taft, for example, that required him to make less of the presidency than his predecessor and sponsor, Theodore Roosevelt. They were of the same time, of the same party and, for some years at least, of the same administrative team. Nor have great demands on the office been the measure of the incumbent's conception of it. As much was required of James Buchanan as of Lincoln, but the former allowed the conditions encountered by him to survive for Lincoln to master; and similarly the conditions unalleviated because of Herbert Hoover's deep convictions about the limits of presidential power were left for Franklin Roosevelt, with his confident views of the strengths of the office, to allay.

The strongest of the Presidents, Lincoln, saw the authority of the President under the conditions of extreme civil strife, as absolute, and incontestable. Among the few times when a tone of impatience crept into his utterances were those occasions when he was responding to dissent from his very clear and—as he thought—wholly logical conviction that there was nothing the President could not do to save the Constitution he had sworn to uphold and to give leadership to a nation he was bound to preserve. Although one of the most astute lawyers of his time, he flatly refused to be stayed by legal strictures.

It is doubtful, however, that the office would have evolved in such a way as to have made the bold concept of Lincoln workable if it had not been for the force of Washington's view of the presidency at the beginning. The prime and stern architect of the presidency, Washington believed that the Constitution's use of the expression "executive power" meant that there was integrally attached to the office, in a quite literal sense, a body of powers independent of the other branches.

Of the thirty-three men who held the office prior to the 1961 inaugural, eight took Washington's view of its capacities and enlarged upon it: Thomas Jefferson, Andrew Jackson, James K. Polk, Abraham Lincoln, Theodore Roosevelt, Woodrow Wilson, Franklin Roosevelt, and Harry Truman. Their combined terms, including Washington's, covered sixty-seven years, over a third of the nation's history. These were strong national leaders, men who took the office and, through vision, courage, political skill, boldness, used it to advance the interests of the nation and of humanity. All of them were men stubborn in purpose, and whose purpose was closely attuned to their times. Each of them was equipped, by gifts of insight and perception, to see the needs of his time and, by gifts of leadership, to respond to them. But each of them had also a more precise quality, and this is the thing that has governed the capacity of any man to grow great in the office: an expanding awareness of the active as contrasted to the merely custodial responsibility of the presidency.

In all these men that sense of active presidential responsibility was so strong that they considered it the only moral check upon presidential powers. Consequently, under each of them the powers of the presidency were greatly expanded. Sometimes this was done, as in the first administration of Franklin Roosevelt, to meet an emergency. Occasionally it was done by extralegal steps, as when, two months after taking office, Lincoln decided, contrary to the provisions of the Constitution, to increase the size of the Army and to tell the Congress about it afterward. But most often it was done by a liberal interpretation and strong application of the existent but previously narrowly confined constitutional powers of the office, as in the case of Jefferson and Polk. Thus there emerge, as a corollary to the active moral awareness of the responsibility of the presidential office, two principles of presidential action that the seven great Presidents shared: first, that to meet his responsibility, a President can assert his leadership only by taking the broadest and not the narrowest view of his constitutional powers; and, secondly, that it is his duty to suggest and shepherd through the Congress temporary legislation to broaden the interpretation of those powers, if no present tenable interpretation of them is sufficient to meet the requirements of the situation that confronts him and that critically affects the public interest. In short, therefore, the great Presidents have been men who welcomed rather than evaded responsibility and who found some way of meeting it.

Historically, the presidency as a strong and independent agency of the people was first asserted by Andrew Jackson in his fight to destroy the private control over the nation's moneys implicit in the deposit of Federal funds in Nicholas Biddle's Bank of the United States. He succeeded in this by withdrawing the government's funds, despite a resolution of confidence in the bank passed by the House. It was further asserted in his direct action to prevent South Carolina from declaring a law of the nation null and void. In this he succeeded by issuing a presidential proclamation that sent the nullifiers into a hasty convention to nullify their own nullification. Abrasively defiant of any checks on the presidency, whether judicial or legislative, Jackson's doctrine was flat and inclusive: "It was settled by the Constitution, the laws, and the whole practice of the government that the entire executive power is vested in the President of the United States . . ."[1]

Both Tyler, in annexing Texas, and Polk, in shaping the final continental integration of the United States, depended heavily on the Jacksonian precedent of broad use of the presidential office, on a leadership independent of the Congress and on direct answerability to the people. Wrote Polk: "The President represents in the executive department the whole people of the United States, as each member of the legislative department represents portions of them."[2] Every strong President has repeated these words over and over again in his writings.

But it was the Republicans, Lincoln and Theodore Roosevelt, who pressed the Jacksonian theory of strong presidential leadership even further. As already noted, Lincoln held that there were not even any constitutional limits on the office when it was functioning to "preserve, protect and defend" the Constitution: ". . . would not the official oath be broken if the government should be overthrown when it was believed that disregarding the single law would tend to preserve it?"[3] So the first Republican President took the view that no limitations on the powers of the President existed if they tended to inhibit his execution of his oath. Lincoln therefore stretched the Jacksonian concept further than it had ever been before or since—and, so doing, saved the Union. (The only occasion when the extremeness of Lincoln's view was duplicated by another man who came near the presidency was in 1933 when Alfred E. Smith, with characteristic impatience at listening to pleas that the Constitution permitted no action against the downward-spiraling Depression, starkly and somewhat recklessly observed that it might be a good thing to put the Constitution "on the shelf" and save the country.)

Lincoln faced peculiar problems, and his particular genius gave, in retrospect, comforting reassurance for his acknowledged disregard for the constitutional limitations on the presidency. It was left to another Republican to find the broadest interpretation of the powers of the office in more or less normal times: Theodore Roosevelt, whose administration certainly faced no historic crisis. To a considerable extent, Roosevelt took advantage of the strides made by Grover Cleveland in his two separated administrations. Cleveland used the influence of the presidential office to carry out presidential policies which often conflicted with Congressional policy. He reduced the tariff and instigated repeal of the Silver Purchase Act and the Tenure of Office Act, which had limited the power of the President in removing officeholders within the Executive Department. Contesting successfully the Whig doctrine of Thaddeus Stevens that the President "is the servant of the people as they shall speak through Congress,"[4] Cleveland echoed Jackson and Polk when he insisted that the President represented the people directly: ". . . it is especially the office related to the people as individuals, in no general, local, or other combination . . ."[5]

Theodore Roosevelt, though of the opposite party, used nearly the same words: ". . . the Executive is or ought to be peculiarly representative of the people as a whole."[6] In intervening in the hard-coal strike of 1902, Roosevelt set a pattern for the extension of the presidential office to the settling of labor disputes that has since become an implied extraconstitutional duty of the office, and today even the stoutest adherent to the old Whig theory would be disturbed if the President of the United States sat idly by as the economic life of the nation was paralyzed by a strike in a basic industry. In 1902, the mining of anthracite stopped entirely, and Roosevelt prepared for action on two fronts: he would have the strike arbitrated under presidential auspices or, if this failed, he would send in the Army to mine the coal. Arbitration finally worked; but until it did, Roosevelt was busy perfecting his operational plans for the Army, with a customary energy never before equaled for presidential boldness of action outside of war.

It was Theodore Roosevelt himself who dubbed his theory of the presidency the "stewardship theory," because he held that he was charged with the welfare of the country by the people and that in carrying out that charge he was as President limited by nothing which was not specified in the Constitution or the statutes. It was thus that he came to his conclusion that the President not only could do everything the Constitution empowered him to do but could also do everything that it did not forbid him to do. More than any other modern President, including Wilson and Franklin Roosevelt, the effectiveness of the presidency today is the product of Theodore Roosevelt. Moreover, he was responsible for the injection of the presidency into the economic life of the nation, both in a regulatory and a creative role: he policed the great corporations, he regulated the meat packers, he split up the railroads and coal mines, he intervened in strikes, he used the influence of the presidency to indict before the public "malefactors of a great wealth," and he set a prototype for TVA by having the government build and operate a public utility, the Panama Canal.

A man of direct and often impetuous action rather than a theorist, Theodore Roosevelt nevertheless revealed in his writings a clear perception that a weak executive in a society of increasing intricacy could never fully perform his general constitutional functions. His language was reminiscent of Lincoln's: "I declined to adopt the view that what was imperatively necessary for the nation could not be done by the President unless he could find some specific authorization to do it. My belief was that it was not only his right but his duty to do anything that the needs of the nation demanded unless such action was forbidden by the Constitution or by the laws. Under this interpretation of executive power I did and caused to be done many things not previously done by the President and the heads of the Departments."[7]

Nor did he see his strengthening of the presidency as merely for his own sake or for his own time: "I have used every ounce of power there was in the office, and I have not cared a rap for the criticisms of those who spoke of my 'usurpation of power'; for I knew the talk was all nonsense and that there was no usurpation. I believe that the efficiency of this government depends upon its possessing a strong, central executive, and whenever I could establish a precedent for strength in the Executive . . . as I did in internal affairs in settling the anthracite coal strike, in keeping order in Nevada this year when the Federation of Miners threatened anarchy, or as I have done in bringing the corporations to book—why in all three actions I have felt, not merely my action was right in itself, but that in showing the strength of, or in giving strength to, the executive office, I was establishing a precedent of value."[8]

But precedents are not easily maintained in the American presidency. Polk, for example, was a model of clear-headed purpose and had no reservations about the competence of his office. Coming to the presidential office with the clearest and most specific program of intentions of any President, Polk had an uncluttered view of the need of presidential leadership to reach out and embrace what he saw as the manifest destiny of the country, and he proceeded to meet that need with energetic directness and with a broad sense of presidential power. A less energetic approach was that of Hayes, perhaps the most conscientious reformer in the White House, coming at certainly a time most demanding of reform. His expression of the power of the presidency was the most sweeping of any President's: "Practically the President holds the nation in his hands."[9]

Two of the strongest Presidents, Jackson and Franklin Roosevelt—men of very considerable achievements in the office because of sure political instincts—had a virtuoso concept of the presidency. Under them the office was very much geared to the popularity of their essentially political personalities, which in themselves made for popular acclaim of them as leaders. Neither brought much thought to a definition of the presidency, however—an intellectual casualness that occasionally led them into abrupt neutralizings by the courts or the Congress.

Jackson faced these defiantly. Of a decision of the Chief Justice of which he disapproved, he is reported to have said, "John Marshall has made his decision; now let him enforce it,"[10] and of the United States Senate, that he "would receive no message from the damned scoundrels."[11] Franklin Roosevelt sought rather crude political solutions—pack the Court and purge the Congress, leaving the rationale to others. Jefferson tried to neutralize the Court, too, not only by political action but by intellectual appeals which pressed the separation of powers doctrine too far for public opinion—which, indeed, reduced it to an absurdity.

Far more thoughtful approaches were made by Presidents whose administrations were historic failures so far as mastering the problems of their times went. Herbert Hoover, for example, took a very sober view of the presidency and seemed almost overawed, not by its powers, but by its limitations. Franklin Pierce, the New Hampshire Democrat, in his veto messages, put forth some exceptionally sharp syllogisms in support not only of presidential weakness but also of congressional incompetence in the face of the doctrine of states' rights. The old Whig general, William Henry Harrison, labored on an eight-thousand-word inaugural address, the longest in history, to leave as the major achievement of his thirty-day administration, the shortest in history, a competent and detailed exposition of the Whig doctrine of presidential impotence and congressional leadership.

Out of the thirty-five Presidents of the United States, eleven (William H. Harrison, Taylor, Fillmore, Grant, Benjamin Harrison, McKinley, Taft, Harding, Coolidge, Hoover, and Eisenhower) were devoted, in one degree or another, to the Whig concept of a weak executive, and two others (Pierce and Buchanan) were so devoted in practice even though they based their concept on strong states' rights rather than on strong legislative powers. Together the tenures of these thirteen covered nearly fifty-three years. On the whole, theirs were the least distinguished administrations in the history of the presidency, periods of national drifting or stagnation or quiescence, and sometimes of outright and tragic floundering, as in the cases of Pierce, Buchanan, Grant, and Hoover. Only three of the passive Presidents were elected to more than one term, whereas fifteen or nearly half of all Presidents were restored to office. The tolerances of democracy, however, have minimized, historically, the effect of an executive who so narrowly interprets his power that its constitutional definition serves only as a catalogue of limitations. In practice it has been demonstrated repeatedly that, under such a pilot, the nation is a ship without a rudder, sometimes coming through safely, sometimes a little shattered from the passage, and sometimes dangerously near to cracking up on the rocks. At the same time, there has yet to be a weak President who did not feel that he did both his best and his most—within his own definition of the capacities of his office. And if he survived, he usually devoted himself to the issuing of periodic alarms about the tendency of his successors to take too wide a measure of presidential powers, although some—for example, Benjamin Harrison, Taft, and Eisenhower—wrote at considerable length to explain their philosophies of presidential restraint.

The activist concept of' presidential leadership had, in summary, its seeds planted by Washington, its historic application by Jackson, and its broadest interpretation by Lincoln. Its development has been bipartisan, and its usage has also been bipartisan. It provided at its best an imaginative and vigorous independent leadership to the nation. The most successful Presidents accepted the leadership challenge from the beginning and pressed the office to its constitutional and statutory limits, and in the cases of one Republican, Lincoln, and one Democrat, Franklin Roosevelt, beyond them, to meet the needs of their times. They were also extremely explicit in their writings, and tended to articulate widely and forcefully their views of presidential power. Yet they were not men of very similar temperaments or intellects.

No two more radically different personalities, unless they were Harding and Coolidge, ever shared more closely the same approximate view of the presidency than Wilson and Franklin Roosevelt. The latter, a much less profound mind than Wilson and a much more extroverted nature, reverted *in toto* to the values and methods of the President whom he had once served. Franklin Roosevelt was not one of the great innovators among American Presidents but was essentially an imitator and improvisor. However, he brought the gifts of a very great and effective personality—perhaps the greatest in American politics—

to the office. And as both the domestic and foreign situations with which he had to cope were more extensive repetitions of those Wilson faced, so Roosevelt's meeting of those situations was an extension of methods already employed by Wilson. The New Deal had its prototype in Wilson's New Freedom; the war powers of World War II had their prototype in the war powers of World War I; and the United Nations had its prototype in the League of Nations. In fact, Franklin Roosevelt's main contribution to the growth of the presidency was the stamp of his personality, particularly in respect to the Wilsonian functions of assuming party and legislative leadership.

Franklin Roosevelt proved the presidential office equal, without constitutional alteration although with statutory enlargement, to the most desperate domestic and foreign crises. His historic significance in the development of presidential leadership is that he used with prompt and exceptional vigor the influence and fullest powers of the presidency to rescue the capitalist sytsem in this country at a time when its real interests had been so badly and so casually served that not only did it invite economic ruin but actually had the nation on the verge of it. In this sense, Roosevelt, who could in 1933 have rallied the nation to the support of a violent and basic social change, proved himself one of the great conservatives of history—for he showed not only that American political institutions were capable of survival through the kind of upheaval that could swamp those in other lands, but also that a free and justly regulated capitalism and a degree of economic security for the individual were not mutually exclusive.

Of the Presidents who were active leaders and met their responsibilities, but were not of the same historic significance to the growth of the Presidency: John Adams, Madison, Monroe, John Quincy Adams, Van Buren, Hayes, Arthur, and Cleveland—all had a less affirmative view of presidential leadership than Franklin Roosevelt and a lesser sense of responsibility to the destiny of his nation than Polk had or to the whole plight of man than Lincoln or Wilson had. They missed greatness because their sense of the office as a source of leadership, while far from narrow, was not so broad as that of the leading Presidents. Indeed, some failed to achieve outstanding records largely because, while they had enough breadth in their concepts of presidential powers to accomplish immediate objectives, they lacked sufficient breadth when considering the long-range effects of their administrations.

Thus, Cleveland, who went to the White House equipped with the best administrative temperament of any President, had a clear insight into the uniqueness of the presidency: "In the scheme of our national government the presidency is preeminently the people's office."[12] But he had an insufficient sense of the leadership role of the presidential office in the new industrialized society, whose problems exploded in the 1894 Pullman strike, to go much beyond the imposition of order by the use of federal troops. Cleveland's predecessor, the imposing Chester A. Arthur, the worst-equipped man to become President, had been nothing more than an elegant New York machine politician, suspended from his appointive office by a predecessor in the presidency, before he was nominated to the vice presidency strictly in political horse trading. But he astonished the people, and everlastingly alienated his own party bosses on Garfield's death, by vigorously supporting civil service reform, prosecuting grafters of his own party, and reorganizing the cabinet. For Arthur, despite his hack-spoilsman background, had a high concept of presidential leadership, and neither adherence to his party machine nor hopes of winning a nomination of his own to the presidency could swerve him from his stubborn loyalty to that concept. Yet Arthur was no more than a good President and quite far from a great one; he confined that sense of responsibility to much too limited an area.

Of the Presidents who either were adequate as national leaders or would have been without congressional harassment—the men who were neither wholly active nor wholly passive as Presidents—all of them had not only a restricted sense of presidential responsibility, so far as national leadership goes, but also either an ineptness in carrying out whatever responsibilities they did recognize or such a restricted idea of the powers of the presidency that they attempted little. It is not insignificant that of the ten adequate Presidents (Tyler, Taylor, Fillmore, Pierce, Johnson, Benjamin Harrison, Taft, Coolidge, Hoover, and Eisenhower), no fewer than four, or over a third, succeeded to the presidency from the vice presidency; and of those four Coolidge was the only one elected to a term of his own.

Tyler was a very special case and a man probably of presidential caliber who was badly inhibited by the circumstances of his administration. Never elected to the presidency, he nevertheless served all but thirty days of a full four-year term after the aged William Henry Harrison died of pneumonia contracted at his own inauguration. He was the first Vice President to succeed to office and had no precedent to follow for guidance. Finally, he was a Democrat on a Whig ticket, whom the Whigs had nominated as Harrison's running mate in the hopes of capturing a few anti-Van Buren Democratic votes. Tyler, a man of principle, consequently was a virtually powerless President, without a mandate from the people, without a party, and without a congressional following. Nevertheless, as Washington's concept of the presidency was the chief force in the permanent definition of the office, the much more difficult problem of the status of a Vice President, particularly as national leader, succeeding to the presidency was determined in great measure by the resolute good sense of John Tyler.

Since of the thirty-five American Presidents, more than a fifth of them, as Vice Presidents, succeeded to the office, the historic importance of Tyler's forceful and persistent example is apparent. In a very real sense, however, it took much more tenacity of purpose for these men to assert and maintain their leadership than it did for men originally elected to the presidency. The quality of their leadership was, on the whole, above average. Fillmore served almost three years of Taylor's term, and used the power of his office to see compromise measures through the Congress to avoid civil war and to enforce them. Arthur, whose background made him the least promising of the eight, showed high character and integrity and assumed a moral leadership based upon convictions considerably ahead of the political mores of his time. Theodore Roosevelt made it clear that he felt that a President who succeeded to the office on the death of an incumbent was President just as fully as though he had been specifically elected; accordingly, he put no limits on his role as the leader of the nation, and pressed it further than it had been since Lincoln. Of the Vice Presidents who succeeded deceased Presidents, only Coolidge took a severely limited view of presidential leadership and avoided making any impression on national and world affairs except one of whimsical and sometimes childlike humor, not always intentional.

Two Vice Presidents, Andrew Johnson and Truman, were plunged into the Presidency in times of great national crisis. One failed to meet the challenge, and the other succeeded. Johnson's failure was due not to any intellectual unawareness of the burden of presidential responsibility or of the necessity for presidential leadership, but to personality deficiencies and to a predatory and almost completely amoral congressional leadership which would have given far more tactful men than Johnson grave troubles. Truman's success, on the other hand, was due not only to his grasp of the historic plight of the democracies but also to a singularly dedicated application to his duties and an unswerving insistence on carrying out the obligations of presidential leadership, even though he seemed to see no reason why that leadership should extend to nongovernmental matters and kept his advisers on edge as to his sometimes compulsive unofficial correspondence and utterances.

The extremely subjective nature of presidential leadership in the United States is nowhere better illustrated than in the presidential career of Dwight Eisenhower. No President had an opportunity for more vigorous, undisputed, aggressive leadership. Not only was he the most popular man ever to be elected President, but he had no real political enemies. Nor was this exceptional public attitude only national. It extended to the entire Western world and even, to a degree, to the Communist world. Eisenhower, however, chose the custodial role, and left the country and the world little changed historically as a result of his eight-year tenure. There is no doubt that Eisenhower, a man of great character and integrity, had serious views on the limitations of presidential powers and responsibilities. But however serious, they were lacking in both depth and sophistication, and the President's odd innocence of history was as striking at the end of his terms as at the beginning. His temperament on the other hand, meshed with the mood of the nation, after two decades of coping with war and depression, and he left the presidency no less well loved than he had entered it. And the part that presidential leadership might play in the history of the nation and the world during the second half of the twentieth century was still to be determined as its first decade came to an end in 1960.

WASHINGTON

As the first of every thing, in our situation, will serve to establish a Precedent, it is devoutly wished on my part, that these precedents may be fixed on true principles.[13]

* * *

The President of the United States wishes to avail himself of your sentiments on the following points:

1st. Whether a line of conduct, equally distant from an association with all kinds of company on the one hand and from a total seclusion from Society on the other, ought to be adopted by him? and, in that case, how is it to be done?

2d. What will be the least exceptionable method of bringing any system, which may be adopted on this subject, before the public and into use?

3d. Whether, after a little time, one day in every week will not be sufficient for receiving visits of Compliment?

4th. Whether it would tend to prompt impertinent applications and involve disagreeable consequences to have it known, that the President will, every Morning at eight Oclock, be at leisure to give Audience to persons who may have business with him?

5th. Whether, when it shall have been understood that the President is not to give general entertainments in the manner the Presidents of Congress have formerly done, it will be practicable to draw such a line of discrimination in regard to persons, as that Six, eight or ten official characters (including in the rotation the members of both Houses of Congress) may be invited informally or otherwise to dine with him on the days fixed for receiving Company, without exciting clamours in the rest of the Community?

6th. Whether it would be satisfactory to the public for the President to make about four great entertainmts. in a year on such great occasions as . . . the Anniversary of the Declaration of Independence . . . the Alliance with France . . . the Peace with Great Britain . . . the Organization of the general Government: and whether arrangements of these two last kinds could be in danger of diverting too much of the Presidents time from business, or of producing the evils which it was intended to avoid by his living more recluse than the Presidts. of Congress have heretofore lived.

7th. Whether there would be any impropriety in the Presidents making informal visits; that is to say, in his calling upon his Acquaintances or public Characters for the purposes of sociability or civility: and what (as to the form of doing it) might evince these visits to have been made in his private character, so as that they may not be construed into visits from the President of the United States? and in what light would his appearance rarely at Tea parties be considered?

8th. Whether, during the recess of Congress, it would not be advantageous to the interests of the Union for the President to make the tour of the United States, in order to become better acquainted with their principal Characters and internal Circumstances, as well as to be more accessible to numbers of well-informed persons, who might give him useful information and advices on political subjects?

9th. If there is a probability, that either of the arrangements may take place, which will eventually cause additional expences, whether it would not be proper that those ideas should come into contemplation, at the time when Congress shall make a permanent provision for the support of the Executive?

REMARKS

On the one side no augmentation can be effected in the pecuniary establishment which shall be made in the first instance, for the support of the Executive. On the other, all monies destined to that purpose beyond the actual expenditures, will be left in the Treasury of the United States or sacredly applied to the promotion of some national objects.

Many things which appear of little importance in themselves

and at the beginning, may have great and durable consequences from their having been established at the commencement of a new general government. It will be much easier to commence the administration, upon a well adjusted system, built on tenable grounds, than to correct errors or alter inconveniences after they shall have been confirmed by habit. The President in all matters of business and etiquette, can have no object but to demean himself in his public character, in such a manner as to maintain the dignity of Office, without subjecting himself to the imputation of superciliousness or unnecessary reserve. Under these impressions, he asks for your candid and undisguised Opinions.[14]

These queries were sent to Vice President Adams, Chief Justice Jay, and Secretary of the Treasury Hamilton.

✟ ✟ ✟

To draw such a line for the conduct of the President as will please every body, I know is impossible, but to mark out and follow one (which by being consonent with reason) will meet general approbation, may be as practicable as it is desireable. The true medium I conceive must lye in pursuing such a course, as will allow him time for all the official duties of his station. This should be the primary object. The next, to avoid as much as may be, the charge of superciliousness, and seclusion from information by too much reserve and too great a withdraw of himself from company on the one hand, and the inconveniences, as well as reduction of respectability by too free an intercourse, and too much familiarity on the other.[15]

✟ ✟ ✟

The President of the United States presents his best respects to the Governor, and has the honor to inform him that he shall be at home 'till 2 o'clock.

The President of the United States need not express the pleasure it will give him to see the Governor; but, at the same time, he most earnestly begs that the Governor will not hazard his health on the occasion.[16]

This was a rebuke. Hancock had insisted that Washington, on visiting Boston, should first call on him as governor. This Washington flatly refused to do, and made it clear. Hancock forthwith mended his manners and called on the President.

✦ ✦ ✦

All see, and most admire, the glare which hovers round the external trappings of elevated office. To me there is nothing in it, beyond the lustre which may be reflected from its connection with a power of promoting human felicity. In our progress toward political happiness my station is new; and, if I may use the expression, I walk on untrodden ground. There is scarcely any part of my conduct wch. may not hereafter be drawn into precedent. Under such a view of the duties inherent to my arduous office, I could not but feel a diffidence in myself on the one hand; and an anxiety for the Community that every new arrangement should be made in the best possible manner on the other. If after all my humble but faithful endeavours to advance the felicity of my Country and mankind, I may indulge a hope that my labours have not been altogether without success, it will be the only real compensation I can receive in the closing of life.[17]

✦ ✦ ✦

The powers of the Executive of the U. States are more definite, and better understood perhaps than those of almost any other Country; and my aim has been, and will continue to be, neither to stretch, nor relax from them in any instance whatever, unless imperious circumstances shd. render the measure indispensible.[18]

JOHN ADAMS

People of the United States!—you know not half the solicitude of your presidents for your happiness and welfare, not a hundredth part of the obstructions and embarrassments they endure from intrigues of individuals of both parties. You must support them in their independence, and turn a deaf ear to all the false charges against them. But, if you suffer them to be overawed and shackled in the exercise of their constitutional powers, either by aristocratical or democratical manoeuvres, you will soon repent of it in bitter anguish. Anarchy and civil war cannot be far off. Whereas, by a steady support of the independence of the president's office, your liberties and happiness will be safe, in defiance of all foreign influence, French or English, and of all popular commotion and aristocratical intrigue.[19]

✓ ✓ ✓

Here, according to the practice, if not the Constitution, the ministers are responsible for nothing, the President for every thing. He is made to answer before the people, not only for every thing done by his ministers, but even for all the acts of the legislature. Witness the alien and sedition laws. In all great and essential measures he is bound by his honor and his conscience, by his oath to the Constitution, as well as his responsibility to the public opinion of the nation, to act his own mature and unbiased judgment, though unfortunately, it may be in direct contradiction to the advice of all his ministers. This was my situation in more than one instance.[20]

✓ ✓ ✓

Without running a parallel between the President of the United States and the King of England, it is certain that the honor, dignity, and consistency of government is of as much importance to the people in one case as the other. The President must issue proclamations, articles of war, articles of the navy, and must make appointments in the army, navy, revenue, and other branches of public service; and these ought all to be announced by authority in some acknowledged gazette. The laws ought to be published in the same. It is certain that a President's printer must be restrained from publishing libels, and all paragraphs offensive to individuals, public bodies, or foreign nations; but need not be forbid advertisements. The gazette need not appear more than once or twice a week. Many other considerations will occur to the minds of the secretaries. The President requests their opinion,

1. Whether a printer can be appointed by the President, either with or without the advice and consent of the Senate?

2. Whether a printer can be obtained, without salary or fees, for the profit which might be made by such a gazette?

3. Where shall we find such a printer?

It is certain that the present desultory manner of publishing the laws, acts of the President, and proceedings of the Executive departments, is infinitely disgraceful to the government and nation, and in all events must be altered.[21]

The post of Government Printer, who was first chosen by the Secretary of the Senate and the Clerk of the House, became a financial plum and political football. Beginning in 1819, the printer was elected by both houses. Resulting evils brought about the opening of the Government Printing Office in 1860.

✔ ✔ ✔

When any portion of executive power has been lodged in popular or aristocratical assemblies, it has seldom, if ever, failed to introduce intrigue. The executive powers lodged in the Senate are the most dangerous to the Constitution, and to liberty, of all the powers in it. The people, then, ought to consider the President's office as the indispensable guardian of their rights. I have ever, therefore, been of opinion, that the electors of President ought to be chosen by the people at large. The people cannot be too careful in the choice of their Presidents; but when they have chosen them, they ought to expect that they will act their own independent judgments, and not be wheedled or intimidated by factious combinations of senators, representatives, heads of departments, or military officers.[22]

JOHN QUINCY ADAMS

That revered instrument [the Constitution] enumerates the powers and prescribes the duties of the Executive Magistrate, and in its first words declares the purposes to which these and the whole action of the Government instituted by it should be invariably and sacredly devoted—to form a more perfect union, establish justice, insure domestic tranquility, provide for the common defense, promote the general welfare, and secure the blessings of liberty to the people of this Union in their successive generations.[23]

✔ ✔ ✔

The example of Washington, of retiring from the Presidency after a double term of four years, was followed by Mr. Jefferson, against the urgent solicitations of several state Legislatures. This second example of voluntary self-chastened ambition, by the decided approbation of public opinion, has been held obligatory upon their successors, and has become a tacit subsidiary Constitutional law. If not entirely satisfactory to the nation, it is rather by its admitting one re-election, than by its interdicting a second. Every change of a President of the United States, has exhibited some variety of policy from that of his predecessor. In more than one case, the change has extended to political and even to moral principle; but the policy of the country has been fashioned far more by the influences of public opinion, and the prevailing humours in the two Houses of Congress, than by the judgment, the will, or the principles of the President of the United States. The President himself is no more than a representative of public opinion at the time of his election; and as public opinion is subject to great and frequent fluctuations, he *must* accommodate his policy to them; or the people will speedily give him a successor; or either House of Congress will effectually control his power. It is thus, and in no other sense that the Constitution of the United States is democratic—for the government of our country, instead of a Democracy the most simple, is the most complicated government on the face of the globe.[24]

JACKSON

The people of the United States formed the Constitution, acting through the State legislatures in making the compact, to meet and discuss its provisions, and acting in separate conventions when they ratified those provisions; but the terms used in its construction show it to be a Government in which the people of all the States, collectively, are represented. We are *one people* in the choice of President and Vice-President. Here the States have no other agency than to direct the mode in which the votes shall be given. The candidates having the majority of all the votes are chosen. The electors of a majority of States may have given their votes for one candidate, and yet another may be chosen. The people, then, and not the States, are represented in the executive branch.[25]

Electors were originally chosen, for the most part, by state legislatures. It was not until Jackson's administration that they were chosen directly by popular vote.

✦ ✦ ✦

But how I ask, is this [repeal of unpopular laws] to be effected? certainly not by conceding to one state authority to declare an act of Congress void, and meet all the consequences and hazard that such a course would produce, far from it; there is a better remedy, one which has heretofore proved successful in the worst of times, and all must admit its power. If Congress, and the Executive, feeling power, and forgetting right, shall overleap the powers the Constitution bestow, and extend their sanction to laws which the power granted to them does not permit, the remedy is with the people—not by avowed opposition— not thro open and direct resistance, but thro the more peaceful and reasonable course of submitting the whole matter to them at their elections, and they by their free suffrage at the polls, will always in the end, bring about the repeal of any obnoxious laws which violate the constitution. Such abuses as these cannot be of long duration in our enlightened country where the people rule. Let all contested matters be brought to the tribunal, and it will decree correctly.[26]

✦ ✦ ✦

This is a government of the people. 1st The House of Representatives are their immediate representative or agent. 2d the senate is their agent elected by their agents in the sovereign state assemblies. 3d The President is their agent elected by their immediate agents the electors. ?who does these represent? the people of the *Union*. as law makers over whom does their jurisdiction extend? over *the people of the union*. who are the people of the union? all those subject to the jurisdiction of the sovereign states, none else. and it is an idle feeling that can advocate any other doctrine, or a total ignorance of the real principles upon which our federal union is based.[27]

VAN BUREN

The President under our system, like the king in a monarchy, never dies.[28]

The reference was to acts of presidential succession, providing that the nation will never be without a President.

✦ ✦ ✦

The Constitution requires from the President, and from him only, that he should, in addition to the oath of office, before he enters upon its duties, swear that he will, to the best of his ability, preserve, protect and defend the Constitution of the United States.[29]

✓ ✓ ✓

. . . the President of the United States—the officer clothed with the whole executive power of the Government; the only officer, except the Vice-President, who is chosen by the whole people of the United States; the champion, designated by the Constitution itself to "preserve, protect, and defend" it in the performance of the executive duties committed to his charge, —duties affecting what Hamilton happily describes as "the general liberty of the people. . . ."[30]

WILLIAM H. HARRISON

It could not but have occurred to the [Constitutional] Convention that in a country so extensive, embracing so great a variety of soil and climate, and consequently of products, and which from the same causes must ever exhibit a great difference in the amount of the population of its various sections, calling for a great diversity in the employments of the people, that the legislation of the majority might not always justly regard the rights and interests of the minority, and that acts of this character might be passed under an express grant by the words of the Constitution, and therefore not within the competency of the judiciary to declare void; that however enlightened and patriotic they might suppose from past experience the members of Congress might be, and however largely partaking, in the general, of the liberal feelings of the people, it was impossible to expect that bodies so constituted should not sometimes be controlled by local interests and sectional feelings. It was proper, therefore, to provide some umpire from whose situation and mode of appointment more independence and freedom from such influences might be expected. Such a one was afforded by the executive department constituted by the Constitution. A person elected to that high office, having his constituents in every section, State, and subdivision of the Union, must consider himself bound by the most solemn sanctions to guard, protect, and defend the rights of all and of every portion, great or small, from the injustice and oppression of the rest. I consider the veto power, therefore, given by the Constitution to the Executive of the United States solely as a conservative power, to be used only first, to protect the Constitution from violation; secondly, the people from the effects of hasty legislation where their will has been probably disregarded or not well understood, and, thirdly, to prevent the effects

of combinations violative of the rights of minorities. In reference
to the second of these objects I may observe that I consider it
the right and privilege of the people to decide disputed points of
the Constitution arising from the general grant of power to Congress to carry into effect the powers expressly given; and I
believe with Mr. Madison that "repeated recognitions under
varied circumstances in acts of the legislative, executive, and
judicial branches of the Government, accompanied by indications
in different modes of the concurrence of the general will of the
nation," as affording to the President sufficient authority for his
considering such disputed points as settled.[31]

TYLER

For the first time in our history the person elected to the Vice-
Presidency of the United States, by the happening of a contingency provided for in the Constitution, has had devolved upon
him the Presidential office. The spirit of faction, which is directly
opposed to the spirit of a lofty patriotism, may find in this occasion for assaults upon my Administration; and in succeeding,
under circumstances so sudden and unexpected and to responsibilities so greatly augmented, to the administration of public
affairs I shall place in the intelligence and patriotism of my people my only sure reliance.[32]

*The accession of Tyler, a Democrat, to the presidency on the death
of Harrison, a Whig, with all but a month of a full term to serve,
was highly annoying to the Whigs, who had nominated him for
the vice presidency only to attract dissident Democrats. When Tyler,
first of the Vice Presidents to succeed on the death of a President,
styled himself "President" and not just "Acting President," as John
Quincy Adams for one thought proper, there were outraged protests.*

✦ ✦ ✦

It is true that the succession of the Vice-President to the
Chief Magistracy has never occurred before and that all prudent
and patriotic minds have looked on this new trial of the wisdom
and stability of our institutions with a somewhat anxious concern.
I have been made to feel too sensibly the difficulties of my unprecedented position not to know all that is intended to be con-
veyed in the reproach cast upon a President without a party.
But I found myself placed in this most responsible station by no

usurpation or contrivance of my own. I was called to it, under Providence, by the supreme law of the land and the deliberately declared will of the people. It is by these that I have been clothed with the high powers which they have seen fit to confide to their Chief Executive and been charged with the solemn responsibility under which those powers are to be exercised. It is to them that I hold myself answerable as a moral agent for a free and conscientious discharge of the duties which they have imposed upon me. It is not as an individual merely that I am now called upon to resist the encroachments of unconstitutional power. I represent the executive authority of the people of the United States, and it is in their name, whose mere agent and servant I am, and whose will declared in their fundamental law I dare not, even were I inclined, to disobey, that I protest against every attempt to break down the undoubted constitutional power of this department without a solemn amendment of that fundamental law.[33]

✦ ✦ ✦

I felt that a high and solemn duty had devolved upon me. My resignation would amount to a declaration to the world that our system of government had failed, from the fact that the provision made for the death of the President was either so defective as to merge all executive powers in the legislative branch of the government, by making the succession the mere instrument of their will, or, by forcing him to give way before the embarrassments of his position, devolve the government on another, the remotest probability of whose succession had not been looked to by the people during the elections, and who would therefore be more feeble and impotent in the exercise of an independent mind and judgment than a vice-president. I considered the path of my duty was clearly marked out before me, and I resolved to pursue it.[34]

POLK

. . . my position as President of the U.S. made (it) my duty to represent all the States & to preserve the harmony of the Union as far as I possessed the power to do so.[35]

FILLMORE

The Constitution has made it the duty of the President to take care that the laws be faithfully executed. In a government like ours, in which all laws are passed by a majority of the representatives of the people, and these representatives are chosen for such short periods that any injurious or obnoxious law can very soon be repealed, it would appear unlikely that any great numbers should be found ready to resist the execution of the laws. But it must be borne in mind that the country is extensive; that there may be local interests or prejudices rendering a law odious in one part which is not so in another, and that the thoughtless and inconsiderate, misled by their passions or their imaginations, may be induced madly to resist such laws as they disapprove. Such persons should recollect that without law there can be no real practical liberty; that when law is trampled under foot tyranny rules, whether it appears in the form of a military despotism or of popular violence. The law is the only sure protection of the weak and the only efficient restraint upon the strong. When impartially and faithfully administered, none is beneath its protection and none above its control.[36]

PIERCE

I acknowledge my obligations to the masses of my countrymen, and to them alone.[37]

✦ ✦ ✦

The determination of the persons who are of right, or contingently, to preside over the administration of the Government is under our system committed to the States and the people. We appeal to them, by their voice pronounced in the forms of law, to call whomsoever they will to the high post of Chief Magistrate.

And thus it is that as the Senators represent the respective States of the Union and the members of the House of Representatives the several constituencies of each State, so the President represents the aggregate population of the United States. Their election of him is the explicit and solemn act of the sole sovereign authority of the Union.[38]

BUCHANAN

Except in this single case, [power of impeachment] the Constitution has invested the House of Representatives with no power, no jurisdiction, no supremacy whatever over the President. In all other respects he is quite as independent of them as they are of him. As a co-ordinate branch of the Government, he is their equal. Indeed, he is the only direct representative on earth of the people of all and each of the sovereign States. To them, and to them alone, is he responsible whilst acting within the sphere of his constitutional duty, and not in any manner to the House of Representatives. The people have thought proper to invest him with the most honorable, responsible, and dignified office in the world; and the individual, however unworthy, now holding this exalted position, will take care, so far as in him lies, that their rights and prerogatives shall never be violated in his person, but shall pass to his successors unimpaired by the adoption of a dangerous precedent. He will defend them to the last extremity against any unconstitutional attempt, come from what quarter it may, to abridge the constitutional rights of the Executive, and render him subservient to any human power except themselves.[39]

This and the following excerpt relate to a House committee's attempt to censure Buchanan for allegedly using patronage to influence the vote of Congressmen. It was a partisan action.

✶   ✶   ✶

The trial of an impeachment of the President before the Senate on charges preferred and prosecuted against him by the House of Representatives would be an imposing spectacle for the world. In the result, not only his removal from the presidential office would be involved, but, what is of infinitely greater importance to himself, his character, both in the eyes of the present and of future generations might possibly be tarnished. The disgrace cast upon him would in some degree be reflected upon the character of the American people who elected him. Hence the precautions adopted by the Constitution to secure a fair trial. On such a trial it declares that "the Chief Justice shall preside." This was doubtless because the framers of the Constitution believed it to be possible that the Vice-President might be biased by the fact that, "in case of the removal of the President from office, the same shall devolve on the Vice-President."[40]

✓ ✓ ✓

Urgent and dangerous emergencies may have arisen, or may hereafter arise in the history of our country, rendering delay disastrous, such as the bombardment of Fort Sumter by the Confederate Government, which would for the moment justify the President in violating the Constitution, by raising a military force without the authority of law, but this only during a recess of Congress. Such extreme cases are a law unto themselves. They must rest upon the principle that it is a lesser evil to usurp, until Congress can be assembled, a power withheld from the Executive, than to suffer the Union to be endangered, either by traitors at home or enemies from abroad. In all such cases, however, it is the President's duty to present to Congress, immediately after their next meeting, the causes which impelled him thus to act, and ask for their approbation; just as, on a like occasion, a British minister would ask Parliament for a bill of indemnity. It would be difficult, however, to conceive of an emergency so extreme as to justify or even excuse a President for thus transcending his constitutional powers whilst Congress, to whom he could make an immediate appeal, was in session.[41]

After the Civil War followed in the wake of his administration, Buchanan set to work on a defensive history.

LINCOLN

As the President in the administration of the government, I hope to be man enough not to know one citizen of the United States from another, nor one section from another.[42]

✓ ✓ ✓

This morning, as for some days past, it seems exceedingly probable that this administration will not be reelected. Then it will be my duty to so cooperate with the President-elect as to save the Union between the election and the inauguration; as he will have secured his election on such ground that he cannot possibly save it afterward.[43]

✓ ✓ ✓

I may not have made as great a President as some other man, but I believe I have kept these discordant elements together as well as anyone could.[44]

✓ ✓ ✓

I shall go just so fast and only so fast as I think I'm right and the people are ready for the step.[45]

ANDREW JOHNSON

How far the duty of the President "to preserve, protect, and defend the Constitution" requires him to go in opposing an unconstitutional act of Congress is a very serious and important question, on which I have deliberated much and felt extremely anxious to reach a proper conclusion. Where an act has been passed according to the forms of the Constitution by the supreme legislative authority, and is regularly enrolled among the public statutes of the country, Executive resistance to it, especially in times of high party excitement, would be likely to produce violent collision between the respective adherents of the two branches of the Government. This would be simply civil war, and civil war must be resorted to only as the last remedy for the worst of evils. Whatever might tend to provoke it should be most carefully avoided. A faithful and conscientious magistrate will concede very much to honest error, and something even to perverse malice, before he will endanger the public peace; and he will not adopt forcible measures, or such as might lead to force, as long as those which are peaceable remain open to him or to his constituents. It is true that cases may occur in which the Executive would be compelled to stand on its rights, and maintain them regardless of all consequences. If Congress should pass an act which is not only in palpable conflict with the Constitution, but will certainly, if carried out, produce immediate and irreparable injury to the organic structure of the Government, and if there be neither judicial remedy for the wrongs it inflicts nor power in the people to protect themselves without the official aid of their elected defender—if, for instance, the legislative department should pass an act even through all the forms of law to abolish a coordinate department of the Government—in such a case the President must take the high responsibilities of his office and save the life of the nation at all hazards. The so-called reconstruction acts, though as plainly unconstitutional as any that can be imagined, were not believed to be within the class last mentioned. The people were not wholly disarmed of the power of self-defense. In all the Northern States they still held in their hands the sacred right of the ballot, and it was safe to believe that in due time they would come to the rescue of their own institutions. It gives me pleasure to add that the appeal to our common constituents was not taken in vain, and that my confidence in their wisdom and virtue seems not to have been misplaced.[46]

✓ ✓ ✓

The President of the United States stands toward the country in a somewhat different attitude from that of any member of Congress. Each member of Congress is chosen from a single district or State; the President is chosen by the people of all the States.[47]

HAYES

I am not liked as a President by the politicians in office, in the press, or in Congress. But I am content to abide the judgment —the sober second thought—of the people.[48]

✓ ✓ ✓

Now, the wisdom of the fathers has given to the President a host of motives to be honest and patriotic. Presidents in the past have always been better than their adversaries have predicted. Take, of course, only those who are so far removed by time that no one's sensibilities will be shocked or even touched by allusions to them—say, from Washington to Jackson inclusive. All were free from the least taint of personal corruption. All were honest men. All were in the best sense gentlemen. Compare them with the chief magistrates of the nations of Europe.[49]

CLEVELAND

He who takes the oath to-day to preserve, protect, and defend the Constitution of the United States only assumes the solemn obligation which every patriotic citizen—on the farm, in the workshop, in the busy marts of trade, and everywhere—should share with him. The Constitution which prescribes his oath, my countrymen, is yours; the Government you have chosen him to administer for a time is yours; the suffrage which executes the will of freemen is yours; the laws and the entire scheme of our civil rule, from the town meeting to the State capitals and the national capital, is yours. Your every voter, as surely as your

Chief Magistrate, under the same high sanction, though in a different sphere, exercises a public trust. Nor is this all. Every citizen owes to the country a vigilant watch and close scrutiny of its public servants and a fair and reasonable estimate of their fidelity and usefulness. Thus is the people's will impressed upon the whole framework of our civil polity—municipal, State, and Federal; and this is the price of our liberty and the inspiration of our faith in the Republic.[50]

✦ ✦ ✦

That the office of President of the United States does represent the sovereignty of sixty millions of free people, is, to my mind, a statement full of solemnity; for this sovereignty I conceive to be the working out or enforcement of the divine right of man to govern himself and a manifestation of God's plan concerning the human race.

Though the struggles of political parties to secure the incumbency of this office, and the questionable methods sometimes resorted to for its possession, may not be in keeping with this idea, and though the deceit practiced to mislead the people in their choice, and its too frequent influence on their suffrage may surprise us, these things should never lead us astray in our estimate of this exalted position and its value and dignity.

And though your fellow-citizen who may be chosen to perform for a time the duties of this highest place should be badly selected, and though the best attainable results may not be reached by his administration, yet the exacting watchfulness of the people, freed from the disturbing turmoil of partisan excitement, ought to prevent mischance to the office which represents their sovereignty, and should reduce to a minimum the danger of harm to the State.

I by no means underestimate the importance of the utmost care and circumspection in the selection of the incumbent. On the contrary, I believe there is no obligation of citizenship that demands more thought and conscientious deliberation than this. But I am speaking of the citizen's duty to the office and its selected incumbent.

This duty is only performed when, in the interest of the entire people, the full. exercise of the powers of the Chief Magistracy is insisted on, and when, for the people's safety, a due regard for the limitations placed upon the office is exacted. These things should be enforced by the manifestation of a calm and enlightened public opinion. But this should not be simulated by the mad clamor of disappointed interest, which, without regard for the general good, or allowance for the exercise of official judgment, would degrade the office by forcing compliance with selfish demands.

If your President should not be of the people and one of your fellow-citizens, he would be utterly unfit for the position, incapable of understanding the people's wants and careless of their desires. That he is one of the people implies that he is subject to human frailty and error. But he should be permitted to claim but little toleration for mistakes; the generosity of his fellow-citizens should alone decree how far good intentions should excuse his shortcomings.

Watch well, then, this high office, the most precious possession of American citizenship. Demand for it the most complete devotion on the part of him to whose custody it may be intrusted, and protect it not less vigilantly against unworthy assaults from without.

Thus will you perform a sacred duty to yourselves and to those who may follow you in the enjoyment of the freest institutions which Heaven has ever vouchsafed to man.[51]

✓ ✓ ✓

He [the President] will find that the rules prescribed for his guidance require for the performance of his duty, not the intellect or attainments which would raise him far above the feeling and sentiment of the plain people of the land, but rather such a knowledge of their condition, and sympathy with their wants and needs as will bring him near to them. And though he may be almost appalled by the weight of his responsibility and the solemnity of his situation, he cannot fail to find comfort and encouragement in the success of the fathers of the Constitution, wrought from their simple, patriotic devotion to the rights and interests of the people. Surely he may hope that, if reverently invoked, the spirit which gave the Constitution life, will be sufficient for its successful operation and the accomplishment of its beneficent purposes.[52]

✓ ✓ ✓

It is a high office, because it represents the sovereignty of a free and mighty people. It is full of solemn responsibility and duty, because it embodies, in a greater degree than any other office on earth, the suffrage and the trust of such a people.[53]

✓ ✓ ✓

The acts of an administration should not be approved as a matter of course, and for no better reason than that it represents a political party; but more unpatriotic than all others are those who, having neither party discontent nor fair ground of criticism to excuse or justify their conduct, rail because of personal disappointment; who misrepresent for sensational purposes, and who profess to see swift destruction in the rejection of their plans for governmental management.

After all, we need have no fear that the American people will permit this high office of President to suffer. There is a patriotic sentiment abroad which, in the midst of all party feeling and of party disappointment, will assert itself and will insist that the office which stands for the people's will shall, in all its vigor, minister to their prosperity and welfare.[54]

✓ ✓ ✓

The world does not afford a spectacle more sublime than is furnished when millions of free and intelligent American citizens select their Chief Magistrate, and bid one of their number to find the highest earthly honor and the full measure of public duty in ready submission to their will.

It follows that a candidate for this high office can never forget that, when the turmoil and the strife which attend the selection of its incumbent shall be heard no more, there must be, in the quiet calm which follows, a complete and solemn self-consecration by the people's chosen President of every faculty and endeavor to the service of a confiding and generous nation of freemen.

These thoughts are intensified by the light of my experience in the Presidential office, which has soberly impressed me with the severe responsibilities it imposes, while it has quickened my love for American institutions and taught me the priceless value of the trust of my countrymen.[55]

✓ ✓ ✓

I have also an idea that the Presidency is preeminently the people's office, and I have been sincere in my constant advocacy of the effective participation in political affairs on the part all our citizens. Consequently, I believe the people should be heard in the choice of their party candidates, and that they themselves should make nominations as directly as is consistent with open, fair, and full party organizations and methods.[56]

＊　＊　＊

If I am ever President of this country again, I shall be President of the whole country, and not of any set of men or class in it.[57]

＊　＊　＊

There is nothing in the highest office that the American people can confer which necessarily makes the President altogether selfish, scheming, and untrustworthy. On the contrary, the solemn duties which confront him tend to a sober sense of responsibility; the trust of the American people and an appreciation of their mission among the nations of the earth should make him a patriotic man, and the tales of distress which reach him from the humble and lowly, and needy and afflicted in every corner of the land, cannot fail to quicken within him every kind impulse and tender sensibility.

After all, it comes to this: The people of the United States have one and all a sacred mission to perform, and your President, not more surely than any other citizen who loves his country, must assume part of the responsibility of the demonstration to the world of the success of popular government. No man can hide his talent in a napkin, and escape the condemnation which his slothfulness deserves, or evade the stern sentence which his faithlessness invites.[58]

＊　＊　＊

In the scheme of our national Government the Presidency is preeminently the people's office . . . When, however, I now speak of the Presidency as being preeminently the people's office, I mean that it is especially the office related to the people as individuals, in no general, local, or other combination, but standing on the firm footing of manhood and American citizenship. The Congress may enact laws; but they are inert and vain without executive impulse. The Federal courts adjudicate upon the rights of the citizen when their aid is invoked. But under the constitutional mandate that the President "shall take care that the laws be faithfully executed," every citizen, in the day or in the night, at home or abroad, is constantly within the protection and restraint of the Executive power—none so lowly as to be beneath its scrupulous care, and none so great and powerful as to be beyond its restraining force.

In view of this constant touch and the relationship thus existing between the citizen and the Executive, it would seem that these considerations alone supplied sufficient reason why his selection should rest upon the direct and independent expression of the people's choice. This reason is reinforced by the fact that inasmuch as Senators are elected by the State legislatures, Representatives in Congress by the votes of districts or States, and judges are appointed by the President, it is only in the selection of the President that the body of the American people can by any possibility act together and directly in the equipment of their national Government. Without at least this much of participation in that equipment, we could hardly expect that a ruinous discontent and revolt could be long suppressed among a people who had been promised a popular and representative government.[59]

✔ ✔ ✔

The President, freed from the Senate's claim of tutelage, became again the independent agent of the people, representing a coordinate branch of their Government, charged with responsibilities which, under his oath, he ought not to avoid or divide with others, and invested with powers, not to be surrendered, but to be used, under the guidance of patriotic intention and an unclouded conscience.[60]

✔ ✔ ✔

What is the use of being elected or reelected, unless you stand for something?[61]

BENJAMIN HARRISON

There is no constitutional or legal requirement that the President shall take the oath of office in the presence of the people, but there is so manifest an appropriateness in the public induction to office of the chief executive officer of the nation that from the beginning of the government the people, to whose service the official oath consecrates the officer, have been called to witness the solemn ceremonial. The oath taken in the presence of the people becomes a mutual covenant. The officer covenants to serve the whole body of the people by a faithful execution of the laws, so that they may be the unfailing defense and security of those who observe them, and that neither wealth, station, nor the power of combinations shall be able to evade their just penalties or to wrest them from a beneficent public purpose to serve the ends of cruelty or selfishness.[62]

✦ ✦ ✦

No evil, however deplorable, can justify the assumption either on the part of the Executive or of Congress of powers not granted, but both will be highly blamable if all the powers granted are not wisely but firmly used to correct these evils.[63]

✦ ✦ ✦

The fears of those who said that the power of the office was such as to enable an ambitious incumbent to secure an indefinite succession of terms have not been realized. In practice the popular opinion has limited the eligibility of the President to one re-election. But some of our leading and most thoughtful public men have challenged the wisdom of the four-year term, and have advocated six years, usually accompanied with a prohibition of a second term. And unless some method can be devised by which a less considerable part of the four-year term must be given to hearing applicants for office and to making appointments, it would be wise to give the President, by extending the term, a better chance to show what he can do for the country. It must be admitted, also, that ineligibility to a second term will give to the Executive action greater independence.[64]

✦ ✦ ✦

Two presidents or three, with equal powers, would as surely bring disaster as three generals of equal rank and command in a single army. I do not doubt that this sense of single and personal responsibility to the people has strongly held our Presidents to a good conscience, and to a high discharge of their great duties.[65]

✦ ✦ ✦

A man who is endowed for the presidency will know how to be President, in fact as well as in name, without any fussy self-assertion.[66]

McKINLEY

I can no longer be called the President of a party; I am now the President of the whole people.[67]

THEODORE ROOSEVELT

The thing in connection with the Presidency which has given me the most satisfaction has been my ability to live up to certain ideals. For instance, on my recent trip instead of having nothing but politicians and contractors with me I had at different times men as diverse as John Burroughs, John Muir, President Butler of Columbia University, President Wheeler of California University, Stewart White the author, Seth Bullock a former Deadwood sheriff, etc.,—because I think them all first-rate types of American citizenship of the kind which ought to be close to and in touch with the President.[68]

✓ ✓ ✓

I am President of the United States, and my business is to see fair play among all men, capitalists or wageworkers, whether they conduct their private business as individuals or as members of organizations.[69]

✓ ✓ ✓

I am President of all the people of the United States, without regard to creed, color, birthplace, occupation, or social condition. My aim is to do equal and exact justice as among them all.[70]

✓ ✓ ✓

I had much rather be a real President for three years and a half than a figurehead for seven years and a half.[71]

✓ ✓ ✓

I am President of all the people. I shall not discriminate for or against a man because he is a Catholic or because he is a Protestant, and Catholic or Protestant ecclesiastics who come here and who are men of reputable character will be received by me with the same courtesy. Surely you must agree with this, and I feel I shall have your sympathy with my attitude when I state that I desire to handle myself toward Catholics exactly as I should wish a Catholic President to handle himself towards Protestants—in other words, as I think an American President should behave toward all honest men of any creed.[72]

✓ ✓ ✓

One thing I want you to understand at the start—I feel myself just as much a constitutionally elected President of the
United States as McKinley was. I was voted for as Vice-President, it is true, but the Constitution provides that in case of the
death or inability of the President the Vice-President shall serve
as President, and therefore, due to the act of a madman, I am
President and shall act in every word and deed precisely as if
I and not McKinley had been the candidate for whom the electors cast the vote for President. I have no superstitions and no
misgivings on that score. That should be understood.[73]

✓ ✓ ✓

I am going to be President of the United States and not of
any section.[74]

✓ ✓ ✓

I know I need not tell you that I appreciate to the full the
burdens placed upon me. All that in me lies to do will be done
to make my work a success. That I shall be able to solve with entire satisfaction to myself or any one else each of the many
problems confronting me, I cannot of course hope for, but I
shall do my best in each case, and in a reasonable number of
cases I shall hope to meet with success. At any rate, I want
you to know one thing. I can conscientiously say that my purpose
is entirely single. I want to make a good President and to keep
the administration upright and efficient; to follow policies external and internal which shall be for the real and ultimate benefit of our people as a whole, and all party considerations will
be absolutely secondary.[75]

✓ ✓ ✓

The other day in a very kindly editorial you spoke of me as
saying that I would do anything in the world not dishonorable
or improper or in violation of my conscience to be reelected as
President. I forget the exact word, but this was the sense. It
seems to me that this is calculated to convey a somewhat wrong
impression of what I said. I do not believe in playing the hypo-
crite. Any strong man fit to be President would desire a renomination and reelection after his first term. Lincoln was President
in so great a crisis that perhaps he neither could nor did feel any
personal interest in his own reelection. I trust and believe that if

the crisis were a serious one I should be incapable of considering my own well-being for a moment in such a contingency. I should like to be elected President just precisely as John Quincy Adams, or McKinley, or Cleveland, or John Adams, or Washington himself, desired to be elected. It is pleasant to think that one's countrymen thought well of one. But I shall not do anything whatever to secure my nomination or election save to try to carry on the public business in such shape that decent citizens will believe I have shown wisdom, integrity and courage. If they believe this with sufficient emphasis to secure my nomination and election—and on no other terms can I or would I, be willing to secure either—why I shall be glad. If they do not I shall be sorry, but I shall not be very much cast down because I shall feel that I have done the best that was in me, and that there is nothing I have yet done of which I have cause to be ashamed, or which I have cause to regret; and that I can go out of office with the profound satisfaction of having accomplished a certain amount of work that was both beneficial and honorable for the country.[76]

♦ ♦ ♦

To me there is something fine in the American theory that a private citizen can be chosen by the people to occupy a position as great as that of the mightiest monarch, and to exercise a power which may for the time being surpass that of Czar, Kaiser, or Pope, and that then, after having filled this position, the man shall leave it as an unpensioned private citizen, who goes back into the ranks of his fellow citizens with entire self-respect, claiming nothing save what on his own individual merits he is entitled to receive. But it is not in the least fine, it is vulgar and foolish, for the President or ex-President to make believe, and, of all things in the world, to feel pleased if other people make believe, that he is a kind of second-rate or imitation king. . . . The effort to combine incompatibles merely makes a man look foolish. The positions of President and King are totally different in kind and degree; and it is silly, and worse than silly, to forget this. It is not of much consequence whether other people accept the American theory of the Presidency; but it is of very much consequence that the American people, including especially any American who has held the office, shall accept the theory and live up to it.[77]

✻ ✻ ✻

No man is fit to hold the position of President of the United States at all unless as President he feels that he represents no party but the people as a whole. So far as in me lies I have tried and shall try so to handle myself that every decent American citizen can feel that I have at least made the effort. Each man has got to carry out his own principles in his own way. If he tries to model himself on some else he will make a poor show of it. My own view has been that if I must choose between taking risks by not doing a thing or by doing it, I will take the risks of doing it.[78]

✻ ✻ ✻

There is very much to be said in favor of the theory that the public has a right to demand as long service from any man who is doing good service as it thinks will be useful; and during the last year or two I have been rendered extremely uncomfortable both by the exultation of my foes over my announced intention to retire, and by the real uneasiness and chagrin felt by many good men because, as they believed, they were losing quite needlessly the leader in whom they trusted, and who they believed could bring to a successful conclusion certain struggles which they regarded as of vital concern to the national welfare. Moreover, it was of course impossible to foresee, and I did not foresee, when I made my public announcement of my intention, that the leadership I then possessed would continue (so far as I am able to tell) unbroken, as has actually been the case; and that the people who believed in me and trusted me and followed me would three or four years later still feel that I was the man of all others whom they wished to see President. Yet such I think has been the case; and therefore, when I felt obliged to insist on retiring and abandoning the leadership, now and then I felt ugly qualms as to whether I was not refusing to do what I ought to do and abandoning great work on a mere fantastic point of honor.

There are strong reasons why my course should be condemned; yet I think that the countervailing reasons are still stronger. Of course, when I spoke I had in view the precedent set by Washington and continued ever since, the precedent which recognizes the fact that as there inheres in the Presidency more power than in any other office in any great republic or constitutional monarchy of modern times, it can only be saved from abuse by having the people as a whole accept as axiomatic the position that no man has held it for more than a limited time. I don't think that any harm comes from the concentration of power in one man's hands, provided the holder does not keep it for more than a certain, definite time, and then returns to the people from whom he sprang.[79]

*   *   *

I think that the President should be a strong man, and that he should make the Presidency the strongest kind of office; but because of this very belief, I feel that he should also make it evident that he has not the slightest intention to grasp at permanent power.[80]

*   *   *

I am ready and eager to do my part, so far as I am able, in solving the problems which must be solved, if we of this, the greatest democratic Republic upon which the sun has ever shone, are to see its destinies rise to the high level of our hopes and its opportunities. This is the duty of every citizen; but it is peculiarly my duty, for any man who has ever been honored by being made President of the United States is thereby forever after rendered the debtor of the American people, and is in honor bound throughout his life to remember this as his prime obligation; and in private life, as much as in public life, so to carry himself that the American people may never have cause to feel regret that once they placed him at their head.[81]

*   *   *

The most important factor in getting the right spirit in my Administration, next to the insistence upon courage, honesty, and a genuine democracy of desire to serve the plain people, was my insistence upon the theory that the executive power was limited only by specific restrictions and prohibition appearing in the Constitution or imposed by the Congress under its Constitutional powers. My view was that every executive officer, and above all every executive officer in high position, was a steward of the people bound actively and affirmatively to do all he could for the people, and not to content himself with the negative merit of keeping his talents undamaged in a napkin. I declined to adopt the view that what was imperatively necessary for the Nation could not be done by the President unless he could find some specific authorization to do it. My belief was that it was not only his right but his duty to do anything that the needs of the Nation demanded unless such action was forbidden by the Constitution or by the laws. Under this interpretation of executive power I did and caused to be done many things not previously done by the President and the heads of the departments. I did not usurp power, but I did greatly broaden the use of executive power. In other words, I acted for the public welfare, I acted for the common well-being of all our people, whenever and in whatever manner was necessary, unless prevented by direct constitutional or legislative prohibition. I did not care a rap for the mere form and show of power; I cared immensely for the use that could be made of the substance.[82]

✦ ✦ ✦

The course I followed, of regarding the executive as subject only to the people, and, under the Constitution, bound to serve the people affirmatively in cases where the Constitution does not explicitly forbid him to render the service, was substantially the course followed by both Andrew Jackson and Abraham Lincoln. Other honorable and well-meaning Presidents, such as James Buchanan, took the opposite and, as it seems to me, narrowly legalistic view that the President is the servant of Congress rather than of the people, and can do nothing, no matter how necessary it be to act, unless the Constitution explicitly commands the action.[83]

✦ ✦ ✦

The President is merely the most important among a large number of public servants. He should be supported or opposed exactly to the degree which is warranted by his good conduct or bad conduct, his efficiency or inefficiency, in rendering loyal, able and disinterested service to the Nation as a whole. Therefore it is absolutely necessary that there should be full liberty to tell the truth about his acts, and this means that it is exactly as necessary to blame him when he does wrong as to praise him when he does right. Any other attitude in an American citizen is both base and servile. To announce that there must be no criticism of the President, or that we are to stand by the President, right or wrong, is not only unpatriotic and servile, but is morally treasonable to the American public. Nothing but the truth should be spoken about him or anyone else. But it is even more important to tell the truth, pleasant or unpleasant, about him than about anyone else.[84]

✓ ✓ ✓

Our Governmental officers, from the President down, are of right the servants of the people, not the rulers of the people. This is the fundamental difference between an autocracy and a democracy. The Hohenzollerns are the rulers of Germany, and the Germans are the subjects of the Hohenzollerns, not their fellow citizens. On the contrary, our Presidents are not the rulers of the American people, but the servants of the American people, and the rest of the people are their fellow citizens. Our duty is to stand by the country. It is our duty to stand by the President— as by every other official—just so long as he stands by the country. It is no less our duty to oppose him whenever, and to the extent that, he does not stand by the country. If we fail to oppose him under such conditions, we are guilty of moral treason to the country. The President and our other public officials are subject to the laws just like the rest of us. It is an infamy untruthfully to assail our public servants—or anyone else. But it is our duty to tell the truth about our public servants, whether the truth be pleasant or unpleasant. Tho higher the public servant and the more important his task, the more careful we should be to speak only the truth about him; and the more necessary it is that we should tell the full truth about him.[85]

✓ ✓ ✓

Our loyalty is due entirely to the United States. It is due to the President only and exactly to the degree in which he efficiently serves the United States. It is our duty to support him when he serves the United States well. It is our duty to oppose him when he serves it badly. This is true about Mr. Wilson now and it has been true about all our Presidents in the past. It is our duty at all times to tell the truth about the President and about every one else, save in the cases where to tell the truth at the moment would benefit the public enemy.[86]

TAFT

While the President's powers are broad, the lines of his jurisdiction are as fixed as a written constitution can properly make them. He has tremendous responsibilities. Every President does the best he can, and while we may differ with him in judgment, while we may think he does not bring the greastest foresight to his task, while we may think that he selects poor instruments for his assistants and therefore we may properly vote against his reelection to the office, we must remember that while he is in office, he is the head of our government. We should indulge in his favor the presumption that he acts under a high sense of duty. Correct ideals and disciplined intelligence should impose a special responsibility on men and women as law-abiding American citizens to be respectful to constituted authority and to the President, because it was the American people who chose him, and for the time being he is the personal embodiment and representative of their dignity and majesty.[87]

✦ ✦ ✦

There is little danger to the public weal from the tyranny or reckless character of a President who is not sustained by the people. The absence of popular support will certainly in the course of two years withdraw from him the sympathetic action of at least one House of Congress, and by the control that that House has over appropriations, the Executive arm can be paralyzed, unless he resorts to a coup d'etat, which means impeachment, conviction and deposition. The only danger in the action of the Executive under the present limitations and lack of limitation of his powers is when his popularity is such that he can be sure of the support of the electorate and therefore of Congress, and when the majority in the legislative halls respond with alacrity and sycophancy to his will. This condition cannot probably be long continued. We have had Presidents who felt the public pulse with accuracy, who played their parts upon the political stage with histrionic genius and commanded the people almost as if they were an army and the President their Commander-in-Chief. Yet in all these cases, the good sense of the people has ultimately prevailed and no danger has been done to our political structure and the reign of law has continued. In such times when the Executive power seems to be all prevailing, there have always been men in this free and intelligent people of ours, who apparently courting political humiliation and disaster have registered protest against this undue Executive domination and this use of the Executive power and popular support to perpetuate itself.

The cry of Executive domination is often entirely unjustified, as when the President's commanding influence only grows out of a proper cohesion of a party and its recognition of the necessity for political leadership; but the fact that Executive domination is regarded as a useful ground for attack upon a successful administration, even when there is no ground for it, is itself proof of the dependence we may properly place upon the sanity and clear perceptions of the people in avoiding its baneful effects when there is real danger. Even if a vicious precedent is set by the Executive, and injustice done, it does not have the same bad effect than an improper precedent of a court may have, for one President does not consider himself bound by the policies or constitutional views of his predecessors.

The Constitution does give the President wide discretion and great power, and it ought to do so. It calls from him activity and energy to see that within his proper sphere he does what his great responsibilities and opportunities require. He is no figurehead, and it is entirely proper that an energetic and active clearsighted people, who, when they have work to do, wish it done well, should be willing to rely upon their judgment in selecting their Chief Agent, and having selected him, should entrust to him all the power needed to carry out their governmental purpose, great as it may be.[88]

WILSON

Whatever strength I have and whatever authority I possess are mine only so long and so far as I express the spirit and purpose of the American people.[89]

*   *   *

I cannot choose as an individual what I shall do; I must choose always as a President, ready to guard at every turn and in every way possible the success of what I have to do for the people. Apparently the little things count quite as much as the big in this strange business of leading opinion and securing action; and I must not kick against the pricks . . . The President is a superior kind of slave, and must content himself with the reflection that the *kind* is superior![90]

COOLIDGE

It is desirable for the President to stay for some time in different sections of the country, but a month or six weeks at the most is ample for him to make such observations and acquaintances as are required for him to understand something of the problems of various localities.[91]

✔ ✔ ✔

The words of the President have an enormous weight and ought not to be used indiscriminately.[92]

✔ ✔ ✔

Yet the President exercises his authority in accordance with the Constitution and the law. He is truly the agent of the people, performing such functions as they have entrusted to him. The Constitution specifically vests him with the executive power. Some Presidents have seemed to interpret that as an authorization to take any action which the Constitution, or perhaps the law, does not specifically prohibit. Others have considered that their powers extended only to such acts as were specifically authorized by the Constitution and the statutes. This has always seemed to me to be a hypothetical question, which it would be idle to attempt to determine in advance. It would appear to be the better practice to wait to decide each question on its merits as it arises. Jefferson is said to have entertained the opinion that there was no constitutional warrant for enlarging the territory of the United States, but when the actual facts confronted him he did not hesitate to negotiate the Louisiana Purchase. For all ordinary occasions the specific powers assigned to the President will be found sufficient to provide for the welfare of the country. That is all he needs.[93]

✔ ✔ ✔

It is because in their hours of timidity the Congress becomes subservient to the importunities of organized minorities that the President comes more and more to stand as the champion of the rights of the whole country.[94]

✔ ✔ ✔

The President has tended to become the champion of the people because he is held solely responsible for his acts, while in the Congress where responsibility is divided it has developed that there is much greater danger of arbitrary action.

It has therefore become increasingly imperative that the President should resist any encroachment upon his constitutional powers. One of the most important of these is the power of appointment. The Constitution provides that he shall nominate, and by and with the advice and consent of the Senate appoint. A constant pressure is exerted by the Senators to make their own nominations and the Congress is constantly proposing laws which undertake to deprive the President of the appointive power. Different departments and bureaus are frequently supporting measures that would make them self-perpetuating bodies to which no appointments could be made that they did not originate. While I have always sought cooperation and advice, I have likewise resisted these efforts, sometimes by refusing to adopt recommendations and sometimes by the exercise of the veto power. One of the farm relief bills, and later a public health measure, had these clearly unconstitutional limitations on the power of appointment. In the defense of the rights and liberties of the people it is necessary for the President to resist all encroachments upon his lawful authority.[95]

HOOVER

I learn more each day as to the relation of the Presidential office to the press. It appears to expect me to perform two separate duties, which occasionally in some degree seem to conflict. One duty is to help the people of the United States to get along peacefully and prosperously without any undue commotion or trouble over their affairs—that is, not to start anything that will occasion conflict and dissension. The other duty, which is almost every day borne in powerfully upon me, is that I should provide the press with exciting news of something about to happen. These are duties difficult at times to perform simultaneously.[96]

*   *   *

The President of the United States is obliged to determine a multitude of questions and policies. By the Constitution he must recommend to Congress such measures as he shall deem necessary and expedient, and he is required to finally pass upon every act of Congress. He is the Chief Executive of the greatest business in the world, which at some point touches upon every single activity of our people.

By his position he must, within his capacities, give leadership to the development of moral, social, and economic forces outside of government which make for betterment of our country.[97]

*   *   *

Our great American experiment has demonstrated that the people will of their own initiative take care of progress if the Government can remove abuse and help put the signs on the road, stimulation to all of which is part of the job of Presidents.[98]

* * *

It is well to remember that the office of Chief Executive is in part a symbol of the nation and that leaders in a nation may differ in their own house but they have instant solidarity in the presence of foreign attack.[99]

* * *

No man can be President without looking back upon the effort given to the country by the thirty Presidents who in my case have preceded me. No man of imagination can be President without thinking of what shall be the course of his country under the thirty more Presidents who will follow him. He must think of himself as a link in the long chain of his country's destiny, past and future.[100]

* * *

The Presidency is more than executive responsibility. It is the symbol of America's high purpose. The President must represent the Nation's ideals, and he must also represent them to the nations of the world.[101]

* * *

The nature of the Presidential office as it has evolved through the history of the Republic is somewhat puzzling. Since the Founding Fathers, we had grown from 3,000,000 population to 135,000,000 and from thirteen to forty-eight states. We had grown from an agricultural country to a complex industrial nation. We had risen in power to the first stature among nations. The original constitutional concept of the President's office had certainly been enlarged. He had become a broader policy-maker in legislation, foreign affairs, economic and social life than the Founding Fathers ever contemplated.

The President is, by his oath, one of the protectors of the Constitution. As "Chief Executive" he is administrator of the government. As "Commander-in-Chief" he has a responsibility in national defense. As "Chief Magistrate" he is the chief Federal law enforcement officer. Through his responsibility for foreign relations, he must keep the peace in a world of increasing perplexities. With the growth of the two-party system, he has become the leader of his party, bearing the responsibility to carry out the platform on which he was elected and to keep the party in power. As adviser to the Congress on the state of the nation, he must demonstrate constant leadership by proposing social and economic reforms made necessary by the increasing complexity of American life. He must be the conserver of national resources, and he must carry forward the great public works in pace with public need. He must encourage all good causes. Presidents have given different emphasis to these functions, depending upon the man and the times. In the end the President has become increasingly the depository of all national ills, especially if things go wrong.[102]

✦ ✦ ✦

The first requisites of a President of the United States are intellectual honesty and sincerity.[103]

FRANKLIN D. ROOSEVELT

You will recognize, I think, that a true function of the head of the Government of the United States is to find among many discordant elements that unity of purpose that is best for the Nation as a whole. This is necessary because government is not merely one of the many coordinate groups in the community or the Nation, but government is essentially the outward expression of the unity and the leadership of all groups.[104]

✦ ✦ ✦

Did you ever stop to think that there are, after all, only two positions in the Nation that are filled by the vote of all of the voters—the President and the Vice-President?[105]

✦ ✦ ✦

Whatever his party affiliations may be, the President of the United States, in addressing the youth of the country—even when speaking to the younger citizens of his own party—should speak as President of the whole people. It is true that the Presidency carries with it, for the time being, the leadership of a political party as well. But the Presidency carries with it a far higher obligation than this—the duty of analyzing and setting forth national needs and ideals which transcend and cut across all lines of party affiliation.[106]

✦ ✦ ✦

Every President of the United States in this generation has been faced by the fact that when labor relations are strained to

the breaking point there remains but one high court of concilia-
tion—the Government of the United States.[107]

✶ ✶ ✶

No man can occupy the office of President without realizing
that he is President of all the people.[108]

✶ ✶ ✶

Any President should welcome any American citizen or group
of citizens who can offer constructive suggestions for the management of government or for the improvement of laws.[109]

✶ ✶ ✶

It is an experience in responsibility and humility to be permitted, as President, to know and share the hopes and the difficulties, the patience and the courage, the victories and the
defeats of this great people.[110]

✶ ✶ ✶

I have thought that it was part of the duty of the Presidency to
keep in touch, personal touch, with the Nation. And so this year,
since January, I have already made one trip through a number
of the Southern states on my way back from catching some fish,
and now I am going out to the Coast for the third time since I
have been President—not counting campaign trips—going out
to take a "look-see," to try to tie together in my own mind the
problems of the Nation, in order that I may, at first hand, know
as much about the questions that affect all the forty-eight states
as possible.[111]

✶ ✶ ✶

It is not by any means the sole task of the Presidency to think
about the present. One of the chief obligations of the Presidency
is to think about the future. We have been, in our one hundred
and fifty years of constitutional existence, a wasteful nation, a
nation that has wasted its natural resources and, very often,
wasted its human resources.

One reason why a President of the United States ought to
travel throughout the country and become familiar with every
State is that he has a great obligation to think about the days
when he will no longer be President, to think about the next
generation and the generation after that.[112]

✦ ✦ ✦

For a President especially it is a duty to think in national terms.

He must think not only of this year but of future years when someone else will be President.

He must look beyond the average of the prosperity and well-being of the country, for averages easily cover up danger spots of poverty and instability.

He must not let the country be deceived by a merely temporary prosperity which depends on wasteful exploitation of resources which cannot last.

He must think not only of keeping us out of war today, but also of keeping us out of war in generations to come.[113]

✦ ✦ ✦

As President, I have willingly defended the interests of each of the Nation's great groups to the others, even if the others were critical. I have been just as glad to defend business to labor and agriculture, and to defend labor to business and agriculture, as I have been to defend agriculture to labor and business. That is part of my public duty.[114]

✦ ✦ ✦

The Presidency is not a prize to be won by mere glittering promises. It is not a commodity to be sold by high-pressure salesmanship and national advertising. The Presidency is a most sacred trust and it ought not to be dealt with on any level other than an appeal to reason and humanity.[115]

✦ ✦ ✦

In spite of what some people say, I seek always to be a constitutional President.[116]

✦ ✦ ✦

No President of the United States can make the American contribution to preserve the peace without the constant, alert, and conscious collaboration of the American people.[117]

TRUMAN

As President of the United States, I am guided by a simple formula: to do, in all cases, from day to day, without regard to narrow political considerations, what seems to me to be best for the welfare of all our people.[118]

✶ ✶ ✶

A speech by the President is one of the principal means of informing the public what the policy of the administration is. Because of this, presidential messages have to be written and rewritten many times.

All presidential messages must begin with the President himself. He must decide what he wants to say and how he wants to say it. Many drafts are usually drawn up, and this fact leads to the assumption that presidential speeches are "ghosted." The final version, however, is the final word of the President himself, expressing his own convictions and his policy. These he cannot delegate to any man if he would be President in his own right.[119]

✶ ✶ ✶

The President's relations with the press are of the utmost importance. By way of the press he maintains a direct contact with the people.[120]

✶ ✶ ✶

The President is the man who decides every major domestic policy, and he is the man who makes foreign policy and negotiates treaties. In doing these things it would be very difficult for him to take the second man in the government—the Vice-President—completely into his confidence. The President, by necessity, builds his own staff, and the Vice-President remains an outsider, no matter how friendly the two may be. There are many reasons for this, but an important one is the fact that both the President and Vice-President are, or should be, astute politicians, and neither can take the other completely into his confidence.[121]

✶ ✶ ✶

Then followed a number of unofficial visitors whom a President has to see, because part of his duties are to receive citizens, leaders and spokesmen of representative organizations. These visits are valuable to the President, for they help him keep in touch with the cross section of American interests and opinion. . . .

It is more than a mere ceremonial duty, and although it is a heavy burden on the President, he cannot share it with anyone, for in the White House he is the only directly elected representative of the people.[122]

✦ ✦ ✦

It is only the President who is responsible to all the people. He alone has no sectional, no occupational, no economic ties. If anyone is to speak for the people, it has to be the President.[123]

✦ ✦ ✦

Admidst all these demands on his time, the President must be ready to perform the necessary functions of a head of state, whether they be ceremonial or informal, and he can, of course, never close his doors to the public and, even less so, to the press.[124]

✦ ✦ ✦

A President cannot always to be popular. He has to be able to say *yes* and *no,* and more often *no* to most of the propositions that are put up to him by partisan groups and special interests who are always pulling at the White House for one thing or another. If a President is easily influenced and interested in keeping in line with the press and the polls, he is a complete washout. Every great President in our history had a policy of his own, which eventually won the people's support.[125]

✦ ✦ ✦

It is characteristic of any system where free expression of opinion prevails that the critics and the malcontents will be heard more often than those who support the established policy. In the first place, people who are satisfied with a policy have no reason to be noisy about it; in the second place, our means of communicating and consolidating public opinion—the press and the radio—emphasize the differences of opinion rather than agreements. A President must not be influenced by this distortion of opinion. He must be able to distinguish between propaganda and the true opinion of the people.[126]

✦ ✦ ✦

There is no office quite like the presidency anywhere else in the world. It has great powers. But these powers must be safeguarded against inroads, just as Congress must look after its powers and prerogatives.[127]

✦ ✦ ✦

When there is danger that a vital portion of the economy will be crippled at a time that is critical to the nation's security, then, in my opinion, the President has a clear duty to take steps to protect the nation.[128]

✦ ✦ ✦

The Constitution states that "the executive power shall be vested in a President of the United States of America." These words put a tremendous responsibility on the individual who happens to be President. He holds an office of immense power. It surely is the greatest trust that can be placed in any man by the American people. It is trust with a power that appalls a thinking man. There have been men in history who have liked power and the glamour that goes with it: Alexander, Caesar, Napoleon, to name only a few. I never did. It was only the responsibility that I felt to the people who had given me this power that concerned me. I believe that the power of the President should be used in the interest of the people, and in order to do that the President must use whatever power the Constitution does not expressly deny him.[129]

✦ ✦ ✦

The man who occupies the high office of President is always aware that he is there only because more people wanted him than wanted the other fellow. But if he is to judge his situation by the people around him, he will hear a hundred voices telling him that he is the greatest man in the world for every one that tells him he is not. A President, if he is to have clear perspective and never get out of touch, must cut through the voices around him, know his history, and make certain of the reliability of the information he gets.[130]

EISENHOWER

I have the conception that although elected by only part of the population, as is evident, anybody occupying this office is President of all the people. He has got the responsibility of attempting to develop a program that is enlightened and progressive and for the benefit of all people. And if the success he has in getting assistance and associates around him in his working with the Congress in an effective way—not just in an apparent, you

might say, out-in-front way, but in an effective way—so as to
secure the enactment of such programs, then those people that
are supporting him, people of his own party, people that are supporting that kind of a program, have a real umbrella under which
to operate. That is the best thing I think he can do, both for, you
might say—for his party, because he is working for his country.

I have no intention of going out and getting into partisan struggles in any district or in any State, because I know that I, for
one, in such a State would resent that kind of intrusion from the
President of the United States.[131]

✓ ✓ ✓

Just as I believe that every President is president of all the
people, there is no such thing as a president of the Republicans,
there is no such thing as a president of the Democrats.[132]

✓ ✓ ✓

To this office—to the President, whoever he may be, there
comes every day from all parts of the land and from all parts of
the world a steady flow of dispatches, reports and visitors. They
tell of the successes and the disappointments of our people in
their efforts to help achieve peace with justice in the world.
They tell, too, of the progress and difficulties in building a sturdy,
prosperous and a just society here at home.

On the basis of this information, decisions, affecting all of us,
have to be made every day. Because your President, aside from
the Vice President, is the only governmental official chosen by a
vote of all the people, he must make his decisions on the basis of
what he thinks best for all the people. He cannot consider only
a district, a state or a region in developing solutions to problems.
He must always use the yardstick of the national interest.[133]

✓ ✓ ✓

The Presidency is not merely an institution. In the minds of
the American public the President is also a personality. They
are interested in his thinking. They like the rather informal ex-
changes that come from the representatives of various types of
publications from various geographical areas, and so on. At the
same time, they believe that the President, who is the one official
with the Vice President that is elected by the whole country,
should be able to speak to the whole country in some way.

Now, this press conference habit, which started back some
years, with each President has undergone some innovations.

As you know, we here started the television and the radio on a live basis, whereas, when these things started, they were on the basis of questions submitted by you people; they were written, they were selected then by the press officer and maybe even drafts of answers given, and the President approved them and that was a press conference.

Now, to my mind, that is just not good enough in modern America. I believe they want to see, is the President, probably, capable of going through the whole range of subjects that can be fired at him, and giving to the average citizen some concept of what he is thinking about the whole works.[134]

✓ ✓ ✓

When I am in some other part of the United States, I cannot see that it makes a very great difference in the way the Presidency is conducted, except, of course, when there are times of real tension and difficulty. So, if you have times when there is a great deal on the legislative platter, you try to take only the weekends when they are not busy and go off.

Now, on the contrary, I don't think that a person, just by sitting in this post, will be doing his job best if he sits in Washington. He is, after all, President of the United States; and I think he has got a right to go any place in the United States he chooses. In fact, you will recall one question I got just last week—someone, I believe a Congressman, reported if I'd go around and see little towns more, I would be a better President. He has got something there.

I do not believe that any individual, whether he is running General Motors or the United States of America, his phase of it, can do the best job by sitting at a desk and putting his face in a bunch of papers.

Actually, when you come down to it, when you think of the interlocking staffs and associates that have to take and analyze all the details of every question that comes to the Presidency, he ought to be trying to keep his mind free of inconsequential detail and doing his own thinking on the basic principles and factors that he believes are important so that he can make clearer and better judgments.

And, I tell you, that is the problem of the Presidency—not to give all the details of why some man was fired for this or some other little thing, but to make clear decisions over the best array of facts that he can get into his own brain.[135]

✓ ✓ ✓

I think that the President, as long as he is President, still has an obligation to every single individual in this Nation. Therefore, the rule of reason and of logic and of good sense has got to apply in these things if a man in such position, concerned with the dignity of the office, concerned with its standing, he cannot just go out and be in the hustings and shouting some of the things that we see stated often irresponsibly. I believe he does have a right to make his views known to Americans wherever they are.[136]

✓ ✓ ✓

Your President, of course, will have to be many things. As Chief of State and of Government, he will be your spokesman, presenting to the world your ideals; your firmness in the right; your strength—in fact, the true image of your country.

To perform this task he must thoroughly think through the problems of our time. In this he cannot succeed unless he is free of rashness; of arrogance; of headlong action; of the inclination to easy compromise.[137]

✓ ✓ ✓

The President has to be concerned with everything that happens to any human in the United States and often abroad and that happens to be brought to his notice. He, therefore, has visitors who come into his office who jump from, let's say, a discussion of the situation in Laos, and the next one may come in and introduce the "Teacher of the Year," something that I've always wanted to do, because the teaching profession—I've always tried to show my respect for it. Then comes maybe a half a dozen boys of the Explorer movement in the Boy Scouts, and again you feel something should be done, and then next you're on a problem of the greatest moment and suddenly you find that your schedule called for you to go over and greet the members of the Advertising Council, or the Chamber of Commerce of the United States, and so on. So that one of the things about the Presidency is the way you have to be prepared to jump just like a mountain sheep from one jag to another jag and you're always on the alert.[138]

KENNEDY

I will—at such time as I think it is most useful and most effective, I will attempt to use the moral authority or position of influence of the Presidency in New Orleans and in other places.[139]

✦ ✦ ✦

The President of a great democracy such as ours, and the editors of great newspapers such as yours, owe a common obligation to the people: an obligation to present the facts, to present them with candor, and to present them in perspective.[140]

✦ ✦ ✦

No President can excuse or pardon the slightest deviation from irreproachable standards of behavior on the part of any member of the executive branch. For his firmness and determination is the ultimate source of public confidence in the government of the United States. And there is no consideration that can justify the undermining of that confidence.[141]

✦ ✦ ✦

I bear the responsibility of the Presidency of the United States, and it is my duty to make decisions that no adviser and no ally can make for me. It is my obligation and responsibility to see that these decisions are as informed as possible, that they are based on as much direct, firsthand knowledge as possible.[142]

✦ ✦ ✦

Every Presidential decision cannot be immediately revealed in a major speech, and every Presidential speech cannot reveal a major decision.[143]

Chapter II

THE PRESIDENT AS ADMINISTRATOR

All that the Constitution says of the presidency as an administrative agency is "He may require the opinion in writing of the principal officer in each of the executive departments," he shall appoint all "officers of the United States for whose appointments the Constitution does not otherwise provide," and "he shall take care that the laws be properly executed." The last of these provisions has occasioned by far the greatest growth in the administrative powers of the President. These apparently increasing administrative powers of the presidency have been the subject of continuing controversy, largely over their implications. In the heat of the defense of partisan doctrinal views, however, some very important basic factors are often overlooked. An examination of the writings of the Presidents is a convincing reminder that these factors were not, on the other hand, far removed from their minds.

Such a basic factor in the history of the American presidency is that its fundamental and constitutional powers have not been altered or augmented in any of the amendments to the Constitution from the beginning. Presidential powers as such have actually been expanded very little. What has happened (and this has been going on since Washington's first administration, although sometimes the process has been accelerated by critical events, such as the Civil War and the Depression of the 1930s, or by strong Presidents, such as Jackson and both Roosevelts) is that the area of national affairs over which the President has been able and required to exercise both his explicit and implied powers has expanded immensely. But, in general, the expansion of this area has been commensurate with the growth in industrial, social, and economic intricacy of the society to the advancement of whose interests the President must apply those powers. Even here, however, the influence of the office has been determined primarily by the view that the incumbent took of it.

The second factor to be remembered is that the real uneasiness has probably been occasioned less by the growth of the presidency in power than by the growth of the government in scope, for every new administrative function of the presidency has had its root in an act of Congress. It is consequently as baseless to indict the presidency for usurping powers because it executes those acts, which is a constitutional duty, as it would be to indict the Congress for usurping power because it passed them, which is a constitutional function as long as the act can survive judicial tests.

This leads to the third factor, which is that what the Congress does by way of enhancing the administrative powers of the presidency is subject to judicial review and to popular review at the polls, and can be annulled in the absence of adequate enabling legislation or repudiated if such legislation is held by the courts to be contrary to the Constitution or by the people at the polls to be contrary to their best interests.

It is necessary, therefore, when one is comparing the views of the Presidents on the domestic powers of the presidency, to remember that the area of national affairs subject to executive powers has grown immeasurably. This can be ascribed, in turn, directly to the changing total context of the national life, particularly its economic and technical progress, which has required more and more legislation to keep the government an effective instrument for serving the interests of the people. As a result, the President has had more laws in more areas to execute. As a result of that, he has had to have more administrative bureaus (some of them added to the Executive Department and some independent of it) to execute them.

It is important to remember, too, that all of these agencies have been established by Congress, and not by presidential fiat, and that they were set up to enforce congressional acts and not, except insofar as these are made to aid such enforcement, executive orders. These orders have themselves been the subject of wide misunderstanding, for actually an executive order springs directly from a congressional authorization of the President to make such regulations as are necessary to give effective expression to legislative acts of the Congress. Reference to such orders as a "lawmaking" power of the presidency is a distortion, for they represent no such implied legislative power in the presidency at all and no President has ever claimed such power. They constitute only a regulatory power within the referential framework of a specific act of Congress.

Nor are such authorizations of regulatory orders casually given by the Congress. Ordinarily they have been authorized when an act could be adequately enforced only if the fulfillment of the intent of the act varied with where or when it was applied, as in the case of conservation laws, or in the case of acts designed to meet emergency situations as they arose without recourse to congressional action on each development, such as the War Powers Acts, or in cases when the Congress was able as a matter of sound common judgment to fix a policy (incorporated in and expressed by the act) but was unequipped technically to formulate the detailed regulations necessary to bring about the desired ends, such as in the Pure Food and Drug Acts. By authorizing the President, or a commission appointed by him, to draft as occasion may require the regulatory measures needed to give its act meaning and effectiveness, the Congress does not thereby delegate any of its own basic legislative functions, nor does it abrogate them.

It is not insignificant that nearly all such regulatory powers vested in bureaus of the Executive Department or in independent, quasi-legislative and quasi-judicial agencies, like the Interstate Commerce Commission and the Federal Communications Commission, are largely related to the economic life of the nation or to technical or scientific developments. The increased activity of the Federal Government in the civil rights field has all stemmed from litigations brought by private parties resulting in more stringent judicial decisions on the application of constitutional law and on the enforcement duties of federal agencies. In the area of economics, in which the government does intrude itself by legislative action more conspicuously than in the past, the pace of growth of the nation itself has been amazingly fast. For in this century the major remaining frontier has been and continues to be an economic one. And just as in the last century, when physical frontiers were important, the government legislated broadly concerning the land, so in this century it legislates broadly in economic terms. Such legislation inevitably involves the President, who not only has to execute the new laws but must also recommend to the Congress those measures which he thinks desirable to the national welfare and veto those which he thinks undesirable. An energetic President is apt to take an active role in the formulation of such legislation and to recommend measures with such vigor that the people will respond by themselves exerting pressure upon the Congress to pass them. But that is a constitutional function of the presidency which has from time to time lapsed into such disuse by passive Presidents that it seemed strangely new when fully exercised by the more active ones. Much of this legislation has necessarily resulted in augmenting the statutory powers of the President, largely because it would otherwise be impossible to enforce new acts at all. But one searches in vain to find, except in the case of Lincoln during the first months of the Civil War, any evidence in presidential writings that such powers were arbitrarily pre-empted by the President.

The most exhaustive study of the Executive Department ever made was presided over by one of the most restrained men to have occupied it, Herbert Hoover. He submitted to the Congress a vast bill of particulars that would strengthen the President's office mechanically and organizationally far beyond its present status. Hoover reported that his commission found "that the President and his department heads do not have authority commensurate with the responsibility they must assume"; that "the President lacks authority to organize the agencies of the Executive branch for the most effective discharge of his executive duties"; that the "tendency to create by statute interdepartmental committees . . . has limited the President's authority to choose his advisors"; that the granting of statutory powers to subordinate officers had denied "authority in certain areas to the President"; and, among many other complaints, that "where executive duties are assigned to the independent regulatory commissions [e.g., the Federal Trade or Maritime Commission] the President's authority is also weakened."[1] If all this seems strange coming from a commission presided over by a man who two decades earlier had taken a very narrow view of the powers of the Executive, it should be remembered that the commission studied the presidency as it ought to be rather than as it was and in antiseptic detachment from partisan philosophies.

WASHINGTON

Matters of mere routine, or Office decision, need never wait for any opinion of the President, or even be referred to him; as it serves to encrease (by the transcripts) your [i.e., Cabinet members'] business, and to withdraw his attention from other concerns.[2]

Another general-President, Eisenhower, took the same view. See page 131.

See page 131.

✓ ✓ ✓

It was not, I conceive, the intention of the Law which established the seat of the general government, that the President of the United States should enter into the detail of the business for the execution of which Commissioners were appointed. But it certainly is his duty, when charges of Malpractice, or improper conduct are exhibited against them, to cause the charges to be fairly examined. This I shall do; in the first instance, by transmitting a copy of your letter, that they may severally know, of what they are accused; that, from the answers I shall receive, ulterior measures may be decided on.

This is the line of conduct I have always pursued. For, as I never, on the one hand, suffer information unfavourable to the character, or conduct of public Officers (who are amenable to the Executive) to pass unnoticed; so, on the other, from motives of delicacy as well as justice, I have conceived it proper to hear, always, what they have to say in their justification before a more formal investigation takes place.[3]

✓ ✓ ✓

Lengthy as this letter is, I cannot conclude it without expressing an *earnest* wish that, some intimate and confidential friend of the President's would give him to understand that, his long absence from the Seat of Government in the present critical conjecture, affords matter for severe animadversion by the friends of government; who speak of it with much disapprobation; while the other party chuckle at and set it down as a favourable omen for themselves. It has been suggested to me to make this communication; but I have declined it, conceiving that it would be better received from a private character, more in the habits of social intercourse and friendship.[4]

Washington was referring to the custom of his successor, John Adams, of spending months at a time away from the capital in his Quincy home. For Adams' comment, see below.

JOHN ADAMS

The people elected me to administer the government, it is true, and I do administer it here at Quincy, as really as I could do at Philadelphia. The Secretaries of State, Treasury, War, Navy, and the Attorney-General, transmit me daily by the post all the business of consequence, and nothing is done without my advice and direction, when I am here, more than when I am in the same city with them. The post goes very rapidly, and I answer by the return of it, so that nothing suffers or is lost.[5]

✓ ✓ ✓

If any one entertains the idea, that, because I am a President of [by] three [electoral] votes only, I am in the power of a party, they shall find that I am no more so than the Constitution forces upon me. If combinations of senators, generals, and heads of department shall be formed, such as I cannot resist, and measures are demanded of me that I cannot adopt, my remedy is plain and certain. I will try my own strength at resistance first, however.[6]

✓ ✓ ✓

The organization of the stamp tax suggests a vexation to me. The bill was worth money, and money was so much wanted for the public service, that I would not put it at risk; otherwise I would have negatived that bill; not from personal feelings, for I care not a farthing for all the personal power in the world. But the office of the secretary of the treasury is, in that bill, premeditatedly set up as a rival to that of the President; and that policy will be pursued, if we are not on our guard, till we have a quintuple or a centuple executive directory, with all the Babylonish dialect which modern pedants most affect.[7]

JEFFERSON

The President is to have the laws executed. He may order an offense then to be prosecuted. If he sees a prosecution put into a train which is not lawful, he may order it to be discontinued and put into legal train.[8]

✓ ✓ ✓

Reserving the necessary right of the President of the U.S. to decide, independently of all other authority, what papers, coming to him as President, the public interests permit to be communicated, & to whom, I assure you of my readiness under that restriction, voluntarily to furnish on all occasions, whatever the purposes of justice may require.[9]

✓ ✓ ✓

For our government although in theory subject to be directed by the unadvised will of the President, is, and from its origin has been, a very different thing in practice. The minor business in each department is done by the head of the department on consultation with the President alone; but all matters of importance or difficulty are submitted to all the heads of departments composing the cabinet. Sometimes, by the President's consulting them separately and successively, as they happen to call on him, but in the gravest cases calling them together, discussing the subject maturely, and finally taking the vote, on which the President counts himself but as one. So that in all important cases the Executive is in fact a directory, which certainly the President might control.[10]

✓ ✓ ✓

. . . the preference of a plural over a singular executive, will probably not be assented to here. When our present government was first established, we had many doubts on this question, and many leanings towards a supreme executive council. It happened that at that time the experiment of such an one was commenced in France, while the single executive was under trial here. We watched the motions and effects of these two rival plans, with an interest and anxiety proportioned to the importance of a choice between them. The experiment in France failed after a short course, and not from any circumstance peculiar to the times or nation, but from those internal jealousies and dissensions in the Directory, which will ever arise among men equal in power, without a principal to decide and control their differences. We had tried a similar experiment in 1784, by establishing a committee of the States, composed of a member from every State, then thirteen, to exercise the executive functions during the recess of Congress. They fell immediately into schisms and dissensions, which became at length so inveterate as to render all co-operation among them impracticable; they dissolved themselves, abandoning the helm of government, and it continued without a head, until Congress met the ensuing winter. This was then imputed to the temper of two or three individuals; but the wise ascribed it to the nature of man. The failure of the French Directory, and from the same cause, seems to have authorized a belief that the form of a plurality, however promising in theory, is impracticable with men constituted with the ordinary passions. While the tranquil and steady tenor of our single executive, during a course of twenty-two years of the most tempestuous times the history of the world has ever presented, gives a rational hope that this important problem is at length solved. Aided by the counsels of a cabinet of heads of departments, originally four, but now five, with whom the President consults, either singly or altogether, he has the benefit of their wisdom and information, brings their views to one centre, and produces an unity of thought on their account, because they knew also they had provided a regulating power which would keep the machine in steady movement. I speak with an intimate knowledge of these scenes, *quorum pars fui;* as I may of others of a character entirely opposite. The third administration, which was of eight years, presented an example of harmony in a cabinet of six persons, to which perhaps history has furnished no parallel. There never arose, during the whole time, an instance of an unpleasant thought or word between the members. We sometimes met under differences of opinion, but scarcely ever failed, by conversing and reasoning, so to modify each other's ideas, as to produce an unanimous result. Yet, able and amicable as these members were, I am not certain this would have been the case, had each possessed equal and inde-

pendent powers. Ill-defined limits of their respective departments, jealousies, trifling at first, but nourished and strengthened
by repetition of occasions, intrigues without doors of designing
persons to build an importance to themselves on the divisions of
others, might, from small beginnings, have produced persevering
oppositions. But the power of decision in the President left no
object for internal dissension, and external intrigue was stifled
in embryo by the knowledge which incendiaries possessed, that
no division they could foment would change the course of the
executive power. I am not conscious that my participations in
executive authority have produced any bias in favor of the single executive; action and direction in all the branches of the
government. The excellence of this construction of the executive
power has already manifested itself here under very opposite
circumstances. During the administration of our first President,
his cabinet of four members was equally divided by as marked
an opposition of principle as monarchism and republicanism
could bring into conflict. Had that cabinet been a directory, like
positive and negative quantities in algebra, the opposing wills
would have balanced each other and produced a state of absolute inaction. But the President heard with calmness the opinions
and reasons of each, decided the course to be pursued, and kept
the government steadily in it, unaffected by the agitation. The
public knew well the dissensions of the cabinet, but never had
an uneasy thought on their account, because the parts I have
acted have been in the subordinate, as well as superior stations,
and because, if I know myself, what I have felt, and what I have
wished, I know that I have never been so well pleased, as when
I could shift power from my own, on the shoulders of others; nor
have I ever been able to conceive how any rational being could
propose happiness to himself from the exercise of power over
others.[11]

MADISON

In general, the Secretary of War, like the Heads of the other
Departments, as well by express statute as by the structure of
the Constitution, acts under the authority and subject to the
decisions and instructions of the President, with the exception
of cases where the law may vest special and independent powers
in the Head of the Department.

From the great number and variety of subjects, however, embraced by that Department, and the subordinate and routine

character of a great portion of them, it cannot be either necessary or convenient that proceedings relative to every subject
should receive a previous and positive sanction of the Executive.
In cases of that minor sort, it is requisite only that they be
subsequently communicated, as far and as soon as a knowledge
of them can be useful or satisfactory.

In cases of a higher character and importance, involving
necessarily, and in the public understanding, a just responsibility
of the President, the acts of the Department ought to be either
prescribed by him or preceded by his sanction.

It is not easy to define in theory the cases falling within
these different classes, or, in practice, to discriminate them with
uniform exactness. But a substantial observance of the distinction is not difficult, and will be facilitated by the confidence
between the Executive and the Head of the Department.[12]

✓ ✓ ✓

Should a Head of Department at any time violate the intentions of the Executive, it is a question between him and the
Executive. In all cases where the contrary does not appear, he
is to be understood to speak and to act with the Executive
sanction, or, in other words, the Executive is presumed to speak
and to act through him.[13]

✓ ✓ ✓

With respect to the Executive department, it appears that
every President, from Washington to the present [Jackson]
inclusive, concurred in the legislative construction of the Constitution [on the power to regulate commerce]. For the reiterated
and emphatic proofs, let me refer to the extracts from Executive
messages appended to the letters of J. Madison to J. C. Cabell,
in a pamphlet published in Richmond in 1829. It will be there
seen, that besides the messages of Mr. Jefferson, the great
weight of whose name has been so loudly claimed for the
adverse construction, his very able and elaborate reports, when
Secretary of State, on the fisheries and on foreign commerce,
inculcated the policy of exercising the protective power, without indicating the slightest doubt of its constitutionality. Nay,
more, it will be seen, that in addition to these high official
sanctions to it, his correspondence, when out of office and at
leisure to review his opinions, shows that he adhered to the
protective principle and policy, without any doubt on the point
of constitutional authority. In the scale opposed to all this

evidence, given at different periods of his long life and under varied circumstances, has been but a brief passage in a letter written a few months before his death to Mr. Giles, which does not necessarily imply any change of opinion; on the contrary, by referring the one there expressed to an erroneous and *"indefinite"* abuse of power, in the case of the tariff equivalent to a usurpation of power, any appearance of inconsistency might be avoided.[14]

*   *   *

How, in justice or in truth, could I join in the charge against the President [Jackson] of claiming a power over the public money, including a right to apply it to whatever purpose he pleased, even to his own? However unwarrantable the removal of the deposits or culpable the mode of effectuating it, the act has been admitted by some of his leading opponents to have been not a usurpation, as charged, but as abuse only of power. And however unconstitutional the denial of a legislative power over the custody of the public money as being an Executive prerogative, there is no appearance of a denial to the Legislature of an absolute and exclusive right to appropriate the public money, or of a claim for the Executive of an appropriating power, the charge, nevertheless, pressed with most effect against him. The distinction is so obvious and so essential between a custody and an appropriation, that candour would not permit a condemnation of the wrongful claim of custody without condemning at the same time the wrongful charge of a claim of appropriation.[15]

MONROE

The Executive is charged officially in the Departments under it with the disbursement of the public money, and is responsible for the faithful application of it to the purposes for which it is raised. The Legislature is the watchful guardian over the public purse. It is its duty to see that the disbursement has been honestly made. To meet the requisite responsibility every facility should be afforded to the Executive to enable it to bring the public agents intrusted with the public money strictly and promptly to account. Nothing should be presumed against them; but if, with the requisite facilities, the public money is suffered to lie long and uselessly in their hands, they will not be the only defaulters, nor will the demoralizing effect be confined to them. It will evince a relaxation and want of tone in the Administration which will be felt by the whole community.[16]

✓   ✓   ✓

The President, in whom the executive power is vested, is made commander in chief of the Army and Navy, and militia when called into the service of the United States. He is authorized, with the advice and consent of the Senate, two-thirds of the members present concurring, to form treaties, to nominate and, with the advice and consent of the Senate, to appoint ambassadors, other public ministers, and consuls, judges of the Supreme Court, and all other officers whose appointments are not otherwise provided for by law. He has power to grant reprieves and pardons for offenses against the United States, except in cases of impeachment. It is made his duty to give to Congress from time to time information of the state of the Union, to recommend to their consideration such measures as he may judge necessary and expedient, to convene both Houses on extraordinary occasions, to receive ambassadors, and to take care that the laws be faithfully executed.[17]

✓   ✓   ✓

The reasons in favor of committing the executive department to an individual appear to be conclusive . . . Standing alone, his decision would in all cases be conclusive, and the ministers under him be compelled promptly to obey his orders. There would, therefore, be more energy in the government. His responsibility would also be increased, since the sectional feeling, even in his own quarter, would be diminished, and there would be none elsewhere. By standing alone also, the suspicion of his abuse of power would be much increased, and in consequence his conduct more closely watched, whereby it might be prevented, and if committed, be more easily detected and punished.[18]

JACKSON

A recent proclamation of the present governor of South Carolina [nullifying an act of Congress] has openly defied the authority of the Executive of the Union, and general orders from the headquarters of the State announced his determination to accept the services of volunteers and his belief that should their country need their services they will be found at the post of honor and duty, ready to lay down their lives in her defense. Under these orders the forces referred to are directed to "hold themselves in readiness to take the field at a moment's warning," and in the city of Charleston, within a collection district, and a port of entry, a rendezvous has been opened for the purpose of enlisting men for the magazine and municipal guard. Thus South Carolina presents herself in the attitude of hostile preparation, and ready even for military violence if need be to enforce her laws for preventing the collection of the duties within her limits.

Proceedings thus announced and matured must be distinguished from menaces of unlawful resistance by irregular bodies of people, who, acting under temporary delusion, may be restrained by reflection and the influence of public opinion from the commission of actual outrage. In the present instance aggression may be regarded as committed when it is officially authorized and the means of enforcing it fully provided. . . .

Under these circumstances there can be no doubt that it is the determination of the authorities of South Carolina fully to carry into effect their ordinance and laws after the 1st of February. It therefore becomes my duty to bring the subject to the serious consideration of Congress, in order that such measures as they in their wisdom may deem fit shall be seasonably provided, and that it may be thereby understood that while the Government is disposed to remove all just cause of complaint as far as may be practicable consistently with a proper regard to the interests of the community at large, it is nevertheless determined that supremacy of the laws shall be maintained.

In the uncertainty, then, that exists as to the duration of the ordinance and of the enactments for enforcing it, it becomes imperiously the duty of the Executive of the United States, acting with a proper regard to all the great interests committed to his care, to treat those acts as absolute and unlimited. They are so far as his agency is concerned. He can not either embrace or lead to the performance of the conditions. He has already discharged the only part in his power by the recommendation in his annual message. The rest is with Congress and the people, and until they have acted his duty will require him to look to the existing state of things and act under them according to his high obligations. . . .

The right of the people of a single State to absolve themselves at will and without the consent of the other States from their most solemn obligations, and hazard the liberties and happiness of the millions composing this Union, can not be acknowledged.

Such authority is believed to be utterly repugnant both to the principles upon which the General Government is constituted and to the objects which it is expressly formed to attain. . . .

These deductions plainly flow from the nature of the federal compact, which is one of limitations, not only upon the powers originally possessed by the parties thereto, but also upon those conferred on the Government and every department thereof. It will be freely conceded that by the principles of our system all power is vested in the people, but to be exercised in the mode and subject to the checks which the people themselves have prescribed. These checks are undoubtedly only different modifications of the same great popular principle which lies at the foundation of the whole, but are not on that account to be less regarded or less obligatory.

Upon the power of Congress, the veto of the Executive and the authority of the judiciary, which is to extend to all cases in law and equity arising under the Constitution and laws of the United States made in pursuance thereof, are the obvious checks, and the sound action of public opinion, with the ultimate power of amendment, are the salutary and only limitation upon the powers of the whole. . . .

The Constitution, which his oath of office obliges him to support, declares that the Executive *"shall take care that the laws be faithfully executed,"* and in providing that he shall from time to time give to Congress information of the state of the Union, and recommend to their consideration such measures as he shall judge necessary and expedient, imposes the additional obligation of recommending to Congress such more efficient provision for executing the laws as may from time to time be found requisite. . . .

The rich inheritance bequeathed by our fathers has devolved upon us the sacred obligation of preserving it by the same virtues which conducted them through the eventful scenes of the Revolution and ultimately crowned their struggle with the noblest model of civil institutions. They bequeathed to us a Government of laws and a Federal Union founded upon the great principle of popular representation. After a successful experiment of forty-four years, at a moment when the Government and the Union are the objects of the hopes of the friends of civil liberty throughout the world, and in the midst of public and individual prosperity unexampled in history, we are called to decide whether these laws possess any force and that Union the means of self-preservation. The decision of this question by an enlightened and patriotic people can not be doubtful. For myself, fellow-citizens, devoutly relying upon that kind Providence which has hitherto watched over our destinies, and actuated by a profound reverence for those institutions I have so much cause to love, and for the American people, whose partiality honored me with their highest trust, I have determined to spare no effort to discharge the duty which in this conjuncture is devolved upon me. That a similar spirit will actuate the representatives of the American people is not to be questioned; and I fervently pray that the Great Ruler of Nations may so guide your deliberations and our joint measures as that they may prove salutary examples not only to the present but to future times, and solemnly proclaim that the Constitution and the laws are supreme and the *Union indissoluble*.[19]

* * *

Having carefully and anxiously considered all the facts and arguments which have been submitted to him relative to a removal of the public deposits from the Bank of the United States [a private institution], the President deems it his duty to communicate in this manner to his Cabinet the final conclusions of his own mind and the reasons on which they are founded, in order to put them in durable form and to prevent misconceptions.

The President's convictions of the dangerous tendencies of the Bank of the United States, since signally illustrated by its own acts, were so overpowering when he entered on the duties of Chief Magistrate that he felt it his duty, notwithstanding the objections of the friends by whom he was surrounded, to avail himself of the first occasion to call the attention of Congress and the people to the question of its recharter. . . .

The object avowed by many of the advocates of the bank was to *put the President to the test*, that the country might know his final determination relative to the bank prior to the ensuing election. Many documents and articles were printed and circulated at the expense of the bank to bring the people to a favorable decision upon its pretensions. Those whom the bank appears to have made its debtors for the special occasion were warned of the ruin which awaited them should the President be sustained, and attempts were made to alarm the whole people by painting the depression in the price of property and produce and the general loss, inconvenience, and distress which it was represented would immediately follow the reelection of the President in opposition to the bank.

Can it now be said that the question of a recharter of the bank was not decided at the election which ensued? Had the veto been equivocal, or had it not covered the whole ground; if it had merely taken exceptions to the details of the bill or to the time of its passage; if it had not met the whole ground of constitutionality and expediency, then there might have been some plausibility for the allegation that the question was not decided by the people. It was to compel the President to take his stand that the question was brought forward at that particular time. He met the challenge, willingly took the position into which his adversaries sought to force him, and frankly declared his unalterable opposition to the bank as being both unconstitutional and inexpedient. On that ground the case was argued to the people; and now that the people have sustained the President, notwithstanding the array of influence and power which was brought to bear upon him, it is too late, he confidently thinks, to say that the question has not been decided. Whatever may be the opinions of others, the President considers his reelection as a decision of the people against the bank. In the concluding paragraph of his veto message he said:

I have now done my duty to my country. If sustained by my fellow-citizens, I shall be grateful and happy; if not, I shall find in the motives which impel me ample grounds for contentment and peace.

He was sustained by a just people, and he desires to evince his gratitude by carrying into effect their decision so far as it depends upon him.[20]

✓ ✓ ✓

It is for the wisdom of Congress to decide upon the best substitute to be adopted in the place of the Bank of the United States, and the President would have felt himself relieved from a heavy and painful responsibility if in the charter to the bank Congress had reserved to itself the power of directing at its pleasure the public money to be elsewhere deposited, and had not devolved that power exclusively on one of the Executive Departments. It is useless now to inquire why this high and important power was surrendered by those who are peculiarly and appropriately the guardians of the public money. Perhaps it was an oversight. But as the President presumes that the charter to the bank is to be considered as a contract on the part of the Government, it is not now in the power of Congress to disregard its stipulations; and by the terms of that contract the public money is to be deposited in the bank during the continuance of its charter unless the Secretary of the Treasury shall otherwise direct. Unless, therefore, the Secretary of the Treasury first acts, Congress have no power over the subject, for they can not add a new clause to the charter or strike one out of it without the consent of the bank, and consequently the public money must remain in that institution to the last hour of its existence unless the Secretary of the Treasury shall remove it at an earlier day. The responsibility is thus thrown upon the executive branch of the Government of deciding how long before the expiration of the charter the public interest will require the deposits to be placed elsewhere; and although according to the frame and principle of our Government this decision would seem more properly to belong to the legislative power, yet as the law has imposed it upon the executive department the duty ought to be faithfully and firmly met, and the decision made and executed upon the the best lights that can be obtained and the best judgment that can be formed. It would ill become the executive branch of the Government to shrink from any duty which the law imposes on it, to fix upon others the responsibility which justly belongs to itself. And while the President anxiously wishes to abstain from the exercise of doubtful powers and to avoid all interference with the rights and duties of others, he must yet with unshaken constancy discharge his own obligations, and can not allow himself to turn aside in order to avoid any responsibility which the high trust with which he has been honored requires him to encounter; and it being the duty of one of the Executive Departments to decide in the first instance, subject to the future action of the legislative power, whether the public deposits shall remain in the Bank of the United States until the end of its existence or be withdrawn some time before, the President has felt himself bound to examine the question carefully and deliberately in order to make up his judgment on the subject, and in his opinion the near approach of the termination of the charter and the public considerations heretofore mentioned are of themselves amply sufficient to justify the removal of the deposits, without reference to the conduct of the bank or their safety in its keeping.[21]

Jackson wrested control of the currency from private hands by ordering withdrawal of public funds from the government-chartered but privately operated Bank of the United States.

✦ ✦ ✦

But in the conduct of the bank [of the United States] may be found other reasons, very imperative in their character, and which require prompt action. Developments have been made from time to time of its faithlessness as a public agent, its misapplication of public funds, its interference in elections, its efforts by the machinery of committees to deprive the Government directors of a full knowledge of its concerns, and, above all, its flagrant misconduct as recently and unexpectedly disclosed in placing all the funds of the bank, including the money of the Government, at the disposition of the president of the bank as means of operating upon public opinion and procuring a new charter, without requiring him to render a voucher for their disbursement. A brief recapitulation of the facts which justify these charges, and which have come to the knowledge of the public and the President, will, he thinks, remove every reasonable doubt as to the course which it is now the duty of the President to pursue.[22]

✦ ✦ ✦

If the question of a removal of the deposits presented itself to the Executive in the same attitude that it appeared before the House of Representatives at their last session, their resolution in relation to the safety of the deposits would be entitled to more weight, although the decision of the question of removal has been confided by law to another department of the Government. But the question now occurs attended by other circumstances and new disclosures of the most serious import. It is true that in the message of the President which produced this inquiry and resolution on the part of the House of Representatives it was his object to obtain the aid of that body in making a thorough examination into the conduct and condition of the bank and its branches in order to enable the executive department to decide whether the public money was longer safe in its hands. The limited power of the Secretary of the Treasury over the subject disabled him from making the investigation as fully and satisfactorily as it could be done by a committee of the House of Representatives, and hence the President desired the assistance of Congress to obtain for the Treasury Department a full knowledge of all the facts which were necessary to guide his judgment. But it was not his purpose, as the language of his message will show, to ask the representatives of the people to assume a responsibility which did not belong to them and relieve the executive branch of the Government from the duty which the law had imposed upon it. It is due to the President that his object in that proceeding should be distinctly understood, and that he should acquit himself of all suspicion of seeking to escape from the performance of his own duties or of desiring to interpose another body between himself and the people in order to avoid a measure which he is called upon to meet. But although as an act of justice to himself he disclaims any design of soliciting the opinion of the House of Representatives in relation to his own duties in order to shelter himself from responsibility under the sanction of their counsel, yet he is at all times ready to listen to the suggestions of the representatives of the people, whether given voluntarily or upon solicitation, and to consider them with the profound respect to which all will admit that they are justly entitled. Whatever may be the consequences, however, to himself, he must finally form his own judgment where the Constitution and the law make it his duty to decide, and must act accordingly; and he is bound to suppose that such a course on his part will never be regarded by that elevated body as a mark of disrespect to itself, but that they will, on the contrary, esteem it the strongest evidence he can give of his fixed resolution conscientiously to discharge his duty to them and the country.[23]

✴ ✴ ✴

It is the desire of the President that the control of the banks and the currency shall, as far as possible, be entirely separated from the political power of the country as well as wrested from an institution which has already attempted to subject the Government to its will. In his opinion the action of the General Government on this subject ought not to extend beyond the grant in the Constitution, which only authorized Congress "to coin money and regulate the value thereof"; all else belongs to the States and the people, and must be regulated by public opinion and the interests of trade.

In conclusion, the President must be permitted to remark that he looks upon the pending question as of higher consideration than the mere transfer of a sum of money from one bank to another. Its decision may affect the character of our Government for ages to come. Should the bank be suffered longer to use the public moneys in the accomplishment of its purposes, with the proofs of its faithlessness and corruption before our eyes, the patriotic among our citizens will despair of success in struggling against its power, and we shall be responsible for entailing it upon our country forever. Viewing it as a question of transcendent importance, both in the principles and consequences it involves, the President could not, in justice to the responsibility which he owes to the country, refrain from pressing upon the Secretary of the Treasury his view of the considerations which impel to immediate action. Upon him has been devolved by the Constitution and the suffrages of the American people the duty of superintending the operation of the Executive Departments of the Government and seeing that the laws are faithfully executed. In the performance of this high trust it is his undoubted right to express to those whom the laws and his own choice have made his associates in the administration of the Government his opinion of their duties under circumstances as they arise. It is this right which he now exercises. Far be it from him to expect or require that any member of the Cabinet should at his request, order, or dictation do any act which he believes unlawful or in his conscience condemns. From them and from his fellow-citizens in general he desires only that aid and support which their reason approves and their conscience sanctions.[24]

✦ ✦ ✦

The custody of the public property, under such regulations as may be prescribed by legislative authority, has always been considered an appropriate function of the executive department in this and all other Governments. In accordance with this principle, every species of property belonging to the United States (excepting that which is in the use of the several coordinate departments of the Government as means to aid them in performing their appropriate functions) is in charge of officers appointed by the President, whether it be lands, or buildings, or merchandise, or provisions, or clothing, or arms and munitions of war. The superintendents and keepers of the whole are appointed by the President, responsible to him, and removable at his will.

Public money is but a species of public property. It can not be raised by taxation or customs, nor brought into the Treasury in any other way except by law; but whenever or howsoever obtained, its custody always has been and always must be, unless the Constitution be changed, intrusted to the executive department. No officer can be created by Congress for the purpose of taking charge of it whose appointment would not by the Constitution at once devolve on the President and who would not be responsible to him for the faithful performance of his duties. The legislative power may undoubtedly bind him and the President by any laws they may think proper to enact; they may prescribe in what place particular portions of the public property shall be kept and for what reason it shall be removed, as they may direct that supplies for the Army or Navy shall be kept in particular stores, and it will be the duty of the President to see that the law is faithfully executed; yet will the custody remain in the executive department of the Government. Were the Congress to assume, with or without a legislative act, the power of appointing officers, independently of the President, to take the charge and custody of the public property contained in the military and naval arsenals, magazines, and storehouses, it is believed that such an act would be regarded by all as a palpable usurpation of executive power, subversive of the form as well as the fundamental principles of our Government. But where is the difference in principle whether the public property be in the form of arms, munitions of war, and supplies or in gold and silver or bank notes? None can be perceived; none is believed to exist. Congress can not, therefore, take out of the hands of the executive department the custody of the public property or money without an assumption of executive power and a subversion of the first principles of the Constitution.[25]

↗ ↗ ↗

It would be an extraordinary result if because the person charged by law with a public duty is one of his Secretaries it were less the duty of the President to see that law faithfully executed than other laws enjoining duties upon subordinate officers or private citizens. If there be any difference, it would seem that the obligation is the stronger in relation to the former, because the neglect is in his presence and the remedy at hand.

It can not be doubted that it was the legal duty of the Secretary of the Treasury to order and direct the deposits of the public money to be made elsewhere than in the Bank of the United States *whenever sufficient reasons existed for making the change.* If in such a case he neglected or refused to act, he would neglect or refuse to execute the law. What would be the sworn duty of the President? Could he say that the Constitution did not bind him to see the law faithfully executed because it was one of his

Secretaries and not himself upon whom the service was specially imposed? Might he not be asked whether there was any such limitation to his obligations prescribed in the Constitution? Whether he is not equally bound to take care that the laws be faithfully executed, whether they impose duties on the highest officer of State or the lowest subordinate in any of the Departments? Might he not be told that it was for the sole purpose of causing all executive officers, from the highest to the lowest, faithfully to perform the services required of them by law that the people of the United States have made him their Chief Magistrate and the Constitution has clothed him with the entire executive power of this Government? The principles implied in these questions appear too plain to need elucidation.[26]

Congress had censured Jackson for removing the Secretary of the Treasury, who had refused to carry out the order to remove public funds from the Bank of the United States.

✦ ✦ ✦

The dangerous tendency of the doctrine which denies to the President the power of supervising, directing, and controlling the Secretary of the Treasury in like manner with the other executive officers would soon be manifest in practice were the doctrine to be established. The President is the direct representative of the American people, but the Secretaries are not. If the Secretary of the Treasury be independent of the President in the execution of the laws, then is there no direct responsibility to the people in that important branch of this Government to which is committed the care of the national finances. And it is in the power of the Bank of the United States, or any other corporation, body of men, or individuals, if a Secretary shall be found to accord with them in opinion or can be induced in practice to promote their views, to control through him the whole action of the Government (so far as it is exercised by his Department) in defiance of the Chief Magistrate elected by the people and responsible to them.

But the evil tendency of the particular doctrine adverted to, though sufficiently serious, would be as nothing in comparison with the pernicious consequences which would inevitably flow from the approbation and allowance by the people and the practice by the Senate of the unconstitutional power of arraigning and censuring the official conduct of the executive in the manner recently pursued. Such proceedings are eminently calculated to unsettle the foundations of the Government, to disturb the harmonious action of its different departments, and to break down the checks and balances by which the wisdom of its framers sought to insure its stability and usefulness.

The honest differences of opinion which occasionally exist between the Senate and the President in regard to matters in which both are obliged to participate are sufficiently embarrassing; but if the course recently adopted by the Senate shall hereafter be frequently pursued, it is not only obvious that the harmony of the relations between the President and the Senate will be destroyed, but that other and graver effects will ultimately ensue. If the censures of the Senate be submitted to by the President, the confidence of the people in his ability and virtue and the character and usefulness of his Administration will soon be at an end, and the real power of the Government will fall into the hands of a body holding their offices for long terms, not elected by the people and not to them directly responsible. If, on the other hand, the illegal censures of the Senate should be resisted by the President, collisions and angry controversies might ensue, discreditable in their progress and in the end compelling the people to adopt the conclusion either that their Chief Magistrate was unworthy of their respect or that the Senate was chargeable with calumny and injustice. Either of these results would impair public confidence in the perfection of the system and lead to serious alterations of its framework or to the practical abandonment of some of its provisions.[27]

VAN BUREN

All executive authority to be exercised under it [the Constitution] was granted to the President, and he was hence spoken of by the writers of the 'Federalist' as the *sole depositary* of executive power.[28]

WILLIAM H. HARRISON

Amongst the other duties of a delicate character which the President is called upon to perform is the supervision of the government of the Territories of the United States.[29]

TYLER

In answer to a resolution of the House of Representatives of the 7th of February, 1842, in the following words—

> *Resolved*, That the President of the United States inform this House under what authority the commission, consisting of George Poindexter and others, for the investigation of the concerns of the New York custom-house was raised; what were the purposes and objects of said commission; how many persons have in any way been connected with it, and the compensation received or to be received by each; and the aggregate amount of every description of said commission, and out of what fund the said expenditures have been or are to be paid—

I have to state that the authority for instituting the commission mentioned in said resolution is the authority vested in the President of the United States to "take care that the laws be faithfully executed, and to give to Congress from time to time information on the state of the Union, and to recommend to their consideration such measures as he shall judge necessary and expedient."[30]

Tyler was telling a hostile Congress, unreconciled to his accession on Harrison's death, that he was doing his job as President.

✦ ✦ ✦

If by the assertion of this claim of right to call upon the Executive for all the information in its possession relating to any subject of the deliberation of the House, and within the sphere of its legitimate powers, it is intended to assert also that the Executive is bound to comply with such call without the authority to exercise any discretion on its part in reference to the nature of the information required or to the interests of the country or of individuals to be affected by such compliance, then do I feel bound, in the discharge of the high duty imposed upon me "to preserve, protect, and defend the Constitution of the United States," to declare in the most respectful manner my entire dissent from such a proposition. The instrument from which the several departments of the Government derive their authority makes each independent of the other in the discharge of their respective functions. The injunction of the Constitution that the President "shall take care that the laws be faithfully executed" necessarily confers an authority commensurate with the obligation imposed to inquire into the manner in which all public agents perform the duties assigned to them by law. To be effective these inquires must often be confidential. They may result in the collection of truth or of falsehood, or they may be incomplete and may require further prosecution. To maintain that the President can exercise no discretion as to the time in which the matters thus collected shall be promulgated or in respect to the character of the information obtained would deprive him at once of the means of performing one of the most salutary duties of his office. An inquiry might be arrested at its first stage and the officers whose conduct demanded investigation may be enabled to elude or defeat it. To require from the Executive the transfer of this discretion to a coordinate branch of the Government is equivalent to the denial of its possession by him and would render him dependent upon that branch in the performance of a duty purely executive.

Nor can it be a sound position that all papers, documents, and information of every description which may happen by any means to come into the possession of the President or of the heads of Departments must necessarily be subject to the call of the House of Representatives *merely* because they relate to a subject of the deliberations of the House, although that subject may be within the sphere of its legitimate powers. It can not be that the only test is whether the information relates to a legitimate subject of deliberation. The Executive Departments and the citizens of this country have their rights and duties as well as the House of Representatives, and the maxim that the rights of one person or body are to be so exercised as not to impair those of others is applicable in its fullest extent to this question. Impertinence or malignity may seek to make the Executive Departments the means of incalculable and irremediable injury to innocent parties by throwing into them libels most foul and atrocious. Shall there be no discretionary authority permitted to refuse to become the instruments of such malevolence?[81]

↑   ↑   ↑

In a communication made by the Secretary of War in 1832 to the Committee of the House on the Public Lands, by direction of President Jackson, he denies the obligation of the Executive to furnish the information called for and maintains the authority of the President to exercise a sound discretion in complying with calls of that description by the House of Representatives or its committees. Without multiplying other instances, it is not deemed improper to refer to the refusal of the President at the last session of the present Congress to comply with a resolution of the House of Representatives calling for the names of the members of Congress who had applied for offices. As no further notice was taken in any form of this refusal, it would seem to be a fair inference that the House itself admitted that there were cases in which the President had a discretionary authority in respect to the transmission of information in the possession of any of the Executive Departments.[32]

✦ ✦ ✦

Since my accession to the presidency I have had to encounter trials of no ordinary character. A great experiment was, under Providence, committed to my hands. It was no other than a test as to the sufficiency of our institutions to meet the contingency which for the first time had occurred in our history, of the death of the president, and the succession of a vice-president to the administration of public affairs. In entering upon the office I had to decide the question whether I would surrender honor, judgment, conscience, and the right of an independent mind, into the hands of a party majority, in whose views and opinions, it became very soon obvious, I could not concur without such surrender; or whether I should brave all consequences in the vindication of the constitutional rights of the executive, and in the discharge of the most sacred obligations of duty to the country. By adopting the first course, I was perfectly aware that my presidential term would throughout be peaceable and tranquil, and that I should receive the zealous and ardent support of a controlling and dominant party; by pursuing the latter, I should incur the most violent denunciations, the bitterest reproaches, the most unrelenting persecutions, while I could look to no active support from any engaged in the administration of public affairs.[33]

PIERCE

Meanwhile information, not only reliable in its nature, but of an official character, was received to the effect that preparation was making within the limits of the United States by private individuals under military organization for a descent upon the island of Cuba with a view to wrest that colony from the dominion of Spain. International comity, the obligations of treaties, and the express provisions of law alike required, in my judgment, that all the constitutional power of the Executive should be exerted to prevent the consummation of such a violation of positive law and of that good faith on which mainly the amicable relations of neighboring nations must depend. In conformity with these convictions of public duty, a proclamation was issued to warn all persons not to participate in the contemplated enterprise and to invoke the interposition in this behalf of the proper officers of the Government. No provocation whatever can justify private expeditions of hostility against a country at peace with the United States. The power to declare war is vested by the Constitution in Congress, and the experience of our past history leaves no room to doubt that the wisdom of this arrangement of constitutional power will continue to be verified whenever the national interest and honor shall demand a resort to ultimate measures of redress. Pending negotiations by the Executive, and before the action of Congress, individuals could not be permitted to embarrass the operations of the one and usurp the powers of the other of these depositaries of the functions of Government.[34]

*   *   *

No citizen of our country should permit himself to forget that he is a part of its Government and entitled to be heard in the determination of its policy and its measures, and that therefore the highest considerations of personal honor and patriotism require him to maintain by whatever of power or influence he may possess the integrity of the laws of the Republic.

Entertaining these views, it will be my imperative duty to exert the whole power of the Federal Executive to support public order in the Territory [of Kansas, in slavery dispute]; to vindicate its laws, whether Federal or local, against all attempts of organized resistance, and so to protect its people in the establishment of their own institutions, undisturbed by encroachment from without, and in the full enjoyment of the rights of self-government assured to them by the Constitution and the organic act of Congress.[35]

*   *   *

In such an event the path of duty for the Executive is plain. The Constitution requiring him to take care that the laws of the United States be faithfully executed, if they be opposed in the Territory of Kansas he may, and should, place at the disposal of the marshal any public force of the United States which happens to be within the jurisdiction, to be used as a portion of the *posse comitatus;* and if that do not suffice to maintain order, then he may call forth the militia of one or more States for that object, or employ for the same object any part of the land or naval force of the United States. So, also, if the obstruction be to the laws of the Territory, and it be duly presented to him as a case of insurrection, he may employ for its suppression the militia of any State or the land or naval force of the United States. And if the Territory be invaded by the citizens of other States, whether for the purpose of deciding elections or for any other, and the local authorities find themselves unable to repel or withstand it, they will be entitled to, and upon the fact being fully ascertained they shall most certainly receive, the aid of the General Government.[36]

BUCHANAN

In one form or other under the acts of 1793 and 1850, both being substantially the same, the fugitive slave law has been the law of the land from the days of Washington until the present moment. Here, then, a clear case is presented, in which it will be the duty of the next President, as it has been my own, to act with vigor in executing this supreme law against the conflicting enactments of State Legislatures. Should he fail in the performance of this high duty, he will then have manifested a disregard of the Constitution and laws, to the great injury of the people of nearly one-half of the States of the Union.[37]

LINCOLN

I cannot run this thing [the presidency] upon the theory that every officeholder must think I am the greatest man in the nation, and I will not.[38]

✦ ✦ ✦

I therefore consider that, in view of the Constitution and the laws, the Union is unbroken; and to the extent of my ability I shall take care, as the Constitution itself expressly enjoins upon me, that the laws of the Union be faithfully executed in all the States. Doing this I deem to be only a simple duty on my part; and I shall perform it so far as practicable, unless my rightful masters, the American people, shall withhold the requisite means, or in some authoritative manner direct the contrary.[39]

✓ ✓ ✓

Upon your [Secretary of State William Seward's] closing propositions—that "whatever policy we adopt, there must be an energetic prosecution of it.

"For this purpose it must be somebody's business to pursue and direct it incessantly.

"Either the President must do it himself, and be all the while active in it, or

"Devolve it on some member of his cabinet. Once adopted, debates on it must end, and all agree and abide"—I remark that if this must be done, I must do it. When a general line of policy is adopted, I apprehend there is no danger of its being changed without good reason, or continuing to be a subject of unnecessary debate; still, upon points arising in its progress I wish, and suppose I am entitled to have, the advice of all the cabinet.[40]

The "some member" Seward had in mind was himself. His proposal to Lincoln was that he, Seward, the Secretary of State, run the administration as the first minister. Lincoln would have none of it.

✓ ✓ ✓

Lest there be some uneasiness in the minds of candid men as to what is to be the course of the government toward the Southern States after the rebellion shall have been suppressed, the executive deems it proper to say it will be his purpose then, as ever, to be guided by the Constitution and the laws; and that he probably will have no different understanding of the powers and duties of the Federal Government relatively to the rights of the States and the people, under the Constitution, than that expressed in the inaugural address.

He desires to preserve the government, that it may be administered for all as it was administered by the men who made it. Loyal citizens everywhere have the right to claim this of their government, and the government has no right to withhold or neglect it. It is not perceived that in giving it there is any coercion, any conquest, or any subjugation, in any just sense of those terms.[41]

✓ ✓ ✓

Something said by the Secretary of State, in his recent speech at Auburn, has been construed by some into a threat that if I shall be beaten at the election I will, between then and the end of my constitutional term, do what I may be able to ruin the government. . . .

I am struggling to maintain the government, not to overthrow it. I am struggling, especially, to prevent others from overthrowing it. I therefore say that if I shall live I shall remain President until the 4th of next March; and that whoever shall be constitutionally elected therefor, in November, shall be duly installed as President on the 4th of March; and that, in the interval, I shall do my utmost that whoever is to hold the helm for the next voyage shall start with the best possible chance to save the ship.

This is due to the people both on principle and under the Constitution. Their will, constitutionally expressed, is the ultimate law for all. If they should deliberately resolve to have immediate peace, even at the loss of their country and their liberty, I know not the power or the right to resist them. It is their own business, and they must do as they please with their own. I believe, however, they are still resolved to preserve their country and their liberty; and in this, in office or out of it, I am resolved to stand by them.[42]

ANDREW JOHNSON

I hold it the duty of the Executive to insist upon frugality in the expenditures, and a sparing economy is itself a great national resource.[43]

* * *

It can not be doubted that the triumphant success of the Constitution is due to the wonderful wisdom with which the functions of government were distributed between the three principal departments—the legislative, the executive, and the judicial—and to the fidelity with which each has confined itself or been confined by the general voice of the nation within its peculiar and proper sphere. While a just, proper, and watchful jealousy of executive power constantly prevails, as it ought ever to prevail, yet it is equally true that an efficient Executive, capable, in the language of the oath prescribed to the President, of executing the laws and, within the sphere of executive action, of preserving, protecting, and defending the Constitution of the United States, is an indispensable security for tranquility at home and peace, honor, and safety abroad. Governments have been erected in many countries upon our model.[44]

✦   ✦   ✦

Within a period less than a year the legislation of Congress has attempted to strip the executive department of the Government of some of its essential powers. The Constitution and the oath provided in it devolve upon the President the power and duty to see that the laws are faithfully executed. The Constitution, in order to carry out this power, gives him the choice of the agents, and makes them subject to his control and supervision. But in the execution of these laws the constitutional obligation upon the President remains, but the power to exercise that constitutional duty is effectually taken away. The military commander is as to the power of appointment made to take the place of the President, and the General of the Army the place of the Senate; and any attempt on the part of the President to assert his own constitutional power may, under pretense of law, be met by official insubordination. It is to be feared that these military officers, looking to the authority given by these laws rather than to the letter of the Constitution, will recognize no authority but the commander of the district and the General of the Army.

If there were no other objection than this to this proposed legislation, it would be sufficient. Whilst I hold the chief executive authority of the United States, whilst the obligation rests upon me to see that all the laws are faithfully executed, I can never willingly surrender that trust or the powers given for its execution. I can never give my assent to be made responsible for the faithful execution of laws, and at the same time surrender that trust and the powers which accompany it to any other executive officer, high or low, or to any number of executive officers. If this executive trust, vested by the Constitution in the President, is to be taken from him and vested in a subordinate officer, the responsibility will be with Congress in clothing the subordinate with unconstitutional power and with the officer who assumes its exercise.

This interference with the constitutional authority of the executive department is an evil that will inevitably sap the foundations of our federal system; but it is not the worst evil of this legislation. It is a great public wrong to take from the President powers conferred on him alone by the Constitution, but the wrong is more flagrant and more dangerous when the powers so taken from the President are conferred upon subordinate executive officers, and especially upon military officers. Over nearly one-third of the States of the Union military power, regulated by

no fixed law, rules supreme. Each one of the five district commanders, though not chosen by the people or responsible to them,
exercises at this hour more executive power, military and civil,
than the people have ever been willing to confer upon the head
of the executive department, though chosen by and responsible
to themselves. The remedy must come from the people themselves. They know what it is and how it is to be applied.[45]

✓ ✓ ✓

I do not claim that a head of Department should have no
other opinions than those of the President. He has the same
right, in the conscientious discharge of duty, to entertain and
express his own opinions as has the President. What I do claim
is that the President is the responsible head of the Administration, and when the opinions of a head of Department are ir-
reconcilably opposed to those of the President in grave matters
of policy and administration there is but one result which can
solve the difficulty, and that is a severance of the official relation.
This in the past history of the Government has always been the
rule, and it is a wise one, for such differences of opinion among
its members must impair the efficiency of any Administration.[46]

*It was Johnson's removal of Stanton, as Secretary of War, who
consistently disagreed with and actively resisted his policies, that
led to Johnson's impeachment.*

✓ ✓ ✓

It is the President upon whom the Constitution devolves, as
head of the executive department, the duty to see that the laws
are faithfully executed: but as he can not execute them in person, he is allowed to select his agents, and is made responsible
for their acts within just limits. So complete is this presumed
delegation of authority in the relation of a head of Department
to the President that the Supreme Court of the United States
have decided that an order made by a head of Department is
presumed to be made by the President himself.

The principal, upon whom such responsibility is placed for
the acts of a subordinate, ought to be left as free as possible in
the matter of selection and of dismissal. To hold him to responsibility for an officer beyond his control; to leave the question of
the fitness of such an agent to be decided *for* him and not *by*
him; to allow such a subordinate, when the President, moved
by "public considerations of a high character," requests his resig-

nation, to assume for himself an equal right to act upon his own views of "public considerations" and to make his own conclusions paramount to those of the President—to allow all this is to reverse the just order of administration and to place the subordinate above the superior.

There are, however, other relations between the President and a head of Department beyond these defined legal relations, which necessarily attend them, though not expressed. Chief among these is mutual confidence. This relation is so delicate that it is sometimes hard to say when or how it ceases. A single flagrant act may end it at once, and then there is no difficulty. But confidence may be just as effectually destroyed by a series of causes too subtle for demonstration. As it is a plant of slow growth, so, too, it may be slow in decay.[47]

GRANT

I am extremely anxious to avoid any appearance of undue interference in State affairs, and if Congress differs from me as to what ought to be done I respectfully urge its immediate decision to that effect; otherwise I shall feel obliged, as far as I can by the exercise of legitimate authority, to put an end to the unhappy controversy which disturbs the peace and prostrates the business of Louisiana, by the recognition and support of that government which is recognized and upheld by the courts of the State.[48]

The disputed 1872 elections left Louisiana with two state governments.

✓ ✓ ✓

The whole subject of Executive interference with the affairs of a State is repugnant to public opinion, to the feelings of those who, from their official capacity, must be used in such such interposition, and to him or those who must direct. Unless most clearly on the side of law, such interference becomes a crime; with the law to support it, it is condemned without a hearing. I desire, therefore, that all necessity for Executive direction in local affairs may become unnecessary and obsolete. I invite the attention, not of Congress, but of the people of the United States, to the causes and effects of these unhappy questions. Is there not a disposition on one side to magnify wrongs and outrages, and on the other side to belittle them or justify them? If public opinion could be directed to a correct survey of what is and to rebuking wrong and aiding the proper authorities in punishing it, a bet-

ter state of feeling would be inculcated, and the sooner we would
have that peace which would leave the States free indeed to
regulate their own domestic affairs. I believe on the part of our
citizens of the Southern States—the better part of them—there is
a disposition to be law abiding, and to do no violence either to
individuals or to the laws existing. But do they do right in ignoring the existence of violence and bloodshed in resistance to constituted authority? I sympathize with their prostrate condition,
and would do all in my power to relieve them, acknowledging
that in some instances they have had most trying governments to
live under, and very oppressive ones in the way of taxation for
nominal improvements, not giving benefits equal to the hard-
ships imposed. But can they proclaim themselves entirely irresponsible for this condition? They can not. Violence has been
rampant in some localities, and has either been justified or denied
by those who could have prevented it. The theory is even raised
that there is to be no further interference on the part of the General Government to protect citizens within a State where the
State authorities fail to give protection. This is a great mistake.
While I remain Executive all the laws of Congress and the provisions of the Constitution, including the recent amendments
added thereto, will be enforced with rigor, but with regret that
they should have added one jot or title to Executive duties or
powers. Let there be fairness in the discussion of Southern questions, the advocates of both or all political parties giving honest,
truthful reports of occurrences, condemning the wrong and up-
holding the right, and soon all will be well. Under existing conditions the negro votes the Republican ticket because he knows
his friends are of that party. Many a good citizen votes the opposite, not because he agrees with the great principles of state
which separate parties, but because, generally, he is opposed to
negro rule. This is a most delusive cry. Treat the negro as a
citizen and a voter, as he is and must remain, and soon parties
will be divided, not on the color line, but on principle. Then we
shall have no complaint of sectional interference.[49]

✓   ✓   ✓

I have deplored the necessity which seemed to make it my
duty under the Constitution and laws to direct such interference.
I have always refused except where it seemed to be my imperative duty to act in such a manner under the Constitution and
laws of the United States. I have repeatedly and earnestly en-
treated the people of the South to live together in peace and

obey the laws; and nothing would give me greater pleasure than to see reconciliation and tranquillity everywhere prevail, and thereby remove all necessity for the presence of troops among them. I regret, however, to say that this state of things does not exist, nor does its existence seem to be desired, in some localities; and as to those it may be proper for me to say that to the extent that Congress has conferred power upon me to prevent it neither Kuklux [sic] Klans, White Leagues, nor any other association using arms and violence to execute their unlawful purposes can be permitted in that way to govern any part of this country; nor can I see with indifference Union men or Republicans ostracized, persecuted, and murdered on account of their opinions, as they now are in some localities.[50]

HAYES

The President is called upon to give his affirmative approval to positive enactments which in effect deprive him of the ordinary and necessary means of executing laws still left in the statuto book and embraced within his constitutional duty to see that the laws are executed. If he approves the bill, and thus gives to such positive enactments the authority of law, he participates in the curtailment of his means of seeing that the law is faithfully executed, while the obligation of the law and of his constitutional duty remains unimpaired.

The appointment of special deputy marshals is not made by the statute a spontaneous act of authority on the part of any executive or judicial officer of the Government, but is accorded as a popular right of the citizens to call into operation this agency for securing the purity and freedom of elections in any city or town having 20,000 inhabitants or upward. Section 2021 of the Revised Statutes puts it in the power of any two citizens of such city or town to require of the marshal of the district the appointment of these special deputy marshals. Thereupon the duty of the marshal becomes imperative, and its nonperformance would expose him to judicial mandate or punishment or to removal from office by the President, as the circumstances of his conduct might require. The bill now before me neither revokes this popular right of the citizens, nor relieves the marshal of the duty imposed by law, nor the President of his duty to see that this law is faithfully executed.[51]

✦ ✦ ✦

It is the right and duty, and the necessity exists, that the President should exhaust his constitutional authority to secure to every American citizen possessing the qualifications of an elector the right to cast at each congressional election one unintimidated ballot and to have it honestly counted.[52]

ARTHUR

Questions which concern the very existence of the Government and the liberties of the people were suggested by the prolonged illness of the late President and his consequent incapacity to perform the functions of his office.

It is provided by the second article of the Constitution, in the fifth clause of its first section, that "in case of the removal of the President from office, or of his death, resignation, or inability to discharge the powers and duties of the said office, the same shall devolve on the Vice-President."

What is the intendment of the Constitution in its specification of "inability to discharge the powers and duties of the said office" as one of the contingencies which calls the Vice-President to the exercise of Presidential functions?

Is the inability limited in its nature to long-continued intellectual incapacity, or has it a broader import?

What must be its extent and duration?

How must its existence be established?

Has the President whose inability is the subject of inquiry any voice in determining whether or not it exists, or is the decision of that momentous and delicate question confided to the Vice-President, or is it contemplated by the Constitution that Congress should provide by law precisely what should constitute inability and how and by what tribunal or authority it should be ascertained?

If the inability proves to be temporary in its nature, and during its continuance the Vice-President lawfully exercises the functions of the Executive, by what tenure does he hold his office?

Does he continue as President for the remainder of the four years' term?

Or would the elected President, if his inability should cease in the interval, be empowered to resume his office?

And if, having such lawful authority, he should exercise it, would the Vice-President be thereupon empowered to resume his powers and duties as such?[53]

*Arthur was bringing up the question because of the three months'
illness of Garfield following his shooting. The question recurred
with the illnesses of Wilson and Eisenhower.*

✓ ✓ ✓

Among the questions which have been the topic of recent debate in the halls of Congress none are of greater gravity than
those relating to the ascertainment of the vote for Presidential
electors and the intendment of the Constitution in its provisions
for devolving Executive functions upon the Vice-President when
the President suffers from inability to discharge the powers and
duties of his office.[54]

✓ ✓ ✓

At the time when the present Executive entered upon his office his death, removal, resignation, or inability to discharge his
duties would have left the Government without a constitutional
head.

It is possible, of course, that a similar contingency may again
arise unless the wisdom of Congress shall provide against its
recurrence.

The Senate at its last session, after full consideration, passed
an act relating to this subject, which will now, I trust, commend
itself to the approval of both Houses of Congress.

The clause of the Constitution upon which must depend any
law regulating the Presidential succession presents also for solution other questions of paramount importance.

These questions relate to the proper interpretation of the
phrase "inability to discharge the powers and duties of said office," our organic law providing that when the President shall suffer from such inability the Presidential office shall devolve upon
the Vice-President, who must himself under like circumstances
give place to such officer as Congress may by law appoint to act
as President.

I need not here set forth the numerous and interesting inquiries which are suggested by these words of the Constitution. . . .

It is greatly to be hoped that these momentous questions will
find speedy solution, lest emergencies may arise when longer delay will be impossible and any determination, albeit the wisest,
may furnish cause for anxiety and alarm.[55]

CLEVELAND

The Constitution declares: "The executive power shall be vested in a President of the United States of America," and this is followed by a recital of the specific and distinctly declared duties with which he is charged, and the powers with which he is invested. The members of the [constitutional] convention were not willing, however, that the executive power which they had vested in the President should be cramped and embarrassed by any implication that a specific statement of certain granted powers and duties excluded all other executive functions; nor were they apparently willing that the claim of such exclusion should have countenance in the strict meaning which might be given to the words "executive power." Therefore we find that the Constitution supplements a recital of the specific powers and duties of the President with this impressive and conclusive additional requirement: "He shall take care that the laws be faithfully executed." This I conceive to be equivalent to a grant of all the power necessary to the performance of his duty in the faithful execution of the laws.[56]

This was essentially a return to Lincoln's view.

✦ ✦ ✦

It is therefore apparent that as the Constitution, in addition to its specification of especial duties and powers devolving upon the President, provides that "he shall take care that the laws be faithfully executed," and as this was evidently intended as a general devolution of power and imposition of obligation in respect to any condition that might arise relating to the execution of the laws, so it is likewise apparent that the convention was not content to rest the sworn obligation of the President solely upon his covenant to "faithfully execute the office of President of the United States," but added thereto the mandate that he should preserve, protect, and defend the Constitution, to the best of his judgment and power, or, as it was afterward expressed, to the best of his ability. Thus is our President solemnly required not only to exercise every power attached to his office, to the end that the laws may be faithfully executed, and not only to render obedience to the demands of the fundamental law and executive duty, but to exert all his official strength and authority for the preservation, protection, and defense of the Constitution.[57]

✦ ✦ ✦

To me it clearly seems my duty to exercise all the powers which the present condition of the law has left in my hands, so far as it may be done independently of the Senate, to protect the interests of the government, to vindicate the laws which have been enacted for the regulation of the postal service, and to impress upon Federal officeholders that no indulgence will be granted by the Executive to those who violate the law or neglect public duty.[58]

✦ ✦ ✦

I believe the most important benefit that I can confer on the country by my presidency is to insist upon the entire independence of the executive and legislative branches of the government, and compel the members of the legislative branch to see that they have responsibilities of their own, grave and well-defined, which their official oaths bind them sacredly to perform. . . . I believe that this is an executive office, and I deem it important that the country should be reminded of it. I have certain executive duties to perform; when that is done my responsibility ends. The office is one of the coordinate branches of the government. The Senators and members have their duties and responsibilities. They put their hands upon the Bible and take the same oath of obligation upon assuming office as does the President.[59]

BENJAMIN HARRISON

A many-headed executive must necessarily lack that vigor and promptness of action which is often a condition of public safety. A distinguished public man is reported, perhaps erroneously, to have very recently expressed the opinion that each Cabinet officer should be independent in the administration of his department, and not subject to control by the President. The adoption of this view would give us eight Chief Executives, exercising, not a joint, but a separate control of specified subdivisions of the Executive power, and would leave the President, in whom the Constitution says "the Executive power shall be vested," no function save that of appointing these eight Presidents. It would be a farming-out of his Constitutional powers.[60]

✓ ✓ ✓

The most comprehensive power is given in these words: "He shall take care that the laws be faithfully executed." This is the central idea of the office. An executive is one who executes or carries into effect. And in a Republic—a Government by the people, through laws appropriately passed—the thing to be executed is the law, not the will of the ruler as in despotic governments. The President cannot go beyond the law, and he cannot stop short of it. His duty and his oath of office take it all in and leave him no discretion, save as to the means to be employed. Laws do not execute themselves. Somebody must look after them. It is the duty of the President to see that every law passed by Congress is executed.[61]

✓ ✓ ✓

In all important matters the President is consulted by all the Secretaries. He is responsible for all executive action, and almost everything that is out of the routine receives some attention from him. Every important foreign complication is discussed with him, and the diplomatic note receives his approval. The same thing is true of each of the departments. Routine matters proceed without the knowledge of interference of the President; but, if any matter of major importance arises the Secretary presents it for the consideration and advice of the President. Only matters of importance affecting the general policy of the administration are discussed in the Cabinet meetings—according to my experience —and votes are of rare occurrence. Any Secretary desiring to have an expression upon any question in his department presents it, and it is discussed; but usually questions are settled in a conference between the President and the head of the particular department. If there is that respect and confidence that should prevail between a President and his Cabinet officers this consultation is on equal terms, and the conclusion is one that both support. There should be no question of making a "mere clerk" of the Cabinet officer; there is a yielding of views, now on one side, now on the other; but it must, of course, follow that when the President has views that he feels he cannot yield, those views must prevail, for the responsibility is his, both in a Constitutional and popular sense. The Cabinet officer is a valued adviser, and it does not often happen that his views and those of the President cannot be reconciled.[62]

✦ ✦ ✦

The laws that the President must enforce are, of course, only the laws of the United States. . . . But the power and duty of the President to suppress mob violence happening in the States is broader than the old thought and practice in such matters.[63]

✦ ✦ ✦

It was also held that the stoppage of trains—freight or passenger—running from one State into another—that is, conducting interstate commerce—or the tearing up of or obstructing the tracks over which such interstate commerce was carried, was an offense against the peace of the United States. Such an offense may be enjoined by the Courts, and the Army of the United States may be used by the President to restore order, without waiting for any call from the State Legislature or the Governor for assistance. It is not "domestic violence," in the sense of the section just quoted, but an attack upon the powers of the National Government, and neither the request nor the consent of the State is needed to give the President a right to use the means placed in his hands by the Constitution, to preserve the peace of the United States, and to see that the mails and interstate commerce are neither stopped nor impeded by violence. A strike of violence affecting a street railway in a city, or a shop or factory or coal mine, or other local interest, or a riot raised for the lynching of a prisoner charged with an offence against the State—all these must be dealt with by the State authorities, save that, as has been seen, the President may be called upon for aid by the Legislature or Governor.[64]

✦ ✦ ✦

It is not a pleasant thing to have the power of life and death. No graver or more oppressive responsibility can be laid upon a public officer. The power to pardon includes the power to commute a sentence, that is, to reduce it. When the sentence is death the President may commute it to imprisonment for life, or for any fixed term; and when the sentence is imprisonment for life, or for a fixed term of years, he may reduce the term, and if a fine is imposed he may reduce the amount, or remit it altogether. . . . There is an increasing amount of pardon business coming to the President's desk, and he often has many cases waiting his action.[65]

✦ ✦ ✦

There is only a door—one that is never locked—between the President's office and what are not very accurately called his private apartments. There should be an Executive Office building, not too far away, but wholly distinct from the dwelling-house. For every one else in the public service there is an un-roofed space between the bedroom and the desk.[66]

THEODORE ROOSEVELT

On three previous occasions the Vice-President had succeeded to the Presidency on the death of the President. In each case there had been a reversal of party policy, and a nearly immediate and nearly complete change in the personnel of the higher offices, especially the Cabinet. I had never felt that this was wise from any standpoint. If a man is fit to be President, he will speedily so impress himself in the office that the policies pursued will be his anyhow, and he will not have to bother as to whether he is changing them or not; while as regards the offices under him the important thing for him is that his subordinates shall make a success in handling their several departments. The subordinate is sure to desire to make a success of his department for his own sake, and if he is a fit man, whose views on public policy are sound, and whose abilities entitle him to his position, he will do excellently under almost any chief with the same purposes.[67]

✦ ✦ ✦

Among the trades unions generally, the wageworkers generally, there was beginning to be ugly talk of a general sympathetic strike, which, happening at the beginning of winter, would have meant a crisis only less serious than the civil war. Even without such a crisis the first long-continued spell of bitter weather meant misery and violence in acute form in our big cities. I did not intend to sit supinely when such a state of things was impending, and I notified Knox and Root that if the contingency arose where I had to take charge of the matter, as President, on behalf of the Federal Government, I should not ask even their advice, but would proceed to take certain definite action which I outlined to them. I explained that I knew that this action would form an evil precedent, and that it was one which I should take most reluctantly, but that it was the only one which I could see (to take) which would be effective in such an emergency; and that I should feel obliged to take it rather than expose our people to the suffering and chaos which would otherwise come.[68]

*   *   *

I was of course not required by the Constitution to attempt this settlement [of a coal strike]; and if I had failed to attempt I should have held myself worthy of comparison with Franklin Pierce and James Buchanan, among my predecessors. For the time being, and in vital fashion, this question was that which beyond all others concerned the entire nation; and, as being for the moment the head of the nation, I obeyed the supreme law of duty to the republic in acting as I did. I think all competent observers agree that if the strike had not been settled there would have been within thirty days the most terrible riots that this country has ever seen, with as their sequence the necessity of drastic, and perhaps revolutionary measures, by the various state governments, or by the national government. The strike certainly would not have been settled if I had not interfered.[69]

*   *   *

I call your especial attention to the telegram sent to you on December 14th by the Secretary of State. This sets out what must be shown as a matter of actual fact to exist in order to warrant the President in acting on the request of the State authorities. The action must be either to suppress an insurrection which the State authorities are unable to suppress, or to secure to some portion or class of the people of the State the equal protection of the laws to which they are entitled under the Constitution of the United States, and which is denied them. Action under this or any other section requires the production of evidence sufficient to sustain a judgment by the President, that the condition described in the statute exists. A mere statement of domestic disturbance, still less a mere statement of apprehension of domestic disturbance, is not sufficient, even tho it comes from as high and unimpeachable a source as the Governor of a State. Such a communication from the Governor or from the legislature warrants the President in taking immediate steps to put himself in readiness to act, in view of the probability of conditions arising which will require his action.[70]

✔ ✔ ✔

Of course I should like to be reelected President, and I shall be disappointed if I am not; and so far as I legitimately can I pay heed to considerations of political expediency—in fact I should be unfit for my position, or for any position of political leadership, if I did not do so. But when questions involve deep and far-reaching principles, then I believe that the real expediency is to be found in straightforward and unflinching adherence to principle, and this without regard to what may be the temporary effect. . . . I should be sorry to lose the Presidency, but I should be a hundredfold more sorry to gain it by failing in every way in my power to try to put a stop to lynching and to brutality and wrong of any kind; or by failing on the one hand to make the very wealthiest and most powerful men in the country obey the law and handle their property (so far as it is in my power to make them) in the public interest; or, on the other hand, to fail to make the laboring men in their turn obey the law, and realize that envy is as evil a thing as arrogance, and that crimes of violence and riot shall be as sternly punished as crimes of greed and cunning.[71]

✔ ✔ ✔

While President I have *been* President, emphatically; I have used every ounce of power there was in the office and I have not cared a rap for the criticisms of those who spoke of my "usurpation of power"; for I knew that the talk was all nonsense and that there was no usurpation. I believe that the efficiency of this Government depends upon its possessing a strong central executive, and wherever I could establish a precedent for strength in the executive, as I did for instance as regards external affairs in the case of sending the fleet around the world, taking Panama, settling affairs of Santo Domingo and Cuba; or as I did in internal affairs in settling the anthracite coal strike, in keeping order in Nevada this year when the Federation of Miners threatened anarchy, or as I have done in bringing the big corporations to book—why, in all these cases I have felt not merely that my action was right in itself, but that in showing the strength of, or in giving strength to, the executive, I was establishing a precedent of value. I believe in a strong executive; I believe in power; but I believe that responsibility should go with power, and that it is not well that the strong executive should be a perpetual executive. Above all and beyond all I believe as I have said

before that the salvation of this country depends upon Washington and Lincoln representing the type of leader to which we are
true. I hope that in my acts I have been a good President, a
President who has deserved well of the Republic; but most of
all, I believe that whatever value my service may have comes
even more from what I *am* than from what I *do*. I may be mistaken, but it is my belief that the bulk of my countrymen, the
men whom Abraham Lincoln called "the plain people"—the
farmers, mechanics, small tradesmen, hard-working professional
men—feel that I am in a peculiar sense their President, that I
represent the democracy in somewhat the fashion that Lincoln
did, that is, not in any demagogic way but with the sincere effort
to stand for a government by the people and for the people.[72]

✦ ✦ ✦

Any man who has occupied the office of President realizes the
incredible amount of administrative work with which the President has to deal even in time of peace. He is of necessity a
very busy man, a much-driven man, from whose mind there can
never be absent, for many minutes at a time, the consideration
of some problem of importance, or of some matter of less importance which yet causes worry and strain. Under such circumstances, it is not easy for a President, even in times of peace,
to turn from the affairs that are of moment to all the people and
consider affairs that are of moment to but one person.[73]

✦ ✦ ✦

I acted on the theory that the President could at any time in
his discretion withdraw from entry any of the public lands of the
United States and reserve the same for forestry, for water-power
sites, for irrigation, and other public purposes. Without such
action it would have been impossible to stop the activity of the
land thieves. No one ventured to test its legality by lawsuit. My
successor, however, himself questioned it, and referred the matter to Congress. Again Congress showed its wisdom by passing a
law which gave the President the power which he had long
exercised, and of which my successor had shorn himself.[74]

✦ ✦ ✦

The President's duty is to act so that he himself and his subordinates shall be able to do efficient work for the people, and this
efficient work he and they cannot do if Congress is permitted to
undertake the task of making up his mind for him as to how he
shall perform what is clearly his sole duty.[75]

✓ ✓ ✓

Very much the most important action I took as regards labor had nothing to do with legislation, and represented executive action which was not required by the Constitution. It illustrated as well as anything that I did the theory which I have called the Jackson-Lincoln theory of the Presidency; that is, that occasionally great national crises arise which call for immediate and vigorous executive action, and that in such cases it is the duty of the President to act upon the theory that he is the steward of the people, and that the proper attitude for him to take is that he is bound to assume that he has the legal right to do whatever the needs of the people demand, unless the Constitution or the laws explicitly forbid him to do it.[76]

TAFT

It is the constitutional duty of the President to issue commissions to all officers of the United States. This, I think, is the greatest manual duty the President has to perform. When you consider all the officers in the government who are entitled to commissions, and in addition to this, the number of letters in the President's correspondence, you can understand that a substantial part of each business day is occupied with signatures. Of course the shorter the President's name, the easier his work.[77]

✓ ✓ ✓

The widest power and the broadest duty which the President has is conferred and imposed by a clause in section three of article two, providing that "he shall take care that the laws be faithfully executed."[78]

✓ ✓ ✓

In the practical provision for the enforcement of law by Congress, that body has found it necessary to impose upon the President or his subordinates not only a purely Executive function, but to enlarge this into what are really quasi-legislative and quasi-judicial duties. Frequently in statutes covering a wide field, Congress confers upon the particular subordinate of the President, who is to execute this law, the power to make rules and regulations under it which are legislative in their nature.[79]

✓ ✓ ✓

The express duties defined in the statute, and distributed to the departments and to the various appointees of the President, create a great permanent organization over which he can exercise only a very general supervision. Under the civil service laws, inadequate as they are in some respects, the continuity of the government in the departments at Washington in routine matters is fairly well settled and is little changed from administration to administration. It would be difficult, if the President chose to exercise the power he has, to impose his personality minutely on the going government. He can insist upon greater economy. He can infuse a new spirit in the service by making plain his earnest desire for greater efficiency, and yet while he is, of course, the real head of the government, there seems to be an impersonal entity in the permanent governmental structure, independent of him, which in some degree modifies his responsibility for its operation. Chiefs of Divisions and clerks of Bureaus in the civil service in Washington have been there for decades. They are loyal to the government, and not especially beholden to any one President.[80]

✓ ✓ ✓

The laws that the President must take care shall be faithfully executed are not confined to acts of Congress. The treaties of the United States with other countries are under the Constitution laws of the United States having the same effect as Congressional enactments, in so far as they are intended to operate in this way and are in form appropriate.[81]

✓ ✓ ✓

The last power of the President which I shall consider is the power of pardon. This is a wide power, and enables the President to pardon any one guilty of an offense against the United States before indictment, after indictment and before conviction, or after conviction. He need not name the persons to be pardoned if he pardons a class and makes provision by which the persons affected shall establish their membership in that class. The pardon under such circumstances is called an amnesty. He is expressly given power to grant reprieves, which means only a suspension of the execution of a sentence for one purpose or another. The Supreme Court said in one case that a pardon reaches both the punishment prescribed for the offense and the guilt of the offender, and when the pardon is full, it relieves the punishment and blots out of existence the guilt, so that in the eye of the law the offender is as innocent as if he never had committed the offense. This is rather a strong statement as some later cases show. It is difficult to clothe Omnipotence with such a power.[82]

* * *

The duty involved in the pardoning power is a most difficult one to perform, because it is so completely within the discretion of the Executive and is lacking so in rules or limitations of its exercise. The only rule he can follow is that he shall not exercise it against the public interest. The guilt of the man with whose case he is dealing is usually admitted, and even if it is not, the judgment of the court settles that fact in all but few cases. The question which the President has to decide is whether under peculiar circumstances of hardship he can exercise clemency without destroying the useful effect of punishment in deterring others fom committing crimes.[83]

WILSON

The more I succeed in directing things the more I am depended on for leadership and expected to do everything, make all parts straight and carry every plan to its completion.[84]

COOLIDGE

The Presidency is primarily an executive office. It is placed at the apex of our system of government. It is a place of last resort to which all questions are brought that others have not been able to answer.[85]

* * *

While it is wise for the President to get all the competent advice possible, final judgments are necessarily his own. No one can share with him the responsibility for them. No one can make his decisions for him. He stands at the center of things where no one else can stand. If others make mistakes, they can be relieved, and oftentimes a remedy can be provided. But he can not retire. His decisions are final and usually irreparable. This constitutes the appalling burden of his office. Not only the welfare of 120,000,000 of his countrymen, but oftentimes the peaceful relations of the world are entrusted to his keeping. At the turn of his hand the guns of an enormous fleet would go into action anywhere in the world, carrying the iron might of death and destruction. His appointment confers the power to administer justice, inflict criminal penalties, declare acts of state legislatures and of the Congress void, and sit in judgment over the very life of the nation. Practically all the civil and military authorities of the government, except the Congress and the courts, hold their office at his discretion. He appoints, and he can remove. The billions of dollars of government revenue are collected and expended under his direction. The Congress makes the laws, but it is the President who causes them to be executed. A power so vast in its implications has never been conferred upon any ruling sovereign.[86]

As he is head of the government, charged with making appointments, and clothed with the executive power, the President has a certain responsibility for the conduct of all departments, commissions and independent bureaus. While I was willing to advise with any of these officers and give them any assistance in my power, I always felt they should make their own decisions and rarely volunteered any advice. Many applications are made requesting the President to seek to influence these bodies, and such applications were usually transmitted to them for their information without comment. Wherever they exercise judicial functions, I always felt that some impropriety might attach to any suggestions from me.[87]

An unofficial adviser to a President of the United States is not a good thing and is not provided for in our form of government.[88]

HOOVER

The essential of the flexible tariff is that with respect to a particular commodity, after exhaustive determination of the facts as to differences of cost of production at home and abroad by a Tariff Commission, comprised of one-half of its members from each political party, whose selection is approved by the Senate, then the President should, upon recommendation of the Commission, promulgate changes in the tariff on that commodity not to exceed 50 percent of the rates fixed by Congress. Under these provisions the President has no authority to initiate any changes in the tariff. No power rests on the Executive until after recommendations by the Commission. Any change must arise from application directly to the Commission, and his authority in the matter becomes a simple act of proclamation of the recommendations of the Commission or, on the other hand, a refusal to issue such a proclamation, amounting to a veto of the conclusions of the Commission. In no sense, therefore, can it be claimed that the President can alter the tariff at will, or that despotic power is conferred upon the Executive. It has been declared a constitutional procedure by the Supreme Court.[89]

✓ ✓ ✓

The first duty of the President under his oath of office is to secure the enforcement of the laws.[90]

There had been some difficulty about it in the case of the Prohibition laws.

✓ ✓ ✓

The President himself cannot pretend to know or to have the time for detailed investigation into every one of the hundreds of subjects in a great people. But the fine minds of our citizens are available and can be utilized for the search.[91]

✓ ✓ ✓

The first obligation of my office is to uphold and defend the Constitution and the authority of the law.[92]

✓ ✓ ✓

. . . the very core of the Presidency was enforcement of the laws.[93]

✓ ✓ ✓

By a series of invasions of the judicial and legislative arms and the independence of the states, accompanied by such measures as managed currency, government operation of some industries and dictation to others, "Planned Economy" quickly developed as a centralization of power in the hands of the President, administered and perpetuated by an enormous Federal bureaucracy.[94]

Hoover was speaking of some of the innovations of his successor, Franklin Roosevelt.

✦ ✦ ✦

The first step of economic Regimentation is a vast centralization of power in the Executive.[95]

✦ ✦ ✦

Is there any single person in America who is so ignorant that he does not know the gigantic growth of the personal power of the President during this last seven years [1933–1940]?[96]

✦ ✦ ✦

There has been a gigantic and insidious building up of personal power of the President during these two terms [1933–1940]. The President himself admits these powers provide shackles upon liberty which may be dangerous. Many of these extraordinary powers have been obtained under claims of emergencies which proved not to exist or to have expired. Despite many promises, there has been no return of these dangerous powers or the unused powers, or those which proved futile or for which emergencies have passed. In building up these powers the independence of the Supreme Court, the Congress and the local government has been degraded.[97]

✦ ✦ ✦

The whole genius of the American people has demonstrated over one hundred and fifty years that when we come to executive action, including the office of the President of the United States, we must have single-headed responsibility. It is just as foolish to set up a board to conduct munitions business as it would be to set up a board to conduct the presidency of the United States.[98]

FRANKLIN D. ROOSEVELT

The [National Industrial Recovery] Act did not itself set up any specified form of administration. It authorized and directed the President to designate such officers and employees as might be necessary, for carrying out its purposes. This flexibility was very desirable in the crisis which had to be met. It was recognized that it would be necessary gradually to work out the best method of administration.

The functions of the Special Industrial Recovery Board were

never very clearly defined and in the course of time the actual day-by-day administration of the Act centered more and more in the Administrator and the President.[99]

But the Supreme Court invalidated the whole plan as unconstitutional in 1935.

✓ ✓ ✓

From my earlier experience in the Navy Department I had long felt that any President would be greatly benefited by a complete change of scene and thought for a week or two during long Congressional sessions.[100]

✓ ✓ ✓

The Committee on Administrative Management points out that no enterprise can operate effectively if set up as is the Government today. There are over 100 separate departments, boards, commissions, corporations, authorities, agencies, and activities through which the work of the Government is being carried on. Neither the President nor the Congress can exercise effective supervision and direction over such a chaos of establishments, nor can overlapping, duplication, and contradictory policies be avoided.

The Committee has not spared me; they say, what has been common knowledge for twenty years, that the President cannot adequately handle his responsibilities; that he is overworked; that it is humanly impossible, under the system which we have, for him fully to carry out his Constitutional duty as Chief Executive because he is overwhelmed with minor details and needless contacts arising directly from the bad organization and equipment of the Government. I can testify to this. With my predecessors who have said the same thing over and over again, I plead guilty.

The plain fact is that the present organization and equipment of the Executive Branch of the Government defeat the Constitutional intent that there be a single responsible Chief Executive to coordinate and manage the departments and activities in accordance with the laws enacted by the Congress. Under these conditions the Government cannot be thoroughly effective in working, under popular control, for the common good.[101]

The adjustment of the presidency to the managerial demands made upon it persisted into the Truman and Eisenhower administrations, despite the efforts of Herbert Hoover's commission set up to make re-organization recommendations.

✦ ✦ ✦

The Presidency as established in the Constitution of the United States has all of the powers that are required. In spite of timid souls in 1787 who feared effective government the Presidency was established as a single, strong Chief Executive office in which was vested the entire Executive power of the national Government, even as the legislative power was placed in the Congress and the judicial in the Supreme Court and inferior courts. What I am placing before you is the request not for more power, but for the tools of management and the authority to distribute the work so that the President can effectively discharge those powers which the Constitution now places upon him. Unless we are prepared to abandon this important part of the Constitution, we must equip the President with authority commensurate with his responsibilities under the Constitution.[102]

✦ ✦ ✦

To the President of the United States there come every day thousand of messages of appeal, of protest, of support, of information and advice, messages from rich and poor, from business man and farmer, from factory employee and relief worker, messages from every corner of our wide domain.[103]

✦ ✦ ✦

To carry out any twentieth century program, we must give the Executive Branch of the Government twentieth century machinery to work with. I recognize that democratic processes are necessarily and rightly slower than dictatorial processes. But I refuse to believe that democratic processes need be dangerously slow.

For many years we have all known that the executive and administrative departments of the Government in Washington are a higgledy-piggledy patchwork of duplicate responsibilities and overlapping powers. The reorganization of this vast government machinery which I proposed to the Congress last winter does not conflict with the principle of the democratic process, as some people say. It only makes that process work more efficiently.[104]

✐ ✐ ✐

As far as powers go, I figured out the other day that there is not a single power I have that Hoover and Coolidge did not have. Can anyone name any power I have today that Hoover and Coolidge did not have? . . .

You spoke this morning about priming the pump again. We are going to spend more money if we can get it out quickly. It is going to help this immediate situation; but it is not that alone, it is the long range end of it that is important. In using that money along that line, somebody has to spend it. If Congress wants to earmark every dollar of it, that is all right. But again, you cannot get Congress to earmark every project. It is impossible. You cannot turn it over to the courts, it would be unconstitutional.

You have to turn it over to the Executive Department under the Constitution. Earmark all you want, as far as you can, but somebody has to spend the money. It is not a power which I desire. It means setting up machinery overnight. I would much rather Congress earmark it, but you know what you would get if they did. You would get a "You scratch my back, I will scratch yours." You would get a pork barrel bill.[105]

✐ ✐ ✐

Forty years ago in 1899 President McKinley could deal with the whole machinery of the Executive Branch through his eight cabinet secretaries and the heads of two commissions; and there was but one commission of the so-called quasi-judicial type in existence. He could keep in touch with all the work through eight or ten persons.

Now, forty years later, not only do some thirty major agencies (to say nothing of the minor ones) report directly to the President, but there are several quasi-judicial bodies which have enough administrative work to require them also to see him on important executive matters.

It has become physically impossible for one man to see so many persons, to receive reports directly from them, and to attempt to advise them on their own problems which they submit. In addition the President today has the task of trying to keep their programs in step with each other or in line with the national policy laid down by the Congress. And he must seek to prevent unnecessary duplication of effort.[106]

✦ ✦ ✦

In other words, the Constitution states one man is responsible. Now that man can delegate, surely, but in the delegation he does not delegate away any part of the responsibility from the ultimate responsibility that rests on him.[107]

✦ ✦ ✦

There were one or two cardinal principles; and one of them is the fact that you cannot, under the Constitution, set up a second President of the United States. In other words, the Constitution states one man is responsible. Now that man can delegate, surely, but in the delegation he does not delegate away any part of the responsibility from the ultimate responsibility that rests on him.[108]

TRUMAN

In my message dated May 24, 1945, it was recommended that permanent legislation be enacted which would authorize the President to submit to the Congress, from time to time, plans providing for the organization of executive agencies, each such plan to become effective unless the Congress should reject it by concurrent resolution.

This type of joint action by the Congress and the President has produced, and will produce, far better results than can be achieved by the usual legislative process in the field of executive reorganization. If proper progress is to be made, it is necessary to permit the President to lay out the machinery for carrying out his responsibility for the conduct of the executive branch, subject to rejection by the two Houses of Congress. Executive initiative, subject to congressional veto, is an effective approach to governmental reorganization.

The responsibility of conducting the executive branch rests upon the President. It is fair and efficient to permit him to lay out the machinery for carrying out that responsibility.

The means for doing this should be generally along the lines of the Reorganization Act of 1939, which gives the initiative to the President, but reserves power to the Congress by a majority vote to nullify any action of the President which does not meet with its approval.[109]

✔ ✔ ✔

The presidency is so tremendous that it is necessary for a President to delegate authority. To be able to do so safely, however, he must have around him people who can be trusted not to arrogate authority to themselves.[110]

✔ ✔ ✔

When a Cabinet member speaks publicly, he usually speaks on authorization of the President, in which case he speaks for the President. If he takes it upon himself to announce a policy that is contrary to the policy the President wants carried out, he can cause a great deal of trouble. I was always careful to discuss all matters of policy in open Cabinet meetings where all members were present, but when it was necessary to elaborate on anything special, they had access to me at any time.

However, once a policy is established, it is the policy of the President of the United States and nobody else. That is the way it has to be if the operation of government is going to be orderly. The President is elected for that purpose; his office is a constitutional one. He is the Chief Executive of the Republic and Commander in Chief of the armed forces.

Cabinet positions, on the other hand, are created by law at the request of the President to help him carry out his duties as Chief Executive under the Constitution. It is a very satisfactory arrangement if the President keeps his hands on the reins and knows exactly what goes on in each department. That he has to do if he is to be successful.

Our political setup is something unique in the history of the world, and it is a matter with which the President himself must be entirely familar. He must know where he is going and why he is going there, and the manner in which he puts his policies into effect is a matter which he discusses with his Cabinet and all his advisers. It is really a most interesting procedure that has to be followed by a President when he is trying his best to run the government in the interest of all the people.[111]

✔ ✔ ✔

The President may have an adviser who is not a Cabinet member, although all Cabinet members are advisers. There are some special issues on which the President needs detailed information from experts, and it is customary to try to discover the man who is best informed on these detailed matters. For instance, when we set up a scientific commission of any sort, it is necessary to find out the scientists who are best informed on the subject. Then it is necessary to find administrators who understand administration and who are willing to take advice from scientists who are doing the work. The President naturally has to consult with them. Sometimes the Congress makes an effort to rob the President of his appointive powers. I would never stand for it.[112]

✦ ✦ ✦

Under the Constitution the President of the United States is alone responsible for the "faithful execution of the laws." Our government is fixed on the basis that the President is the only person in the executive branch who has the final authority. Everyone else in the executive branch is an agent of the President. There are some people, and sometimes members of the Congress and the press, who get mixed up in their thinking about the powers of the President. The important fact to remember is that the President is the only person in the executive branch who has final authority, and if he does not exercise it, we may be in trouble. If he exercises his authority wisely, that is good for the country. If he does not exercise it wisely, that is too bad, but it is better than not exercising it at all.[113]

✦ ✦ ✦

The difficulty with many career officials in the government is that they regard themselves as the men who really make policy and run the government. They look upon the elected officials as just temporary occupants. Every President in our history has been faced with this problem: how to prevent career men from circumventing presidential policy.[114]

✦ ✦ ✦

A President needs political understanding to *run* the government, but he may be *elected* without it.[115]

✦ ✦ ✦

In government there can never be an end to study, improvement, and the evaluation of new ideas, and no one is more conscious of this than the President, for he can see how the machinery of government operates.[116]

✦ ✦ ✦

The President cannot function without advisers or without advice, written or oral. But just as soon as he is required to show what kind of advice he has had, who said what to him, or what kind of records he has, the advice he receives will become worthless.[117]

✦ ✦ ✦

A President must decide not only on the facts he has but the experience and preparation he brings to them. It is a terrible handicap for a new President to step into office and be confronted with a whole series of critical decisions without adequate briefing. I thought it was an omission in our political tradition that a retiring President did not make it his business to facilitate the transfer of the government to his successor.[118]

EISENHOWER

The ultimate responsibility for the conduct of all parts of the executive branch of the Government rests with the President of the United States. That responsibility cannot be delegated to another branch of Government. It is, of course, likewise the responsibility of the President and his associates to account for their stewardship of public affairs. All of us recognize the right of the people to know how we are meeting this responsibility and the congressional right to inquire and investigate into every phase of our public operations.[119]

✦ ✦ ✦

Sometimes, as I stand outside the White House, I look at it, and I note that the first President that occupied it, John Adams, had his entire office, all his office force, and his living quarters, all within the main part of the building. Succeeding Presidents have built on wings. We have now gone across and taken over one building that used to house three great departments of Government, and we still don't have room for the President's office and the separate offices that are attached to him. This is indicative of what has happened to us in the United States, in the complexities of our economy and industries, and in Government and its complexities. And while this has all happened, that Government and our daily lives have likewise become intertwined.[120]

✓ ✓ ✓

The very basis of our individual rights and freedoms rests upon the certainty that the President and the Executive Branch of Government will support and insure the carrying out of the decisions of the Federal Courts, even, when necessary with all the means at the President's command.

Unless the President did so, anarchy would result.[121]

✓ ✓ ✓

I think when you come to talking about the expanding of the National Security Council, we want to remember this one thing: the National Security Council, like any other body that surrounds the President, is for advisory purposes. You cannot get away from the fact that the President has to make the decisions.

Now, therefore, the President is free to call upon anybody, indeed, as I have frequently, on elder statesmen, on sometimes organized and sometimes unorganized bodies, to come and consult.[122]

✓ ✓ ✓

If a President is going to participate in all of the basic studies and the initial partial decisions, then you are going to have, again, something that is just not possible.

The President must know the general purpose of everything that is going on, the general problem that is there, whether or not it is being solved or the solution is going ahead according to principles in which he believes and which he has promulgated; and, finally, he must say "yes" or "no."[123]

✓ ✓ ✓

A President has a very large organization to run. I have given my beliefs about the need for keeping certain information confidential until it can be published; and as quickly as it can be published in conformity with the security or other interests of the United States, then it should be given promptly because only with that kind of information can a public make up its mind as to what its own government should be.[124]

✓ ✓ ✓

I have told you people several times that I believe the Presidency should be relieved of detail and many of its activities by

proper officials who can take delegated authority and exercise
it in his name.[125]

✦ ✦ ✦

The President should have, not people to whom he turned
over his own duties, but people who in particular areas could
assist him on a big and broad basis. It is necessary, as I see it,
for the President at least once a week to hear, at the same time
and in the same meeting, the conflicting views, let's say of the
State Department and of the A.E.C. and Defense Department
on disarmament. He should hear them and then make up his
own mind—but these things are developing day by day and the
President can't give day by day all his time to one great function.
A single assistant could. So my theory was to set up a man who
in everything touching on foreign affairs did for the President
what the President had to do as his major job all the time, but
he wasn't dealing with the details all the time. So I wanted
a man that I called the First Secretary of the Government for
Foreign Affairs. And then, on the other side—on the domestic
side, I wanted a business manager, who would give us rules
that businessmen could understand when they were talking with
Interior or Defense or State or with the Commerce or anything
else. That kind of thing; not to be in any sense over these other
Cabinet officers, but to take one function and on behalf of the
President to make sure that day by day, it was working properly.
Now, of course, if ever they tried to change policy, they had to
come right to the President. No President can ever delegate his
power of decision. This is his. There's no voting. There is no
consensus of opinion. What he has to make up his mind to do
must be on the best facts and best analyses he has brought before
him. But those best analyses and best interpretations of facts
can be brought before him by people who are doing nothing
else. Now, this is, in its general outline, the kind of reorganization that I think would be better for the Presidency.[126]

✦ ✦ ✦

First of all, the President, by the Constitution, is the head of
the Executive Branch. It is his duty to execute the laws of the
land. They're passed by Congress. They're interpreted by the
judges and the Supreme Courts, but the President is the one
that has to execute them. And in an extreme case, he can even
call upon the Armed Forces, as I did in Little Rock, not to

participate in the struggles that were going on then, between those who were for integration and those who are not, but to make certain that no organized or unorganized resistance, in any place, could interfere with the carrying out of the proper orders of a Federal judge, and that was all it was for. As quick as it was done, why of course, the troops were gotten out.[127]

KENNEDY

The President also has his responsibilities with respect to the operation of these [regulatory] agencies. In addition to a constitutional duty to see that the laws are faithfully executed, and other inherent Executive powers, it is his duty to staff the regulatory agencies, granted to him, with men and women competent to handle the responsibilities vested in them and dedicated to the goals set forth in the legislation they are appointed to implement. The President, moreover, is charged in many instances by the Congress with the specific responsibility of removing agency members for misfeasance, inefficiency or the neglect of duty. Coupled with this is the discretionary exercise of his duty to reward faithful public service by the reappointment of agency members, which requires him to form opinions as to the capability of his or his predecessor's appointees to handle the affairs that the Congress has entrusted to them. In short, the President's responsibilities require him to know and evaluate how efficiently these agencies dispatch their business, including any lack of prompt decision of the thousands of cases which they are called upon to decide, any failure to evolve policy in areas where they have been charged by the Congress to do so, or any other difficulties that militate against the performance of their statutory duties.[128]

*   *   *

I think sometimes we overstate the administerial difficulties of the Presidency. I think really, in many ways, it's a judicial function, where alternatives are suggested which involve great matters, and finally the President must make a decision. That is really the most onerous and important part of the burdens of being President. President Truman used to have a sign on this desk which said: "The buck stops here"—these matters which involve national security and our national strength finally come to rest here—but the matter of our staff, therefore, should serve only to make sure that these important matters are brought here in a way which permits a clear decision after alternatives have been presented. Occasionally, in the past, I think the staff has been used to get a prearranged agreement which is only confirmed at the President's desk, and that I don't agree with.[129]

Chapter III

THE APPOINTIVE AND REMOVAL POWER

Until the reforms of the Hayes period and the establishment of a civil service qualifying and merit system, the bane of every President's existence was the office seeker or the officeholder who bespoke his cause. The papers of the early Presidents are replete with protests at the unconscionable way the office seekers besieged them, clambering up and down the stairways of the White House, lolling in the corridors, fastening themselves like leeches on the body politic.

From the beginning, most Presidents tried to be conscientious about the vast appointive responsibilities of their office, to set high and honorable standards, and diligently sought to prevent favoritism, nepotism, and parasitism.

But the pace at which the nation and the government were growing made the President dependent upon the advice of others in making an ever increasing number of appointments. By Jackson's time, the political spoils system was in, and for decades the most consistently scandalous feature of American political life was the way that public service positions constituted a vast patronage system to pay off party hacks. Moreover, it had the avid support of Senators and Representatives in Congress, who were not above deceiving the President, as Polk noted more than once, to pay off political debts.

By the end of the Grant administration, the situation was so corrupt that Hayes moved to correct it and restore honor to federal employment. But he was ahead of the political party managers and denied a second nomination. Garfield, however, showed no signs of allowing an all-out return to spoilsmanship, and his own assassination at the hands of a disappointed office seeker dramatized the need for reform. It was years later, however, before this was finally achieved on any major scale, and both Republican and Democratic Presidents contributed to the reformation. In the present century, the appointive and removal responsibilities of the office ceased to be a major burden of the office.

At a wholly different level, the appointive and removal powers have been the focal point of a grand conflict between the President and the Congress over control of the machinery of government. This came to a head in the only case of a presidential inpeachment. Andrew Johnson had held, as had all other Presidents, that as the President had sole power of appointment so also he had sole power of removal. It would seem obvious, of course, that in the case of his closest aides and advisers, if the President were forced to keep those who were uncongenial, unsympathetic, or outrightly disloyal to him, the presidency could no longer function. This was exactly the case with Edwin Stanton's removal by President Johnson. Stanton was not only against the President's policies but acted as an informer to members of the Congress who opposed those policies. To prevent his removal, the Congress passed the Tenure of Office Act, making removals from appointive offices by the President valid only with congressional sanction. Johnson fought it on both moral and legal grounds by removing Stanton, and was impeached. Conviction required a two-thirds vote by the Senate, sitting as a jury, and it failed by one vote.

Personalities were involved, Johnson, Stanton, and the leaders of the Senate and House all being fiery temperaments, and such inflammatory immediate issues as the status of the newly subjected South also played a part. But the impeachment of Johnson was, so far as the institutional political history of the United States goes, far more. It determined whether or not the President was to be subservient to Congress, the whole executive establishment beholden to it for its life. Had Johnson, whatever his personal political or diplomatic failings, yielded on the issue of the removal power or had his impeachment resulted in conviction or had the Tenure of Office Act been upheld by the courts, the nation might very well have drifted into some form of parliamentary government that would seriously have diminished the presidency.

Most Presidents were quick to see the fundamental relationship of the appointive and removal powers to the safeguarding of basic political institutions in America. Several made the relationship clear in their writings, not the least persuasive of which are those of Andrew Johnson.

WASHINGTON

I have no conception of a more delicate task, than that [appointments to office] which is imposed by the Constitution on the Executive. . . . Perfectly convinced I am, that, if injudicious or unpopular measures should be taken by the Executive under the New Government with regards to appointment, the Government itself would be in the utmost danger of being utterly subverted by those measures.[1]

* * *

I anticipate that one of the most difficult and delicate parts of the duty of my Office will be that which relates to nominations for appointments.[2]

* * *

No part of my duty will be more delicate, and, in many instances, more unpleasing, than that of nominating or appointing persons to offices. It will undoubtedly often happen that there will be several candidates for the same office whose pretensions, abilities and integrity may be nearly equal, and who will come forward so equally supported in every respect as almost to require the aid of supernatural intuition to fix upon the right. I shall, however, in all events have the satisfaction to reflect that I entered upon my administration unconfined by a single engagement, uninfluenced by any ties of blood or friendship, and with the best intentions and fullest determination to nominate to office those persons only, who, upon every consideration, were the most deserving, and who would probably execute their several functions to the interest and credit of the American Union, if such characters could be found by my exploring every avenue of information respecting their merits and pretensions that it was in my power to obtain.[3]

✦ ✦ ✦

I foresaw the numerous applications which would be made for nominations to offices, and readily conceived that amidst the variety of candidates, it would be one of the most delicate and difficult duties of the President to disseminate those characters which, upon every account, were best fitted to fill the several offices. I have entered into Public life without the restraint of blood or friendship: I shall, therefore, use my best endeavors to find out such persons as are most suitable, on every account, to fill the respective offices, and such only shall I nominate.[4]

✦ ✦ ✦

My political conduct in nominations, even if I was influenced by principle, must be exceedingly circumspect and proof against just criticism, for the eyes of Argus are upon me, and no slip will pass unnoticed that can be improved into a supposed partiality for friends or relatives.[5]

✦ ✦ ✦

My present Ideas are that as they [appointments] point to a single object unconnected in its nature with any other object, they had best be made by written messages. In this case the Acts of the President, and the Acts of the Senate will stand upon clear, distinct and responsible ground.

Independent of this consideration, it could be no pleasing thing I conceive, for the President, on the one hand to be present and hear the propriety of his nominations questioned; nor for the Senate on the other hand to be under the smallest restraint from his presence from the fullest and freest inquiry into the Character of the Person nominated. The President in a situation like this would be reduced to one of two things: either to be a silent witness of the decision by Ballot, if there are objections to the nomination; or in justification thereof (if he should think it right) to support it by argument. Neither of which might be agreeable; and the latter improper; for as the President has a right to nominate without assigning his reasons, so has the Senate a right to dissent without giving theirs.[6]

JOHN ADAMS

If a President of the United States has not authority enough to change his own secretaries, he is no longer fit for his office. If he must enter into a controversy in pamphlets and newspapers, in vindication of his measures, he would have employment enough for his whole life, and must neglect the duties and business of his station.[7]

✦ ✦ ✦

It has been the constant usage, now twelve years, for the President to answer no letters of solicitation of recommendation for office.[8]

✦ ✦ ✦

By the Constitution the President has power, by and with the advice of the Senate, to *appoint* officers, and by the same Constitution the President shall commission all the officers of the United States. A question occurred to me whether the signature of the commission is not the act of appointment, and whether any other evidence of appointment will be admitted by the courts of law; in short, whether there can be an officer without a commission.[9]

✦ ✦ ✦

It is not upon the act of the 3d of March ultimo, that I ground the claim of an authority to appoint the officers in question, but upon the Constitution itself. Whenever there is an office that is not full, there is a vacancy, as I have ever understood the Constitution. To suppose that the President has power to appoint judges and ambassadors, in the recess of the Senate, and not officers of the army, is to me a distinction without a difference, and a Constitution not founded in law or sense, and very embarrassing to the public service. All such appointments, to be sure, must be nominated to the Senate at their next session, and subject to their ultimate decision. I have no doubt that it is my right and my duty to make the provisional appointments.[10]

✦ ✦ ✦

Must a President publish a justificatory Proclamation containing all his Reasons, for dismissing a Secretary of State? And when every one of his Reasons is contradicted, misrepresented, abused, insulted, must he answer all these Libells? How many Clerks and Secretaries must he employ? or must he write all this himself? Twenty Scribes would not be Sufficient. What would become of the Business of the State?

What are the Qualifications of a Secretary of State? He ought to be a Man of universal Reading in Laws, Governments, History.

Our whole terrestrial Universe ought to be summarily comprehended in his Mind.

Suppose a President has a Secretary, fastened upon him by a Predecessor, whom he finds incompetent to the high Duties of his office, and thinks it necessary to dismiss him for his Incapacity; or suppose he knows another, infinitely better qualified: must he reveal the whole History of his Administration, and detail every Fact upon which he grounded his opinion? Every Fact will be denied, every Inference disputed. How long must this Controversy continue. It will be a Subject of dispute with Posterity as well as the present Age.[11]

JEFFERSON

The public will never be made to believe that an appointment of a relative is made on the ground of merit alone, uninfluenced by family views; nor can they ever see with approbation offices, the disposal of which they entrust to their Presidents for public purposes, divided out as family property. Mr. Adams degraded himself infinitely by his conduct on this subject, as Genl. Washington had done himself the greatest honor. With two such examples to proceed by, I should be doubly inexcusable to err. It is true that this places the relations of the President in a worse situation than if he were a stranger, but the public good, which cannot be affected if it's confidence be lost, requires this sacrifice. Perhaps, too, it is compensated by sharing in the public esteem.[12]

✦ ✦ ✦

I had foreseen, years ago, that the first republican President who should come into office after all the places in the government had become exclusively occupied by federalists, would have a dreadful operation to perform. That the republicans would consent to a continuation of everything in federal hands, was not to be expected, because neither just nor politic. On him, then, was to devolve the office of an executioner, that of lopping off.[13]

✦ ✦ ✦

Recommendations, when honestly written should detail the bad as well as good qualities of the person recommended. That gentleman may do freely, if they know their letter is to be confined to the president or the head of a department. But if communicated further it may bring on them troublesome quarrels. In Gl. Washington's time he resisted every effort to bring forth his recommendations. In Mr. Adams time I only know that the republicans knew nothing of them. I have always considered the controul of the Senate as meant to prevent any bias or favoritism in the President towards his own relations, his own religion, towards particular states &c. and perhaps to keep very abnoxious persons out of offices of the first grade. But in all subordinate cases I have ever thought that the selection made by the President ought to inspire a general confidence that it has been made on due inquiry and investigation of character, and that the Senate should interpose their negative only in those particular cases where something happens to be within their knowledge, against the character of the person and unfitting him for the appointment. To Mr. Tracy at any rate no exhibition or information of recommendations ought to be communicated. He may be told that the President does not think it regular to communicate the grounds or reasons of his decision.[14]

✦ ✦ ✦

The fact is that we have put down the great mass of offices which gave such patronage to the President of the U.S. These had been so numerous, that presenting themselves to the public eye at all times & places, office began to be looked to as a resource for every man whose affairs were getting into derangement, or who was too indolent to pursue his profession, and for young men just entering into life. In short it was poisoning the very source of industry, by presenting an easier resource for a livelihood and was corrupting the principles of the great mass of those who passed a wishful eye on office. The case is now quite changed. We have almost nothing to give.[15]

✦ ✦ ✦

. . . and altho' no person wishes more than I do to learn the opinions of respected *individuals,* because they enable me to examine, and often to correct my own, yet I am not satisfied that I ought to admit the addresses even of those bodies of men which are organized by the Constitution, (the houses of legislature for instance) to influence the appointment to office for which the Constitution has chosen to rely on the independence and integrity of the Executive, controlled by the Senate, chosen both of them by the whole union.[16]

✓ ✓ ✓

My nominations are sometimes made on my own knolege of
the persons; sometimes on the information of others given either
voluntarily, or at my request & in personal confidence to me.
This I could not communicate without a breach of confidence,
not I am sure, under the contemplation of the committee. They
are sensible the Constitution has made it my duty to nominate;
and has not made it my duty to lay before them the evidences
or reasons whereon my nominations are founded: & of the correctness of this opinion the established usage in the intercourse
between the Senate & President is a proof. During nearly the
whole of the time this Constitution has been in operation I have
been in situations of intimacy with this part of it & may observe
from my own knolege that it has not been the usage for the
President to lay before the Senate or a committee, the information on which he makes his nominations.[17]

MADISON

The law terminating appointments at periods of four years is
pregnant with mischiefs such as you describe. It overlooks the
important distinction between repealing or modifying the office
and displacing the officer. The former is a legislative, the latter
an Executive function; and even the former, if done with a view
of re-establishing the office and letting in a new appointment,
would be an indirect violation of the theory and policy of the
Constitution. If the principle of the late statute be a sound one,
nothing is necessary but to limit appointments held during pleasure to a single year, or the next meeting of Congress, in order to
make the pleasure of the Senate a tenure of office, instead of
that of the President alone. If the error be not soon corrected,
the task will be very difficult; for it is of a nature to take a deep
root.[18]

✓ ✓ ✓

You call my attention with much emphasis to the principle
openly avowed by the President [Jackson] and his friends, that
offices and emoluments were the spoils of victory, the personal
property of the successful candidate for the Presidency, to be
given as rewards for electioneering services, and in general to be
used as the means of rewarding those who support, and of punishing those who do not support, the dispenser of the fund. I fully

agree in all the odium you attach to such a rule of action. But I have not seen any avowal of such a principle by the President, and suspect that few if any of his friends would openly avow it. The first, I believe, who openly proclaimed the right and policy in a successful candidate for the Presidency to reward friends and punish enemies by removals and appointments, is now the most vehement in branding the practice. Indeed, the principle if avowed without the practice, or practised without the avowal, could not fail to degrade any Administration; both together, completely so. The odium itself would be an antidote to the poison of the example, and a security against the permanent danger apprehended from it.[19]

✦ ✦ ✦

The claim [of the Senate] on *constitutional* ground, to a share in the removal as well as appointment of officers, is in direct opposition to the uniform practice of the Government from its commencement. It is clear that the innovation would not only vary, essentially, the existing balance of power, but expose the Executive, occasionally, to a total inaction, and at all times to delays fatal to the due execution of the laws.[20]

✦ ✦ ✦

Another innovation of great practical importance espoused by the Senate, relates to the power of the Executive to make diplomatic and consular appointments in the recess of the Senate. Hitherto it has been the practice to make such appointments to places calling for them, whether the places had or had not before received them. Under no Administration was the distinction more disregarded than under that of Mr. Jefferson, particularly in consular appointments, which rest on the same text of the Constitution with that of public ministers. It is now assumed that the appointments can only be made for occurring vacancies; that is, places which had been previously filled. The error lies in confounding foreign missions under the law of nations with municipal officers under the local law. If they were officers in the *constitutional* sense, a legislative creation of them being expressly required, they could not be created by the President and Senate. If, indeed, it could be admitted that as offices they would *ipso facto* be created by the appointment from the President and Senate, the office would expire with the appointment, and the next appointment would create a new office, not fill a vacant one. By regarding those missions not as offices, but as stations or agencies, always existing under the law of nations for governments agreeing, the one to send the other to receive the proper functionaries, the case, though not perhaps altogether free from difficulty, is better provided for than by any other construction. The doctrine of the Senate would be as injurious in practice as it is unfounded in authority. It might and probably would be of infinitely greater importance to send a public minister where one had never been sent, than where there had been a previous mission. If regarded as offices, it follows, moreover, that the President would be bound, as in case of other offices, to keep them always filled, whether the occasion required it or not; the opposite extreme of not being permitted to provide for the occasion, however urgent.[21]

MONROE

In executing this very delicate and important trust I acted with the utmost precaution.' Sensible of what I owed to my country, I felt strongly the obligation of observing the utmost impartiality in selecting those officers who were to be retained. In executing this law I had no personal object to accomplish or feeling to gratify—no one to retain, no one to remove. Having on great consideration fixed the principles on which the reduction should be made, I availed myself of the example of my predecessor [Madison] by appointing through the proper department a board of general officers to make the selection, and whose report I adopted. . . .

In filling original vacancies—that is, offices newly created—it is my opinion, as a general principle, that Congress have no right under the Constitution to impose any restraint by law on the power granted to the President so as to prevent his making a free selection of proper persons for these offices from the whole body of his fellow-citizens. . . .

Having already suggested my impression that in filling offices newly created, to which on no principle whatever anyone could have a claim of right, Congress could not under the Constitution restrain the free selection of the President from the whole body of his fellow-citizens, I shall only further remark that if that impression is well founded all objection to these appointments must cease.[22]

✶ ✶ ✶

Your view of the Constitution, as to the powers of the Executive in the appointment of public Ministers, is in strict accord with my own, and is, as I understand, supported by numerous precedents, under successive administrations. A foreign mission is not an office, in the sense of the Constitution, which authorizes the President to fill vacancies in the recess of the Senate. It is not an office created by law, nor subject to the rules applicable to such offices. It exists only when an appointment is made, and terminates when it ceases, whether by the recall, death, or resignation of the Minister. It exists in the contemplation of the Constitution, with every power, and may be filled with any, or terminated with either, as circumstances may require, according to the judgment of the Executive. If an appointment can be made by the Executive, in the recess of the Senate, to a court at which we have been represented, to fill a vacancy created by the death or resignation of the Minister, I am of opinion that it may be made to a court at which we have never been represented.[23]

JOHN QUINCY ADAMS

Mr. Tracy, member of the House of Representatives from New York, was here this morning, and made some enquiries respecting the principle of re-appointment to offices the tenure of which is limited to four years. I told him that the Act of Congress of 15th May, 1820, by which all the offices employed in the collection of the revenue were thus limited, had not answered the purpose for which it was intended: that the ostensible object under color of which it had been carried through Congress had been to secure the accountability of those officers, for which other enactments should have been much better suited; that its real and immediate object was to promote the election of W. H. Crawford as President of the United States in 1825. It placed the whole body of Executive officers of the General Government throughout the Union at the mercy, for their continuance in office, of the Secretary of the Treasury and of a majority of the Senate. It was drawn up by Mr. Crawford, as he himself told me. It was introduced into the Senate by Mahlon Dickerson, of New Jersey, then one of his devoted partisans, and its design was to secure for Mr. Crawford the influence of all the incumbents in office, at the peril of displacement, and of five or ten

times an equal number of ravenous office-seekers, eager to sup-
plant them. This object succeeded so far as to enlist a multitude
of most active electioneering partisans in Crawford's cause. The
Custom-House officers throughout the Union, the District Attorneys, Marshals, Registers of the Land Offices, Receivers of Public Moneys, Paymasters in the army, and all their family connec-
tions, were ardent Crawfordites. The Senate was conciliated by
the permanent increase of their power, which was the principal
ultimate effect of the Act, and every Senator was flattered by
the power conferred upon himself of multiplying chances to provide for his friends and dependants. But the gravity of the mass
was disproportioned to the length of the lever. Mr. Monroe un-
warily signed the bill without adverting to its real character. He
told me that Mr. Madison considered it as in principle unconstitutional. He thought the tenure of all subordinate Executive
offices was necessarily the pleasure of the chief by whom they
were commissioned. If they could be limited by Congress to four
years, they might to one—to a month—to a day—and the Executive power might thus be annihilated. Mr. Monroe himself inclined to the same opinion, but the question had not occurred
to him when he signed the bill. In carrying the Act into execution, he adopted the principle of renominating every officer at
the expiration of his commission, unless some charge of misdemeanor should be adduced and proved against him, and during
the last eighteen months' of that Administration Mr. Crawford
was disabled, both physically and politically, from making the
use of this Act which he had intended. I have proceeded upon
the principle established by Mr. Monroe, and have renominated
every officer, friend or foe, against whom no specific charge of
misconduct has been brought. The result of the Act has been
to increase the power of patronage exercised by the President,
and still more that of the Senate, and of every individual Senator.[24]

✓ ✓ ✓

Stephen Fitch, a man having the appearance and manners of
a Quaker, came, and told me that he had come hither with Red
Jacket and two others of the New York Seneca and Oneida Indians to complain of wrongs in regard to the purchase of their
lands; that he himself had been extremely anxious to see me,
and although he had been advised not to come, and told that I
should probably not receive him, he had yet determined to make
the experiment, and Red Jacket was equally desirous to see his

father the President. . . . The direct access to the President in all their transactions with this Government, and especially in the representation of all their grievances, they take greatly to heart, and with much more reason than the white hunters—that is, office-hunters. This access I have never denied to any one, of any color, and, in my opinion of the duties of a Chief Magistrate of the United States, it ought never to be denied. The place-hunters are not pleasant visitors or correspondents, and they consume an enormous disproportion of time. To this personal importunity the President ought not to be subjected; but it is perhaps not possible to relieve him from it without secluding the man from the intercourse of the people more than comports with the nature of our institutions.[25]

*   *   *

I said that the discretionary power of the President to remove was settled by law, and by the uniform practice of forty years. I though it correctly settled; but if the discretion was palpably abused, I thought it impeachable misdemeanor. In questioning, however, this abuse of power, I thought it would be unsafe, and certainly unsuccessful, to advance any new principle.[26]

*   *   *

The Constitution had prescribed that the President should *nominate*, and by and with the advice and consent of the Senate, should *appoint*, all the officers of the United States, with the exception that Congress might by law vest the appointment of such inferior officers as they should think proper in the President alone, in the courts of law, or in the heads of departments. The Constitution had also provided, that the President should commission *all* the officers of the United States—and that the judges both of the supreme and inferior courts should hold their offices during good behaviour. But it had prescribed no term of duration to executive offices, civil or miliatry, nor how, nor by whom, nor for what, they should be removable from office. The institution of the first Executive Department gave rise to that question. After a long and able discussion, it was ultimately settled, that by the investment of the executive power in the President, and the duty imposed upon him to take care that the laws should be faithfully executed, the discretionary power of removing all subordinate executive offices must necessarily be vested in him; and the law was accordingly so expressed. It must be admitted that this, like all other discretionary powers, is susceptible of great abuse—but while exercised as it always must be, under the powerful influence of public opinion, its abuse cannot be so pernicious to the welfare of the community, as would be a tenure of ministerial office, independent of the superior, responsible for its faithful execution.[27]

JACKSON

While members of Congress can be constitutionally appointed to offices of trust and profit it will be the practice, even under the most conscientious adherence to duty, to select them for such stations as they are believed to be better qualified to fill than other citizens; but the purity of our Government would doubtless be promoted by their exclusion from all appointments in the gift of the President, in whose election they may have been officially concerned. The nature of the judicial office and the necessity of securing in the Cabinet and in diplomatic stations of the highest rank the best talents and political experience should, perhaps, except these from the exclusion.[28]

✓ ✓ ✓

You may assure Mr. Richie that his Washington correspondent knows nothing of what will be the course of the President in appointments, or he would have known that the President has not, nor will he ever, make an appointment but with a view, to the public good, and the security of the fiscal concerns of the nation. He never has, nor will he, appoint a personal friend to office, unless by such appointment the public will be faithfully served. I cannot suppose mr Richie would have me proscribe my friends, merely because they are so. If my personal friends are qualified and patriotic, why should I not be permitted to bestow a *few* offices on them? For my own part I can see no well founded objections to it. In my Cabinet, it is well known that there is but one man with whom I have had an intimate and particular acquaintance, tho' they are all my friends, and in whom I have the greatest confidence. But even if it were as mr Richie supposes, I have only followed the examples of my illustrious predecessors, Washington and Jefferson. They took from their own state, bosom friends and placed them in the Cabinet. Not only this, but Genl Washington went even farther —besides placing two of his friends from Virginia near him, he brought into his cabinet Genl Hamilton with whom, if possible, he was upon more intimate terms than I am with any member of my Cabinet.[29]

✓ ✓ ✓

The most disagreeable duty I have to perform is the removals, and appointments to office. There is great distress here, and it appears, that all who possess office, depend upon the emolument for support, and thousands who are pressing for office to it upon the ground, that they are starving, and their families, and must perish without they can be relieved by the emolument of some office. These hungry expectants, as well as those who enjoy office, are dangerous contestants over the public purse, unless possessed of the purest principles of integrity, and honesty, and when any and every man can get recommendations of the strongest kind, it requires great circumspection to avoid imposition, and select honest men.

You will see from the public journals we have begun reform, and that we are trying to cleans the augean stables, and expose to view the corruption of some of the agents of the late administration.[30]

✓ ✓ ✓

Permit me to premise, that in appointing persons to office it is not incumbent on the President to assign the reasons which govern his conduct. To appoint one, and reject another, is by the Constitution left to his discretion and if he errs in the former case, the Senate affords a safe guarantee. It is by his acts that he is in this respect to be judged by his constituents.[31]

✓ ✓ ✓

By the Constitution "the executive power is vested in a President of the United States." Among the duties imposed upon him, and which he is sworn to perform, is that of "taking care that the laws be faithfully executed." Being thus made responsible for the entire action of the executive department, it was but reasonable that the power of appointing, overseeing, and controlling those who execute the laws—a power in its nature executive— should remain in his hands. It is therefore not only his right, but the Constitution makes it his duty, to "nominate and, by and with the advice and consent of the Senate, appoint" all "officers of the United States whose appointments are not in the Constitution otherwise provided for," with a proviso that the appointment of inferior officers may be vested in the President alone, in the courts of justice, or in the heads of Departments.

The executive power vested in the Senate is neither that of

"nominating" nor "appointing." It is merely a check upon the Executive power of appointment. If individuals are proposed for appointment by the President by them deemed incompetent or unworthy, they may withhold their consent and the appointment can not be made. They check the action of the Executive, but can not in relation to those very subjects act themselves nor direct him. Selections are still made by the President, and the negative given to the Senate, without diminishing his responsibility, furnishes an additional guaranty to the country that the subordinate executive as well as the judicial offices shall be filled with worthy and competent men.[32]

✓ ✓ ✓

The whole executive power being vested in the President, who is responsible for its exercise, it is a necessary consequence that he should have a right to employ agents of his own choice to aid him in the performance of his duties, and to discharge them when he is no longer willing to be responsible for their acts. In strict accordance with this principle, the power of removal, which, like that of appointment, is an original executive power, is left unchecked by the Constitution in relation to all executive officers, for whose conduct the President is responsible, while it is taken from him in relation to judicial officers, for whose acts he is not responsible. In the Government from which many of the fundamental principles of our system are derived the head of the executive department originally had power to appoint and remove at will all officers, executive and judicial. It was to take the judges out of this general power of removal, and thus make them independent of the Executive, that the tenure of their offices was changed to good behavior. Nor is it conceivable why they are placed in our Constitution upon a tenure different from that of all other officers appointed by the Executive unless it be for the same purpose.

But if there were any just ground for doubt on the face of the Constitution whether all executive officers are removable at the will of the President, it is obviated by the contemporaneous construction of the instrument and the uniform practice under it.

The power of removal was a topic of solemn debate in the Congress of 1789 while organizing the administrative departments of the Government, and it was finally decided that the President derived from the Constitution the power of removal so far as it regards that department for whose acts he is responsible. Although the debate covered the whole ground, embracing the Treasury as well as all the other Executive Departments, it arose on a motion to strike out of the bill to establish a Department of Foreign Affairs, since called the Department of State, a clause declaring the Secretary "to be removable from office by the President of the United States." After that motion had been decided in the negative it was perceived that these words did not convey the sense of the House of Representatives in relation to the true source of the power of removal. With the avowed object of preventing any future inference that this power was exercised by the President in virtue of a grant from Congress, when in fact that body considered it as derived from the Constitution, the words which had been the subject of debate were struck out, and in lieu thereof a clause was inserted in a provision concerning the chief clerk of the Department, which declared that "whenever the said principal officer shall be removed from office by the President of the United States, or in any other case of vacancy," the chief clerk should during such vacancy have charge of the papers of the office. This change having been made for the express purpose of declaring the sense of Congress that the President derived the power of removal from the Constitution, the act as it passed has always been considered as a full expression of the sense of the Legislature on this important part of the American Constitution.

Here, then, we have the concurrent authority of President Washington, of the Senate, and the House of Representatives, numbers of whom had taken an active part in the convention which framed the Constitution and in the State conventions which adopted it, that the President derived an unqualified power of removal from that instrument itself, which is "beyond the reach of legislative authority." Upon this principle the Government has now been steadily administered for about forty-five years, during which there have been numerous removals made by the President or by his direction, embracing every grade of executive officers from the heads of Departments to the messengers of bureaus.

No joint power of appointment is given to the two Houses of Congress, nor is there any accountability to them as one body; but as soon as any office is created by law, of whatever name or character, the appointment of the person or persons to fill it devolves by the Constitution upon the President, with the advice and consent of the Senate, unless it be an inferior office, and the appointment be vested by the law itself "in the President alone, in the courts of law, or in the heads of Departments."[33]

✦ ✦ ✦

Thus was it settled by the Constitution, the laws, and the whole practice of the Government that the entire executive power is vested in the President of the United States; that as incident to that power the right of appointing and removing those officers who are to aid him in the execution of the laws, with such restrictions only as the Constitution prescribes, is vested in the President; that the Secretary of the Treasury is one of those officers; that the custody of the public property and money is an Executive function which, in relation to the money, has always been exercised through the Secretary of the Treasury and his subordinates; that in the performance of these duties he is subject to the supervision and control of the President, and in all important measures having relation to them consults the Chief Magistrate and obtains his approval and sanction. . . .[34]

VAN BUREN

The constitution directs, in express terms, that the officers of the Federal Government shall be appointed by the President, but is silent in regard to the authority by which they may be removed. A question was raised at the commencement of the Government, upon the latter point, was elaborately discussed, and as was supposed, was finally decided by the first Congress, in favor of the power of removal by the President. That construction had since been generally acquiesced in, and had been acted upon, without intermission, by every President.[35]

✦ ✦ ✦

The appointment is made by the Constitution to consist of three acts—the nomination, the approach by the Senate, and the commissioning. The first and last devolve on the President.[36]

WILLIAM H. HARRISON

By making the President the sole distributer of all the patronage of the Government the framers of the Constitution do not appear to have anticipated at how short a period it would become a formidable instrument to control the free operations of the

State governments. Of trifling importance at first, it had early in Mr. Jefferson's Administration become so powerful as to create great alarm in the mind of that patriot from the potent influence it might exert in controlling the freedom of the elective franchise. If such could have then been the effects of its influence, how much greater must be the danger at this time, quadrupled in amount as it certainly is and more completely under the control of the Executive will than their construction of their powers allowed or the forbearing characters of all the early Presidents permitted them to make. But it is not by the extent of its patronage alone that the executive department has become dangerous, but by the use which it appears may be made of the appointing power to bring under its control the whole revenues of the country. The Constitution has declared it to be the duty of the President to see that the laws are executed, and it makes him the Commander in Chief of the Armies and Navy of the United States. If the opinion of the most approved writers upon that species of mixed government which in modern Europe is termed *monarchy* in contradistinction to despotism is correct, there was wanting no other addition to the powers of our Chief Magistrate to stamp a monarchical character on our Government by the control of the public finances; and to me it appears strange indeed that anyone should doubt that the entire control which the President possesses over the officers who have the custody of the public money, by the power of removal with or without cause, does, for all mischievous purposes at least, virtually subject the treasure also to his disposal.[37]

TYLER

The patronage incident to the Presidential office, already great, is constantly increasing. Such increase is destined to keep pace with the growth of our population, until, without a figure of speech, an army of officeholders may be spread over the land. The unrestrained power exerted by a selfishly ambitious man in order either to perpetuate his authority or to hand it over to some favorite as his successor may lead to the employment of all the means within his control to accomplish his object. The right to remove from office, while subjected to no just restraint, is inevitably destined to produce a spirit of crouching servility with the official corps, which, in order to uphold the hand which feeds them, would lead to direct and active interference in the elections, both State and Federal, thereby subjecting the course of State legislation to the dictation of the chief executive officer and making the will of that officer absolute and supreme.[38]

✦ ✦ ✦

All appointments to office made by a President become from the date of their nomination to the Senate official acts, which are matter of record and are at the proper time made known to the House of Representatives and to the country. But applications for office, or letters respecting appointments, or conversations held with individuals on such subjects are not official proceedings, and can not by any means be made to partake of the character of official proceedings unless after the nomination of such person so writing or conversing the President shall think proper to lay such correspondence or such conversations before the Senate. Applicants for office are in their very nature confidential, and if the reasons assigned for such applications or the names of the applicants were communicated, not only would such implied confidence be wantonly violated, but, in addition, it is quite obvious that a mass of vague, incoherent, and personal matter would be made public at a vast consumption of time, money, and trouble without accomplishing or tending in any manner to accomplish, as it appears to me, any useful object connected with a sound and constitutional administration of the Government in any of its branches.

But there is a consideration of a still more effective and lofty character which is with me entirely decisive of the correctness of the view that I have taken of this question. While I shall ever evince the greatest readiness to communicate to the House of Representatives all proper information which the House shall deem necessary to a due discharge of its constitutional obligations and functions, yet it becomes me, in defense of the Constitution and laws of the United States, to protect the executive department from all encroachment on its powers, rights, and duties. In my judgment a compliance with the resolution which has been transmitted to me would be a surrender of duties and powers which the Constitution has conferred exclusively on the Executive, and therefore such compliance can not be made by me nor by the heads of Departments by my direction. The appointing power, so far as it is bestowed on the President by the Constitution, is conferred without reserve or qualification. The reason for the appointment and the responsibility of the appointment rest with him alone. I can not perceive anywhere in the Constitution of the United States any right conferred on the House of Representatives to hear the reasons which an applicant may urge for an appointment to office under the executive department, or any duty resting upon the House of Representatives by which it may become responsible for any such appointment.[39]

POLK

I am thoroughly satisfied that the patronage of the Government greatly weakens any President of the U. States, so much so, indeed, that I doubt whether any President will ever again be re-elected. Members of Congress and others occupying high positions in Society, make representations to procure appointments for their friends, upon which I cannot rely, & constantly lead me into error. I begin, more than I have ever done before, to distrust the disinterestedness and honesty of all mankind. Some selfish or petty local feeling seems to influence even members of Congress in their recommendations for office, much more than principle. When I act upon the information which they give me, and make a mistake, they leave me to bear the responsibility, and never have the manliness to assume it themselves.[40]

For the thirty-two years between the second election of Jackson and that of Lincoln no President was re-elected. In the twentieth century every President except Taft and Hoover was returned to office.

✓ ✓ ✓

In every appointment which the President makes he disappoints half a dozen or more applicants and their friends, who, actuated by selfish and sordid motives, will prefer any other candidate in the next election, while the person appointed attributes the appointment to his own superior merit and does not even feel obliged by it. The number of office seekers has become so large that they probably hold the balance of power between the two great parties in the country, and if disappointed in getting place under one administration they will readily unite themselves with the party and candidate of opposite politics, so as to increase their chances for place. Another great difficulty in making appointments which the President encounters is that he cannot tell upon what recommendations to rely. Members of Congress and men of high station in the country sign papers of recommendation, either from interested personal motives or without meaning what they say, and thus the President is often imposed on, and induced to make bad appointments. When he does so the whole responsibility falls on himself, while those who have signed papers of recommendation and misled him, take special care never to avow the agency they have had in the matter, or to assume any part of the responsibility. I have had some remarkable instances of this during my administration. One or two of them I think worthy to be recorded as illustrations of many others. In the recess of Congress shortly after the commencement of my administration I made an appointment upon the letter of recommendation of a senator. I sent the nomination to the Senate at the last session & it was rejected, and, as I learned, at the instance of the same Senator who had made the recommendation. A few days afterwards the Senator called to recommend another person for the same office. I said to him, well, you rejected the man I nominated; O yes, he replied, he was without character & wholly unqualified. I then asked him if he knew upon whose recommendation I had appointed him, to which he replied that he did not. I then handed to him his own letter & told him that that was the recommendation upon which I had appointed him. He appeared confused and replied, Well, we are obliged to recommend our constituents when they apply to us. The Senator was Mr. Atchison of Missouri, and the person appointed & rejected was Mr. Hedges as Surveyor of the port of St. Louis.[41]

✦ ✦ ✦

I then stated that a Bill had passed the Senate, & might pass the House, to create a Board of Commissioners to decide on claims of the people of California against the U. S., and that this Bill had designated by description the three persons who were to be the commissioners, and this I considered to be a violation of the Constitution. The Constitution confers upon the President the power to make all appointments to office by and with the advice & consent of the Senate, except the appointment of inferior officers which might be vested by law in the President alone, in the Heads of Departments, or in the Judicial tribunals. By the Bill referred to, Congress [would] undertake to make the appointments by law. The Cabinet were unanimously of opinion that such a law would be unconstitutional, and that if it passed I ought to veto it. I told the Cabinet I would certainly veto it if it passed.[42]

✦ ✦ ✦

The office of President is generally esteemed a very high & dignified position, but really I think the public would not so regard it if they could look in occasionally and observe the kind of people by whom I am often annoyed. I cannot seclude myself but must be accessible to my fellow-citizens, and this gives an opportunity to all classes and descriptions of people to obtrude themselves upon me about matters in which the public has not the slightest interest. There is no class of our population by whom I am annoyed so much, or for whom I entertain a more sovereign contempt, than for the professed office-seekers who have beseiged me ever since I have been in the Presidential office.[43]

FILLMORE

The appointing power is one of the most delicate with which the Executive is invested. I regard it as a sacred trust, to be exercised with the sole view of advancing the prosperity and happiness of the people. It shall be my effort to elevate the standard of official employment by selecting for places of importance individuals fitted for the posts to which they are assigned by their known integrity, talents, and virtues. In so extensive a country, with so great a population, and where few persons appointed to office can be known to the appointing power, mistakes will sometimes unavoidably happen and unfortunate appointments be made notwithstanding the greatest care. In such cases the power of removal may be properly exercised; and neglect of duty or malfeasance in office will be no more tolerated in individuals appointed by myself than in those appointed by others.[44]

✦ ✦ ✦

The Constitution declares, that, "the President shall have power to fill up all vacancies, that may happen during the recess of the Senate, by granting commissions, which shall expire at the end of their next session. . . ." Yet the intention of the framers of the Constitution evidently was, that these appointments should be submitted to the consideration of the Senate at the first session after they were made. This it is true was done in all these cases, and the Senate had an opportunity to approve or disapprove those appointments, but it is difficult to see how that fact can effect [sic] the authority of the President of appointing to

fill the vacancy without its approval, and we must therefore conclude that the President might exercise this power, without
having previously nominated the officer to the Senate; the consequence of which would be that by continued temporary commissions and an omission on the part of the President to nominate
to the Senate he might continue to fill these offices without its
concurrence. This would evidently be a violation of the spirit of
the Constitution. But it would certainly be in the power of Congress to make such an omission a high crime or misdemeanor,
and then to impeach the President for his neglect of duty in
omitting to nominate the officers to the Senate.[45]

✦ ✦ ✦

It is possible to be mistaken in men of the best repute and
those having abundance of recommendation. The applicants for
office were generally entered on a list, during my Administration, by the chiefs of the departments to whom they applied.
When vacancies were to be filled and a man was selected for
appointment inquiries were made as to his character and ability,
and not as to his political achievements. If I found the man selected was capable of discharging the duties of the office I sent
his name forward to Congress for confirmation. But, then, any
mistakes or abuse of confidence can readily be remedied by the
recalling power vested in the President.[46]

BUCHANAN

The distribution of the patronage of the Government is by far
the most disagreeable duty of the President. Applicants are so
numerous, and their applications are pressed with such eagerness
by their friends both in and out of Congress, that the selection
of one for any desirable office gives offence to many.[47]

LINCOLN

I must myself be the judge how long to retain in and when to
remove any of you from his position. It would greatly pain me to
discover any of you endeavoring to procure another's removal, or
in any way to prejudice him before the public. Such endeavor
would be a wrong to me, and, much worse, a wrong to the
country. My wish is that on this subject no remark be made nor
question asked by any of you, here or elsewhere, now or hereafter.[48]

ANDREW JOHNSON

That the power of removal is constitutionally vested in the President of the United States is a principle which has been not more distinctly declared by judicial authority and judicial commentators than it has been uniformly practiced upon by the legislative and executive departments of the Government.[49]

✦ ✦ ✦

A construction which denied the power of removal by the President was further maintained by arguments drawn from the danger of the abuse of the power; from the supposed tendency of an exposure of public officers to capricious removal to impair the efficiency of the civil service; from the alleged injustice and hardship of displacing incumbents dependent upon their official stations without sufficient consideration; from a supposed want of responsibility on the part of the President, and from an imagined defect of guaranties against a vicious President who might incline to abuse the power. On the other hand, an exclusive power of removal by the President was defended as a true exposition of the text of the Constitution. It was maintained that there are certain causes for which persons ought to be removed from office without being guilty of treason, bribery, or malfeasance, and that the nature of things demands that it should be so.[50]

✦ ✦ ✦

The question, thus ably and exhaustively argued, was decided by the House of Representatives, by a vote of 34 to 20, in favor of the principle that the executive power of removal is vested by the Constitution in the Executive, and in the Senate by the casting vote of the Vice-President.

The question has often been raised in subsequent times of high excitement, and the practice of the Government has, nevertheless, conformed in all cases to the decision thus early made.[51]

✦ ✦ ✦

The power of appointment of all officers of the United States, civil or military, where not provided for in the Constitution, is vested in the President, by and with the advice and consent of the Senate, with this exception, that Congress "may by law vest

the appointment of such inferior officers as they think proper in
the President alone, in the courts of law, or in the heads of Departments."[52]

*   *   *

The President may be thoroughly convinced that an officer is
incapable, dishonest, or unfaithful to the Constitution, but under
the law which I have named [Tenure of Office Act] the utmost
he can do is to complain to the Senate and ask the privilege of
supplying his place with a better man. If the Senate be regarded
as personally or politically hostile to the President, it is natural,
and not altogether unreasonable, for the officer to expect that it
will take his part as far as possible, restore him to his place, and
give him a triumph over his Executive superior. The officer has
other chances of impunity arising from accidental defects of evidence, the mode of investigating it, and the secrecy of the hearing. It is not wonderful that official malfeasance should become
bold in proportion as the delinquents learn to think themselves
safe. I am entirely persuaded that under such a rule the President can not perform the great duty assigned to him of seeing
the laws faithfully executed, and that it disables him most especially from enforcing that rigid accountability which is necessary
to the due execution of the revenue laws.

The Constitution invests the President with authority to *decide*
whether a removal should be made in any given case; the act
of Congress declares in substance that he shall only *accuse* such
as he supposes to be premises, but the statute takes away his
jurisdiction, transfers it to the Senate, and leaves him nothing
but the odious and sometimes impracticable duty of becoming a
prosecutor. The prosecution is to be conducted before a tribunal
whose members are not, like him, responsible to the whole people, but to separate constituent bodies, and who may hear his accusation with great disfavor. The Senate is absolutely without any
known standard of decision applicable to such a case. Its judgment can not be anticipated, for it is not governed by any rule.
The law does not define what shall be deemed good cause for
removal. It is impossible even to conjecture what may or may not
be so considered by the Senate. The nature of the subject forbids
clear proof. If the charge be incapacity, what evidence will support it? Fidelity to the Constitution may be understood or mis-
understood in a thousand different ways, and by violent party
men, in violent party times, unfaithfulness to the Constitution
may even come to be considered meritorious. If the officer be

accused of dishonesty, how shall it be made out? Will it be inferred from acts unconnected with public duty, from private history, or from general reputation, or must the President await the
commission of an actual misdemeanor in office? Shall he in the
meantime risk the character and interest of the nation in the
hands of men to whom he can not give his confidence? Must he
forbear his complaint until the mischief is done and can not be
prevented? If his zeal in the public service should impel him to
anticipate the overt act, must he move at the peril of being tried
himself for the offense of slandering his subordinate? In the present circumstances of the country someone must be held responsible for official delinquency of every kind. It is extremely difficult
to say where that responsibility should be thrown if it be not left
where it has been placed by the Constitution. But all just men
will admit that the President ought to be entirely relieved from
such responsibility if he can not meet it by reason of restrictions
placed by law upon his action.

The unrestricted power of removal from office is a very great
one to be trusted even to a magistrate chosen by the general
suffrage of the whole people and accountable directly to them
for his acts. It is undoubtedly liable to abuse, and at some periods
of our history perhaps has been abused. If it be thought desirable
and constitutional that it should be so limited as to make the
President merely a common informer against other public agents,
he should at least be permitted to act in that capacity before
some open tribunal, independent of party politics, ready to investigate the merits of every case, furnished with the means of
taking evidence, and bound to decide according to established
rules. This would guarantee the safety of the accuser when he
acts in good faith, and at the same time secure the rights of the
other party. I speak, of course, with all proper respect for the
present Senate, but it does not seem to me that any legislative
body can be so constituted as to insure its fitness for these functions.[53]

✔ ✔ ✔

The uniform practice from the beginning of the Government,
as established by every President who has exercised the office,
and the decisions of the Supreme Court of the United States
have settled the question in favor of the power of the President
to remove all officers excepting a class holding appointments of
a judicial character. No practice nor any decision has ever ex-

cepted a Secretary of War from this general power of the President to make removals from office.

It is only necessary, then, that I should refer to the power of the Executive, under the laws of the United States, to remove from office a Secretary of War. The resolution denies that under these laws this power has any existence. In other words, it affirms that no such authority is recognized or given by the statutes of the country.

What, then, are the laws of the United States which deny the President the power to remove that officer? I know but two laws which bear upon this question. The first in order of time is the act of August 7, 1789, creating the Department of War, which, after providing for a Secretary as its principal officer, proceeds as follows:

> Sec. 2. *And be it further enacted,* That there shall be in the said Department an inferior officer, to be appointed by the said principal officer, to be employed therein as he shall deem proper, and to be called the chief clerk in the Department of War, and who, whenever the said principal officer shall be removed from office by the President of the United States, or in any other case of vacancy, shall during such vacancy have the charge and custody of all records, books, and papers appertaining to the said Department.

It is clear that this act, passed by a Congress many of those members participated in the formation of the Constitution, so far from denying the power of the President to remove the Secretary of War, recognizes it as existing in the Executive alone, without the concurrence of the Senate or of any other department of the Government. Furthermore, this act does not purport to confer the power by legislative authority, nor in fact was there any other existing legislation through which it was bestowed upon the Executive. The recognition of the power by this act is therefore complete as a recognition under the Constitution itself, for there was no other source or authority from which it could be derived.[54]

✓ ✓ ✓

It is assuredly proper that the President should have the same power to fill temporarily a vacancy occasioned by removal as he has to supply a place made vacant by death or the expiration of a term. If, for instance, the incumbent of an office should be found to be wholly unfit to exercise its functions, and the public service should require his immediate expulsion, a remedy should exist and be at once applied, and time be allowed the President to select and appoint a successor, as is permitted him in case of a vacancy caused by death or the termination of an official term.[55]

✦ ✦ ✦

This respondent was informed and verily believed that it was practically settled by the First Congress of the United States, and had been so considered and uniformly and in great numbers of instances acted on by each Congress and President of the United States, in succession, from President Washington to and including President Lincoln, and from the First Congress to the Thirty-ninth Congress, that the Constitution of the United States conferred on the President, as part of the executive power and as one of the necessary means and instruments of performing the executive duty expressly imposed on him by the Constitution of taking care that the laws be faithfully executed, the power at any and all times of removing from office all executive officers for cause to be judged of by the President alone. This respondent had, in pursuance of the Constitution, required the opinion of each principal officer of the Executive Departments upon this question of constitutional executive power and duty, and had been advised by each of them, including the said Stanton, Secretary for the Department of War, that under the Constitution of the United States this power was lodged by the Constitution in the President of the United States, and that, consequently, it could be lawfully exercised by him, and the Congress could not deprive him thereof; and this respondent, in his capacity of President of the United States, and because in that capacity he was both enabled and bound to use his best judgment upon this question, did, in good faith and with an earnest desire to arrive at the truth, come to the conclusion and opinion, and did make the same known to the honorable the Senate of the United States by a message dated on the 2d day of March, 1867. . . . that the power last mentioned was conferred and the duty of exercising it in fit cases was imposed on the President by the Constitution of 'the United States, and that the President could not be deprived of this power or relieved of this duty, nor could the same be vested by law in the President and the Senate jointly, either in part or whole; and this has ever since remained and was the opinion of this respondent at the time when he was forced as aforesaid to consider and decide what act or acts should and might lawfully be done by this respondent, as President of the United States, to cause the said Stanton to surrender the said office.[56]

GRANT

There is no duty which so much embarrasses the Executive and heads of Departments as that of appointments, nor is there any such arduous and thankless labor imposed on Senators and Representatives as that of finding places for constituents. The present system does not secure the best men, and often not even fit men, for public place.[57]

HAYES

. . . My experience in the executive duties has strongly confirmed the belief in the great advantage the country would find in observing strictly the plan of the Constitution, which imposes upon the Executive the sole duty and responsibility of the selection of those Federal officers who by law are appointed, not elected, and which in like manner assigns to the Senate the complete right to advise and consent to or to reject the nominations so made, whilst the House of Representatives stands as the public censor of the performance of official duties, with the prerogative of investigation and prosecution in all cases of dereliction. The blemishes and imperfections in the civil service may, as I think, be traced in most cases to a practical confusion of the duties assigned to the several Departments of the Government. My purpose in this respect has been to return to the system established by the fundamental law, and to do this with the heartiest cooperation and most cordial understanding with the Senate and House of Representatives.

The practical difficulties in the selection of numerous officers for posts of widely varying responsibilities and duties are acknowledged to be very great. No system can be expected to secure absolute freedom from mistakes, and the beginning of any attempted change of custom is quite likely to be more embarrassed in this respect than any subsequent period. It is here that the Constitution seems to me to prove its claim to the great wisdom accorded to it. It gives to the Executive the assistance of the knowledge and experience of the Senate, which, when acting upon nominations as to which they may be disinterested and impartial judges, secures as strong a guaranty of freedom from errors of importance as is perhaps possible in human affairs.

In addition to this, I recognize the public advantage of making all nominations, as nearly as possible, impersonal, in the sense of being free from mere caprice or favor in the selection; and in those offices in which special training is of greatly increased value I believe such a rule as to the tenure of office should obtain as may induce men of proper qualifications to apply themselves industriously to the task of becoming proficients. Bearing these things in mind, I have endeavored to reduce the number of changes in subordinate places usually made upon the change of the general administration, and shall most heartily cooperate with Congress in the better systematizing of such methods and rules of admission to the public service and of promotion within it as may promise to be most successful in making thorough competency, efficiency, and character the decisive tests in these matters.[58]

❧ ❧ ❧

The capital mistake is to attempt to build up an administration or a party by the use of the offices as patronage. The offices should be filled for the good of the service. Country first and party afterwards.[59]

❧ ❧ ❧

To secure needed legislation and to give the Executive independence and strength, the absolute and entire separation of Senators and Representatives from the exercise of the power of appointment is the essential feature of any wise plan of reform. With this established the rest will follow.[60]

ARTHUR

The civil list now comprises about 100,000 persons, far the larger part of whom must, under the terms of the Constitution, be selected by the President either directly or through his own appointees.

In the early years of the administration of the Government the personal direction of appointments to the civil service may not have been an irksome task for the Executive, but now that the burden has increased fully a hundredfold it has become greater than he ought to bear, and it necessarily diverts his time and attention from the proper discharge of other duties no less delicate and responsible, and which in the very nature of things can not be delegated to other hands.

In the judgment of not a few who have given study and reflection to this matter, the nation has outgrown the provisions which the Constitution has established for filling the minor offices in the public service.

But whatever may be thought of the wisdom or expediency of changing the fundamental law in this regard, it is certain that much relief may be afforded, not only to the President and to the heads of the Departments, but to Senators and Representatives in Congress, by discreet legislation.[61]

CLEVELAND

This dreadful, damnable office-seeking hangs over me and surrounds me—and makes me feel like resigning.[62]

✓ ✓ ✓

I go to bed after a long day with the feeling that I must be the meanest man in the world, for I seem to say only "no" where I would be only too glad to say "yes." But this office-seeking is a disease—I am entirely satisfied of that. It is even catching. Men get it, and they lose the proper balance of their minds. I've known men to come here to Washington on other business, with no thought of office, but when they had been here a couple of weeks they had caught it. They seem suddenly to get a mania.[63]

✓ ✓ ✓

The d——d everlasting clatter for office continues to some extent, and makes me feel like resigning, and Hell is to pay generally.[64]

✓ ✓ ✓

It will not be denied, I suppose, that the President may suspend a public officer in the entire absence of any papers or documents to aid his official judgment and discretion; and I am quite prepared to avow that the cases are not few in which suspensions from office have depended more upon oral representations made to me by citizens of known good repute and by members of the House of Representatives and Senators of the United States than upon any letters and documents presented for my examination. I have not felt justified in suspecting the veracity, integrity, and patriotism of Senators, or ignoring their representations, because they were not in party affiliation with the majority of their associates; and I recall a few suspensions which bear the approval of individual members identified politically with the majority in the Senate.

While, therefore, I am constrained to deny the right of the Senate to the papers and documents described, so far as the right to the same is based upon the claim that they are in any view of the subject official, I am also led unequivocally to dispute the right of the Senate by the aid of any documents whatever, or in any way save through the judicial process of trial on impeachment, to review or reverse the acts of the Executive in the suspension, during the recess of the Senate, of Federal officials.

I believe the power to remove or suspend such officials is vested in the President alone by the Constitution, which in express terms provides that "the executive power shall be vested in a President of the United States of America," and that "he shall take care that the laws be faithfully executed."

The Senate belongs to the legislative branch of the Government. When the Constitution by express provision superadded to its legislative duties the right to advise and consent to appointments to office and to sit as a court of impeachment, it conferred upon that body all the control and regulation of Executive action supposed to be necessary for the safety of the people; and this express and special grant of such extraordinary powers, not in any way related to or growing out of general Senatorial duty, and in itself a departure from the general plan of our Government, should be held, under a familiar maxim of construction, to exclude every other right of interference with Executive functions.

In the first Congress which assembled after the adoption of the Constitution, comprising many who aided in its preparation, a legislative construction was given to that instrument in which the independence of the Executive in the matter of removals from office was fully sustained.

I think it will be found that in the subsequent discussions of this question there was generally, if not at all times, a proposition pending to in some way curtail this power of the President by legislation, which furnishes evidence that to limit such power it was supposed to be necessary to supplement the Constitution by such legislation.

The first enactment of this description was passed under a

stress of partisanship and political bitterness which culminated in the President's impeachment.

This law provided that the Federal officers to which it applied could only be suspended during the recess of the Senate when shown by evidence satisfactory to the President to be guilty of misconduct in office, or crime, or when incapable or disqualified to perform their duties, and that within twenty days after the next meeting of the Senate it should be the duty of the President "to report to the Senate such suspension, with the evidence and reasons for his action in the case."

This statute, passed in 1867, when Congress was overwhelmingly and bitterly opposed politically to the President, may be regarded as an indication that even then it was thought necessary by a Congress determined upon the subjugation of the Executive to legislative will to furnish itself a law for that purpose, instead of attempting to reach the object intended by an invocation of any pretended constitutional right.

The law which thus found its way to our statute book was plain in its terms, and its intent needed no avowal. If valid and now in operation, it would justify the present course of the Senate and command the obedience of the Executive to its demands. It may, however, be remarked in passing that under this law the President had the privilege of presenting to the body which assumed to review his executive acts his reasons therefor, instead of being excluded from explanation or judged by papers found in the Departments.

Two years after the law of 1867 was passed, and within less than five weeks after the inauguration of a President in political accord with both branches of Congress, the sections of the act regulating suspensions from office during the recess of the Senate were entirely repealed, and in their place were substituted provisions which, instead of limiting the causes of suspension to misconduct, crime, disability, or disqualification, expressly permitted such suspension by the President "in his discretion," and completely abandoned the requirement obliging him to report to the Senate "the evidence and reasons" for his action.

With these modifications and with all branches of the Government in political harmony, and in the absence of partisan incentive to captious obstruction, the law as it was left by the amendment of 1869 was much less destructive of Executive discretion. And yet the great general and patriotic citizen who on the 4th day of March, 1869, assumed the duties of Chief

Executive, and for whose freer administration of his high office the most hateful restraints of the law of 1867 were, on the 5th day of April 1869, removed, mindful of his obligation to defend and protect every prerogative of his great trust, and apprehensive of the injury threatened the public service in the continued operation of these statutes even in their modified form, in his first message to Congress advised their repeal and set forth their unconstitutional character and hurtful tendency in the following language:

> It may be well to mention here the embarrassment possible to arise from leaving on the statute books the so-called "tenure-of-office acts," and to earnestly recommend their total repeal. It could not have been the intention of the framers of the Constitution, when providing that appointments made by the President should receive the consent of the Senate, that the latter should have the power to retain in office persons placed there by Federal appointment against the will of the President. The law is inconsistent with a faithful and efficient administration of the Government. What faith can an Executive put in officials forced upon him, and those, too, whom he has suspended for reason? How will such officials be likely to serve an Administration which they know does not trust them?

I am unable to state whether or not this recommendation for a repeal of these laws has been since repeated. If it has not, the reason can probably be found in the experience which demonstrated the fact that the necessities of the political situation but rarely developed their vicious character.

And so it happens that after an existence of nearly twenty years of almost innocuous desuetude these laws are brought forth—apparently the repealed as well as the unrepealed—and put in the way of an Executive who is willing, if permitted, to attempt an improvement in the methods of administration.

The constitutionality of these laws is by no means admitted. But why should the provisions of the repealed law, which required specific cause for suspension and a report to the Senate of "evidence and reasons," be now in effect applied to the present Executive, instead of the law, afterwards passed and unrepealed, which distinctly permits suspensions by the President "in his discretion" and carefully omits the requirement that "evidence and reasons for his action in the case" shall be reported to the Senate.

The requests and demands which by the score have for nearly three months been presented to the different Departments of the Government, whatever may be their form, have but one complexion. They assume the right of the Senate to sit in judgment upon the exercise of my exclusive discretion and Executive function, for which I am solely responsible to the people from whom I have so lately received the sacred trust of office. My oath to support and defend the Constitution, my duty to the people who have chosen me to execute the powers of their great office and not to relinquish them, and my duty to the Chief Magistracy, which I must preserve unimpaired in all its dignity and vigor, compel me to refuse compliance with these demands.

To the end that the service may be improved, the Senate is invited to the fullest scrutiny of the persons submitted to them for public office, in recognition of the constitutional power of that body to advise and consent to their appointment. I shall continue, as I have thus far done, to furnish, at the request of the confirming body, all the information I possess touching the fitness of the nominees placed before them for their action, both when they are proposed to fill vacancies and to take the place of suspended officials. Upon a refusal to confirm I shall not assume the right to ask the reasons for the action of the Senate nor question its determination. I can not think that anything more is required to secure worthy incumbents in public office than a careful and independent discharge of our respective duties within their well-defined limits.

Though the propriety of suspensions might be better assured if the action of the President was subject to review by the Senate, yet if the Constitution and the laws have placed this responsibility upon the executive branch of the Government it should not be divided nor the discretion which it involves relinquished.

It has been claimed that the present Executive having pledged himself not to remove officials except for cause, the fact of their suspension implies such misconduct on the part of a suspended official as injures his character and reputation, and therefore the Senate should review the case for his vindication.

I have said that certain officials should not, in my opinion, be removed during the continuance of the term for which they were appointed solely for the purpose of putting in their place those in political affiliation with the appointing power, and this declaration was immediately followed by a description of official partisanship which ought not to entitle those in whom it was exhibited to consideration. It is not apparent how an adherence to the course thus announced carries with it the consequences described. If in any degree the suggestion is worthy of consideration, it is to be hoped that there may be a defense against unjust suspension in the justice of the Executive.

Every pledge which I have made by which I have placed a limitation upon my exercise of executive power has been faithfully redeemed. Of course the pretense is not put forth that no mistakes have been committed; but not a suspension has been made except it appeared to my satisfaction that the public welfare would be improved thereby. Many applications for suspension have been denied, and the adherence to the rule laid down to govern my action as to such suspensions has caused much irritation and impatience on the part of those who have insisted upon more changes in the offices.

The pledges I have made were made to the people, and to them I am responsible for the manner in which they have been redeemed. I am not responsible to the Senate, and I am unwilling to submit my actions and official conduct to them for judgment.[65]

ᕽ ᕽ ᕽ

The discussion arose upon a bill then before the Congress, providing for the organization of the State Department, which contained a provision that the head of the department to be created should be removable from office by the President. This was opposed by a considerable number on the ground that as the Senate cooperated in the appointment, it should also be consulted in the matter of removal; it was urged by others that the power of removal in such cases was already vested in the President by the Constitution, and that the provision was therefore unnecessary; and it was also contended that the question whether the Constitution permitted such removal or not should be left untouched by legislative action, and be determined by the courts.

Those insisting upon retaining in the bill the clause permitting removal by the President alone, claimed that such legislation would remove all doubt on the subject, though they asserted that the absolute investiture of all executive power in the President, reinforced by the constitutional command that he should take care that the laws be faithfully executed, justified their position that the power already existed, especially in the absence of any adverse expression in the Constitution. They also insisted that the removal of subordinate officers was an act so executive in its character, and so intimately related to the faithful execution of the laws, that it was clearly among the President's constitutional prerogatives, and that if it was not sufficiently declared in the Constitution, the omission should be supplied by the legislation proposed. . . .

The discussion developed the fact that from the first a decided majority were of the opinion that the Executive should have power of independent removal, whether already derived from the Constitution or to be conferred by supplementary legislation. It will be recalled that the debate arose upon the clause in a pending bill providing that the officer therein named should "be removable by the President," and that some of the members of the House, holding that such power of removal was plainly granted to the Constitution, insisted that it would be useless and improper to assume to confer it by legislative enactment. Though a motion to strike from the bill the clause objected to had been negatived by a large majority, it was afterward proposed, in deference to the opinions of those who suggested that the House should go no further than to give a legislative construction to the Constitution in favor of executive removal, that in lieu of the words contained in the bill, indicating a grant of the power, there should be inserted a provision for a new appointment in case of a vacancy occurring in the following manner:

"Whenever the said principal officer shall be removed from office by the President of the United States, or in any other case of vacancy."

This was universally acknowledged to be a distinct and unequivocal declaration that, under the Constitution, the right of removal was conferred upon the President; and those supporting that proposition voted in favor of the change, which was adopted by a decisive majority. The bill thus completed was sent to the Senate, where, if there was opposition to it on the ground that it contained a provision in derogation of senatorial right, it did not avail; for the bill was passed by that body, though grudgingly, and, as has been disclosed, only by the vote of the Vice-President, upon an equal division of the Senate.[66]

BENJAMIN HARRISON

The Tenure of Office law was passed in 1867, during the heated controversy between President Johnson and the Congress; and the constitutionality of the law was denied by many able lawyers. It prohibited the removal of any officer during his term without the advice and consent of the Senate, but gave the President power to suspend until the end of the next session of the Senate. The law was repealed in 1887.[67]

*   *   *

The power of removal has been generally regarded as an incident of the power of appointment, and as necessary to enable the President to fulfil his duty to see the laws executed; but during the sessions of the Senate he cannot put any person into an office until the nomination is confirmed. Of course, the power of removal does not extend to such officers as judges, who are appointed for life and are only removable on impeachment.[68]

*   *   *

It has come to be a custom that, in the appointment of officers whose duties relate wholly to a Congressional district, or some part of it, the advice of the Congressman—if he is of the President's party—is accepted. This is a mere matter of custom, but it has become so settled a custom that the President finds himself in not a little trouble if he departs from it. In the Congressional districts represented by Congressmen of the party opposed to the President the custom is that the Senator or Senators —if of the President's party—make the recommendations for the local appointments; as they also do for appointments in their States not of a local character. These recommendations are followed as a rule, unless something against the character or fitness of the applicant is alleged. In such case the President exercises his prerogative to make a selection of his own upon such other representations and recommendations as are made to him. When he does this the confirmation of the appointment, however good and unexceptionable in itself, is often held up in the Senate upon the objection of the Senator whose recommendation has not been followed, and the nomination is sometimes rejected—not upon the merits, but out of "Senatorial courtesy." The power and duty of selection are vested by the Constitution in the President, but appointments are made "by and with the advice and consent of the Senate." It would seem that the power vested in the Senate relates only to the competency, fitness, and character of the person appointed, but this view is much varied in practice. Some Senators practically assert the right to select as well as to consent.

There can be no doubt that the participation of the Senate in the matter of appointments is larger than the Constitution contemplates. But as the President can, in the nature of things, know but little about the applicants for local offices, and must depend upon some one better informed than he to give him the necessary information, it is quite natural that he should give great weight to the advice of the Senator or Representative. It ought, however, to be admitted that as the responsibility rests upon the President he must be satisfied as to the fitness of the appointment. That being satisfactorily established, the public interests are saved, for the choice between fit men is not very important. If there is any objection to the appointment, growing out of the character or habits of the applicant, it is pretty sure to be brought out; and on the whole, considering the number of appointments the President is required to make without any personal knowledge of the appointees, the public service is well and honestly conducted.[69]

✦ ✦ ✦

The Civil Service Law has removed a large number of minor offices in the departments at Washington, and in the postal and other services, from the scramble of politics, and has given the President, the Cabinet officers and the Members of Congress great relief; but it still remains true that in the power of appointment to office the President finds the most exacting, unrelenting, and distracting of his duties. In the nature of things he begins to make enemies from the start, and has no way of escape—it is fate; and to a sensitive man involves much distress of mind. His only support is in the good opinion of those who chiefly care that the public business shall be well done, and are not disturbed by the consideration whether this man or that man is doing it; but he hears very little directly from this class. No President can conduct a successful administration without the support of Congress, and this matter of appointments, do what he will, often weakens that support. It is for him always a sort of compromise between his ideal and the best attainable thing.[70]

✦ ✦ ✦

The applicants for office are generally respectable and worthy men, and many of them are the personal friends of the President. They are entitled to a respectful and kindly hearing, but at the end of one hundred days of this work the President should not be judged too harshly if he shows a little wear, a little loss of effusiveness, and even a hunted expression in his eyes.[71]

✦ ✦ ✦

The duty devolved by law upon the President to nominate and, by and with the advice and consent of the Senate, to appoint all public officers whose appointment is not otherwise provided for in the Constitution or by act of Congress has become very burdensome and its wise and efficient discharge full of difficulty. The civil list is so large that a personal knowledge of any large number of the applicants is impossible. The President must rely upon the representations of others, and these are often made inconsiderately and without any just sense of responsibility.[72]

THEODORE ROOSEVELT

To clear up any possible misapprehension, I would like, at the outset, to say that the Senators do not select postmasters in any State while I am President. I consult them always, and in the vast majority of cases act on the recommendations they make; but the selection is mine and not theirs, and time and again during the three years I have been President I have positively refused to select individuals suggested to me for nomination as postmaster by various Senators.[73]

✦ ✦ ✦

No law can take away my power of appointment or force me to make appointments, any more than I could by Executive order decree that I had the power to make appropriations. The legislature cannot usurp the functions of the Executive any more than the Executive can unsurp the functions of the Legislature.[74]

✦ ✦ ✦

But the great point to consider is that under the Constitution the President alone has power to appoint, just as the Legislature alone has power to pass laws and appropriate money. The

Legislature may think that the Legislature ought to pass a particular law; but neither side can make the other perform the act which that other is alone competent to perform, without a complete, and I may add, an exceedingly inadvisable, change in the Constitution. I am often accused of violating the Constitution (the accusation being usually made with especial vehemence when I am carrying on a lawsuit, which the courts themselves decide); but no action of which I have been even accused is so clearly a violation of the Constitution as the attempted usurpation by one branch of the Government of the power of another branch of the Government; such would be the effort (and, I may add, the futile effort) to deprive me of my power of appointment.[75]

✓ ✓ ✓

About appointments I was obliged by the Constitution to consult the Senate; and the long-established custom of the Senate meant that in practice this consultation was with individual Senators and even with big politicians who stood behind the Senators. I was only one-half the appointing power; I nominated; but the Senate confirmed. . . . In consequence the Constitution itself forced the President and the Senators from each State to come to a working agreement on the appointments in and from that State.[76]

TAFT

I hate to use the patronage as a club unless I have to.[77]

✓ ✓ ✓

One of the functions which in a practical way gives the President more personal influence than any other is that of appointments. The prestige that a President has in the outset of his administration is in part due to this power. Even in the case of the most popular President, his prestige wanes with Congress as the term wears on and the offices are distributed.[78]

✓ ✓ ✓

It was settled, as long ago as the first Congress, at the instance of Madison, then in the Senate, and by deciding the vote of John Adams, then Vice-President, that even where the advice and consent of the Senate was necessary to the appointment of an officer, the President had the absolute power to remove him without consulting the Senate. This was on the principle that the power of removal was incident to the Executive power and must be untrammeled.[79]

✦ ✦ ✦

In the days before the present civil service law, a sense of obligation to the President for the places held, made practically all the civil employees his political henchmen. In those halcyon times, even the humblest charwoman or the most poorly paid janitor felt a throb of deep personal interest in the political health of the President.[80]

✦ ✦ ✦

In my judgment, the President should not be required to exercise his judgment to make appointments except to fill the most important offices. In the Executive department, he should be limited to the selection of those officers, the discharge of whose duties involves discretion in the carrying out of the political and governmental policy of his administration. He therefore ought to have the appointment of his Cabinet officers, and he ought also to have the appointment of a political under-secretary in each department to take the place of the head of the department when for any reason the head of the department is not able to discharge his usual duties.[81]

✦ ✦ ✦

The President of course should appoint the Supreme Judges, as the Constitution requires, and the inferior judges of the Federal judiciary. He ought, too, to appoint the general officers of the army and the flag officers to the navy, and he ought also to appoint the leading Ambassadors and Ministers. Other appointments, it seems to me, might well be left to a system of promotion, to be carried on under civil service rules as interpreted and enforced by a Commission and the heads of departments.[82]

COOLIDGE

The President is responsible to the people for his conduct relative to the retention or dismissal of public officials. I assume that responsibility, and the people may be assured that as soon as I can be advised so that I may act with entire justice to all parties concerned and fully protect the public interests, I shall act.[83]

HOOVER

It is a handicap to any man to succeed a member of his own party as President. He has little patronage with which to reward his personal supporters.[84]

✦ ✦ ✦

Each President must have his own major policy-making officials sympathetic with his ideas, irrespective of the appointments of his predecessors.[85]

✦ ✦ ✦

Appointments of district and circuit judges, district attorneys and marshals offer a special problem in political pressures to all Presidents. As the Senate must confirm these officials, the senators over the years had assumed that they could make unofficial nominations. If the President did not accept their views, then, because of the common interest among senators, anyone not of their selection stood little chance of securing confirmation. With this club the judicial appointments below the Supreme Court had become practically a perquisite of the senators. And conversely the custom of the President asking the senators for suggestions as to such appointments had become a basis of amity.[86]

✦ ✦ ✦

I cannot believe that you . . . overlook the primary responsibility which rests upon the President of the United States. That responsibility is one of the most sacred which he assumes upon his oath of office. It is that he shall, to his utmost capacity, appoint men to public office who will execute the laws of the United States with integrity and without fear, favor or political collusion. The appointive responsibility rests in the President, not in any organization.[87]

✦ ✦ ✦

The resolution raises the question of the independence of the Executive arm of the Government in respect of the appointment and removal of executive officials. Many Presidents have had to meet this particular encroachment upon the Executive power in some form. Every one of them has repelled it, and every President has handed on this authority unimpaired. It reaches to the very fundamentals of independence and vigor of the Executive, whose power comes from the people alone and the maintenance of which is vital to the protection of public interest and the integrity of the Constitution.

The President is responsible to the people to see that honest and capable officials are employed by or appointed to the various administrative agencies of the Government.[88]

FRANKLIN D. ROOSEVELT

Senator Glass in his letter asked if Federal appointments, for which Senate approval was necessary, would be subjected to the effective veto of the Governor of Virginia.

To this I replied on March 18th, explaining to the Senator the difference between the appointive power, which is in the President, and the power of confirmation, which is in the Senate. I pointed out to the Senator that time-hallowed courtesy permits Senators and others to make recommendations for nomination, and, at the same time, that every President has sought information from any other source deemed advisable.[89]

✦ ✦ ✦

In regard to the original newspaper article suggesting that Governor Price had been given the veto over Federal appointments, this and similar stories are, of course, not worth answering or bothering about, for the very simple reason that no person—no Governor, no Senator, no member of the Administration—has at any time had, or ever will have, any right of veto over Presidential nominations. Every person with common sense knows this.[90]

✦ ✦ ✦

In other cases nominations by former Presidents of men of outstanding ability and character have been denied confirmation by the Senate, not on the plea that they were unfitted for office but on the sole ground that they were personally obnoxious to the Senator or Senators from the State from which they came.

During this whole period Presidents have recognized that the constitutional procedure is for a President to receive advice, i.e., recommendations, from Senators.

Presidents have also properly received advice, i.e., recommendations, from such other sources as they saw fit.

Thereupon Presidents have decided on nominations in accordance with their best judgment—and in most cases basing their judgment on the character and ability of the nominee. In many cases, of course, the recommendations of Senators have been followed, but in many other cases thay have not been followed by Presidents in making the nominations.[91]

Chapter IV

THE PRESIDENCY AND THE CONGRESS

The President's specified duty to report to the Congress on the state of the Union, to recommend measures, to convene the Congress and adjourn it if the two houses disagree about adjournment, and to approve or disapprove enacted bills (Congress can ignore disapproval by enlisting two thirds of its own members to override it) is all the Constitution provides concerning the relationship of the President to the Congress.

Yet, though Washington, with incomparable insight and creative statesmanship of an almost unmatched order, determined that the American executive was not to be a version of a European prime minister, subservient and answerable to a congressional majority—despite the vagueness of the advise and consent clause—much of the continuing political discourse in the United States has centered on the Whig theory of the supremacy of congressional over presidential power. Even Presidents with very positive views of executive powers and with wide popular support have become victims, to some extent, of this doctrine when it has had powerful congressional advocates; and some strong-minded Presidents have been paralyzed by it, as the case of Johnson demonstrated in the extreme. Weak Presidents, on the other hand, have been content to accept the Whig view, and in some cases have even welcomed it with eagerness.

The Whigs insisted upon a parliamentary version of the presidency because they valued the weaknesses that presidential answerability to the Congress would create in the office. Wilson, on the other hand, in his early days as a political scientist, gravitated toward a parliamentary version because of what he regarded as its strengths. His aspirations for a union of presidential and congressional government extended well into his first ad-

ministration and undoubtedly accounted for his reviving the custom—dormant since John Adams—of delivering the annual presidential State of the Union message in person. Wilson was later,
of course, to discover sadly that the plausibility of a ministerial
responsibility to the legislature diminished significantly when
viewed from the executive's office under the pressure of controversial events which demanded prompt administrative decisions
and prompt presidential actions.

For under the demands imposed by history upon the presidential office, the role of the American presidency evolved from
the beginning as a creative one, while the role of the Congress,
also from the beginning, evolved as a critical one, capable of
action largely by compromise. And because the leading Presidents have created new policies, often without either direct or
collateral precedent, they have also—as has already been noted—
had to create from time to time new methods to put those policies into effective operation. This has been the more necessary
because the Congress, in its traditionally critical role, has almost
always been suspicious of anything new and has frequently been
outrightly hostile. Indeed, perhaps too often minorities in the
Congress—and not infrequently the majorities—have been moved
to assume that Presidents have been guilty in the conduct of their
office until proved innocent and that the appropriate function
of the Congress has been to use all legal devices at its disposal
to impede them in the execution of their policies. As a result,
the Presidents have conceived as within the powers of the office
the introduction of novel devices to carry out their policies—devices which have intentionally reduced or bypassed congressional impedimenta. As the substance of much of the writings
of the Presidents on the presidency has been in defense of presidential responsibility against congressional incursions, so much
presidential action has been directed at forcing necessary measures through in spite of hostile or indifferent blocs.

Increasingly numerous, for example, in diplomatic history in
place of conventional treaties are foreign compacts which have
been arrived at by the President through executive agreements
and then submitted to the Congress for confirmation by joint

resolution. The obvious advantage of this procedure over a treaty is that it is often easier to secure a simple majority vote of assent from both houses than the two thirds required of the Senate by a treaty. In the twentieth century, epitomized by the reciprocal trade and lend-lease agreements of Franklin Roosevelt, an increasing volume of United States foreign affairs has been conducted through this device of joint resolution, which was first applied to a major problem by John Tyler in the annexation of Texas. It was one of Tyler's few winning battles, during a term that lasted all but one month of a full four years.

By April, 1844, three years after Tyler had succeeded to the presidency on Harrison's death, the Texas Republic, through its president, Sam Houston, had three times offered to join the United States and had been twice rejected for internal, sectional reasons within the United States. Tyler, in 1844, was determined to see the annexation through. In April he sent a treaty of annexation to the Senate, which that body rejected under the two-thirds rule after two months' delay. In the fall, during the Polk-Clay campaign of 1844, the annexation was a major issue, and Polk, outspokenly in favor, won the election. Tyler interpreted this as popular endorsement of his policy and again proposed annexation—this time by joint resolution of the Senate and the House. With the power of the Senate to veto a treaty by a vote of one-third plus one thus bypassed, the resolution, requiring only a simple majority in both houses, carried easily three days before Tyler was to leave office. Texas was annexed, and the presidency had introduced, for permanent use, a method of wiping out a basically undemocratic technique for obstructing its foreign policies.

The steady growth of the use of joint resolutions is one of the most workable products of the evolution of representative government in the United States. For in effect the treaty-making power of the Senate, with its requirement of a two-thirds vote for ratification, actually merely subjected the will of the President, elected by all the people, and frequently also the will of a majority of the Senate, to a strangling veto by one third of the Senate. Indeed, it is mathematically possible under the two-thirds rule for senators from seventeen states, representing 12,000,000 of the nation's 180,000,000 people, to defeat completely the will of the senatorial representation of the remaining 168,000,000 in thirty-three states. If all one hundred senators are present, ratification of a treaty requires sixty-seven votes. Thus, the votes of thirty-four senators can defeat it. If those thirty-four came from the States of Alaska, Arizona, Colorado, Delaware, Hawaii, Idaho, Maine, Nebraska, Nevada, New Hampshire, New Mexico, North Dakota, Rhode Island, South Dakota, Utah, Vermont, and Wyoming—little more than one-fifteenth of the nation's population could stop dead in its tracks the will of the other fourteen-fifteenths. In view of such possibilities as this, it is difficult now —except among senators themselves—to work up much popular resentment or even to find any logical arguments against the increasingly employed system of confirming executive agreements with other countries by joint congressional resolution. Originally designed to protect the regional interests of an agricultural nation, the geographic distribution of senators—it now seems generally agreed—bears no proper relationship to either the democratic or the efficient conduct of foreign affairs.

In contrast to the fate of the League of Nations at the hands of twenty-three senators in rejecting the Treaty of Versailles as it stood without reservations in 1919, United States backing of the United Nations was assured by the Participation Act of 1945, a joint Congressional Act which required only a majority in each house.

Since answerability of the leadership to the people, whatever the governmental structure, is the *sine qua non* of a democracy, foreign commitments entered into with confirmation of an executive agreement by a majority of both houses of Congress are unquestionably more expeditiously referred to the electorate than a ratification by two thirds of the Senate would be. Senators who might ratify an unpopular treaty can be charged with their actions at the polls only once in six years, while a President who made a foreign agreement unacceptable to the people can be held answerable once in four years, and the entire membership of the House which confirmed it by joint resolution could be turned out of office to a man in two years at most. There is consequently less to fear, by way of answerability to the people, in executive agreements confirmed by congressional joint resolution than by formal treaties ratified by the Senate.

Many Presidents, however, especially in the nineteenth century, have not sought the enlargement of executive power but have, in fact, resisted the use of powers clearly granted them. The old Whig theory, inherited by a majority but not all of the Republican Presidents, held that the presidency is limited strictly to following the Congress and adhering to the letter of the Constitution, that it could reasonably suggest fields in which legislation was required but no legislative program itself, and that the veto power should be used sparingly and mainly on the question of an act's constitutionality rather than its desirability.

This view was pressed to its extreme by the ancient and ill-fated William Henry Harrison, at his inauguration in 1841, in a long tribute to the impotence of the American presidency. His inaugural address, taking him an hour and forty-five minutes to read and by far the longest on record, was an inventory of inferred limitations on presidential powers. Harrison even viewed the veto power with caution: "I consider the veto power, therefore, given by the Constitution to the executive of the United States solely as a conservative power. . . ."[1] He obviously thought of the President as a kind of office manager of the nation, not capable of determining or even of suggesting policy and certainly not constitutionally competent to exercise any kind of leadership. His theory of the presidency was dictated by Whig adherents to congressional supremacy, their spokesman, Daniel Webster, revising the inaugural address after the old soldier flatly refused to read one entirely of Webster's composition. Dying thirty days following this strange inauguration, Harrison had no time to put his feeble appraisal of his office into practice, although he did affirm his belief in congressional leadership by calling the Congress into emergency session to cope with a financial crisis.

Harrison left the office to John Tyler, the first Vice President to succeed, to serve all but thirty days of a full term. Tyler was a Democrat and did not share the Whig theory of a weak presidency. He took an activist view of presidential powers, including a forthright use of the veto power as a means of asserting presidential leadership in the construction of national policy. A Whig cabal in Congress responded by suggesting such radical antidotes as a constitutional amendment barring the veto, and the impeachment of the President for "abuse" of the power.

Not until Zachary Taylor, another aging warrior, went into office in 1849 was the Whig ideal of passive Presidents restored. Taylor lived only sixteen months, when the Vice President, Millard Fillmore, succeeded to finish his term for him. The two succeeding Democrats, Pierce and Buchanan, also saw the presidency as a passive office, expecting at best merely to act as conciliators of opposing elements of the Congress, and, without formally subscribing to the Whig theory of presidential incompetence, nevertheless left the country without any executive leadership at all. After the ultimate conflict of congressional and presidential power in the Johnson impeachment, the Whig theory gained presidential support again when Ulysses S. Grant was inaugurated, and under him it was given full indulgence. If Harrison had thought of himself as a kind of national office manager, Grant regarded himself, for the most part, as the office boy, although—as can be observed in his writings late in his second term—he belatedly sought to contest congressional dominance over the presidency.

The next three Presidents—Hayes, Garfield, and Arthur—all of them from the Republican Party, which had inherited much of Whig doctrine—reacted to the theory of a presidency subservient to the Congress with sufficient force to jolt the party managers, and neither Hayes nor Arthur were renominated.

Garfield, like both his predecessor Hayes and his successor Arthur, set out, as he said, to determine "whether the President is registering clerk of the Senate or the Executive of the United States."[2] But he was struck down by an assassin in four months, and died before making a record. Grover Cleveland had come and gone before the Whig theory again asserted itself in the White House with Benjamin Harrison, elected over Cleveland in 1888, though he received nearly 100,000 less popular votes. Harrison was inclined, however, to take a less constricted attitude toward the office than his grandfather. Cleveland had served a second presidential term before the Whig theory was again restored with McKinley, and endured, with two major interruptions and with varying narrowness, down through Taft, Harding, Coolidge, and Hoover, and then, after a twenty-year hiatus, the two administrations of Eisenhower, the only Republican in the twentieth century to be twice elected. All these regarded the major responsibility for the destiny of the nation as resting with Congress, to which they were necessarily subservient, although Eisenhower also delegated a great deal to Cabinet ministers and others. But Congress never rose to the opportunities for positive action given it by the passive Presidents.

The Jacksonian revolution, coming after the twenty years of presidential subservience to Congress from Madison through John Quincy Adams, was the product as much of congressional ineptness as of a strong presidential estimate of the role of the executive. Its acceptance by the people was to no small extent the acceptance of the lesser of two evils, for there was in the American character a wariness of a strong executive as well as an impatience of a fumbling legislature. But the strong Presidents were more sensitive on the whole to the spirit of their times than were the Congresses. They acted with courage, and they did not drift.

Briefly, in direct opposition to the Whig theory, the activist concept holds that the presidency is, equally with the Congress and the Supreme Court, an independent branch of the Federal Government; that it has inherent powers not catalogued in the Constitution but implied in the inclusive and unqualified language of Article Two: "The Executive power shall be vested in a President"; that the President is responsible directly to the people and not to the Congress; that he also derives his mandate from the people and not from the unwieldy sum of their representatives; that he should furnish a leadership for the nation's legislative processes and not, as Herbert Hoover insisted, limit himself to pointing out where legislation is needed—which is to say that he should direct the fire engines at the fire and not just ring the alarm; that the office is an opportunity for service rather than an exercise in restraint.

Both Wilson and the second Roosevelt associated the strength of the presidency with legislative leadership, while Theodore Roosevelt seemed to prefer to act independently. In this respect, Wilson and Franklin Roosevelt guided the evolution of the presidency along safer democratic channels and made it, both in theory and in fact, much less government by one man. Theodore Roosevelt derived his strength, and seemed also to derive his satisfaction, from a vigorous and independent course of individual action, without much dependence on Congress. Wilson and Franklin Roosevelt acted in concert with Congress, and appealed to the people, in cases of discord, to bring pressure upon their representatives and senators. Indeed, since Franklin Roosevelt's administration was historically merely a resumption and extension of Woodrow Wilson's, Wilson might—next only to Washington—be called the most creative statesman to sit in the White House, for he—interested in constitutional processes all his life—depended not on the direct action of Lincoln or the thunder of the first Roosevelt but on the building of the presidency as a legislative influence, though he ultimately saw need for the President often to go it alone.

The development of the President's legislative influence had also been a goal of Theodore Roosevelt: "In theory the Executive has nothing to do with legislation. . . . [but] As often as not the action of the Executive offers the only means by which the people can get the legislation they demand and ought to have. Therefore a good executive under the present conditions of American political life must take a very active interest in getting the right kind of legislation. . . ."[3] But he was himself too devoted to the dramatic action and had come toward the end of too long a period of congressional supremacy to go far in the direction of legislative leadership.

Wilson, in his first administration, worked in quieter and more informed ways with a predominantly new kind of Congress. As a student of government, he was profoundly aware of the evolutionary character of political institutions and of the fact that their interplay was forever changing. Before his inauguration and during his first administration, he seemed most hopeful that the drift of the presidency and the Congress would be toward one another—toward a kind of parliamentary system; and the separation of powers meant far less to him than to some of the other strong Presidents. "It must be clear to everybody who has studied our political institutions," he wrote a few days before his first inauguration, "that the character of the presidency is passing through a transitional stage. . . . He is expected by the nation to be the leader of his party as well as the chief executive officer of the government and the country will take no excuses from him. He must play the part and play it successfully or lose the country's confidence. He must be prime minister, as much concerned with the guidance of legislation as with just and orderly execution of the law. . . ."[4]

In addition to exceptional erudition in political science, Wilson had a practical political insight of a high order, though he lacked the flexibility to put it to consistent good use. When he delivered the annual message in person to the Congress, nevertheless, it was for the first time in a hundred and twelve years, ending a practice—as he put it—of the President "hailing the Congress from some isolated island of jealous power."[5] And his reform program passed both Houses with a speed unparalleled in legislative history until 1933. For five years he was the guiding force behind Congress, primarily because he understood the appropriate role of an extraconstitutional institution, the political party, in accomplishing strictly constitutional legislative purposes. His acquaintance with the operational character of the Congress led him to depend less on floor leaders than on committee chairmen. Wilson thus established at once the party leadership and the legislative leadership of the presidency and, going beyond this, established it also as an office of moral leadership. But, after the congressional elections of 1918 resulted in revolt of the Congress, he relied solely on the moral strength of the presidency. He fought congressional dissenters instead of coping with them, and gave up the fight only after his physical collapse.

Despite his high sense of the responsibility of his office and his awareness of its powers, however, Wilson was not inclined to set aside the Congress. He preferred joint presidential and congressional action and, far from being satisfied with unilateral action as President, was always disturbed when it was necessary, as it was, for example, in arming American merchant vessels before our entry into World War I. His vast war powers were not assumed, as Lincoln had assumed them, but granted by the Congress. And when it came time to make the peace and to decide on the extent of American participation in the League of Nations, Wilson still stuck to constitutional processes and spent his last able days attempting to rally public opinion to influence two thirds of a Senate under hostile leadership to ratify the treaty. This very devotion to the Constitution no doubt accounted for the failure of the United States to join the League. Had Wilson followed in Tyler's footsteps and presented the question of American participation as the subject of a joint resolution, it would not have failed, for on two test votes in the Senate it received a majority in favor. The constitutional flaw that permits the killing of treaties if one short of two thirds of the senators favor them and one more than one third oppose them spelled the ultimate death of the League and was an ironic defeat indeed to the one strong President in American history who sought to avoid compromising the power of the Congress.

WASHINGTON

The President has "the power by and with the advice and consent of the Senate, to make treaties and to appoint Officers."

The Senate when these powers are exercised, is evidently a Council only to the President, however its concurrence may be to his Acts. It seems incident to this relation between them, that not only the time but the place and manner of consultation should be with the President. It is probable that the place may vary. The indisposition or inclination of the President may require, that the Senate should be summoned to the President's House. Whenever the Government shall have buildings of its own, an executive Chamber will no doubt be provided, where the Senate will generally attend the President. It is not impossible that the place may be made to depend in some degree on the nature of the business. In the appointment to offices, the agency of the Senate is purely executive, and they may be summoned to the President. In treaties, the agency is perhaps as much of a legislative nature and the business may possibly be referred to their deliberations in their legislative chamber. The occasion for this distinction will be lessened, if not destroyed, when a chamber shall be appropriated for the joint business of the President and the Senate.

The manner of consultation may also vary. The indisposition of the President may supersede the mere question of conveniency. The inclination or ideas of different Presidents may be different. The opinions both of President and Senators as to the proper manner may be changed by experience. In some kinds of business it may be found best for the President to make his propositions orally and in person, in others by written message. On some occasions it may be most convenient that the President should attend the deliberations and decisions on his propositions; on others that he should not; or that he should not attend the whole of the time. In other cases again, as in Treaties of a complicated nature, it may happen that he will send his propositions in writing and consult the Senate in person after time shall have been allowed for consideration. Many other varieties may be suggested as to the mode, by practice.

If these remarks be just, it would seem not amiss, that the Senate should accommodate their rules to the uncertainty of the particular mode and place that may be preferred; providing for the reception of either oral written propositions, and for giving their consent and advice in either the presence or absence of the President, leaving him free to use the mode and place that may be found most eligible and accordant with other business which may be before him at the time.[6]

Once Washington tried getting the advice of the Senate in person, was kept idly waiting while a Senate committee pondered the matter, and abandoned the practice—which was never resumed by him or any other President.

✓ ✓ ✓

Before the curtain drops on my political life, which it will do this evening, I expect for ever; I shall acknowledge, although it be in a few hasty lines only, the receipt of your kind and affectionate letter of the 23d. of January last.

When I add, that according to custom, all the Acts of the Session; except two or three very unimportant Bills, have been presented to me within the last four days, you will not be surprised at the pressure under which I write at present; but it must astonish others who know that the Constitution allows the President ten days to deliberate on each Bill that is brought before him that he should be allowed by the Legislature less than half that time to consider all the business of the Session; and in some instances, scarcely an hour to revolve [*sic*] the most important. But as the scene is closing, with me, it is of little avail now to let it be with murmers.[7]

JOHN ADAMS

The causes of the two parties I have already shown to be permanent and unchangeable. Both must be represented in the legislature, and there must be a mediator between them in the executive. This mediator must have power for the purpose. He must calm and restrain the ardor of both, and be more impartial between them than any president ever yet has been. And the senators themselves must not constrain him to be partial, as they so often have done. Their power to do so, instead of being increased, as Mr. Hillhouse proposes, ought to be wholly taken from them. They ought to have nothing to do with executive power.[8]

✓ ✓ ✓

But is not man, in the shape of a senator or a representative, as fond of power as a president? . . . are not ambition and favoritism, and all other vicious passions and sinister interests, as strong and active in a senator or a representative as in a president? Cannot, indeed, the members of the legislature conceal their private views and improper motives more easily than a president?[9]

✓ ✓ ✓

Mr. Tracy, of Connecticut, who indeed was always in my confidence, came to me, I believe, at the opening of the special session of Congress, which I called soon after my inauguration, and produced a long, elaborate letter from Mr. Hamilton, containing a whole system of instruction for the conduct of the President, the Senate, and the House of Representatives. I read it very deliberately, and really thought the man was in a delirium. It appeared to me a very extraordinary instance of volunteer empiricism thus to prescribe for a President, Senate, and House of Representatives, all desperately sick and in a state of deplorable debility, without being called.[10]

✓ ✓ ✓

"Mischief has been done by the Senate of U.S." I have known and felt more of this mischief, than Washington, Jefferson and Madison altoge[the]r. But this has been all caused by the constitutional Power of the Senate in Executive Business, which ought to be immediately, totally and eternally abolished.[11]

Adams was referring to the confirmation of appointments and the ratification of treaties.

✓ ✓ ✓

The legislative and executive authorities are too much blended together. While the Senate of the United States have a negative on all appointments to office, we can never have a national President. In spite of his own judgment, he must be the President, not to say the tool, of a party.[12]

MADISON

Without entering into a general review of the relations in which the Constitution has placed the several departments of the Government to each other, it will suffice to remark that the Executive and Senate, in the cases of appointments to office and of treaties, are to be considered as independent of and coordinate with each other. If they agree, the appointments or treaties are made; if the Senate disagree, they fail. If the Senate wish information previous to their final decision, the practice, keeping in view the constitutional relations of the Senate and the Executive, has been either to request the Executive to furnish it or to refer the subject to a committee of their body to communicate, either formally or informally, with the head of the proper department. The appointment of a committee of the Senate to confer immediately with the Executive himself appears to lose sight of the coordinate relation between the Executive and the Senate which the Constitution has established, and which ought therefore to be maintained.

The relation between the Senate and House of Representatives, in whom legislative power is concurrently vested, is sufficiently analogous to illustrate that between the executive and Senate in making appointments and treaties. The two Houses are in like manner independent of and coordinate with each other, and the invariable practice of each in appointing committees of conference and consultation is to commission them to confer not with the coordinate body itself, but with a committee of that body; and although both branches of the Legislature may be too numerous to hold conveniently a conference with committees, were they to be appointed by either to confer with the entire body of the other, it may be fairly presumed that if the whole number of either branch were not too large for the purpose the objection to such a conference, being against the principle as derogating from the coordinate relations of the two Houses, would retain all its force.[13]

✓ ✓ ✓

Serious danger seems to be threatened to the genuine sense of the Constitution [by midnight sessions of expiring Congresses], not only by an unwarrantable latitude of construction, but by the use made of precedents which cannot be supposed to have had in the view of their Authors, the bearing contended for, and even where they may have crept, thro' inadvertence, into acts of Cong. & been signed by the Executive at a midnight hour, in the midst of a group scarcely admitting perusal, & under a weariness of mind as little admitting a vigilant attention.[14]

Before the inauguration of new administrations and Congresses was advanced from March 4 to January 20, old Congresses had four months of life after new ones were elected. Frequently they passed the time in pushing through legislation that the President had insufficient time to consider before approving or vetoing.

✓ ✓ ✓

It is obvious that the Constitution meant to allow the President an adequate time to consider the bills, &c., presented to him, and to make his objections to them; and, on the other hand, that Congress should have time to consider and overrule the objections. A disregard on either side of what it owes to the other must be an abuse for which it would be responsible under the forms of the Constitution. An abuse on the part of the President, with a view sufficiently manifest, in a case of sufficient magnitude to deprive Congress of the opportunity of overruling objections to their bills, might doubtless be a ground for impeachment. But nothing short of the signature of the President, or a lapse of ten days without a return of his objections to their bills, might doubtless be a ground for impeachment. But nothing short of the signature of the President, or a lapse of ten days without a return of his objections, or an overruling of the objections by two-thirds of each House of Congress, can give legal validity to a bill.[15]

✦ ✦ ✦

The place of a foreign minister or consul is not an *office* in the constitutional sense of the term.

1. It is not created by the Constitution.

2. It is not created by a law authorized by the Constitution.

3. It cannot, as an office, be created by the mere appointment for it, made by the President and Senate, who are to fill, not create offices. These must be "established by law," and therefore by Congress only.

4. On the supposition even that the appointment could create an office, the office would expire with the expiration of the appointment, and every new appointment would create a new office, not fill an old one. A law reviving an expired law is a new law.

The place of a foreign minister or consul is to be viewed as created by the law of nations, to which the United States, as an independent nation, is a party, and as always open for the proper functionaries, when sent by the constituted authority of one nation and received by that of another. The Constitution, in providing for the appointment of such functionaries, presupposes this mode of intercourse as a branch of the law of nations.

The question to be decided is, What are the cases in which the President can make appointments without the concurrence of the Senate? and it turns on the construction of the power "to fill up all vacancies that may happen during the recess of the Senate."

The term "all" embraces both foreign and municipal [i.e., internal] cases; and in examining the power in the foreign, however failing in exact analogy to the municipal, it is not improper to notice the extent of the power in the municipal.

If the text of the Constitution be taken literally, no municipal officer could be appointed by the President alone to a vacancy not *originating* in the recess of the Senate. It appears, however, that under the sanction of the maxim, *qui hoeret in litera hoeret in cortice*, and of the *argumentum ab inconvenienti*, the power has been understood to extend, in cases of necessity or urgency, to vacancies happening to exist in the recess of the Senate, though not coming into existence in the recess. In the case, for example, of an appointment to a vacancy by the President and Senate of a person dead at the time, but not known to be so till after the adjournment and dispersion of the Senate, it has been deemed within the reason of the constitutional provision that the vacancy should be filled by the President alone, the object of the provision being to prevent a failure in the execution of the laws, which, without such a scope to the power, must very inconveniently happen, more especially in so extensive a country. Other cases of like urgency may occur; such as an appointment by the President and Senate rendered abortive by a refusal to accept it.

If it be admissible at all to make the power of the President, without the Senate, applicable to vacancies happening unavoidably to exist, though not to originate in the recess of the Senate, and which the public good requires to be filled in the recess, the reasons are far more cogent for considering the sole power of the President as applicable to the appointment of foreign functionaries, inasmuch as the occasions demanding such appointments may not only be far more important, but, on the farther consideration, that, unlike appointments under the municipal law, the calls for them may depend on circumstances altogether under foreign control, and sometimes on the most improbable and sudden emergencies, and requiring, therefore, that a competent authority to meet them should be always in existence. It would be a hard imputation on the framers and ratifiers of the Constitution, that while providing for casualties of inferior magnitude, they should have intended to exclude from the provisions the means usually employed in obviating a threatened war; in putting an end to its calamities; in conciliating the friendship or neutrality of powerful nations; or even in seizing a favorable moment for commercial or other arrangements material to the public interest. And it would surely be a hard rule of construction that would give to the text of the Constitution an operation so injurious, in preference to a construction that would avoid it, and not be more liberal than would be applied to a remedial statute. Nor ought the remark to be omitted, that by rejecting such a construction this important function, unlike some others, would be excluded altogether from our political system, there being no pretension to it in any other department of the General Government, or in any department of the State Governments. To regard the power of appointing the highest functionaries employed in foreign missions, though a specific and substantive provision in the Constitution, as incidental merely, in any case, to a subordinate power, that of a provisional negotiation by the President alone, would be a more strained construction of the text than that here given to it.

The view which has been taken of the subject overrules the distinction between missions to foreign courts, to which there had before been appointments and to which there had not been. Not to speak of diplomatic appointments destined, not for stations at foreign courts, but for special negotiations, no matter where, and to which the distinction would be inapplicable, it cannot bear a rational or practical test in the cases to which it has been applied. An appointment to a foreign court at one time, unlike an appointment to a municipal office always requiring it, is no evidence of a need for the appointment at another time; while an appointment where there had been none before, may, in the recess of the Senate, be of the greatest urgency. The distinction becomes almost ludicrous when it is asked for what length of time the circumstance of a former appointment is to have the effect assigned to it on the power of the President. Can it be seriously alleged, that after the interval of a century, and the political changes incident to such a lapse of time, the original appointment is to authorize a new one without the concurrence of the Senate, while a like appointment to a new court, or even a new nation, however immediately called for, is barred by the circumstance that no previous appointment to it had taken place? The case of diplomatic missions belongs to the law of nations, and the principles and usages on which that is founded are entitled to a certain influence in expounding the provisions of the Constitution which have relation to such missions. The distinction between courts to which there had, and to which there had not been previous missions, is believed to be recorded in none of the oracular works on international law, and to be unknown to the practice of Governments, where no question was involved as to the *de facto* establishment of a Government.[16]

MONROE

As to the mode of securing complete responsibility in this officer to the people, and the faithful discharge of his duties, none can be devised so effectual as by committing the right of impeachment to the popular branch of the legislature, and of trial to the other. The legislature is by far the most numerous; the election of its members is more frequent; they come from every part of the country, and are absent from their constituents a short term only. It is the branch which stands nearest to the people, and is more immediately identified with them; their duties are also of a nature corresponding more with those which the people could perform, if they exercised the government themselves en masse. It is that branch, a misconduct in any of whose members should be punishable by the loss of confidence and non-election only. In every view, therefore, it is the branch on which the people must depend, principally, for their safety, and to which they must commit all those powers in regard to the supervision of the conduct of those in the other departments which they cannot execute, as the sovereign power, directly themselves. To suffer the punishment for misconduct in the chief executive magistrate to rest on the loss of confidence, and non-election by the people only, would neither suit the nature of the office, nor a violation of many of its important powers. The force of the country being in his hands; the intercourse with foreign powers; the supervision and control of the administration, in all its departments, in peace and war; with the appointment to office, and the patronage incident to it; misconduct in many ways might endanger the system, and would evince a perfidy, which would require the severest punishment. Even neglect or idleness, distinctly proved, to the public injury, would not escape notice or censure. The legislature is the only branch within the pale of the system which can exercise this power with effect. Being present, and a party in the government, and in some views, a rival one, the deposit of the power with it will in itself form a great check on misconduct in the other. In this mode, the machine will be kept in motion by its own powers, and on a proper balance. If the power should be taken from the legislature, and vested elsewhere, a new feature would be introduced into the government which would weaken it in all its parts, and might disorganize it. It could not be committed, with propriety, to the judiciary, for that would connect it with the political movement, and the parties which may occasionally be formed by it, which would be incompatible with its duties. A new branch could not be instituted for the purpose, without making the system more complicated, and exposing it to a like danger. The right of impeachment and of trial by the legislature is the main spring of the great machine of government. It is the pivot on which it turns. If preserved in full vigor, and exercised with perfect integrity, every branch will perform its duty, and the people be left to the performance of theirs, in the most simple form, and with complete effect, as the sovereign power of the state. It is not believed that this right could be abused by the legislature. An attack on the executive would draw the public attention to it, and if unfounded, rather benefit, than injure the individual. The whole proceeding would be before the public, in the case of trial, and if innocent, the sympathies of the people would be excited in his favor.[17]

✓ ✓ ✓

It is indispensable that the three branches be made independent of, and a check on each other. By vesting in the legislature the right to impeach and try the chief executive officer and the members of the judiciary for misconduct, this object will be fully accomplished, as to that branch. Even without this resource, the legislature is less exposed to encroachments from the other branches, than they from it. If the executive should transcend its powers, by acts not authorized by the Constitution or a law, the breach would be so palpable, that it would be immediately discovered, and the incumbent be called to account and punished for it. For the judiciary to make encroachments on either of the branches seems to be impossible, the nature of its powers and duties being so different and obvious. The object most difficult to be provided for, is to arm these two branches with the means of preventing encroachment on them by the legislature; and none occur, which it is thought are so competent, and free from objection, as to invest the executive with the right to negative acts of the legislature, and the judiciary with that to declare a law, which it should deem unconstitutional, void. By vesting these branches with these powers no injury could result, and much benefit might, in many ways. If the right in the executive to negative acts be qualified, as it might be, it would bring the subject again before the legislature, with new light thrown on it, and secure to it a more deliberate consideration. The division between the two branches would draw the attention of the people to the subject, and should the act pass, and be exposed to the objections made to it by the executive, the judiciary, if repugnant to the Constitution, might declare it void; or if consistent with the Constitution, and the power in itself be objectionable, the people might correct the evil, by an amendment of the Constitution. If objectionable on other ground, the people might furnish a remedy, by the declaration of their sentiments respecting it, which might be done in different ways, and with effect. Instances might occur in the progress of affairs, of a political nature, in which the better opportunity enjoyed by the executive to acquire full information, might enable it to negative a bill with advantage to the country.[18]

JOHN QUINCY ADAMS

I found no article or clause in the Constitution of the United States delegating the right or the power to define, limit, or declare what are or are not the constitutional powers of the President.[19]

✓ ✓ ✓

I said the Senate might dispose of it [a resolution criticizing the President's action in foreign affairs] as they should think proper, if they should not pass it. But if the Senate were to take an attitude of positive hostility to the Administration, I thought this was ground upon which the Executive would stand defensively stronger than perhaps any other that could be taken—a secret tribunal or inquisition of state, in which they constitute themselves accusers, triers, judges, and executioners against the President of the United States upon impeachable matters, without hearing him, without even informing him that they are receiving charges against him.[20]

✓ ✓ ✓

In the spirit of the Constitution of the United States, the executive is not only separated from the legislative power, but made dependent upon, and responsible to it. Until a very recent period of our history, all reference, in either House of Congress, to the opinions or wishes of the President, relating to any subject in deliberation before them, was regarded as an outrage upon the rights of the deliberative body, among the first of whose duties it is to spurn the influence of the dispenser of patronage and power. Until very recently, it was sufficient greatly to impair the influence of any member to be suspected of personal subserviency to the Executive; and any allusion to his wishes, in debate, was deemed a departure not less from decency than from order.[21]

Adams was speaking here as a Congressman, constantly at odds with his successors in the presidency. When he held the office himself, he entertained other views.

✦ ✦ ✦

It has perhaps never been duly remarked, that under the Constitution of the United States the powers of the executive department explicitly and emphatically concentrated in one person, are vastly more extensive and complicated than those of the legislative. The language of the instrument, in conferring legislative authority is, "*All* legislative powers herein granted, shall be vested in a Congress of the United States, which shall consist of a Senate and House of Representatives." But the executive trust it committed in unrestricted terms: "THE executive power shall be vested in a President of the United States of America." The legislative powers of Congress are, therefore, limited to specific grants contained in the Constitution itself, all restricted on one side by the power of internal legislation within the separate States, and on the other, by the laws of nations, otherwise and more properly called the rights of war and peace, consisting of all the rules of intercourse between independent nations. These are not subject to the legislative authority of any one nation, and they are, therefore, not included within the powers of Congress. But *the* executive power vested in the President of the United States, confers upon him the power, and enjoins upon him the duty, of fulfilling all the duties and of exacting all the rights of the nation in her intercourse with all the other nations of the earth. The powers of *declaring* war, of *regulating* commerce, of *defining* and *punishing* piracies and felonies committed on the high seas, and *offences* AGAINST THE LAW OF NATIONS, are among the special grants to Congress, but over that law itself, thus expressly recognised, and all-comprehensive as it is, Congress has no alterative power. While *the* power of executing it, is conferred in unlimited terms upon the President of the United States.[22]

JACKSON

It is due to candor, as well as to my own feelings, that I should express the reluctance and anxiety which I must at all times experience in exercising the undoubted right of the Executive to withhold his assent from bills on other grounds than their constitutionality. That this right should not be exercised on slight occasions all will admit. It is only in matters of deep interest, when the principle involved may be justly regarded as next in importance to infractions of the Constitution itself, that such a step can be expected to meet with the approbation of the people . . . In the discharge of this delicate and highly responsible duty I am sustained by the reflection that the exercise of this power has been deemed consistent with the obligation of official duty by several of my predecessors, and by the persuasion, too, that whatever liberal institutions may have to fear from the encroachments of Executive power, which has been everywhere the cause of so much strife and bloody contention, but little danger is to be apprehended from a precedent by which that authority denies to itself the exercise of powers that bring in their train influence and patronage of great extent, and thus excludes the operation of personal interests, everywhere the bane of official trust. I derive, too, no small degree of satisfaction from the reflection that if I have mistaken the interests and wishes of the people the Constitution affords the means of soon redressing the error by selecting for the place their favor has bestowed upon me a citizen whose opinions may accord with their own.[23]

✦ ✦ ✦

The executive is a coordinate and independent branch of the Government equally with the Senate, and I have yet to learn under what constitutional authority that branch of the Legislature has a right to require of me an account of any communication, either verbally or in writing, made to the heads of Departments acting as a Cabinet council. As well might I be required to detail to the Senate the free and private conversations I have held with those officers on any subject relating to their duties and my own.

Feeling my responsibility to the American people, I am willing upon all occasions to explain to them the grounds of my conduct, and I am willing upon all proper occasions to give to either branch of the Legislature any information in my possession that can be useful in the execution of the appropriate duties confided to them.

Knowing the constitutional rights of the Senate, I shall be the last man under any circumstances to interfere with them. Knowing those of the Executive, I shall at all times endeavor to maintain them agreeably to the provisions of the Constitution and the solemn oath I have taken to support and defend it.[24]

✦ ✦ ✦

I disclaim all pretension of right on the part of the President officially to inquire into or call in question the reasons of the Senate for rejecting any nomination whatsoever. As the President is not responsible to them for the reasons which induce him to make a nomination, so they are not responsible to him for the reasons which induce them to reject it. In these respects each is independent of the other and both responsible to their respective constituents.[25]

✦ ✦ ✦

It appears by the published Journal of the Senate that on the 26th of December last a resolution was offered by a member of the Senate, which after a protracted debate was on the 28th day of March last modified by the mover and passed by the votes of twenty-six Senators out of forty-six who were present and voted, in the following words, viz:

Resolved, That the President, in the late Executive proceedings in relation to the public revenue, has assumed upon himself authority and power not conferred by the Constitution and laws, but in derogation of both.

Having had the honor, through the voluntary suffrages of the American people, to fill the office of President of the United States during the period which may be presumed to have been referred to in this resolution, it is sufficiently evident that the censure it inflicts was intended for myself. Without notice, unheard and untried, I thus find myself charged on the records of the Senate, and in a form hitherto unknown in our history, with the high crime of violating the laws and Constitution of my country.

It can seldom be necessary for any department of the Government, when assailed in conversation or debate or by the strictures of the press or of popular assemblies, to step out of its ordinary path for the purpose of vindicating its conduct or of pointing out any irregularity or injustice in the manner of the attack; but when the Chief Executive Magistrate is, by one of the most important branches of the Government in its official capacity, in a public manner, and by its recorded sentence, but without precedent, competent authority, or just cause, declared guilty of a breach of the laws and Constitution, it is due to his station, to public opinion, and to a proper self-respect that the officer thus denounced should promptly expose the wrong which has been done.

In the present case, moreover, there is even a stronger necessity for such a vindication. By an express provision of the Constitution, before the President of the United States can enter on the execution of his office he is required to take an oath or affirmation in the following words:

> I do solemnly swear (or affirm) that I will faithfully execute the office of President of the United States and will to the best of my ability preserve, protect, and defend the Constitution of the United States.

The duty of defending so far as in him lies the integrity of the Constitution would indeed have resulted from the very nature of his office, but by thus expressing it in the official oath or affirmation, which in this respect differs from that of any other functionary, the founders of our Republic have attested their sense of its importance and have given to it a peculiar solemnity and force. Bound to the performance of this duty by the oath I have taken, by the strongest obligations of gratitude to the American people, and by the ties which unite my every earthly interest with the welfare and glory of my country, and perfectly convinced that the discussion and passage of the above-mentioned resolution were not only unauthorized by the Constitution, but in many respects repugnant to its provisions and subversive of the rights secured by it to other coordinate departments, I deem it an imperative duty to maintain the supremacy of that sacred instrument and the immunities of the department intrusted to my care by all means consistent with my own lawful powers, with the rights of others, and with the genius of our civil institutions. To this end I have caused this my *solemn protest* against the aforesaid proceedings to be placed on the files of the executive department and to be transmitted to the Senate.

It is alike due to the subject, the Senate, and the people that the views which I have taken of the proceedings referred to, and which compel me to regard them in the light that has been mentioned, should be exhibited at length, and with the freedom and firmness which are required by an occasion so unprecedented and peculiar.[26]

✓ ✓ ✓

Under the Constitution of the United States the powers and functions of the various departments of the Federal Government and their responsibilities for violation or neglect of duty are clearly defined or result by necessary inference. The legislative power is, subject to the qualified negative of the President, vested in the Congress of the United States, composed of the Senate and House of Representatives; the executive power is vested exclusively in the President, except that in the conclusion of treaties and in certain appointments to office he is to act with the advice and consent of the Senate; the judicial power is vested exclusively in the Supreme and other courts of the United States, except in cases of impeachment, for which purpose the accusatory power is vested in the House of Representatives and that of hearing and determining in the Senate. But although for the special purposes which have been mentioned there is an occasional intermixture of the powers of the different departments, yet with these exceptions each of the three great departments is independent of the others in its sphere of action, and when it deviates from that sphere is not responsible to the others further than it is expressly made so in the Constitution. In every other respect each of them is the coequal of the other two, and all are the servants of the American people, without power or right to control or censure each other in the service of their common superior, save only in the manner and to the degree which that superior has prescribed.[27]

*   *   *

The responsibilities of the President are numerous and weighty. He is liable to impeachment for high crimes and misdemeanors, and on due conviction to removal from office and perpetual disqualification; and not withstanding such conviction, he may also be indicted and punished according to law. He is also liable to the private action of any party who may have been injured by his illegal mandates or instructions in the same manner and to the same extent as the humblest functionary. In addition to the responsibilities which may thus be enforced by impeachment, criminal prosecution, or suit at law, he is also accountable at the bar of public opinion for every act of his Administration. Subject only to the restraints of truth and justice, the free people of the United States have the undoubted right, as individuals or collectively orally or in writing, at such times and in such language and form as they may think proper, to discuss his official conduct and to express and promulgate their opinions concerning it. Indirectly also his conduct may come under review in either branch of the Legislature, or in the Senate when acting in its executive capacity, and so far as the executive or legislative proceedings of these bodies may require it, it may be exercised by them. These are believed to be the proper and only modes in which the President of the United States is to be held accountable for his official conduct.

Tested by these principles, the resolution of the Senate is wholly unauthorized by the Constitution, and in derogation of its entire spirit. It assumes that a single branch of the legislative department may for the purposes of a public censure, and without any view to legislation or impeachment, take up, consider, and decide upon the official acts of the Executive. But in no part of the Constitution is the President subjected to any such responsibility, and in no part of that instrument is any such power conferred on either branch of the Legislature.[28]

* * *

That the Senate possesses a high judicial power and that instances may occur in which the President of the United States will be amenable to it is undeniable; but under the provisions of the Constitution it would seem to be equally plain that neither the President nor any other officer can be rightfully subjected to the operation of the judicial power of the Senate except in the cases and under the forms prescribed by the Constitution.

The Constitution declares that "the President, Vice-President, and all civil officers of the United States shall be removed from office on impeachment for and conviction of treason, bribery, or other high crimes and misdemeanors;" that the House of Representatives "shall have the sole power of impeachment;" that the Senate "shall have the sole power to try all impeachments;" that "when sitting for that purpose they shall be on oath or affirmation;" that "when the President of the United States is tried the Chief Justice shall preside;" that "no person shall be convicted without the concurrence of two-thirds of the members present," and that "judgment shall not extend further than to removal from office and disqualification to hold and enjoy any office of honor, trust, or profit under the United States."

The resolution above quoted charges, in substance, that in certain proceedings relating to the public revenue the President has usurped authority and power not conferred upon; him by the Constitution and laws, and that in doing so he violated both. Any such act constitutes a high crime—one of the highest, indeed, which the President can commit—a crime which justly exposes him to impeachment by the House of Representatives, and, upon due conviction, to removal from office and to the complete and immutable disfranchisement prescribed by the Constitution. The resolution, then, was in substance an impeachment of the President, and in its passage amounts to a declaration by a majority of the Senate that he is guilty of an impeachable offense. As such it is spread upon the journals of the Senate, published to the nation and to the world, made part of our enduring archives, and incorporated in the history of the age. The punishment of removal from office and future disqualification does not, it is true, follow this decision, nor would it have followed the like decision if the regular forms of proceeding had been pursued, because the requisite number did not concur in the result. But the moral influence of a solemn declaration by a majority of the Senate that the accused is guilty of the offense charged upon him has been as effectually secured as if the like declaration had been made upon an impeachment expressed in the same terms. Indeed, a greater practical effect has been gained, because the votes given for the resolution, though not sufficient to authorize a judgment of guilty on an impeachment, were numerous enough to carry that resolution.

That the resolution does not expressly allege that the assumption of power and authority which it condemns was intentional and corrupt is no answer to the preceding view of its character and effect. The act thus condemned necessarily implies volition and design in the individual to whom it is imputed, and, being unlawful in its character, the legal conclusion is that it was prompted by improper motives and committed with an unlawful intent. The charge is not of a mistake in the exercise of supposed powers, but of the assumption of powers not conferred by the Constitution and laws, but in derogation of both, and nothing is suggested to excuse or palliate the turpitude of the act. In the absence of any such excuse or palliation there is only room for one inference, and that is that the intent was unlawful and corrupt. Besides, the resolution not only contains no mitigating suggestions, but, on the contrary, it holds up the act complained of as justly obnoxious to censure and reprobation, and thus as distinctly stamps it with impurity of motive as if the strongest epithets had been used.

The President of the United States, therefore, has been by a majority of his constitutional triers accused and found guilty of an impeachable offense, but in no part of this proceeding have the directions of the Constitution been observed.[29]

✓ ✓ ✓

If by a mere denunciation like this [Senate] resolution the President should ever be induced to act in a matter of official duty contrary to the honest convictions of his own mind in compliance with the wishes of the Senate, the constitutional independence of the executive department would be as effectually destroyed and its power as effectually transferred to the Senate as if that end had been accomplished by an amendment of the Constitution. But if the Senate have a right to interfere with the Executive powers, they have also the right to make that interference effective, and if the assertion of the power implied in the resolution be silently acquiesced in we may reasonably apprehend that it will be followed at some future day by an attempt at actual enforcement. The Senate may refuse, except on the condition that he will surrender his opinions to theirs and obey their will, to perform their own functions, to pass the necessary laws, to sanction appropriations proposed by the House of Representatives, and to confirm proper nominations made by the President. It has already been maintained (and it is not conceivable that the resolution of the Senate can be based on any other principle) that the Secretary of the Treasury is the officer of Congress and independent of the President; that the President has no right to control him, and consequently none to remove him. With the same propriety and on similar grounds may the Secretary of State, the Secretaries of War and the Navy, and the Postmaster-General each in succession be declared independent of the President, the subordinates of Congress, and removable only with the concurrence of the Senate. Followed to its consequences, this principle will be found effectually to destroy one coordinate department of the Government, to concentrate in the hands of the Senate the whole executive power, and to leave the President as powerless as he would be useless—the shadow of authority after the substance had departed.[30]

✓ ✓ ✓

This is another of those calls for information made upon me by the Senate which have, in my judgment, either related to the subjects exclusively belonging to the executive department or otherwise encroached on the constitutional powers of the Executive. Without conceding the right of the Senate to make either of these requests, I have yet, for the various reasons heretofore assigned in my several replies, deemed it expedient to comply with several of them. It is now, however, my solemn conviction that I ought no longer, from any motive nor in any degree, to yield to these unconstitutional demands. Their continued repetition imposes on me, as the representative and trustee of the American people, the painful but imperious duty of resisting to the utmost any further encroachment on the rights of the Executive. This course is especially due to the present resolution. The President in cases of this nature possesses the exclusive power of removal from office, and, under the sanctions of his official oath and of his liability to impeachment, he is bound to exercise it whenever the public welfare shall require. If, on the other hand, from corrupt motives he abuses this power, he is exposed to the same responsibilities. On no principle known to our institutions can he be required to account for the manner in which he discharges this portion of his public duties, save only in the mode and under the forms prescribed by the Constitution. The suggestion that the charges a copy of which is requested by the Senate "may contain information necessary to their action" on a nomination now before them can not vary the principle. There is no necessary connection between the two subjects, and even if there were the Senate have no right to call for that portion of these matters which appertains to the separate and independent action of the Executive. The intimation that these charges may also be necessary "to the investigation now in progress respecting frauds in the sales of public lands" is still more insufficient to authorize the present call. Those investigations were instituted and have thus far been conducted by the Senate in their legislative capacity, and with the view, it is presumed, to some legislative action. If the President has in his possession any information on the subject of such frauds, it is his duty to communicate it to Congress, and it may undoubtedly be called for by either House sitting in its legislative capacity, though even from such a call all matters properly belonging to the exclusive duties of the President must of necessity be exempted.[31]

✓ ✓ ✓

The duty of the Legislature to define, by clear and positive enactments, the nature and extent of the action which it belongs to the Executive to superintend springs out of a policy analogous to that which enjoins upon all the branches of the Federal Government an abstinence from the exercise of powers not clearly granted.

In such a Government, possessing only limited and specific powers, the spirit of its general administration can not be wise or just when it opposes the reference of all doubtful points to the great source of authority, the States and the people, whose number and diversified relations, securing them against the influences and excitements which may mislead their agents, make them the safest depository of power. In its application to the Executive, with reference to the legislative branch of the Government, the same rule of action should make the President ever anxious to avoid the exercise of any discretionary authority which can be regulated by Congress. The biases which may operate upon him will not be so likely to extend to the representatives of the people in that body.[32]

❧ ❧ ❧

It is due to the character of our institutions that the diplomatic intercourse of this Government should be conducted with the utmost directness and simplicity, and that in all cases of importance the communications received or made by the Executive should assume the accustomed official form. It is only by insisting on this form that foreign powers can be held to full responsibility, that their communications can be officially replied to, or that the advice or interference of the Legislature can with propriety be invited by the President. This course is also best calculated, on the one hand, to shield that officer from unjust suspicions, and on the other to subject this portion of his acts to public scrutiny, and, if occasion shall require it, to constitutional animadversion.[33]

VAN BUREN

Everybody knows that an act which is contrary to the Constitution is a nullity, although it may have passed according to the forms of the Constitution. That instrument creates several departments, whose duty it may become to act upon such a bill, in the performance of their respective functions. The theory of the Constitution is that these departments are coordinate and independent of each other, and that when they act in their appropriate spheres they each have a right, and it is the duty of each to judge for themselves in respect to the authority and requirements of the Constitution, without being controled or interfered with by their co-departments, and are each responsible to the people alone who made them for the manner in which they discharge their respective duties in that regard. It is not therefore to be presumed that that instrument, after making it the President's especial duty to take an oath to preserve and uphold the Constitution and prevent its violation, intended to deny to him the right to withhold his assent from a measure which he might conscientiously believe would have that effect, and to impose upon him the necessity of outraging his conscience, by making himself a party to such a violation. The Constitution, which was framed by great men, the form of which has been so much and so justly admired, is not so imperfect nor subject to such a reproach. The matter does not necessarily end with a refusal on the part of the executive to do an act which he believes congress had no right, under the Constitution, to require his department to perform. Although the President, representing one of the three great departments of the Government, possesses in this respect a right which neither the citizen nor any other officer or officers of the Government, not having the control of such a department, can exercise, yet if he allows himself to be governed by unworthy motives he is liable to impeachment and expulsion from office. It is in this way, or by his removal by the people, that the wrong he does to the public is redressed.[34]

✦ ✦ ✦

The Houses of the legislature, in every law or resolution that they pass, have to consider whether it is authorized by the Constitution to which they have sworn to conform, and the President and Senate, when they make a treaty, are bound to consider and decide the same question. The President, as the sole depositary of the executive power, is under a similar obligation. His first inquiry is, whether the Constitution authorizes him to apply the power of his department to the execution of the business before him, or, if it is one of the numerous functions which the legislature is in the constant habit of calling upon him to perform, has the legislature power under the Constitution to direct the thing to be done, and can he do it consistently with his oath to preserve and uphold that instrument?[35]

WILLIAM H. HARRISON

But if there is danger to public liberty from the acknowledged defects of the Constitution in the want of limit to the continuance of the Executive power in the same hands, there is, I apprehend, not much less from a misconstruction of that instrument as it regards the powers actually given. I can not conceive that by a fair construction any or either of its provisions would be found to constitute the President a part of the legislative power. It can not be claimed from the power to recommend, since, although enjoined as a duty upon him, it is a privilege which he holds in common with every other citizen; and although there may be something more of confidence in the propriety of the measures recommended in the one case than in the other, in the obligations of ultimate decision there can be no difference.[36]

✦ ✦ ✦

It may be said, indeed, that the Constitution has given to the Executive the power to annul the acts of the legislative body by refusing to them his assent. So a similar power has necessarily resulted from that instrument to the judiciary, and yet the judiciary forms no part of the Legislature. There is, it is true, this difference between these grants of power: The Executive can put his negative upon the acts of the Legislature for other cause than that of want of conformity to the Constitution, whilst the judiciary can only declare void those which violate that instrument. But the decision of the judiciary is final in such a case, whereas in every instance where the veto of the Executive is applied it may be overcome by a vote of two-thirds of both Houses of Congress. The negative upon the acts of the legislative by the executive authority, and that in the hands of one individual, would seem to be an incongruity in our system. Like some others of a similar character, however, it appears to be highly expedient, and if used only with the forebearance and in the spirit which was intended by its authors it may be productive of great good and be found one of the best safeguards to the Union.[37]

✦ ✦ ✦

And it is preposterous to suppose that a thought could for a moment have been entertained that the President, placed at the capital, in the center of the country, could better understand the wants and wishes of the people than their own immediate representatives, who spend a part of every year among them, living with them, often laboring with them, and bound to them by the triple tie of interest, duty, and affection. To assist or control Congress, then, in its ordinary legislation could not, I conceive, have been the motive for conferring the veto power on the President. This argument acquires additional force from the fact of its never having been thus used by the first six

Presidents—and two of them were members of the Convention, one presiding over its deliberations and the other bearing a larger share in consummating the labors of that august body than any other person. But if bills were never returned to Congress by either of the Presidents above referred to upon the ground of their being inexpedient or not as well adapted as they might be to the wants of the people, the veto was applied upon that of want of conformity to the Constitution or because errors had been committed from a too hasty enactment.[38]

* * *

Upon another occasion I have given my opinion at some length upon the impropriety of Executive interference in the legislation of Congress—that the article in the Constitution making it the duty of the President to communicate information and authorizing him to recommend measures was not intended to make him the source in legislation, and, in particular, that he should never be looked to for schemes of finance. It would be very strange, indeed, that the Constitution should have strictly forbidden one branch of the Legislature from interfering in the origination of such bills and that it should be considered proper that an altogether different department of the Government should be permitted to do so.[39]

* * *

The Senate, in relation to revenue bills, have the right to propose amendments, and so has the Executive by the power given him to return them to the House of Representatives with his objections. It is in his power also to propose amendments in the existing revenue laws, suggested by his observations upon their defective or injurious operation. But the delicate duty of devising schemes of revenue should be left where the Constitution has placed it—with the immediate representatives of the people. For similar reasons the mode of keeping the public treasure should be prescribed by them, and the further removed it may be from the control of the Executive the more wholesome the arrangement and the more in accordance with the republican principle.[40]

TYLER

I readily admit that whilst the qualified *veto* with which the Chief Magistrate is invested should be regarded and was intended by the wise men who made it a part of the Constitution as a great conservative principle of our system, without the exercise of which on important occasions a mere representative majority might urge the Government in its legislation beyond the limits fixed by its framers or might exert its just powers too hastily or oppressively, yet it is a power which ought to be most cautiously exerted, and perhaps never except in a case eminently involving the public interest or one in which the oath of the President, acting under his conviction, both mental and moral, imperiously requires its exercise. In such a case he has no alternative. He must either exert the negative power intrusted to him by the Constitution chiefly for its own preservation, protection, and defense or commit an act of gross moral turpitude. Mere regard to the will of a majority must not in a constitutional republic like ours control this sacred and solemn duty of a sworn officer. The Constitution itself I regard and cherish as the embodied and written will of the whole people of the United States. It is their fixed and fundamental law, which they unanimously prescribe to the public functionaries, their mere trustees and servants. This *their* will and the law which *they* have given us as the rule of our action have no guard, no guaranty of preservation, protection, and defense, but the oaths which it prescribes to the public officers, the sanctity with which they shall religiously observe those oaths, and the patriotism with which the people shall shield it by their own sovereign will, which has made the Constitution supreme. It must be exerted against the will of a mere representative majority or not at all. It is alone in pursuance of that will that any measure can reach the President, and to say that because a majority in Congress have passed a bill he should therefore sanction it is to abrogate the power altogether and to render its insertion in the Constitution a work of absolute supererogation.[41]

✦   ✦   ✦

When I was a member of either House of Congress I acted under the conviction that *to doubt* as to the constitutionality of a law was sufficient to induce me to give my vote against it; but I have not been able to bring myself to believe that *a doubtful opinion* of the Chief Magistrate ought to outweigh the solemnly pronounced opinion of the representatives of the people and of the States.[42]

✓ ✓ ✓

For having declined of late to unite in giving away a fruitful source of revenue, from a Treasury which has become nearly exhausted, I have been charged with a desire to dictate to Congress, when my sole object is to carry out a law of this very Congress on the subject of public lands. The welkin is made to resound with charges of executive dictation, because I have not seen cause to approve the repeal or suspension of an act passed as late as the 4th of September last.

My reply is, that if it was right to pass that act then, it must be wrong to repeal it now, when the Treasury requires the use of every dollar which it can rightfully claim. Executive dictation! I repel the imputation. I would gladly harmonize with Congress in the enactment of all necessary measures if the majority would permit me. Most gladly would I approve any bill having revenue for its object, and the protection of manufacturing industry as its incident, which should be presented to me unconnected with matters having no necessary affiliation, and which are only calculated to embarrass the executive action. Each branch of the government is independent of every other, and Heaven forbid that the day should ever come when either can dictate to the other. The Constitution never designed that the executive should be a mere cipher. On the contrary, it denies to Congress the right to pass any law without his approval, thereby imparting to it, for wise purposes, an active agency in all legislation.[43]

✓ ✓ ✓

Nothing can be more painful to any individual called upon to perform the Chief Executive duties under our limited Constitution than to be constrained to withhold his assent from an important measure adopted by the Legislature. Yet he would neither fulfill the high purposes of his station nor consult the true interests or the solemn will of the people—the common constituents of both branches of the Government—by yielding his well-considered, most deeply fixed, and repeatedly declared opinions on matters of great public concernment to those of a coordinate department without requesting that department seriously to reexamine the subject of their difference. The exercise of some independence of judgment in regard to all acts of legislation is plainly implied in the responsibility of approving them. At all times a duty, it becomes a peculiarly solemn and imperative one when the subjects passed upon by Congress happen to involve, as in the present instance, the most momentous issues, to affect variously the various parts of a great country, and to have given rise in all quarters to such a conflict of opinion as to render it impossible to conjecture with any certainty on which side the majority really is.[44]

* * *

The Executive can to no more than apply the means which Congress places in its hands for the support of Government, and, happily for the good of the country and for the preservation of its liberties, it possesses no power to levy exactions on the people or to force from them contributions to the public revenue in any form. It can only recommend such measures as may in its opinion be called for by the wants of the public service to Congress, with whom alone rests the power to "lay and collect taxes, duties, imposts, and excises."[45]

POLK

The preservation of the Constitution from infraction is the President's highest duty. He is bound to discharge that duty at whatever hazard of incurring the displeasure of those who may differ with him in opinion. He is bound to discharge it as well by his obligations to the people who have clothed him with his exalted trust as by his oath of office, which he may not disregard. Nor are the obligations of the President in any degree lessened by the prevalence of views different from his own in one or both Houses of Congress. It is not alone hasty and inconsiderate legislation that he is required to check; but if at any time Congress shall, after apparently full deliberation, resolve on measures which he deems subversive of the Constitution or of the vital interests of the country, it is his solemn duty to stand in the breach and resist them. The President is bound to approve or disapprove every bill which passes Congress and is presented to him for his signature. The Constitution makes this his duty, and he can not escape it if he would. He has no election. In deciding upon any bill presented to him he must exercise his own best judgment. If he can not approve, the Constitution commands him to return the bill to the House in which it originated with his objections, and if he fail to do this within ten days (Sundays excepted) it shall become a law without his signature. Right or wrong, he may be overruled by a vote of two-thirds of each House, and in that event the bill becomes a law without his sanction. If his objections be not thus overruled, the subject is only postponed, and is referred to the States and the people for their consideration and decision. The President's power is negative merely, and not affirmative. He can enact no law. The only effect, therefore, of his withholding his approval of a bill passed by Congress is to suffer the existing laws to remain unchanged, and the delay occasioned is only that required to enable the States and the people to consider and act upon the subject in the election of public agents who will carry out their wishes and instructions. Any attempt to coerce the President to yield his sanction to measures which he can not approve would be a violation of the spirit of the Constitution, palpable and flagrant, and if successful would break down the independence of the executive department and make the President, elected by the people and clothed by the Constitution with power to defend their rights, the mere instrument of a majority of Congress. A surrender on his part of the powers with which the Constitution has invested his office would effect a practical alteration of that instrument without resorting to the prescribed process of amendment.

With the motives or considerations which may induce Congress to pass any bill the President can have nothing to do. He must presume them to be as pure as his own, and look only to the practical effect of their measures when compared with the Constitution or the public good.

But it has been urged by those who object to the exercise of this undoubted constitutional power that it assails the representative principle and the capacity of the people to govern themselves; that there is greater safety in a numerous representative body than in the single Executive created by the Constitution, and that the Executive veto is a "one-man power," despotic in its character. To expose the fallacy of this objection it is only necessary to consider the frame and true character of our system. Ours is not a consolidated empire, but a confederated union. The States before the adoption of the Constitution were coordinate, co-equal, and separate independent sovereignties, and by its adoption they did not lose that character. They clothed the Federal Government with certain powers and reserved all others, including their own sovereignty, to themselves. They guarded their own rights as States and the rights of the people by the very limitations which they incorporated into the Federal Constitution, whereby the different departments of the General

Government were checks upon each other. That the majority should govern is a general principle controverted by none, but they must govern according to the Constitution, and not according to an undefined and unrestrained discretion, whereby they may oppress the minority.[46]

✔ ✔ ✔

The people, by the Constitution, have commanded the President, as much as they have commanded the legislative branch of the Government, to execute their will. They have said to him in the Constitution, which they require he shall take a solemn oath to support, that if Congress pass any bill which he can not approve "he shall return it to the House in which it originated with his objections." In withholding from it his approval and signature he is executing the will of the people, constitutionally expressed, as much as the Congress that passed it. No bill is presumed to be in accordance with the popular will until it shall have passed through all the branches of the Government required by the Constitution to make it a law. A bill which passes the House of Representatives may be rejected by the Senate, and so a bill passed by the Senate may be rejected by the House. In each case the respective Houses exercise the veto power on the other.

Congress, and each House of Congress, hold under the Constitution a check upon the President, and he, by the power of the qualified veto, a check upon Congress. When the President recommends measures to Congress, he avows in the most solemn form his opinions, gives his voice in their favor, and pledges himself in advance to approve them if passed by Congress. If he acts without due consideration, or has been influenced by improper or corrupt motives, or if from any other cause Congress, or either House of Congress, shall differ with him in opinion, they exercise their veto upon his recommendations and reject them; and there is no appeal from their decision but to the people at the ballot box. These are proper checks upon the Executive, wisely interposed by the Constitution. None will be found to object to them or to wish them removed. It is equally important that the constitutional checks of the Executive upon the legislative branch should be preserved.

If it be said that the Representatives in the popular branch of Congress are chosen directly by the people, it is answered, the people elect the President. If both Houses represent the States and the people, so does the President. The President represents in the executive department the whole people of the United States, as each member of the legislative department represents portions of them.

In the exercise of the power of the veto the President is responsible not only to an enlightened public opinion, but to the people of the whole Union, who elected him, as the representatives in the legislative branches who differ with him in opinion are responsible to the people of particular States or districts, who compose their respective constituencies. To deny to the President the exercise of this power would be to repeal that provision of the Constitution which confers it upon him. To charge that its exercise unduly controls the legislative will is to complain of the Constitution itself.

If the Presidential veto be objected to upon the ground that it checks and thwarts the popular will, upon the same principle the equality of representation of the States in the Senate should be stricken out of the Constitution. The vote of a Senator from Delaware has equal weight in deciding upon the most important measures with the vote of a Senator from New York, and yet the one represents a State containing, according to the existing apportionment of Representatives in the House of Representatives, but one thirty-fourth part of the population of the other. By the constitutional composition of the Senate a majority of that body from the smaller States represent less than one-fourth of the people of the Union. There are thirty States, and under the existing apportionment of Representatives there are 230 Members in the House of Representatives. Sixteen of the smaller States are represented in that House by but 50 Members, and yet the Senators from these States constitute a majority of the Senate. So that the President may recommend a measure to Congress, and it may receive the sanction and approval of more than three-fourths of the House of Representatives and of all the Senators from the large States, containing more than three-fourths of the whole population of the United States, and yet the measure may be defeated by the votes of the Senators from the smaller States. None, it is presumed, can be found ready to change the organization of the Senate on this account, or to strike that body practically out of existence by requiring that its action shall be conformed to the will of the more numerous branch.[47]

✦ ✦ ✦

One great object of the Constitution in conferring upon the President a qualified negative upon the legislation of Congress was to protect minorities from injustice and oppression by majorities. The equality of their representation in the Senate and the veto power of the President are the constitutional guaranties which the smaller States have that their rights will be respected. Without these guaranties all their interests would be at the mercy of majorities in Congress representing the larger States. To the smaller and weaker States, therefore, the preservation of this power and its exercise upon proper occasions demanding it is of vital importance. They ratified the Constitution and entered into the Union, securing to themselves an equal representation with the larger States in the Senate; and they agreed to be bound by all laws passed by Congress upon the express condition, and none other, that they should be approved by the President or passed, his objections to the contrary notwithstanding, by a vote of two-thirds of both Houses. Upon this condition they have a right to insist as a part of the compact to which they gave their assent.

A bill might be passed by Congress against the will of the whole people of a particular State and against the votes of its Senators and all its Representatives. However prejudicial it might be to the interests of such State, it would be bound by it if the President shall approve it or it shall be passed by a vote of two-thirds of both Houses; but it has a right to demand that the President shall exercise his constitutional power and arrest it if his judgment is against it. If he surrender this power, or fail to exercise it in a case where he can not approve, it would make his formal approval a mere mockery, and would be itself a violation of the Constitution, and the dissenting State would become bound by a law which had not been passed according to the sanctions of the Constitution.[48]

✓ ✓ ✓

The power of the Executive veto was exercised by the first and most illustrious of my predecessors and by four of his successors who preceded me in the administration of the Government, and it is believed in no instance prejudicially to the public interests. It has never been and there is but little danger that it ever can be abused. No President will ever desire unnecessarily to place his opinion in opposition to that of Congress. He must always exercise the power reluctantly, and only in cases where his convictions make it a matter of stern duty, which he can not escape. Indeed, there is more danger that the President, from the repugnance he must always feel to come in collision with Congress, may fail to exercise it in cases where the preservation of the Constitution from infraction, or the public good, may demand it than that he will ever exercise it unnecessarily or wantonly.[49]

TAYLOR

The Executive has authority to recommend (not to dictate) measures to Congress. Having preformed that duty, the executive department of the Government can not rightfully control the decision of Congress or any subject of legislation until that decision shall have been officially submitted to the President for approval. The check provided by the Constitution in the clause confining the qualified veto will never be exercised by me except in the cases contemplated by the fathers of the Republic. I view it as an extreme measure, to be resorted to only in extraordinary cases, as where it may become necessary to defend the executive against the encroachments of the legislative power or to prevent hasty and inconsiderate or unconstitutional legislation.[50]

PIERCE

In the organization of the Government of the United States the legislative and executive functions were separated and placed in distinct hands. Although the President is required from time to time to recommend to the consideration of Congress such measures as he shall judge necessary and expedient, his participation in the formal business of legislation is limited to the single duty, in a certain contingency, of demanding for a bill a particular form of vote prescribed by the Constitution before it can become a law. He is not invested with power to defeat legislation by an absolute veto, but only to restrain it, and is charged with the duty, in case he disapproves a measure, of invoking a second and a more deliberate and solemn consideration of it on the part of Congress. It is not incumbent on the President to sign a bill as a matter of course, and thus merely to authenticate the action of Congress, for he must exercise intelligent judgment or be faithless to the trust reposed in him. If he approve a bill, he shall sign it, but if not he shall return it with his objections to that House in which it shall have originated for such further action as the Constitution demands, which is its enactment, if at all, not by a bare numerical majority, as in the first instance, but by a constitutional majority of two-thirds of both Houses.

While the Constitution thus confers on the legislative bodies the complete power of legislation in all cases, it proceeds, in the spirit of justice, to provide for the protection of the responsibility of the President. It does not compel him to affix the signature of approval to any bill unless it actually have his approbation; for while it requires him to sign if he approve, it, in my judgment, imposes upon him the duty of withholding his signature if he do not approve. In the execution of his official duty in this respect he is not to perform a mere mechanical part, but is to decide and act according to conscientious convictions of the rightfulness or wrongfulness of the proposed law. In a matter as to which he is doubtful in his own mind he may well defer to the majority of the two Houses. Individual members of the respective Houses, owing to the nature, variety, and amount of business pending, must necessarily rely for their guidance in many, perhaps most, cases, when the matters involved are not of popular interest, upon the investigation of appropriate committees, or, it may be, that of a single member, whose attention has been particularly directed to the subject. For similar reasons, but even to a greater extent, from the number and variety of subjects daily urged upon his attention, the President naturally relies much upon the investigation had and the results arrived at by the two Houses, and hence those results, in large classes of cases, constitute the basis upon which his approval rests. The President's responsibility is to the whole people of the United States, as that of a Senator is to the people of a particular State, that of a Representative to the people of a State or district; and it may be safely assumed that he will not resort to the clearly defined and limited power of arresting legislation and calling for reconsideration of any measure except in obedience to requirements of duty. When, however, he entertains a decisive and fixed conclusion, not merely of the unconstitutionality, but of the impropriety, or injustice in other respects, of any measure, if he declare that he approves it he is false to his oath, and he deliberately disregards his constitutional obligations.[51]

BUCHANAN

The most important business of each session is generally crowded into its last hours, and the alternative presented to the President is either to violate the constitutional duty which he owes to the people, and approve bills which, for want of time, it is impossible he should have examined, or, by his refusal to do this, subject the country and individuals to great loss and inconvenience.

Besides, a practice has grown up of late years to legislate in appropriation bills, at the last hours of the session, on new and important subjects. This practice constrains the President either to suffer measures to become laws which he does not approve, or to incur the risk of stopping the wheels of the government by vetoing an appropriation bill. Formerly, such bills were confined to specific appropriations for carrying into effect existing laws and the well-established policy of the country, and little time was then required by the President for their examination.[52]

*   *   *

In former times it was believed to be the true character of an appropriation bill simply to carry into effect existing laws, and the established policy of the country. A practice has, however, grown up of late years to ingraft on such bills, at the last hours of the session, large appropriations for new and important objects not provided for by preexisting laws, and when no time is left to the Executive for their examination and investigation. No alternative is thus left to the President but either to approve measures without examination, or, by vetoing an appropriation bill, seriously to embarrass the operations of the Government.[53]

*   *   *

The people have not confined the President to the exercise of executive duties. They have also conferred upon him a large measure of legislative discretion. No bill can become a law without his approval, as representing the people of the United States, unless it shall pass after his veto by a majority of two-thirds of both Houses. In his legislative capacity, he might, in common with the Senate and the House, institute an inquiry to ascertain any facts which ought to influence his judgment in approving or vetoing any bill.

This participation in the performance of legislative duties between the co-ordinate branches of the Government ought to inspire the conduct of all of them, in their relations towards each other, with mutual forbearance and respect. At least each has a right to demand justice from the other. The cause of complaint is, that the constitutional rights and immunities of the Executive have been violated in the person of the President.[54]

✦ ✦ ✦

The sovereign people of the several States have elected him
[the President] to the highest and most honorable office in the
world. He is their only direct representative in the Government.
By their Constitution they have made him commander-in-
chief of their army and navy. He represents them in their intercourse with foreign nations. Clothed with their dignity and
authority, he occupies a proud position before all nations, civilized and savage. With the consent of the Senate, he appoints all
the important officers of the Government. He exercises the veto
power, and to that extent controls the legislation of Congress.
For the performance of these high duties he is responsible to
the people of the several States, and not in any degree to the
House of Representatives.

Shall he surrender these high powers, conferred upon him as
the representative of the American people, for their benefit, to
the House, to be exercised under their overshadowing influence
and control? Shall he alone of all the citizens of the United
States be denied a fair trial? Shall he alone not be "informed of
the nature and cause of the accusation" against him? Shall he
alone not "be confronted with the witnesses" against him? Shall
the House of Representatives, usurping the powers of the Senate,
proceed to try the President through the agency of a secret
committee of the body where it is impossible he can make any
defence, and then, without affording him an opportunity of
being heard, pronounce a judgment of censure against him? The
very same rule might be applied for the very same reason to
every judge of every court of the United States. From what
part of the Constitution is this terrible secret inquisitorial power
derived? No such express power exists. From which of the
enumerated powers can it be inferred? It is true the House
cannot pronounce the formal judgment against him of "removal
from office," but they can, by their judgment of censure, asperse
his reputation, and thus, to the extent of their influence, render
the office contemptible.[55]

LINCOLN

I will show them at the other end of the Avenue whether I
am President or not![56]

*"At the other end of the Avenue" was Congress, with whom Lin-
coln had as little as possible to do.*

ANDREW JOHNSON

I know it has been urged that the executive department is more likely to enlarge the sphere of its action than either of the other two branches of the Government, and especially in the exercise of the veto power conferred upon it by the Constitution. It should be remembered, however, that this power is wholly negative and conservative in its character, and was intended to operate as a check upon unconstitutional, hasty, and improvident legislation and as a means of protection against invasions of the just powers of the executive and judicial departments.[57]

✶ ✶ ✶

The necessity of some such check in the hands of the Executive is shown by reference to the most eminent writers upon our system of government, who seem to concur in the opinion that encroachments are most to be apprehended from the department in which all legislative powers are vested by the Constitution.[58]

✶ ✶ ✶

Gentlemen of the Cabinet: You no doubt are aware that certain evil-disposed persons have formed a conspiracy to depose the President of the United States, and to supply his place by an individual of their own selection. Their plan of operations seems to contemplate certain accusations against the President, which are to take the form of Articles of Impeachment, and that hereupon, before hearing or trial, he is, under color of law, to be placed under arrest, and suspended or removed from office.

The first intention, apparently, was to proceed by regular impeachment, in the mode prescribed by the Constitution. This, however, requires some credible evidence of an official act, criminal in its nature, and of a grade high enough to justify such proceeding before an enlightened and impartial public. Failing to obtain, after efforts of the most extraordinary and unscrupulous character, any plausible grounds for such an accusation, the persons engaged in this scheme discover that, to accomplish their purpose, they must now resort to a revolution changing the whole organic system of our Government.

Such a design has been openly and publicly avowed, in language unambiguous in meaning, by persons of great notoriety and much influence. While it is hoped that their declarations may be the mere ebullitions of intense party excitement, it must be remembered that at the present time the temper of many political leaders is desperate and extremely reckless, and that the most prominent among them have admitted and proclaimed that the Constitution has been set aside and repudiated by Congress.

The temptation to join in a revolutionary enterprise for the overthrow of our institutions is extremely strong at the present moment. A combination of men directing the operations of Government without regard to law, or under a Constitution, which they hold themselves authorized to repudiate at pleasure, would be absolute masters of all the wealth of the country, the richest in the world, and they could hold at their mercy the life and liberty of every individual within our territorial limits. Supreme and irresponsible power is always dangerous and seductive; but here, in the present condition of American affairs, with our large army and powerful navy and our vast resources, it is a prize so dazzling that we can not wonder that the desire to grasp it should overcome the public virtue of some ambitious men. The coveted power, once usurped, would easily find means to make itself perpetual.

It can not be doubted that nine-tenths of the American people are true to the Constitution and the free institutions established by their fathers. So, in 1861, were the people of the South; yet they were misled by a few designing men, and forced into a disastrous revolution. A revolutionary party, once in full possession of the Government, with the entire control of the monetary affairs of the country and the immense revenue now paid annually into the Treasury, with universal suffrage and military supervision of elections, might even maintain some external show of popular approbation for its worst excesses.

Without attempting to set forth all the facts and circumstances which tend to establish the existence of a formidable conspiracy for the overthrow of the Government by the deposition of the Chief Executive Magistrate, it is clear that those who are engaged in it regard the present Executive as the main obstacle to the assumption and exercise by them of unwarranted and arbitrary authority over the people. It is believed that if the Executive had united with the majority of Congress in the passage of measures which he deemed subversive of the fundamental principles of free government, he would have had their approbation. Their unqualified animosity has been excited by the effort he has made faithfully to fulfill his solemn obligation.

It has never once occurred to him, however, that upon the mere demands of illegal and revolutionary violence he could surrender his office to a usurper, and thus yield the high duty imposed upon him by his oath "to preserve, protect, and defend the Constitution." To do so would be to betray the most sacred trust committed to human hands. I can not deliver the great charter of our Nation's liberty to men who, by the very act of usurping it, would show their determination to disregard and trample it under foot. The strong probability that such a demand will be made, and the certainty that if made, it must, from a high sense of official obligation on my part, be resisted with all the legal and Constitutional means at the disposal of the President, thus bringing on a conflict between the co-ordinate branches of the Government, makes it absolutely necessary that the Executive and the heads of the several Departments should, upon a question so momentous, understand one another without any reserve whatever.

To that end, I request your separate opinions, in writing, on the following questions:

First. Can the President be removed from office in any other mode than that prescribed in the Constitution; viz., "on impeachment for and conviction of treason, bribery, or other high crimes and misdemeanors?"

Second. Pending impeachment, and before conviction and judgment, can the President, by an act of Congress and otherwise, be suspended from office, and the president *pro tempore* of the Senate, or other officer provided by law, be authorized to act as President during such suspension?

Third. If a law providing for such suspension and such exercise of the office by any officer other than the President should be passed, would it be the duty of the President to surrender his office and withdraw from the exercise of his official duties, or continue to exercise them and to maintain his authority?

Fourth. Whether such deposition or arrest of the President, and the transfer of his official functions to another person, would be less a violation of the organic law, if attempted or done by members of Congress, or at their instigation, than if attempted or effected by private parties?[59]

If the impeachment of Johnson had succeeded—it lost by one vote —the President of the Senate would have become President of the United States.

GRANT

The duty of opposition to filibustering has been admitted by every President.[60]

*   *   *

The mere rejection by the Senate of a treaty negotiated by the President only indicates a difference of opinion between two co-ordinate departments of the Government, without touching the character or wounding the pride of either. But when such rejection takes place simultaneously with charges openly made of corruption on the part of the President or those employed by him the case is different. Indeed, in such case the honor of the nation demands investigation.[61]

*   *   *

Assuming from the action of the last Congress in appointing a Committee on Privileges and Elections to prepare and report to this Congress a constitutional amendment to provide a better method of electing the President and Vice-President of the United States, and also from the necessity of such an amendment, that there will be submitted to the State legislatures for ratification such an improvement in our Constitution, I suggest two others for your consideration:

First. To authorize the Executive to approve of so much of any measure passing the two Houses of Congress as his judgment may dictate, without approving the whole, the disapproved portion or portions to be subjected to the same rules as now, to wit, to be referred back to the House in which the measure or measures originated, and, if passed by a two-thirds vote of the two Houses, then to become a law without the approval of the President. I would add to this a provision that there should be no legislation by Congress during the last twenty-four hours of its sitting, except upon vetoes, in order to give the Executive an opportunity to examine and approve or disapprove bills understandingly.

Second. To provide by amendment that when an extra session of Congress is convened by Executive proclamation legislation during the continuance of such extra session shall be confined to such subjects as the Executive may bring before it from time to time in writing.[62]

✦ ✦ ✦

I have given very attentive consideration to a resolution of the House of Representatives passed on the 3d of April, requesting the President of the United States to inform the House whether any executive offices, acts, or duties, and, if any, what, have within a specified period been performed at a distance from the seat of Government established by law, etc.

I have never hesitated and shall not hesitate to communicate to Congress, and to either branch thereof, all the information which the Constitution makes it the duty of the President to give, or which my judgment may suggest to me or a request from either House may indicate to me will be useful in the discharge of the appropriate duties confided to them. I fail, however, to find in the Constitution of the United States the authority given to the House of Representatives (one branch of the Congress, in which is vested the legislative power of the Government) to require of the Executive, an independent branch of the Government, coordinate with the Senate and House of Representatives, an account of his discharge of his appropriate and purely executive offices, acts, and duties, either as to when, where, or how performed.

What the House of Representatives may require as a right in its demand upon the Executive for information is limited to what is necessary for the proper discharge of its powers of legislation or of impeachment.

The inquiry in the resolution of the House as to where executive acts have within the last seven years been performed and at what distance from any particular spot or for how long a period at any one time, etc., does not necessarily belong to the province of legislation. It does not profess to be asked for that object.

If this information be sought through an inquiry of the President as to his executive acts in view or in aid of the power of impeachment vested in the House, it is asked in derogation of an inherent natural right, recognized in this country by a constitutional guaranty which protects every citizen, the President as well as the humblest in the land, from being made a witness against himself.

During the time that I have had the honor to occupy the position of President of this Government it has been, and while I continue to occupy that position it will continue to be, my earnest endeavor to recognize and to respect the several trusts and duties and powers of the coordinate branches of the Government, not encroaching upon them nor allowing encroachments upon the proper powers of the office which the people of the United States have confided to me, but aiming to preserve in their proper relations the several powers and functions of each of the coordinate branches of the Government, agreeably to the Constitution and in accordance with the solemn oath which I have taken to "preserve, protect, and defend" that instrument.

In maintenance of the rights secured by the Constitution to the executive branch of the Government I am compelled to decline any specific or detailed answer to the request of the House for information as to "any executive offices, acts, or duties, and, if any, what, have been performed at a distance from the seat of Government established by law, and for how long a period at any one time and in what part of the United States."

If, however, the House of Representatives desires to know whether during the period of upward of seven years during which I have held the office of President of the United States I have been absent from the seat of Government, and whether during that period I have performed or have neglected to perform the duties of my office, I freely inform the House that from the time of my entrance upon my office I have been in the habit, as were all of my predecessors (with the exception of one, who lived only one month after assuming the duties of his office, and one whose continued presence in Washington was necessary from the existence at the time of a powerful rebellion), of absenting myself at times from the seat of Government, and that during such absences I did not neglect or forego the obligations or the duties of my office, but continued to discharge all of the executive offices, acts, and duties which were required of me as the President of the United States. I am not aware that a failure occurred in any one instance of my exercising the functions and powers of my office in every case requiring their discharge, or of my exercising all necessary executive acts, in whatever part of the United States I may at the time have been. Fortunately, the rapidity of travel and of mail communication and the facility of almost instantaneous correspondence with the offices at the seat of Government, which the telegraph afford to the President in whatever section of the Union he may be, enable him in these days to maintain as constant and almost as quick intercourse with the Departments at Washington as may be maintained while he remains at the capital.

The necessity of the performance of executive acts by the President of the United States exists and is devolved upon him, wherever he may be within the United States, during his term of office by the Constitution of the United States.

His civil powers are no more limited or capable of limitation as to the place where they shall be exercised than are those which he might be required to discharge in his capacity of Commander in Chief of the Army and Navy, which latter powers it is evident he might be called upon to exercise, possibly, even without the limits of the United States. Had the efforts of those recently in rebellion against the Government been successful in driving a late President of the United States from Washington, it is manifest that he must have discharged his functions, both civil and military, elsewhere than in the place named by law as the seat of Government.

No act of Congress can limit, suspend, or confine this constitutional duty. I am not aware of the existence of any act of Congress which assumes thus to limit or restrict the exercise of the functions of the Executive. Were there such acts, I should nevertheless recognize the superior authority of the Constitution, and should exercise the powers required thereby of the President.

The act to which reference is made in the resolution of the House relates to the establishing of the seat of Government and the providing of suitable buildings and removal thereto of the offices attached to the Government, etc. It was not understood at its date and by General Washington to confine the President in the discharge of his duties and powers to actual presence at the seat of Government. On the 30th of March, 1791, shortly after the passage of the act referred to, General Washington issued an Executive proclamation having reference to the subject of this very act from Georgetown, a place remote from Philadelphia, which then was the seat of Government, where the act referred to directed that "all offices attached to the seat of Government" should for the time remain.

That none of his successors have entertained the idea that their executive offices could be performed only at the seat of Government is evidenced by the hundreds upon hundreds of such acts performed by my predecessors in unbroken line from Washington to Lincoln, a memorandum of the general nature and character of some of which acts is submitted herewith; and no question has ever been raised as to the validity of those acts or as to the right and propriety of the Executive to exercise the powers of his office in any part of the United States.[63]

HAYES

Upon assembling of this Congress, in pursuance of a call for an extra session, which was made necessary by the failure of the Forty-fifth Congress to make the needful appropriations for the support of the Government, the question was presented whether the attempt made in the last Congress to ingraft by construction a new principle upon the Constitution should be persisted in or not. This Congress has ample opportunity and time to pass the appropriation bills, and also to enact any political measures which may be determined upon in separate bills by the usual and orderly methods of proceeding. But the majority of both Houses have deemed it wise to adhere to the principles asserted and maintained in the last Congress by the majority of the House of Representatives. That principle is that the House of Representatives has the sole right to originate bills for raising revenue, and therefore has the right to withhold appropriations upon which the existence of the Government may depend unless the Senate and the President shall give their assent to any legislation which the House may see fit to attach to appropriation bills. To establish this principle is to make a radical, dangerous, and unconstitutional change in the character of our institutions. The various departments of the Government and the Army and the Navy are established by the Constitution or by laws passed in pursuance thereof. Their duties are clearly defined and their support is carefully provided for by law. The money required for this purpose has been collected from the people and is now in the Treasury, ready to be paid out as soon as the appropriation bills are passed. Whether appropriations are made or not, the collection of the taxes will go on. The public money will accumulate in the Treasury. It was not the intention of the framers of the Constitution that any single branch of the Government should have the power to dictate conditions upon which this treasure should be applied to the purpose for which it was collected. Any such intention, if it had been entertained, would have been plainly expressed in the Constitution.

That a majority of the Senate now concurs in the claim of the House adds to the gravity of the situation, but does not alter the question at issue. The new doctrine, if maintained, will result in a consolidation of unchecked and despotic power in the House of Representatives. A bare majority of the House will become the Government. The Executive will no longer be what the framers of the Constitution intended—an equal and independent branch of the Government. It is clearly the constitutional duty of the President to exercise his discretion and judgment upon all bills presented to him without constraint or duress from any other branch of the Government. To say that a majority of either or both of the Houses of Congress may insist upon the approval of a bill under the penalty of stopping all of the operations of the Government for want of the necessary supplies is to deny to the Executive that share of the legislative power which is plainly conferred by the second section of the seventh article of the Constitution. It strikes from the Constitution the qualified negative of the President. It is said that this should be done because it is the peculiar function of the House of Representatives to represent the will of the people. But no single branch or department of the Government has exclusive authority to speak for the American people. The most authentic and solemn expression of their will is contained in the Constitution of the United States. By that Constitution they have ordained and established a Government whose powers are distributed among coordinate branches, which, as far as possible consistently with a harmonious cooperation, are absolutely independent of each other. The people of this country are unwilling to see the supremacy of the Constitution replaced by the omnipotence of any one department of the Government.

The enactment of this bill into a law will establish a precedent which will tend to destroy the equal independence of the several branches of the Government. Its principle places not merely the Senate and the Executive, but the judiciary also, under the coercive dictation of the House. The House alone will be the judge of what constitutes a grievance, and also of the means and measure of redress. An act of Congress to protect elections is now the grievance complained of; but the House may on the same principle determine that any other act of Congress, a treaty made by the President with the advice and consent of the Senate, a nomination or appointment to office, or that a decision or opinion of the Supreme Court is a grievance, and that the measure of redress is to withhold the appropriations required for the support of the offending branch of the Government.

Believing that this bill is a dangerous violation of the spirit and meaning of the Constitution, I am compelled to return it to the House in which it originated without my approval. The qualified negative with which the Constitution invests the President is a trust that involves a duty which he can not decline to perform. With a firm and conscientious purpose to do what I can to preserve unimpaired the constitutional powers and equal independence, not merely of the Executive, but of every branch of the Government, which will be imperiled by the adoption of the principle of this bill, I desire earnestly to urge upon the House of Representatives a return to the wise and wholesome usage of the earlier days of the Republic, which excluded from appropriation bills all irrelevant legislation. By this course you will inaugurate an important reform in the method of Congressional legislation; your action will be in harmony with the fundamental principles of the Constitution and the patriotic sentiment of nationality which is their firm support, and you will restore to the country that feeling of confidence and security and the repose which are so essential to the prosperity of all of our fellow-citizens.[64]

✓ ✓ ✓

The President under the Constitution is part of the law-making power. The people have willed that no measure shall become a law unless he approves until Congress a second time acts on the bill and by a two-thirds vote passes it again.[65]

✓ ✓ ✓

The Democrats will attempt by coercion of the President to secure a repeal of legislation which I deem wise and important. This is to place the Executive "under the coercive dictation" of a bare majority of the two houses of Congress. This is a mode of evading the constitutional provision as to the President's participation in legislation. It is a "measure of coercion," a revolutionary measure.

I must resist it to the last extremity. I say, first, I object to the repeal of important legislation designed to protect the elections, to secure the purity, the honesty, the sanctity of the ballot-box.

But what is of far more importance, I object to the bill because it is an unconstitutional and revolutionary attempt to deprive the Executive of one of his most important prerogatives; to coerce him to approve a measure which he in fact does not approve. The measure is "attached to an appropriation bill as a means of coercion."

No precedent shall be established with my consent to a measure which is tantamount to coercion of the Executive. I stand for "the equal" and constitutional "independence of the Executive." The independence of the different departments of the Government are [is] essential to the progress and the existence of good government.[66]

✔   ✔   ✔

The repeal, for example, of the discretionary test oath is attached to an appropriation bill as a measure of coercion. I will not consider the merits of the bill so presented. The appropriation bill is essential to the continuance of the Government. It is perfectly well known that the Executive approves it. It is the duty of Congress to pass it. The rider is attached to it to get rid of the constitutional exercise of the veto power to defeat that measure in case the President does not approve it. This is the first attempt in our history to break down the functions of the Executive by coercion. I cannot approve it.[67]

✔   ✔   ✔

The attempt to pass a measure under a menace that the Government shall be stopped if the President declines to yield his convictions of duty has never yet succeeded—has never before been made. To consent to it is to make a radical change in the character of the Government. The House of Representatives, in case this principle is established, becomes the Government. With the sole power to originate the measures upon which the existence of government depends, and with the doctrine established that the House may legitimately refuse to act unless the other branches of the Government obey its commands, the House of Representatives will become a despotism with unlimited power.[68]

✔   ✔   ✔

If the two houses of Congress make the approval of any measure of general legislation a condition without which they will refuse to make the requisite appropriations to carry on the Government, should the President yield to that coercion?[69]

✔   ✔   ✔

But if it is sought to repeal this or any other legislation and to obtain the approval of the President by the threat that Congress will grant no supplies to carry on the Government unless such approval is had, I am compelled by my convictions of duty to use every constitutional authority (means) at my command to prevent the repeal upon such terms.

Every measure should stand or fall on its own merits. This should be the fundamental principle in legislation.[70]

✦ ✦ ✦

The President's right is to exercise his discretion and judgment upon all bills presented to him, without constraint or duress laid upon him by a coordinate branch of the Government.[71]

✦ ✦ ✦

This is a controversy which cannot and ought not to be compromised. The revolutionists claim that a bare majority in the House of Representatives shall control all legislation by tacking the measures they can't pass through the Senate, or over the President's objections, to the appropriation bills which are required to carry on the Government. They claim the right to do this under the Constitution and say it is according to the practice and precedents in England. In the presence of this claim it is idle to talk of compromises as to the particular measures which are used as riders on the appropriation bills. These measures may be wise or unwise. It is enough to say in regard to them, that used as they are to establish a doctrine which overthrows the constitutional distribution of power between the different Departments of the Government, and consolidates in the House of Representatives the whole lawmaking power of the Government, and with it the judicial and executive authority as well, we will not discuss or consider them when they are so presented.

Let the appropriation bills be passed in the usual and orderly course of legislation. Let there be no attempt to coerce either the Senate or the Executive. And then, at the proper time and in the proper way, we will be prepared by repeal or amendment to get rid of whatever is objectionable in the existing legislation. I am not a believer in the continuance of the test oaths. I do not wish to see soldiers either under the state or the national authority at the polls. I would have all of the regulations as to the safeguards of the elections impartial, fair, and economical. But none of these questions ought to be even considered under the revolutionary threat that unless the President yields up his discretion and judgment concerning them, the revolutionists will destroy the Government.

Unquestionably, the true rule of legislation is that each measure should stand or fall on its own merits. This wise and salutary rule has, however, been departed from so often, and the practice has been so long established by the action of all parties, that I may not now insist upon its nonobservance as a ground for withholding my approval to bills submitted to me. There are also, it is believed, several cases in which the House has practically carried its point against the Senate or the Executive by tacking (under pain of losing) the measure to the appropriation bills. But no example has been found in our legislative history in which this has been attempted on the ground that the [whole line blank], until the opening of this controversy at the close of the last Congress.

To tack political measures to appropriation bills and to threaten that no appropriations will be made unless the political measures are approved, is not in my judgment constitutional conduct.[72]

* * *

To incorporate political measures in appropriation bills and think to make the approval of such legislation by the President the condition on which appropriation bills for the support of the Government can alone be passed, is revolutionary and unconstitutional.

To attach conditions to an appropriation bill is revolutionary and unconstitutional. I cannot consent to consider, even to discuss conditions attached to appropriation bills for the purpose— the purpose not disguised, but openly avowed and asserted to be a proper and constitutional exercise of the power of a mere majority in the two houses of Congress—to compel the President to give up his right to exercise his discretion and judgment upon all bills presented to him. It is the principle of coercion embodied in this bill which can under no circumstances receive my approval. It is an attempt to compel the President to approve a measure of general legislation under the penalty of, if he withholds his approval, of stopping the operations of Government by denying the supplies necessary to carry them on.

The object of this struggle is the removal of national authority in any efficient form from the polls, even at national elections. State authority with force at its back, both military and civil, is to be permitted to remain, but all national authority, whether military or civil, is denied.

No case has been presented in the debates on the question in which a bare majority of the two houses of Congress has claimed the right or undertaken to coerce the President by tacking political legislation to appropriation bills.[73]

✦ ✦ ✦

The practice of annexing general legislation to appropriation [bills] has become a serious abuse. Every measure should stand on its own bottom. The two houses of Congress and the Executive should insist upon a return to the old method of legislation on this subject. If there were no other objection to this measure than the fact that it embodies in an appropriation bill, essential to the support of the Government, legislation which is not pertinent to the general purpose of the bill, [that] would be a sufficient objection—the bill having passed by a bare majority vote—to justify the President in withholding his approval of the bill.[74]

✦ ✦ ✦

The executive power to approve or return [bills] without approval, according to the conscience and judgment of the President, is a *trust*. It can't be given away without a violation of official oath.[75]

✦ ✦ ✦

My first veto maintained the prerogatives of the Executive and the separate and independent authority of each branch of it [the Government] against the grasping ambition of the House of Representatives. The second maintained the right of the executive branch to exercise power enough to enforce the laws.[76]

✦ ✦ ✦

The traditions and courtesies of the Senators and Representatives stand in the way of the Executive, however, as defined by the Constitution, and no man who is trained in the congressional school fails to suffer by them in a way that men of merely executive experience know nothing of.[77]

GARFIELD

It better be known in the outset whether the President is the head of the government, or the registering clerk of the Senate.[78]

ARTHUR

Is it not advisable that grants of considerable sums of money for diverse and independent schemes of internal improvement should be made the subjects of separate and distinct legislative enactments? It will scarcely be gainsaid, even by those who favor the most liberal expenditures for such purposes as are sought to be accomplished by what is commonly called the river and harbor bill, that the practice of grouping in such a bill appropriations for a great diversity of objects, widely separated either in their nature or in the locality with which they are concerned, or in both, is one which is much to be deprecated unless it is irremediable. It inevitably tends to secure the success of the bill as a whole though many of the items, if separately considered, could scarcely fail of rejection. By the adoption of the course I have recommended every member of Congress, whenever opportunity should arise for giving his influence and vote for meritorious appropriations, would be enabled so to do without being called upon to sanction others undeserving his approval. So also would the Executive be afforded thereby full opportunity to exercise his constitutional prerogative of opposing whatever appropriations seemed to him objectionable without imperling the success of others which commended themselves to his judgment.[79]

CLEVELAND

The Constitution, which requires those chosen to legislate for the people to annually meet in the discharge of their solemn trust, also requires the President to give to Congress information of the state of the Union and recommend to their consideration such measures as he shall deem necessary and expedient. At the threshold of a compliance with these constitutional directions it is well for us to bear in mind that our usefulness to the people's interests will be promoted by a constant appreciation of the scope and character of our respective duties as they relate to Federal legislation. While the Executive may recommend such measures as he shall deem expedient, the responsibility for legislative action must and should rest upon those selected by the people to make their laws.[80]

✦ ✦ ✦

The Constitution imposes upon the President the duty of recommending to the consideration of Congress from time to time such measures as he shall judge necessary and expedient.

I am so deeply impressed with the importance of immediately and thoughtfully meeting the problem which recent events and a present condition have thrust upon us, involving the settlement of disputes arising between our laboring men and their employers, that I am constrained to recommend to Congress legislation upon this serious and pressing subject.[81]

✔ ✔ ✔

At last it occurred to me that there was nothing in the Constitution which required that the annual message should, as is usual, go over the entire public business. The Constitution only says, that the President "shall from time to time, give to the Congress information of the state of the Union." There was no reason why the message should not be confined to a single subject. I spoke to several persons about it: sometimes they would say at first: "Oh, no, that can't be done;" then after thinking about it, they would say: "But why not? Why certainly, it's a good idea: it is just the thing to do."[82]

✔ ✔ ✔

I am President of all the people, good, bad, or indifferent, and as long as my opinions are known, ought perhaps to keep myself out of their squabbles. I must attempt to cooperate with Congress during another session in the interest of needed legislation, and perhaps ought not to unnecessarily further alienate that body and increase its hatred of me, and if I take an active and affirmatively aggressive position it may aid the cause we have *not* at heart, in increasing the effectiveness of the cry of presidential interference.[83]

BENJAMIN HARRISON

The Constitution provides that the President "shall from time to time give to the Congress information of the state of the Union, and recommend to their consideration such measures as he shall judge necessary and expedient." Out of this provision, as well as the obvious necessity of the case, the annual message of the President has come.[84]

✔ ✔ ✔

The President, by the power of the veto, becomes a very large factor in determining whether a bill shall become a law.[85]

✔ ✔ ✔

If Congress adjourns before the expiration of the ten days given to the President for the consideration of a bill, and he does not sign it, but retains it without action, it fails, as has been said. This is called a "pocket veto." It will be seen, therefore, that as to bills presented to the President during the last ten days of a session of Congress his veto is an absolute, not a qualified, one. He has only to do nothing, and the bill fails. The object clearly was to secure to the President proper time for the examination of all bills. If a flood of bills could be thrown upon him in the last ten days of the session, thus depriving him of a proper time for examining them, and they were to become laws unless he stated his objections in veto messages, it would practically abrogate, as to many bills, the veto power. In fact, just such a flood of bills is usually passed, many in the very last hours of the session, when the attendance in the Houses is small, the members wearied by night sessions, and many of the leading members absent from their seats, serving on conference committees. Every interval in the consideration of the appropriation bills is eagerly watched for and utilized by members who have some personal relief bill or some bill of a local character that they want to get through. This hasty legislation needs especial scrutiny, and it is well that when he is in doubt, and has no time to investigate, the President can use the "pocket veto."[86]

✦ ✦ ✦

There is another practice in legislation that greatly restrains the freedom of the President in using the veto power. What are called "riders" are often placed on general appropriation bills— that is, legislation of a general character, having nothing to do with appropriations, is put into an appropriation bill. This is equivalent to saying to the President, "Give your approval to this general legislation or go without the appropriations necessary to carry on the government." President Hayes resisted attempts by this method to impair the Constitutional powers of the Executive, and vetoed five appropriation bills because general legislation had been incorporated to which he could not give his assent.[87]

✦ ✦ ✦

There are other practical restraints upon the freedom of the President in the exercise of the veto power. Very many laws contain more than one proposition—some a number of such—and the President must deal with them as thus associated. In each of the great appropriation bills many hundreds of distinct appropriations are made. Some of these the President may think to be wrong, either as matter of policy, or of Constitutional power; but he cannot single these out; he must deal with the bill as a whole.[88]

✦ ✦ ✦

It has been much contended that the veto was given to enable the President to defeat legislative attempts to encroach upon his Constitutional powers, and to protect those of the Judiciary; and that he should use the veto only where he finds Constitutional objections to a bill. But the power is not so limited, and from the beginning has been exercised upon the ground of the inexpediency or unwisdom of the legislation proposed, as well as upon Constitutional grounds. The President, however, does not deal with bills submitted for his approval upon the principle that he should approve only such as he would have voted for if he had been a member of Congress. Much deference is due to the Congress, and vetoes have customarily been used only when the fault in the proposed legislation was serious in itself, or as a precedent. Washington used the veto but twice; once for Constitutional objections, and once for reasons affecting only the wisdom and expediency of the bill.[89]

✦ ✦ ✦

A proposition that the officer impeached should be suspended from office pending the trial was wisely rejected by the [constitutional] convention, and the officer now continues to exercise his office until a judgment of conviction is entered. The other rule would have put it in the power of the House of Representatives to suspend the President from office and to cast the office temporarily upon another. This would have fatally weakened the Executive and offered to partisanship a dangerous temptation.[90]

McKINLEY

It has been the uniform practice of each President to avoid, as far as possible, the convening of Congress in extraordinary session. It is an example which, under ordinary circumstances and in the absence of a public necessity, is to be commended. But a failure to convene the representatives of the people in Congress in extra session when it involves neglect of a public duty places the responsibility of such neglect upon the Executive himself.[91]

THEODORE ROOSEVELT

The President can recommend the passage of legislation and set forth the need of it . . . If the people at large, and therefore their representatives in Congress, take an interest in the subject and back up the President the laws will pass. If they do not take the interest in the subject, there is nothing he can do that will secure their passage. I very earnestly wish that the philanthropic people who take, as they ought to take, a disinterested concern in matters of genuine public importance . . . would learn to appreciate the limitations on the President's power and the line dividing what he can do from what he cannot.[92]

*   *   *

It is eminently desirable that the President and the majority leaders in Congress shall be in such touch that the President will back whatever legislation they put through and will not veto it, even though, as of course must be the case, he continually disapproves of things more or less substantial in the various bills. So it is eminently desirable that the State Department shall be in such close touch with the leaders and the Senate committee on foreign affairs that they shall be able to agree in substance in advance upon what shall be done in treaties, and we shall be spared—and that without regard to which side is at fault—the irritation and indeed the humiliation of starting to negotiate treaties, of committing ourselves to them in the eyes of foreign people, and then of failing to put them through; and what is even more important, prevent treaties which are important from the standpoint of national policy from getting into such shape that the one country or the other refuses to ratify them. I don't want to start anything the Senate won't approve.[93]

*   *   *

Some of the things the Senate does really work to increase the power of the Executive. They are able so effectually to hold up action when they are consulted, and are so slow about it, that they force a President who has any strength to such individual action as I took in both Panama and Santo Domingo. In neither case would a President a hundred years ago have ventured to act without previous assent by the Senate. But though in each case I should have had the hearty support of the best men in the Senate, including an enormous majority of my own party, yet the opposition, from inertness, timidity, from the spirit of mere academic doctrinaire opposition, and from ignorant and ferocious partisanship, had produced a condition which rendered it in my opinion necessary to try a course of some little hazard. In this nation, as in any nation which amounts to anything, those in the end must govern who are willing actually to do the work of governing; and in so far as the Senate becomes a merely obstructionist body it will run the risk of seeing its power pass into other hands.[94]

✓ ✓ ✓

. . . the President looks at things from the national standpoint and the Senator naturally looks at things from his own special standpoint and therefore may at any time vote to reject a treaty which is greatly for the national good as a whole because there is some special interest in his locality which is hurt.[95]

✓ ✓ ✓

I have a very strong feeling that it is a President's duty to get on with Congress if he possibly can, and that it is a reflection upon him if he and Congress come to a complete break.[96]

✓ ✓ ✓

The President's duty is to act so that he himself and his subordinates shall be able to do efficient work for the people, and this efficient work he and they cannot do if Congress is permitted to undertake the task of making up his mind for him as to how he shall perform what is clearly his sole duty.[97]

TAFT

I think, too, it would have been better to bring the Executive a little closer in touch with Congress in the initiation of legislation and its discussion, notably in the matter of budgets and the economical administration of governmental affairs.[98]

✓ ✓ ✓

It is true that a parliamentary government offers an opportunity for greater effectiveness in that the same mind or minds control the executive and the legislative action, and the one can be closely suited to the other; whereas our President has no initiative in respect to legislation given him by law except that of mere recommendation, and no method of entering into the argument and discussion of the proposed legislation while pending in Congress, except that of a formal message or address. To one charged with the responsibilities of the President, especially where he has party pledges to perform, this seems a defect, but whatever I thought while in office, I am inclined now to think that the defect is more theoretical than actual. It usually happens that the party which is successful in electing a President is also successful in electing a Congress to sustain him. The natural party cohesion and loyalty, and a certain power and prestige which the President has when he enters office, make his first Congress one in which he can exercise much influence in the framing and passage of legislation to fulfil party promises.[99]

✓ ✓ ✓

But it is said that not infrequently the second Congress of an administration contains a majority politically adverse to the President in either one or both of its Houses which makes affirmative legislation impossible and limits congressional action to appropriation bills and nonpolitical measures, if there are any such. The President in such a case naturally chafes under his inability to put through important bills, which he deems of the highest value.[100]

✓ ✓ ✓

The President has both legislative and executive power. Among his executive functions we shall find those which are purely executive and those which are quasi-legislative and are quasi-judicial.

The character of the veto power is purely legislative. The Constitution provides that after both Houses shall have passed a bill, it shall be presented to the President; that if he approve it, he shall sign it, but, if not, that he shall return it, with his objection, to the House in which it originated, which shall proceed to reconsider it; and that if two-thirds of the House agree to pass the bill, it shall be sent with the objections of the President to the other House, where it shall be reconsidered, and if approved by two-thirds of that House, it shall become a law.

It has been suggested by some that the veto power is executive. I do not quite see how. Of course the President has no power to introduce a bill into either House. He has the power of recommending such measures as he shall judge necessary and expedient to the consideration of Congress. But he takes no part in the running discussion of the bill after it is introduced or in its amendments. He has no power to veto parts of the bill and allow the rest to become a law. He must accept it or reject it, and his rejection of it is not final unless he can find one more than one-third of one of the Houses to sustain him in his veto. But even with these qualifications, he is still a participant in the legislation. Except for his natural and proper anxiety not to oppose the will of the two great legislative bodies, and to have harmony in the government, the reasons which control his action must be much like those which affect the action of the members of Congress.[101]

↗ ↗ ↗

It has been contended that the President may not exercise the veto power except when the bill presented to him is unconstitutional. Such a view of his duty is supposed to find color of support in a proposal made and strongly advocated in the Constitutional Convention. It provided for the revision of bills which had passed both Houses by a Council, to include the President and the Supreme Judges, with the power to reject bills which had passed both Houses when they transgressed the constitutional limits of Congressional discretion. It cannot be said, however, that the provision for the Executive veto as adopted in the Constitution implies any such limitation. It is true that the power is one of negation only, but the history of its origin shows that even in its qualified form it is legislative in its nature, a brake rather than a steam chest, but nevertheless a very important part of the machinery for making laws. The Constitution makes the President's veto turn on the question whether he approves the bill or not. The term "approve" is much too broad to be given the narrow construction by which it shall only authorize the President to withhold his signature when the reason for his disapproval of the bill is its invalidity. No better word could be found in the language to embrace the idea of passing on the merits of the bill. If anything has been established by actual precedents, it is that a President in signing or withholding signature, must consider the wisdom of the bill as one of those responsible for its character and effect.[102]

↗ ↗ ↗

In the exercise of the veto power, the truth is that it often happens that the President more truly represents the entire country than does the majority vote of the two Houses. His constituency is the electorate of the United States, and by reason of of that he is much freer from the influence of local prejudices and of the play of those special territorial and state interests, which, brought together by log-rolling methods, sometimes constitute a majority in both Houses for extravagant or unwise legislation.[103]

✓ ✓ ✓

In considering a bill presented to him for signature, it is the duty of the President of course to veto a bill no matter how much he approves its expediency, if he believes that it is contrary to the constitutional limitations upon the power of Congress. He has taken an oath to the best of his ability "to preserve, protect and defend the Constitution of the United States," and he cannot escape his obligation to do so when the question before him is whether he shall approve the bill passed by both Houses which violates the Constitution he has given his plighted faith to maintain and enforce. His duty is as high and exacting in this matter as is the duty of the Supreme Court of the United States.[104]

✓ ✓ ✓

The Constitution provides that if the President does not return the bill presented to him within ten days (Sundays excepted) after its presentation, it is to become law just as if he had signed it, unless Congress by adjourning prevents its return, in which case it is not to become a law. This enables the President, at the close of a session, when bills are presented to him in great number, and when he usually goes to the Capitol for the purpose of signing them, just before the adjournment of Congress, to defeat a bill by what is called a pocket veto, that is by failing to sign it. If he does not return it to Congress with his objections, there is no opportunity for Congress to pass it over his veto, and therefore his failure to sign is final.[105]

✓ ✓ ✓

The language of the Constitution with reference to what the President shall do with a bill leaves only two alternatives, one that if he approve it, he shall sign it, the other that if he does not approve it, he shall return it with his objections to Congress. It does provide that if he fails to return it within ten days, it shall become a law, but this would seem to be only a provision for his neglect. In practice, however, some Presidents have allowed bills to become law without their signature, with the idea, I presume, that their objections to the bill do not justify a veto . . . My own judgment is that the wiser course in such a case is for the President to sign the bill, with a memorandum of his reasons for doing so, in spite of his objections.[106]

✔ ✔ ✔

The Federal Executive veto does not include the power to veto a part of a bill. The lack of such a power in the President has enabled Congress at times to bring to bear a pressure on him to permit legislation to go through that otherwise he would veto. Appropriation bills are necessary for the life of the government, and if Congress by putting what is called a "rider" of general legislation on one of these says, "We'll hamstring the government in respect to the departments that these appropriation bills support, unless you consent to this," puts the President in an embarrassing situation.[107]

✔ ✔ ✔

While for some purposes, it would be useful for the Executive to have the power of partial veto, if we could always be sure of its wise and conscientious exercise, I am not entirely sure that it would be a safe provision. It would greatly enlarge the influence of the President, already large enough from patronage and party loyalty and other causes. I am inclined to think that it is better to trust to the action of the people in condemning the party which becomes responsible for such riders, than to give, in such a powerful instrument like this, a temptation to its sinister use by a President eager for continued political success. This use by Congress of riders upon appropriation bills to force a President to consent to legislation which he disapproves shows a spirit of destructive factionalism and a lack of a sense of responsibility for the maintenance of the government.[108]

✔ ✔ ✔

The power and duty of the President to inform Congress on the state of the Union, and to recommend measures for its adoption, need very little comment, except to say that President Washington and President Adams treated the discharge of this duty as the occasion for visiting Congress in person and delivering their communications orally . . . Jefferson had no pleasure or facility in public speaking. When he came into the office of President, therefore, he preferred to send to Congress written messages, and his practice was so formidable a precedent that this has been the custom of the Presidents down to the present administration, when President Wilson has introduced again the old practice of a personal address to both Houses. I think the change is a good one. Oral addresses fix the attention of the country on Congress more than written communications, and by fixing the attention of the country on Congress, they fix the attention of Congress on the recommendations of the President.[109]

✦ ✦ ✦

No one has as good opportunity to know Senators and Congressmen as the President, because in asking the Presidential favor, the Senator or Congressman frequently bares his motives and discloses his inmost traits of character in the confidence and secrecy of the Executive office. It is more or less an unconscious confessional. It enables the President to measure the characters of men in public life.[110]

✦ ✦ ✦

In theory, the Executive power and the Legislative power are independent and separate, but it is not always easy to draw the line and to say where Legislative control and direction to the Executive must cease, and where his independent discretion begins. In theory, all the Executive officers appointed by the President directly or indirectly are his subordinates, and yet Congress can undoubtedly pass laws definitely limiting their discretion and commanding a certain course by them which it is not within the power of the Executive to vary. Fixing the method in which Executive power shall be exercised is perhaps one of the chief functions of Congress. Indeed, by its legislation, it often creates a duty in the Executive which did not before exist. Then in prescribing how that duty is to be carried out, it imposes restrictions that the Executive is bound to observe.[111]

✦ ✦ ✦

In the matter of appointments, Presidents have been quick to resent encroachments by Congress. The power of appointment is not in Congress.[112]

✦ ✦ ✦

The President is required by the Constitution from time to time to give to Congress information on the state of the Union, and to recommend for its consideration such measures as he shall judge necessary and expedient, but this does not enable Congress or either House of Congress to elicit from him confidential information which he has acquired for the purpose of enabling him to discharge his constitutional duties, if he does not deem the disclosure of such information prudent or in the public interest.[113]

HOOVER

Never has there been a session of Congress when somebody did not waste vast energy building a Scylla and a Charybdis for the President to navigate, or did not elaborately spread those old traps known as the devil and the deep blue sea. At various points in every important debate the opposition never fails to call vigorously upon the Executive to exert leadership, to give direction, to use the big stick. If he yields to these temptations, he is immediately discovered to be meddling in the responsibilities of the independent arm of the Government. This is the oldest form of the devil-and-deep-blue-sea trap.[114]

✓ ✓ ✓

There has been an increasing ascendancy of the Executive over the Legislative arm, which has run to great excesses. The President's veto was not often used in the first seventy years of the Republic as legislative power but was held as a safeguard of constitutionality of legislation. Gradually this power of the veto has expanded until he possesses one-third of the legislative authority. Far from merely advising Congress, he is expected to blast reforms out of it. With the growth of the Federal expenditure the Congress has lost much of its control of the purse, the original citadel of parliamentary power.[115]

✓ ✓ ✓

Thus one of the astonishing evidences of legislative weakening has been the surrender of the parliamentary principle that the control of the purse was the surest check upon the Executive for which parliaments have fought and men have died over centuries. In place of this hard-won legislative control we have now the curious idea that the Executive must protect the people from legislative endeavors to please group and sectional interests by huge and wasteful expenditures. It evidences an enormous surrender and shift of powers.[116]

ꜰ ꜰ ꜰ

This rise of personal power of the President over the last seven years has been accomplished by the disastrous weakening of the legislative and judicial branches.

The sinister word "must" still rings in our ears. Legislative action has been repeatedly jammed through without debate or consideration. Nobody will deny that the majority of the Congress have been reduced to a rubber stamp for the Executive. They don't deny it themselves.[117]

ꜰ ꜰ ꜰ

The structure of our government makes the responsibility of the President and the legislative body entirely independent, and for good reasons. Our Cabinet, in fact, is only a body of operating vice presidents, in charge of administrative departments, and meets for purposes of coordinating administrative action. It has no power over the President. It has no power to originate presidential policies. It is sometimes an advisory body, depending on the President. An American Coalition Cabinet would have no effective part in formulating presidential policies even in war, unless the President would bind himself to abide by the joint and collective vote of the Cabinet. That he would not do.[118]

ꜰ ꜰ ꜰ

But Presidents cannot always kick evil-minded persons out of the front door. Such persons are often selected by the electors to represent them.[119]

ꜰ ꜰ ꜰ

The President does not make the laws. He is required to call public needs to the consideration of Congress.[120]

FRANKLIN D. ROOSEVELT

It is to be hoped that the normal balance of Executive and legislative authority may be wholly adequate to meet the unprecedented task before us. But it may be that an unprecedented demand and need for undelayed action may call for temporary departure from that normal balance of public procedure.

I am prepared under my constitutional duty to recommend the measures that a stricken Nation in the midst of a stricken world may require. These measures, or such other measures as the

Congress may build out of its experience and wisdom, I shall seek, within my constitutional authority, to bring to speedy adoption.

But in the event that the Congress shall fail to take one of these two courses, and in the event that the national emergency is still critical, I shall not evade the clear course of duty that will then confront me. I shall ask the Congress for the one remaining instrument to meet the crisis—broad Executive power to wage a war against the emergency, as great as the power that would be given to me if we were in fact invaded by a foreign foe.

For the trust reposed in me I will return the courage and the devotion that befit the time. I can do no less.[121]

✦ ✦ ✦

The members of Congress realized that the methods of normal times had to be replaced in the emergency by measures which were suited to the serious and pressing requirements of the moment. There was no actual surrender of power, Congress still retained its constitutional authority, and no one has the slightest desire to change the balance of these powers. The function of Congress is to decide what has to be done and to select the appropriate agency to carry out its will. To this policy it has strictly adhered. The only thing that has been happening has been to designate the President as the agency to carry out certain of the purposes of the Congress. This was constitutional and in keeping with the past American tradition.[122]

✦ ✦ ✦

Before the adjournment of the Special Session I want to convey to you and to the members of the House of Representatives an expression of my thanks for making possible, on the broad average, a more sincere and whole-hearted cooperation between the legislative and the executive branches of the United States Government than has been witnessed by the American people in many a long year.

This spirit of teamwork has in most cases transcended party lines. It has taken cognizance of a crisis in the affairs of our Nation and of the world. It has grasped the need for a new approach to problems both new and old. It has proven that our form of government can rise to an emergency and can carry through a broad program in record time.[123]

✓ ✓ ✓

But we also were in general agreement with the thought that Congress should, in some way, keep in touch with the administrative procedure from day to day and week to week through the year. In other words—now this is off the record just so as to give you the thought in the back of my head—it would be a great deal better for the Government as a whole if Congress could keep in very close touch with the operations of the administrative branch of the Government right straight through the year. The custom in the past has been for Congress, every once in so often, to conduct an investigation which goes back two or three or four or five years. It doesn't do anybody any particular good, because, if the Administration is doing anything it should not do, it would be a great deal better to have it known right away.

So, for a long time, I have been trying to work out some practical method of keeping the Congress in touch, day in and day out, with what the Administration is doing, so that there won't be an accumulation of things which may result after a long period of years in scandal or investigation. At the same time we could keep perfectly clear the separation of functions.[124]

✓ ✓ ✓

And then he [Theodore Roosevelt] clenched his fist and said, "Sometimes I wish I could be President and Congress too."

Well, I suppose if the truth were told, he is not the only President that has had that idea.[125]

✓ ✓ ✓

The proper legislative function is to fix the amount of expenditure, the means by which it is to be raised and the general principles under which the expenditures are to be made. The details of expenditure, particularly in view of the great present emergency [the Depression], can be more wisely and equitably administered through the Executive.[126]

✓ ✓ ✓

For the first time in our national history a President delivers his Annual Message to a new Congress within a fortnight of the expiration of his term of office. While there is no change in the Presidency this year, change will occur in future years. It is my belief that under this new constitutional practice, the President

should in every fourth year, in so far as seems reasonable, review the existing state of our national affairs and outline broad
future problems, leaving specific recommendations for future
legislation to be made by the President about to be inaugurated.[127]

*In 1937, the beginning of new presidential terms was advanced from
March 4 to January 20.*

✓ ✓ ✓

On the Congress of the United States falls the primary responsibility for the adoption of methods, but on the President
falls the responsibility of recommending objectives. This is in
accordance with the Constitution.[128]

✓ ✓ ✓

About two months ago you wrote me in regard to the problem
of the "item veto." Since then I have talked with Alben Barkley
and he agrees with us that riders are foreign to the objectives of
appropriation bills or other specific subject legislation; that they
constitute a bad practice and that the President ought to have,
as many Governors have, the right to veto such a rider without
having to veto the whole bill.[129]

✓ ✓ ✓

I want you to know that I completely agree with your criticism of legislative "riders" on tax and appropriation bills. Regardless of the merits or demerits of any such "riders"—and I do
not enter that phase of the discussion at the moment—the manifest fact remains that this practice robs the Executive of legitimate and essential freedom of action in dealing with legislation.[130]

✓ ✓ ✓

Appropriation item veto: An important feature of the fiscal
procedure in the majority of our States is the authority given to
the Executive to withhold approval of individual items in an appropriation bill, and, while approving the remainder of the bill to
return such rejected items for the further consideration of the
legislature. This grant of power has been considered a consistent corollary of the power of the legislature to withhold approval of items in the Budget of the Executive; and the system
meets with general approval in the many States which have

adopted it. A respectable difference of opinion exists as to whether a similar item-veto power could be given to the President by legislation or whether a constitutional amendment would be necessary. I strongly recommend that the present Congress adopt whichever course it may deem to be the correct one.[131]

✓ ✓ ✓

The primary obligation and responsibility for determining the general objectives and direction of any administration naturally lie with the President himself. However, he can do little alone, without the cooperation of the Congress.[132]

✓ ✓ ✓

The inclusion of tariff revisions as parts of or as riders on other legislation creates a difficult situation for the Congress and a much more difficult situation for the Executive. It imposes upon the President the necessity of accepting tariff rate revisions which he may consider contrary to the public interest in order to preserve the main legislation. His only alternative is to veto the whole act and thereby delay and perhaps endanger the desirable and major portions of the Act.[133]

✓ ✓ ✓

It is not correct to infer that legislative powers have been transferred from the Congress to the Executive Branch of the Government. Everyone recognizes that general tariff legislation is a Congressional function; but we know that, because of the stupendous task involved in the fashioning and the passing of a general tariff law, it is advisable to provide at times of emergency some flexibility to make the general law adjustable to quickly changing conditions.[134]

✓ ✓ ✓

The Congress and the Chief Executive constitute a team where the defense of the land is concerned.[135]

✓ ✓ ✓

This system of attaching riders to bills relating to a wholly different subject has been used by former Congresses in a number of notable cases. Such abuses of sound legislative procedure have been protested by many former Presidents, and the practice has been condemned by sound opinion.[136]

TRUMAN

The Constitution has placed upon the President the duty of considering bills for approval or disapproval. It has always been possible for the Congress to hamper the President's exercise of this duty by combining so many subjects into a single bill that he can not disapprove an objectionable item without holding up necessary legislation.[137]

✶ ✶ ✶

The President bears the responsibility for recommending to the Congress a comprehensive set of proposals on all Government activities and their financing. In formulating policies, as in preparing budgetary estimates, the Nation and the Congress have the right to expect the President to adjust and coordinate the views of the various departments and agencies to form a unified program.[138]

✶ ✶ ✶

Congressional criticisms are heard, not infrequently, concerning deficiencies in the Executive Branch of the Government. I should be less than frank if I failed to point out that the Congress cannot consistently advance such criticisms and at the same time deny the President the means of removing the causes at the root of such criticisms.[139]

✶ ✶ ✶

As a practical proposition, the executive branch of the government can no more operate by itself than can the Congress. There have always been a few congressmen who act as if they would like to control everything on the executive side, but they find out differently when the responsibility of administration is on their shoulders. But no President has ever attempted to govern alone. Every President knows and must know that the congressional control of the purse has to be reckoned with. And so Presidents, as a practical proposition, have usually leaned over backward in providing the Congress with information about the operations of the executive departments.[140]

✶ ✶ ✶

Congress, of course, is anxious to obtain as many facts as it can; most of the time this is for legitimate reasons of legislation, but sometimes it is for the sole purpose of embarrassing and hamstringing the President—in other words, for partisan political reasons. When that happens, it is the President's solemn duty to resist the demands for fishing expeditions into his private files. Not even the so-called weak Presidents would stand for it.[141]

✓ ✓ ✓

Whenever the President of the United States finds it necessary to veto a major bill which has been approved by both Houses of the Congress, he is sure to find himself in the center of a bitter controversy involving large groups both inside and outside the federal government.[142]

✓ ✓ ✓

The veto power of the President is one of the most important instruments of his authority, even though the legislation he rejects may later be passed over his veto by the Congress. In the veto message the Chief Executive has an opportunity to set forth clearly and in detail before the nation the policies of his administration.[143]

✓ ✓ ✓

One important lack in the presidential veto power, I believe, is authority to veto individual items in appropriations bills. The President must approve the bill in its entirety, or refuse to approve it, or let it become law without his approval. He cannot veto any separate item of which he may disapprove, for fear of killing an otherwise sound piece of legislation.[144]

EISENHOWER

It has long been recognized that to assist the Congress in achieving its legislative purposes every Executive Department or Agency must, upon the request of a Congressional Committee, expeditiously furnish information relating to any matter within the jurisdiction of the Committee, with certain historical exceptions—some of which are pointed out in the attached memorandum from the Attorney General. This Administration has been and will continue to be diligent in following this principle. However, it is essential to the successful working of our system that the persons entrusted with power in any one of the three great branches of Government shall not encroach upon the authority confided to the others. The ultimate responsibility for the conduct of the Executive Branch rests with the President.

Within this Constitutional framework each branch should cooperate fully with each other for the common good. However, throughout our history the President has withheld information whenever he found that what was sought was confidential or its disclosure would be incompatible with the public interest or jeopardize the safety of the Nation.

Because it is essential to efficient and effective administration that employees of the Executive Branch be in a position to be completely candid in advising with each other on official matters, and because it is not in the public interest that any of their conversations or communications, or any documents or reproductions, concerning such advice be disclosed, you will instruct employees of your Department that in all of their appearances before the Subcommittee of the Senate Committee on Government Operations regarding the inquiry now before it they are not to testify to any such conversations or communications or to produce any such documents or reproductions. This principle must be maintained regardless of who would be benefitted by such disclosures.[145]

✦ ✦ ✦

History shows that when the Executive and Legislative Branches are politically in conflict, politics in Washington runs riot. In these conditions, the public good goes begging while politics is played for politics' sake. Meanwhile, in the eyes of the world, we appear divided in council and uncertain in purpose.[146]

✦ ✦ ✦

The Congress has the power and the right to grant or to deny an appropriation. But once an appropriation is made the appropriation must, under the Constitution, be administered by the executive branch of the Government alone, and the Congress has no right to confer upon its committees the power to veto Executive action or to prevent Executive action from becoming effective.

Since the organization of our Government, the President has felt bound to insist that Executive functions be maintained unimpaired by legislative encroachment, just as the legislative branch has felt bound to resist interference with its power by the Executive.[147]

⚑ ⚑ ⚑

Now, what I do want to make clear is this: I most earnestly believe that the Congress and the White House should be occupied and controlled by the same party, whenever this is humanly possible that this could be done, for the reason then you can fix responsibility. We get into the picture of who is taking credit for what. I recall in the last election that some of the other party were claiming credit for having thought of the soil bank first, and now this year the soil bank money has been cut out in the House. Incidentally, I hope it will be restored in the Senate.

But, the point is: who is responsible for these things in the minds of the people? And I believe, therefore, that a President should stand for the organization of the House and the Senate by his party; and to that extent, of course, I am for whoever the Republicans of any particular State or district nominate. But when it comes down to who I am for enthusiastically, and who I am for merely because they are Republican, there is a very wide difference.[148]

⚑ ⚑ ⚑

Mostly the work of a President with Congress in my opinion is done in a quiet conversational way by the telephone and informal meetings. You don't influence Congress, in my opinion, by threats, by anything except trying to convince them of the soundness and the logic of your views.[149]

⚑ ⚑ ⚑

After careful consideration of the requests from your and several other committees for the so-called Killian and Gaither Panel reports, I have concluded that I cannot properly furnish these reports to the Congress or release them for publication.

In reaching this decision I am mindful of the need for the branches of our government to cooperate with each other for the common good within the Constitutional framework, and accordingly Executive Branch witnesses have not sought to withhold any information pertinent to your inquiry. However, throughout our history the President has withheld information whenever he found that what was sought was confidential or that its disclosure would jeopardize the nation's safety or the proper functioning of our Government.

I mention this consideration because of my conviction, which I am sure you share, that in such a matter as this we must be careful to maintain the proper separation of powers between the Executive and Legislative Branches of the Government. This separation is vital to preclude the exercise of arbitrary power by any one branch of government. This thought I believe we should keep in mind in relation to my decision not to release the Killian and Gaither Panel reports.

As for these reports specifically, you realize, of course, that from time to time the President invites groups of specially qualified citizens to advise him on complex problems. These groups give this advice after intensive study, with the understanding that their advice will be kept confidential. Only by preserving the confidential nature of such advice is it possible to assemble such groups or for the President to avail himself of such advice.[150]

✓ ✓ ✓

Well, now, to say when you will veto something, when you will not, is a very difficult thing to decide in advance of the event, because you know this: we do not have the item veto where you could be quite specific about such things. Also, we have a habit of taking a bill that is a very necessary one, a good one, and by some maneuvering get into it various types of what I would call undesirable legislation. Now, the problem is very difficult for the Executive—what are you vetoing and what do you do when you do take this action?

After all, the Constitution puts the President right square into the legislative business by saying he must approve legislation after it is enacted; and then there is, of course, a method for the overriding. So he can't escape his responsibility.[151]

✓ ✓ ✓

When it comes down to the relations of any President with a Congress controlled by the opposite party, I just say this: it is no bed of roses.[152]

✓ ✓ ✓

I have said time and again that it is clear that I am, or the Presidency is, a part of the legislative process, so stated by the Constitution; it states just exactly how he may act and then what Congress can do.

And if he didn't exercise his own judgment as to what is best for this country in this case, I think he'd be derelict of his duty; that's what I think he is.[153]

✦ ✦ ✦

Future Presidents should have the authority to veto items of appropriation measures without the necessity of disapproving an entire appropriation bill. Many Presidents have recommended that this authority be given to our Chief Executive, and more than 80% of the States have given it to their Governors. It is a necessary procedure for strengthening fiscal responsibility. As in the case of other vetoes, the Congress should have the authority to override an item veto.[154]

✦ ✦ ✦

Our people expect their President and the Congress to find essential agreement on issues of great moment, the wise resolution of which will better shape the future of the Nation.[155]

✦ ✦ ✦

If a President had a Congress, like that of, say, Mr. Roosevelt's, in the early years of his Administrations, well, they were quite ready to go along with everything he wanted to do. The country was in an emergency and they followed along—the first hundred days of his Administration were almost fabulous in the amount of legislation that was brought about. But even in the first two years of my Administration, for example, we came into power—the Republicans did—for the first time in twenty years. There was not a single Republican in the Senate, when I came in, who had ever served under a Republican President. Now, as a result, they were raised in this tradition of antagonism between the Executive and the Legislature, and it was very, very difficult for Republican Senators, at first, to remember that their job was now to cooperate with the President and he with them. On the contrary, they felt they had to cut him down at first. It was instinctive. Our party frequently was split in the Congress, and indeed, the only way I could get anything constructive done in the last six years of my two terms, was to get some kind of Democratic help, or otherwise, I couldn't pass anything, and sometimes that help was given even enthusiastically, and I was very grateful for it, but it had to be done with a hostile Congress. I mean, it's politically hostile—not personally. And this takes a different kind of strength and of patience, and of work, than it does when a man has everything his own way—just pound the table and say, "Now this, or else."[156]

✦ ✦ ✦

There's no possibility of the Congress limiting the powers of the President. And the President, once—if he's got the authority to act, there's nobody that could stop. He could have—one hundred per cent of his staff can be against him and his decision is final. And so, it is merely said "if the President shall determine." That's all there is to it.[157]

✦ ✦ ✦

This [Congressional] investigation process often seeks publicity. I had a number of those cases, and as a matter of fact, every President, so far as I know—I know George Washington did and every other President has had to say, "Here, the vital interest of the United States or its very security is involved, and I will not give you these records." Now, they've tried a number of ways of breaking down that executive privilege by saying, "You cannot use certain amounts of money for certain amounts of purposes unless you give the information that we want." Well, that's unconstitutional, in my opinion, and I never gave way to that. I just wouldn't let them get away with it.[158]

KENNEDY

It is much easier in many ways for me—and for other Presidents, I think, who felt the same way—when Congress is not in town. . . .[159]

✦ ✦ ✦

Our Constitution wisely assigns both joint and separate roles to each branch of the government; and a President and a Congress who hold each other in mutual respect will neither permit nor attempt any trespass. For my part, I shall withhold from neither the Congress nor the people any fact or report, past, present, or future, which is necessary for an informed judgment of our conduct and hazards. I shall neither shift the burden of executive decisions to the Congress, nor avoid responsibility for the outcome of those decisions.[160]

✐ ✐ ✐

So that they are two separate offices and two separate powers, the Congress and the Presidency. There's bound to be conflict. But they must cooperate to the degree that's possible. But that's why no President's program is ever put in. The only time a President's program is put in quickly and easily is when the program is insignificant. But if it's significant and affects important interests and is controversial, therefore, then there's a fight and then the President is never wholly successful.[161]

✐ ✐ ✐

It's a tremendous change to go from being a Senator to being President. The first months it's a—are very difficult—but I have no reason to believe that a President with the powers of this office and responsibilities placed on it, if he has the judgment, and something needs to be done, I think he can do it just as well a second time as the first, depending of course on the makeup of the Congress. The fact is, I think the Congress looks more powerful, sitting here, than it did when I was there in the Congress. But that's because when you're in Congress you're one of a hundred in the Senate, or one of 435 in the House. So that your power is so divided. But from here I look at a Congress, and I look at the collective power of the Congress, particularly to block action, which, if it wants to, is substantial power.[162]

✐ ✐ ✐

Congressmen are always advising Presidents to get rid of presidential advisers. That's one of the most constant threads that run through American history, and Presidents ordinarily do not pay attention.[163]

Chapter V

THE PRESIDENCY AND THE JUDICIARY

Although there are few aspects of the presidency that have at times attracted greater interest than its relationship with the judiciary, particularly the Supreme Court, the Presidents have been notably abstemious in their writings on the subject.

Actually there is more adequate historic explanation for this than sensitivity about the separation of powers—as witness the voluminous and often gratuitous presidential comments on the Congress. The facts of the matter are that the number of Presidents whom the forces of history (far more than any conflict of personality) have put in crucial opposition to the Supreme Court has been limited to a very few; that, though it has taken from time to time a very stern view of the limits of Congressional powers and, beginning with *Marbury* v. *Madison* in 1803, has never hesitated to spell them out, the Supreme Court has been notably reluctant to treat even the implied powers of the presidency quite so categorically; and, finally, that the Supreme Court has, for the most part, tended to share the view of the strong and active Presidents that, far from being inhibited by the Constitution's failure to specify precise powers of the President, presidential action can be greatly enlarged by such omissions. The Court has, generally, been a source of support for Theodore Roosevelt's doctrine that the President could not only do anything the Constitution authorized him to do but also anything the Constitution did not forbid him to do.

The occasional differences between the Presidents and the Court have often centered on the hypothesis that, just as there are implied powers in the Constitution, there may be implied limitations—an ambiguous enough premise which has made *stare decisis* an all but obsolete judicial attitude as far as marginal presidential powers go. The Court has a most contradictory, puzzling history on some uses of presidential power, such as the emergency seizures of private property, and a sublimely sweeping consistency on others, such as the status of executive agreements with foreign powers.

Such clashes with the courts as those of Jefferson, Jackson, and Franklin Roosevelt on substantive aspects of judicial decisions are conspicuous for their rarity rather than their frequency. Unfortunately, they have contributed very little—considerably less than the opinions of the Court and its minorities—to the dialogue, which ought to be sober and thoughtful, on the political role of the Supreme Court. Indeed, if the reputations of Jefferson, Jackson, or Franklin Roosevelt were to rest on their statements on the Court, they would constitute a slender reed upon which to rest their cases before the verdict of history. And one searches in vain for any very profound passage in presidential writings either in protest or in support of judicial supremacy.

As for presidential action with regard to appointments to the Supreme Court, and for that matter presidential utterances, the seriousness, the lack of cynicism, the sense of responsibility with which the appointive power has been used are enormously impressive. Despite the fact that its method is litigatory, and its references and rituals legal, the Supreme Court of the United States is one of the most powerful political entities on earth. It is only because of presidential restraint in treating it politically —including, though with occasional lapses, the use of the appointive powers—that it remains one of the most useful, valuable, and honored.

JEFFERSON

You seem to think it devolved on the judges to decide on the validity of the sedition law. But nothing in the constitution has given them a right to decide for the executive, more than to the Executive to decide for them. Both magistracies are equally independant in the sphere of action assigned to them. The judges, believing the law constitutional, had a right to pass a sentence of fine and imprisonment, because that power was placed in their hands by the constitution. But the Executive, believing the law to be unconstitutional, was bound to remit the execution of it; because that power has been confided to him by the constitution. That instrument meant that its co-ordinate branches should be checks on each other. But the opinion which gives to the judges the right to decide what laws are constitutional, and what not, not only for themselves in their own sphere of action, but for the legislature and executive also in their spheres, would make the judiciary a despotic branch.[1]

Jackson and Franklin Roosevelt took the same line of reasoning. History, public opinion, and the courts themselves have decided otherwise.

✦ ✦ ✦

. . . for to a commission, a deed, a bond, *delivery* is essential to give validity. Until, therefore, the commission is delivered out of the hands of the Executive & his agents, it is not his deed. He may withhold or cancel it at pleasure, as he might his private deed in the same situation. The Constitution intended that the three great branches of the government should be co-ordinate, & independent of each other. As to acts, therefore, which are to be done by either, it has given no controul to another branch. A judge, I presume, cannot sit on a bench without a commission, or a record of a commission; & the Constitution having given to the judiciary branch no means of compelling the executive either to *deliver* a commission, or to make a record of it, shews it did not intend to give the judiciary that control over the executive, but that it should remain in the power of the latter to do it or not.[2]

✦ ✦ ✦

The leading principle of our Constitution is the independence of the Legislature, executive and judiciary of each other, and none are more jealous of this than the judiciary. But would the executive be independent of the judiciary, if he were subject to the *commands* of the latter, and to imprisonment for disobedience; if the several courts could bandy him from pillar to post, keep him constantly trudging from north to south and east to west, and withdraw him entirely from his constitutional duties? The intention of the Constitution, that each branch should be independent of the others, is further manifested by the means it has furnished to each, to protect itself from enterprises of force attempted on them by the others, and to none has it given more effectual or diversified means than to the executive. Again; because ministers can go into a court in London as witnesses, without interruption to their executive duties, it is inferred that they would go to a court one thousand or one thousand five hundred miles off, and that ours are to be dragged from Maine to Orleans by every criminal who will swear that their testimony "may be of use to him." The Judge says, "it is *apparent* that the President's duties as chief magistrate do not demand his whole time, and are not unremitting." If he alludes to our annual retirement from the seat of government, during the sickly season, he should be told that such arrangements are made for carrying on the public business, at and between the several stations we take, that it goes on as unremittingly there, as if it were at the seat of government. I pass more hours in public business at Monticello than I do here, every day; and it is much more laborious, because all must be done in writing.[3]

✓ ✓ ✓

Our judges are as honest as other men, and not more so. They have, with others, the same passions for party, for power, and the privilege of their corps. Their maxim is *"boni judicis est ampliare jurisdictionem,"* and their power the more dangerous as they are in office for life, and not responsible, as the other functionaries are, to the elective control. The constitution has erected no such single tribunal, knowing that to whatever hands confided, with the corruptions of time and party, its members would become despots. It has more wisely made all the departments co-equal and co-sovereign within themselves. If the legislature fails to pass laws for a census, for paying the judges and other officers of government, for establishing a militia, for naturalization as prescribed by the constitution, or if they fail to meet in congress, the judges cannot issue their mandamus to them; if the President fails to supply the place of a judge, to appoint other civil or military officers, to issue requisite commissions, the judges cannot force him. They can issue their mandamus or distringas to no executive or legislative officer to enforce the fulfilment of their official duties, any more than the president or legislature may issue orders to the judges or their officers. Betrayed by English example, and unaware, as it should seem, of the control of our constitution in this particular, they have at times overstepped their limit by undertaking to command executive officers in the discharge of their executive duties; but the

constitution, in keeping three departments distinct and independent, restrains the authority of the judges to judiciary organs,
as it does the executive and legislative to executive and legislative organs. The judges certainly have more frequent occasion to
act on constitutional questions, because the laws of *meum* and
tuum and of criminal action, forming the great mass of the system
of law, constitute their particular department. When the legislative or executive functionaries act unconstitutionally, they are
responsible to the people in their elective capacity. The exemp-
tion of the judges from that is quite dangerous enough. I know
no safe depository of the ultimate powers of the society but the
people themselves; and if we think them not enlightened enough
to exercise their control with a wholesome discretion, the remedy
is not to take it from them, but to inform their discretion by education. This is the true corrective of abuses of constitutional
power.[4]

*The presidency never succeeded in converting public opinion to the
idea of limiting the scope of judicial review of legislative acts or
executive actions.*

MADISON

. . . the Executive of the U. States is not only unauthorized to
prevent the execution of a Decree sanctioned by the Supreme
Court of the U. States, but is especially enjoined by statute to
carry into effect any such decree, where opposition may be made
to it.[5]

✦   ✦   ✦

In a Government whose vital principle is responsibility, it never
will be allowed that the Legislative and Executive Departments
should be compleatly subjected to the Judiciary, in which that
characteristic feature is so faintly seen.[6]

*The power of the judiciary continued to be as worrisome to the
presidency as the power of the President was to the Congress.*

JACKSON

If the opinion of the Supreme Court covered the whole ground
of this act, it ought not to control the coordinate authorities of
this Government. The Congress, the Executive, and the Court
must each for itself be guided by its own opinion of the Constitu-

tion. Each public officer who takes an oath to support the Constitution swears that he will support it as he understands it, and not as it is understood by others. It is as much the duty of the House of Representatives, of the Senate, and of the President to decide upon the constitutionality of any bill or resolution which may be presented to them for passage or approval as it is of the supreme judges when it may be brought before them for judicial decision. The opinion of the judges has no more authority over Congress than the opinion of Congress has over the judges, and on that point the President is independent of both. The authority of the Supreme Court must not, therefore, be permitted to control the Congress or the Executive when acting in their legislative capacities, but to have only such influence as the force of their reasoning may deserve.[7]

Jackson's doctrine of the restricted power of the courts did not gain public acceptance, as did neither Jefferson's before him nor Franklin Roosevelt's after.

VAN BUREN

From the nature of their action, members of Congress do not subject themselves to personal responsibility, except when they act corruptly. But the situation of the incumbent of the executive department is less favorable. Deprived of all discretion, and bound to thus understand his position, he encounters personal responsibility, in certain cases, whichever way he may act. If he find a law upon the statute book, approved by one of his predecessors—and to relieve the country from which has perhaps been one of the reasons for the removal of the latter from office—a law which he deems unauthorized by the Constitution, but which the Supreme Court holds to be constitutional, he must either violate his oath of office and execute it, or refuse to do so and expose himself to impeachment for a failure in the discharge of his official duties. If he persists in the observance of a law which the Supreme Court has, in a private suite, held to be unconstitutional, he incurs a similar responsibility; and if he omits its observance, he does violence to his own conscience by failing to perform his official duties according to his oath.[8]

This dilemma has been resolved for modern Presidents by the rise in power of judicial decisions.

BENJAMIN HARRISON

Political questions are left by the Constitution to the political departments—namely, the Congress and the President; and the Supreme Court will not consider them. Chief-Justice Marshall said: "Questions in their nature political, or which are by the Constitution and laws submitted to the Executive, can never be made in this court." Political questions are such as the recognition of the sovereignty of another nation and of its territorial limits, the recognition of a particular organization as the true Government of a State, or the determination by the President when called upon to aid in suppressing a domestic insurrection in a State, as to which is the lawful Government.[9]

FRANKLIN D. ROOSEVELT

The Constitution provides that the President "shall from time to time give to the Congress information of the State of the Union, and recommend to their consideration such measures as he shall judge necessary and expedient." No one else is given a similar mandate. It is therefore the duty of the President to advise the Congress in regard to the Judiciary whenever he deems such information or recommendation necessary.[10]

⁁ ⁁ ⁁

Last Thursday I described the American form of Government as a three horse team provided by the Constitution to the American people so that their field might be plowed. The three horses are, of course, the three branches of government—the Congress, the Executive and the Courts. Two of the horses are pulling in unison today; the third is not. Those who have intimated that the President of the United States is trying to drive that team, overlook the simple fact that the President, as Chief Executive, is himself one of the three horses.[11]

Roosevelt proposed legislation to permit adding one new justice to the Supreme Court for every one over seventy who did not retire. In 1937, six of the nine on the bench were over seventy. The proposal died in committee in the Senate. Five Presidents, however, have changed the size of the courts or approved congressional moves to change it: John Adams, Jefferson, Jackson, Lincoln, and Grant.

✦ ✦ ✦

If by that phrase "packing the Court" it is charged that I wish to place on the bench spineless puppets who would disregard the law and would decide specific cases as I wished them to be decided, I make this answer: that no President fit for his office would appoint, and no Senate of honorable men fit for their office would confirm, that kind of appointees to the Supreme Court.[12]

EISENHOWER

I do not believe it is the function or indeed it is desirable for a President to express his approval or disapproval of any Supreme Court decision. His job, for which he takes an oath, is to execute the laws.

If he, in advance of such execution, says "I don't like it but I will do it," and in the other cases "I do like it, I will do it," he is constantly laying the whole law enforcement processes of the Federal Government open to the suspicion that he is doing his duty one time well and the other time not well.[13]

Chapter VI

THE PRESIDENCY AND FOREIGN RELATIONS

The President shall "appoint ambassadors, other public ministers and consuls"[1] and receive those from other countries and make treaties with the advice and consent of the Senate is all that the Constitution says of the presidency and foreign relations.

Without going into details or even proposing an executive machinery, the Constitution thus launched the presidency, by implication more than specifics, along the great and critical course of its development as the agency for conduct of foreign affairs. To this power, since the days of Washington, the executive has clung more consistently than to any other, and the writings of the Presidents vary less on their interpretations of the power. With regard to this function, too, Presidents have been less challenged, with certain conspicuous exceptions, by the other two divisions of the government.

Of the need to centralize foreign relations in the presidency, the first Committee on Foreign Relations of the Senate itself was appropriately aware when it reported in 1816: "The President is the Constitutional representative of the United States with regard to foreign nations. He manages our concern with foreign nations and must necessarily be most competent to determine when, how, and upon what subject negotiations may be urged with the greatest prospect of success. For his conduct he is responsible to the Constitution. The committee considers this responsibility the surest pledge for the faithful discharge of his duties. They think the interference of the Senate in the direction of foreign negotiations [is] calculated to diminish that responsibility and thereby to impair the best security for the national safety. The nature of transactions with foreign nations, moreover, requires caution and unity of design."[2]

One reason for the singular consistency of views on executive responsibility for foreign relations is that there is actually in the government of the United States no machinery that would lend itself to the conduct of relations with foreign nations other than the presidency. The Congress has no constitutional authority to participate directly in—that is, to conduct—foreign affairs and has been limited fairly explicitly by the Constitution to such indirect participation as the Senate's power to approve treaties and the House's authorization to appropriate money. Consequently Congress has had to amplify and sometimes to distort these powers in order to nullify the intent of the executive, without feeling called upon to present an alternative and equally constructive program of its own. The Supreme Court has virtually nothing to do with foreign affairs, since they are seldom the subject of laws but more often of diplomatic conversations, negotiations, and the individual activities of the President, his ambassadors, and his special advisers. Moreover, when such negotiations conclude in a treaty, that treaty becomes, in the language of the Constitution, "the supreme law of the land"—i.e., on a level with the Constitution itself and no more subject to judicial review by the Supreme Court than the constitutional articles establishing the presidency or the Court itself. The Supreme Court has, in fact, largely limited its concern with foreign affairs to the review of occasional early attempts of individual states to deal directly with foreign powers on such minor matters as the extradition of fugitives—of which attempts the Court has always taken a negative view.

The Congress, never for long afflicted with the same sense of restraint that has sometimes characterized the judiciary, has from time to time resisted the power of the presidency in foreign affairs. But beginning with Washington, Presidents, whatever their philosophic views of the capacities of their office or their political party affiliations, have been stubborn in defending what they regarded as presidential prerogatives in the area, even though many delegated them to the Secretary of State. Eisenhower, for example, was quick to attack the Bricker amendment, which would have shifted much of the treaty-making power to the

Congress. It is due, in no small measure, to such presidential alertness that the role of the executive as the nation's implement for the conduct of foreign relations has been steadily strengthened. Today, high among the extraconstitutional powers of the President of the United States is an awesome capacity to influence world order, economic and social as well as political and military.

The whole process began when Washington saw very clearly that nothing could be more disastrous to the infant republic, and nothing more inviting to chaos, than having the foreign correspondence of the nation carried on simultaneously by two or three independent agencies of the government, with no one sure what the other was saying. Among the first principles that he established was that the presidency is the only official agency in the United States with which foreign governments can properly communicate. Seven months after his inauguration he made this clear when King Louis XVI of France communicated to "The President and Members of the General Congress of the United States" the news that his son, the heir apparent, had died. Washington did not send the letter, or even a copy of it, to the Congress but merely informed the two houses of its receipt, telling them that he would send the King an answer, which began with the unequivocal information that "By the change which has taken place in the national government of the United States, the honor of receiving and answering your Majesty's letter of the 7th of June to 'the President and Members of Congress' has devolved upon me."[3] The careful use of the word "receiving" was not lost on the foreign ministries of Europe.

In that same month of October, 1789, Washington also made it clear that the President had the right to structure the mechanics of foreign relations as he saw fit and to use extraconstitutional and extrastatutory methods if he wished. He started a custom—neither affirmed nor denied by the Constitution—which has been often and notably revived in American government, particularly in the twentieth century by Woodrow Wilson and Franklin Roosevelt: that of sending private emissaries, without official position and therefore not subject to Senate approval, to deal on the President's behalf with foreign governments. Washington did this, in the first year of his first administration, when he asked a private United States citizen, Gouverneur Morris, to talk with British leaders about the terms of a possible treaty of commerce and other matters. His letter to Morris stating, "I desire you . . . on the authority and Credit of this Matter, to converse with His Brittanic Majesty's Ministers on these Points,"[4] bears a striking resemblance to the manner in which Franklin Roosevelt empowered Harry Hopkins to carry out top-level diplomatic missions: "I am asking you to convey a communication . . . to His Majesty King George VI.[5]

[Washington said that his purpose in sending Morris to hold conversations with the British on the execution of the Treaty of Peace in 1791 was that the nation would be "less committed" if the talks were conducted by "a private rather than a public person."[6] Probably what he really sought to avoid was any accountability to the Congress for the mission's commitments until he was sure they would work out; and since Morris was not theoretically appointed to a public office and thus not liable to Senate confirmation, Washington regarded the whole affair as a "private" one of the President.]

Other Presidents, less attached to the quality of privacy for its own sake, have used the same method to avoid conflict with the Senate on confirmation of the personal representative or, since 1855, to avoid the necessity of asking the Congress to create a public office. Madison sent two special representatives to Europe in 1813 to work with his minister, John Quincy Adams, in negotiating a treaty to end the War of 1812, and later supplemented this "commission" with two more representatives. All four were appointed without confirmation by the Senate and without his consulting it. Similarly, in 1831 Jackson sent special representatives, without consulting the Senate, to Turkey. In 1893 Cleveland sent J. H. Blount to Hawaii as a special agent, while the conversations incidental to annexation were going on. In 1917 Wilson sent Elihu Root to Russia, and in 1940 Franklin Roosevelt sent Myron Taylor to the Vatician. All these, and many more such special emissaries, were usually named to accomplish or inquire into some specific course of action determined solely by the President. Usually, too, their appointments were related to a conscious effort on the part of the President to avoid involving the Congress in any way. With the appointment of Colonel House by Wilson in 1914 as a kind of "roving" ambassador and of Harry L. Hopkins by Franklin Roosevelt in 1941 to go to London and Moscow, the fundamental propriety of such special agents of the President came to be accepted.

What is more important, they appear on the whole to have strengthened the presidency as the agency for carrying on relations with the rest of the world, and eliminated much of the slowness and ponderousness that democratic processes involve —often to a point where the end is no longer pressing or desirable by the time the methods to reach it have been effectively employed. Moreover, without involving the Department of State and ordinary diplomatic channels, special agents have permitted the President, who cannot himself be long absent from Washington, to acquire information and responses vital to the construction of sound policy. For whether or not the Congress has ever been totally reconciled to it, the conduct of foreign affairs was left by the Constitution as so much more a personal function of the President than any other of his great duties that it would take major changes in the Constitution itself ever to change it. It is significant that the Commission on Organization of the Executive Branch of the Government, headed by Herbert Hoover, in all its scores of reports of 1949, nowhere suggested intervention in the President's personal command of foreign relations or advocated the establishment of any executive procedure that would have made such command less personal, and that even a relatively passive President, Eisenhower, lashed out vigorously at such measures as the Bricker amendment designed to reduce presidential power in this area.

Another major extraconstitutional device evolved by the presidency to control and expedite the conduct of foreign affairs is the executive agreement, which has frequently replaced a formal treaty when the President was certain that he could not count on the support of the two thirds of the Senate constitutionally required for a treaty's ratification, or when there was no time to seek it. In some cases such agreements have been reached and put into effect without any congressional participation whatsoever. McKinley, who tended to be a much more decisive President when he was acting independently than when he was worrying about pressure from others, used it in the annexation of Hawaii in 1898; and in 1901, he did not even advise, let alone enlist the support of, the Congress when he entered into the Boxer Indemnity Protocol, which provided for the payment of damages and the punishment of Chinese officials after the Boxer Rebellion against foreign legations in Peking.

It was McKinley's successor, however, the impatient, assertive Theodore Roosevelt, who brought the executive agreement to real stature as a vigorous weapon of the presidency in concluding terms with foreign powers without bothering with the formality and delay of going to the Senate for approval. In 1904, the little Caribbean republic of Santo Domingo feared that European creditors might force the intervention of European powers in its affairs. To protect the collecting of Santo Domingan customs, Roosevelt agreed, through a special emissary and the American minister to Santo Domingo, to put the collectors under United States control, to turn over forty-five per cent of the collections to the Dominican Government and to dole out the rest to its creditors. Mindful of the dangers that might result if, in the absence of United States protection, any of the European creditor nations intervened in the little republic, Roosevelt did not propose to see his project bog down in the Senate; he put it into immediate effect as an executive agreement, without Senate approval.

Of his action, Roosevelt later said: "The Constitution did not explicitly give me power to bring out the necessary agreement with Santo Domingo. But the Constitution did not forbid my doing what I did. I put the agreement into effect, and I continued its execution for two years before the Senate acted; and I would have continued it until the end of my term, if necessary, without any action by Congress."[7] Roosevelt went on to point out that he would have preferred a treaty confirmed by the senators (but "all that they had really done was to shirk their duty. Somebody had to do that duty, and accordingly, I did it.") on the grounds that a treaty would be the law of the land while an executive agreement would terminate, as he thought, with the end of his term. He might have been relieved perhaps to know that thirty-three years later, in 1937, the Supreme Court, in considering the force of Franklin Roosevelt's agreement of 1933 embodying the terms of United States recognition of Russia, maintained that such executive agreements were as much the law of the land as a treaty. Franklin Roosevelt unquestionably found comfort in this decision in September 1940, after the fall of France, when he agreed to turn over fifty destroyers to Great Britain without asking Congress to ratify his action.

The pivotal power to recognize other governments was first assumed for the presidency by Washington. After the French monarchy was turned out in 1792, Washington received an envoy from the new French Republic, Citizen Edmond Genêt—an act which in itself constituted recognition of the new republic.

John Quincy Adams, years later, cited Washington's precedent as grounds for stopping Clay's moves to get Congress "to acknowledge" foreign governments by legislative act: "Instead of admitting the Senate or House of Representatives to any share in the act of recognition," wrote Adams, "I would expressly avoid that form of doing it which would require the concurrence of those bodies."[8]

The neutrality status of the United States, as to belligerents in foreign wars, was also assumed by Washington as a matter of presidential determination. In the Franco-British War of 1793, he issued a proclamation of neutrality, which led to a storm of protest from adherents to the concept of congressional supremacy, who took the view that since Congress had the sole right to declare war it had also the sole right to declare neutrality. The fury that the proclamation aroused resulted in Congress passing its own Neutrality Act of 1794, but Washington's action succeeded in establishing the principle that the President had all powers involved in foreign relations except those, like the declaring of war, that were specifically reserved to the Congress by the Constitution.

Among these few exceptions was the Senate's right of "advice and consent" on the making of treaties, a phrase which Washington was inclined at the beginning to take quite literally. During his first year in office, he proposed to the Senate that they "advise" him on a treaty to be made with some Indian tribes. He visited the Senate in person for such advice, but to Washington's disgust the senators turned the whole matter over to a committee and asked the President to come back a week later. Washington never repeated the experiment and afterward started a long tradition of presenting the Senate with a treaty as a *fait accompli*, for its approval or disapproval, with no consultation.

As his terms progressed, it became increasingly obvious to Washington that the executive should be in effect the sole agency not only for the conduct of foreign relations but also for the determination and definition of foreign policy. Moreover, Washington concluded that the machinery set up to carry out the policy, or to arrive at it, was the business only of the executive.

The first major treaty in United States history was effected, not through the ordinary channels of the Department of State or the regular executive establishment, but by the Chief Justice of the United States, John Jay, whom Washington sent to London in 1794, when relations between the United States and Britain had so deteriorated that war appeared to be inevitable. (In the autumn of 1948, when relations between Russia and the United States had similarly deteriorated, President Truman proposed publicly to send another Chief Justice, Fred Vinson, to Moscow to arrive at a settlement. Truman's action was severely criticized as the most revolutionary proposal in the history of American diplomacy, and he yielded to the criticism. Actually, had Vinson gone on the mission, he could not have had a more exact precedent than that of his predecessor Jay's mission for Washington.) The Senate agreed to a conditional ratification of Jay's treaty, after lengthy debate, and after President Washington had submitted copies of all relevant correspondence with Jay. To put Jay's treaty in effect, however, the House of Representatives was

required to make an appropriation and, before doing so, requested from the President all papers that passed between the
President and Jay leading to the treaty. In a sharp and farsighted
reprimand, Washington told the House that he had no intention
of furnishing any such papers: "A just regard to the Constitution
and to the duty of my office, under all the circumstances of this
case, forbids a compliance with your request."[9] The effort of the
House to use its constitutional power to appropriate moneys to
invade the executive power to make treaties had most serious implications of congressional ascendancy over the President. Washington recognized their significance and dealt with the matter of
submitting to the House's demand with sufficient force to have
lasting effect. But congressional insistence on seeing presidential
papers has remained a recurring source of contention, and the
writings of most Presidents contain sharp refusals.

The present world status of the American presidency is ultimately traceable to Washington's handling of the office. Without
the strength of his character, his competence, his persistent adherence to the theory of a strong executive, his inexplicable skill
in statecraft, the office might well have wallowed in a sea of impotence in foreign affairs. Moreover, his example has been readily
seized upon by American Presidents ever since.

Of the chief executives succeeding Washington, ten can be said
to have distinguished themselves in the area of foreign relations:
John Adams, Jefferson, Tyler, Polk, Lincoln, Cleveland, Theodore
Roosevelt, Wilson, Franklin Roosevelt, and Truman. Each of
these leaned heavily on the precedents set by Washington,
especially on his insistence upon the presidency as being not the
servant of the Congress in foreign relations but the sole and, to a
considerable extent, the independent agency of the government
for the conduct of foreign affairs and for the initiation of treaties.
Jefferson saw the foreign relations role as inclusive, maintaining
that "The transaction of the business is executive altogether!"[10]
It is easy to oversimplify the "ifs" of history, but it seems evident
that without the insistence of these ten Presidents upon the development of the presidency as a strong agency in international
affairs, the United States would have been not one or two but at

least three and possibly four small nations. For the Congress has always been so sectional in its interests and viewpoints that each congressional delegation saw its own proportionate strength lessened with the addition of new states and therefore of more representatives and senators, and would have preferred not to have that strength diluted by an increase in the size of the Union which inevitably led to an increase in the size of the Congress. The growth of the original area of the United States to more than triple its original area was accomplished by such assertive Presidents as Jefferson, Tyler, and Polk, through the broad use of presidential powers and sometimes almost in spite of Congress. The Louisiana Purchase was entirely an executive operation in which Jefferson—reading the power into the presidency, there being neither constitutional provision nor precedent for the acquisition of new territory—arranged the purchase and then called Congress into special session to approve it. Anticipating trouble with the Northeast representation, which had no desire to have its strength counterbalanced by new Western and Southern territory, he had a senator from Kentucky round up Western senators and representatives for the first day of the session, thus forcing through the necessary ratification and appropriation in spite of New England opposition.

Tyler, first of the Vice Presidents to succeed to the presidency and with no sure following in the Congress, acquired Texas by depending on a joint resolution of the House and Senate, which required a simple majority, rather than by drafting a treaty, which would have required a two-thirds vote of approval by the Senate—of which he had slim hopes. When his single term began in 1845, Polk set, as his major objectives in foreign affairs, the settling of the Oregon boundary dispute with Great Britain and the acquisition of California. He toiled without ceasing and accomplished both purposes among several others, renounced any ambition for re-election, and died, to a considerable degree due to overwork, three months after the end of his term, as what George Bancroft called "one of the very best and most honest and successful Presidents the country ever had."[11] It was Polk's arduous, farsighted labors, indeed, that resulted in the United

States spanning the continent, and he stands as the only exception in the long succession of ineffectives between Jackson and Lincoln.

If the normal diplomatic responsibility of the presidency is to maintain peaceful and mutually beneficial relations with other countries or, when war is inevitable, to maintain as successful alliances as possible, then those men who as Presidents took an unequivocal view of the power of the presidency to give direction and purpose to our foreign policy best realized the potentialities of their office: Washington, clear in his vision and forthright in his action; John Adams, who, despite the belligerence of Congress and his own party, avoided open war with France (in contrast to Madison and, later McKinley, both of whom yielded to pressures and fought wars which they did not think really necessary); Jefferson, whose bold action resulted in the Louisiana Purchase; Polk, who seized the initiative; Lincoln, who used all his immense wisdom in dealing with people to prevent Britain and France from recognizing the Confederacy; Cleveland and Theodore Roosevelt, both of whom so reaffirmed the Monroe Doctrine that it was never successfully challenged until the Cuban revolution in the Eisenhower administration; and the three world statesmen America has produced in this century, Wilson, Franklin Roosevelt, and Truman, all of whom saw, in the words of Wilson, that "what affects mankind is inevitably our affair"[12] and that the "principle of public right must henceforth take precedence over the individual interests of nations."[13] Wilson's vision of a world order under law; Roosevelt's drive for a united world; Truman's prompt action to save Greece and Turkey, his practical sense of the relationship of economic health to the restoration of a free Europe in the Marshall Plan and Point Four programs, his initiative in the United Nations action in eastern Asia—all these were essentially expressions of advanced concepts of presidential influence in world affairs.

In general, moreover, the diplomatic history of the United States has tended to justify the insistence of the strong Presidents upon the presidency as the agency for not only the conduct but to a large extent the determination of our foreign policy. The nation's diplomatic history has seen three major divisions, in all of which presidential rather than congressional determination of policy has worked most advantageously. The first period, lasting from 1789 to 1825, was one of consolidating before the world the independence and status of the new republic. It was highlighted by Washington's conduct of the infant republic's foreign affairs, Adams' handling of France, Jefferson's masterly purchase of the Louisiana Territory, and Monroe's farsighted doctrine. The second period, from 1825 to 1900, was one largely of continental expansion and integration, distinguished by Tyler's annexation of Texas, Polk's acquisitions in the Far West, the arbitration of the Northwest dispute with Great Britain, and Lincoln's skilled averting of a foreign war during the Rebellion. The third period, beginning shortly after the turn of the century, and still continuing, is one of American leadership in world affairs, summarized best by Woodrow Wilson before America entered the First World War: "We are participants, whether we would or not, in the life of the world. The interests of all nations are our own also. We are partners with the rest."[14]

In each of these phases of the diplomatic history of the United States, the interests of the nation and of mankind have always been best served by those American Presidents whose high sense of responsibility of their office before the world and posterity has been accompanied by a broad concept of its powers. Conversely, those Presidents, like Madison and McKinley, who yielded too readily to the pressure of congressional groups or to the more inflammatory elements of the press, or who never even attempted to exert leadership in foreign affairs because of personal inadequacies, have very frequently done less than little, in this respect, to vindicate their ever having held the office. And their writings on the subject have been on the whole muddy and unconvincing.

WASHINGTON

The impossibility that one man should be able to perform all the great business of the State, I take to have been the reason for instituting the great Departments, and appointing officers therein, to assist the supreme Magistrate in discharging the duties of his trust. And, perhaps, I may be allowed to say of myself, that the supreme Magistrate of no State can have a greater variety of important business to perform in person, than I have at this moment. Very many things will doubtless occur to you, Sir, as being incident to the office of President in the commencement of the Government, which cannot be done by the intervention of a third person. You will give me leave to say likewise, that no third person (were there a disposition for it) shall ever have it in his power to erect a wall between me and the Diplomatic Corps; that is to say, to prevent necessary communications. Nor has anybody insinuated that it would be beneath the dignity of a President of the United States occasionally to transact business with a foreign Minister. But in what light the public might view the establishment of a precedent for negotiating the business of a Department, without any agency of the Head of the Department who was appointed for that very purpose, I do not at present pretend to determine: Nor whether a similar practice, in that case, must not of right be extended hereafter to all Diplomatic characters of the same rank.[15]

✓ ✓ ✓

In all matters respecting Treaties, oral communications seem indispensably necessary; because in these a variety of matters are contained, all of which not only require consideration, but some of them may undergo much discussion; to do which by written communications would be tedious without being satisfactory.

Oral communications may be proper also for discussing the propriety of sending Representatives to foreign Courts, and ascertaining the Grade or character in which they are to appear and may be so in other cases.

But it may be asked where are these oral communications to be made? If in the Senate Chamber, how are the President and Vice President to be arranged? The latter by the Constitution being ex-officio President of the Senate, Would the Vice President be disposed to give up the Chair? If not Ought the President of the United States to be placed in an awkward situation when there? These are matters which require previous consideration and adjustment for meetings in the Senate Chamber or elsewhere.[16]

✓ ✓ ✓

To our great and beloved Friend and Ally, his Most Christian Majesty.

By the change which has taken place in the national government of the United States, the honor of receiving and answering your Majesty's letter of the 7th. of June, to "the President and Members of Congress" has devolved upon me.[17]

This was Washington's firm and final way of making it known that only the President—and not the Congress—was to receive and acknowledge communications from a foreign power.

✓ ✓ ✓

Information being given by Mr. Van Berkel, that Mr. Cazenove just arrived from Holland, and of a principal Mercantile House there had letters for me which he wished to deliver with his own hands and requested to know when he might be presented for that purpose. It was thought, before this should be done, it might be proper to know whether they were of a public nature, and whether he was acting in a public character. If so, then to let them come to me through the Secretary of State—if not, then for him to send them, that the purport might be known before he was introduced, which might be at the next Levee, when he might be received and treated agreeably to the consequence he might appear to derive from the testimonials of the letters. It being conceived that etiquette of this sort is essential with all foreigners to give a respect to the Chief Magistrate, and the dignity of the Government, which would be lessened if every person who could procure a letter of introduction should be presented otherwise than at Levee hours in a formal manner.[18]

✓ ✓ ✓

Had some conversation with Mr. Madison on the propriety of consulting the Senate on the plans to which it would be necessary to send persons in the Diplomatic line, and Consuls; and with respect to the grade of the first—his opinion coincides with Mr. Jay's and Mr. Jefferson's—to wit—that they have no Constitutional right to interfere with either, and that it might be impolitic to draw it into a precedent, their powers extending no farther than to an approbation or disapprobation of the person nominated by the President, all the rest being Executive and vested in the President by the Constitution.[19]

*   *   *

I trust that no part of my conduct has ever indicated a disposition to withhold any information which the Constitution has enjoined upon the President as a duty to give, or which could be required of him by either House of Congress as a right; And with truth I affirm, that it has been, as it will continue to be, while I have the honor to preside in the Government, my constant endeavour to harmonize with the other branches thereof; so far as the trust delegated to me by the People of the United States, and my sense of the obligation it imposes to "preserve, protect and defend the Constitution" will permit.

The nature of foreign negotiations requires caution; and their success must often depend on secrecy: and even when brought to a conclusion, a full disclosure of all the measures, demands, or eventual concessions, which may have been proposed or contemplated, would be extremely impolitic: for this might have a pernicious influence on future negotiations; or produce immediate inconveniences, perhaps danger and mischief, in relation to other powers. The necessity of such caution and secrecy was one cogent reason for vesting the power of making Treaties in the President, with the advice and consent of the Senate, the principle on which that body was formed confining it to a small number of Members.

To admit then a right in the House of Representatives to demand, and to have as a matter of course, all the Papers respecting a negotiation with a foreign power, would be to establish a dangerous precedent.

It does not occur that the inspection of the papers asked for, can be relative to any purpose under the cognizance of the House of Representatives, except that of an impeachment, which the resolution has not expressed. I repeat, that I have no disposition to withhold any information which the duty of my station will permit, or the public good shall require to be disclosed: and in fact, all the Papers affecting the negotiation with Great Britain were laid before the Senate, when the Treaty itself was communicated for their consideration and advice.

The course which the debate has taken, on the resolution of the House, leads to some observations on the mode of making treaties under the Constitution of the United States.

Having been a member of the General Convention, and knowing the principles on which the Constitution was formed, I have ever entertained but one opinion on this subject; and from the first establishment of the Government to this moment, my conduct has exemplified that opinion, that the power of making treaties is exclusively vested in the President, by and with the advice and consent of the Senate, provided two thirds of the Senators present concur, and that every treaty so made, and promulgated, thenceforward became the Law of the land. It is thus that the treaty making power has been understood by foreign Nations: and in all the treaties made with them, we have declared, and they have believed, that when ratified by the President with the advice and consent of the Senate, they became obligatory. In this construction of the Constitution every House of Representatives has heretofore acquiesced; and until the present time, not a doubt or suspicion has appeared to my knowledge that this construction was not the true one. Nay, they have more than acquiesced: for till now, without controverting the obligation of such treaties, they have made all the requisite provisions for carrying them into effect.[20]

↑ ↑ ↑

Do you suppose that the Executive, in the recess of the Senate, has power in such a case as the one before us, especially if the measure should not be avowed by authority, to send a special character to Paris, as Envoy Extraordinary, to give, and receive explanations? And if there be a doubt, whether it is not probable, nay, more than probable, that the French Directory would, in the present state of things, avail themselves of the unconstitutionallity of the measure, to decline receiving him? The policy of delay, to avoid explanations, would induce them to adopt any pretext to accomplish it. Their reliance upon a party in this country for support, would stimulate them to this conduct; And we may be assured they will not be deficient in the most minute details of every occurrence, and every opinion, worthy of communication. If then an Envoy cannot be sent to Paris without the Agency of the Senate, will the information you have received, admitting it should be realized, be sufficient ground for convening that body?

These are serious things; they may be productive of serious consequences; and therefore require very serious and cool deliberation. Admitting, however, that the Powers of the President during the recess, were adquate to such an appointment, where is the character who would go, that unites the proper qualifications for such a Mission; and would not be obnoxious to one party or the other? And what should be done with Mr. M—— [James Monroe] in that case?

As the affairs of this country in their administration, receive great embarrassment from the conduct of characters among ourselves; and as every act of the Executive is mis-represented, and tortured with a view to make it appear odious, the aid of the friends to government is peculiarly necessary under such circumstances; and at such a crises as the present: It is unnecessary therefore to add, that I should be glad upon the present, and all other important occasion, to receive yours: and as I have great confidence in the abilities, and purity of Mr. Jays views, as well as in his experience, I should wish that his sentiments on the purport of this letter; and other interesting matters as they occur, may accompany yours; for having no other wish than to promote the true and permanent interests of this country, I am anxious, always, to compare the opinions of those in whom I confide with one another; and those again (without being bound by them) with my own, that I may extract all the good I can.[21]

Washington saw a need for occasional special emissaries of the President in addition to regular ambassadors. Later Presidents availed themselves of the precedent set by him.

JOHN ADAMS

The Constitution of the United States makes it my duty to communicate to Congress from time to time information of the state of the Union, and to recommend to their consideration measures which appear to me necessary or expedient. While in discharge of this duty, I submit, with entire resignation, to the responsibility established in the Constitution, I hold myself accountable to no crowned head or Executive Directory, or other foreign power on earth, for the communications which my duty obliges me to make . . .[22]

The French Directory and Talleyrand had indicated that if Adams recalled the U.S. envoy from Paris, France would declare war. The "quasi-war" with France was the major preoccupation in foreign affairs of the Adams administration. Talleyrand also disliked the tone of Adams' messages to Congress on the subject.

✓ ✓ ✓

Sovereign to sovereign, and minister to minister, is a maxim in the cabinets of Europe, and although neither the President of the United States, nor the executive Directory, are sovereigns in their countries, the same relations exist between them and their ministers, and, therefore, the reason of the maxim is applicable to them. It is far below the dignity of the President of the United States to take any notice of Talleyrand's impertinent regrets, and insinuations of superfluities.[23]

✓ ✓ ✓

. . . a President can declare war and can conclude peace without being hurled from his chair.[24]

JEFFERSON

The constitution has given to the President and Senate alone the power (with the consent of the foreign nation) of enacting peace. Their treaty for this purpose is an absolute repeal of the declaration of war, and of all laws authorizing or modifying war measures.[25]

✓ ✓ ✓

The Executive of the Union is, indeed, by the Constitution, made the channel of communication between *foreign* powers and the United States. But citizens, whether individually, or in bodies corporate, or associated, have a right to apply directly to any department of their government, whether legislative, executive, or judiciary, the exercise of whose powers they have a right to claim; and neither of these can regularly offer its intervention in a case belonging to the other.[26]

✓ ✓ ✓

It has never, I believe, been denied that the President may reject a treaty after it's ratification has been advised by the Senate, then certainly he may before that advice; and if he has made up his mind to reject it, it is more respectful to the Senate to do it without, than against their advice. It must not be said that their advice may cast new light on it. Their advice is a bald resolution of yea or nay, without assigning a single reason or motive.[27]

MADISON

The new doctrine involves a difficulty also in providing for treaties, even treaties of peace, on favorable emergencies, the functionaries not being officers in a constitutional sense, nor perhaps ministers to any foreign government. An attempt was, I believe made by a distinguished individual to derive a power in the President to provide for the case of terminating a war, from his military power to establish a truce. This would have opened a wider door for construction than has yet been contended for.

I might add the claim for the Senate of a right to be consulted by the President, and to give their advice previous to his foreign negotiations; a course of proceeding which I believe was condemned by the result of a direct or analogous experiment, and which it was presumed would not again be revived. That the secrecy generally essential in such negotiations would be safe in a numerous body, however individually worthy of the usual confidence, would be little short of a miracle.[28]

JOHN QUINCY ADAMS

The pretension that the President of the United States was to be considered by the ministers of foreign nations, not as the chief magistrate of the country, but as ranking as a minister of state, subordinate to the sovereign in European governments was not confined to the Count de Moustier [French royal envoy]. It was afterward reproduced in still more offensive form, by the first minister from France in her republican transformation. It was then again repelled and finally withdrawn. Since then the President of the United States, in their intercourse with foreign nations represents them as their chief, and the ministers of foreign powers negotiate with the Secretary of State under his direction, and instructions.

At the same time, President Washington fully understood that by the investment of the executive power, he was authorized to enter directly into negotiation with foreign nations, formally or informally, through the department of State, or by agents privately accredited by himself at his discretion.[29]

JACKSON

Nor has any deliberate inquiry ever been instituted in Congress or in any of our legislative bodies as to whom belonged the power of originally recognizing a new [foreign] State—a power the exercise of which is equivalent under some circumstances to a declaration of war; a power nowhere expressly delegated, and only granted in the Constitution as it is necessarily involved in some of the great powers given to Congress, in that given to the President and Senate to form treaties with foreign powers and to appoint ambassadors and other public ministers, and in that conferred upon the President to receive ministers from foreign nations.

In the preamble to the resolution of the House of Representatives it is distinctly intimated that the expediency of recognizing the independence of Texas should be left to the decision of Congress. In this view, on the ground of expediency, I am disposed to concur, and do not, therefore, consider it necessary to express any opinion as to the strict constitutional right of the Executive, either apart from or in conjunction with the Senate, over the subject. It is to be presumed that on no future occasion will a dispute arise, as none has heretofore occurred, between the Executive and Legislature in the exercise of the power of recognition. It will always be considered consistent with the spirit of the Constitution, and most safe, that it should be exercised, when probably leading to war, with a previous understanding with that body by whom war can alone be declared, and by whom all the provisions for sustaining its perils must be furnished.[30]

VAN BUREN

Our course of foreign policy has been so uniform and intelligible as to constitute a rule of Executive conduct which leaves little to my discretion, unless, indeed, I were willing to run counter to the lights of experience and the known opinions of my constituents.[31]

⚡ ⚡ ⚡

Recent experience on the southern boundary of the United States and the events now daily occurring on our northern frontier have abundantly shown that the existing laws are insufficient to guard against hostile invasion from the United States of the territory of friendly and neighboring nations.

The laws in force provide sufficient penalties for the punishment of such offenses after they have been committed, and provided the parties can be found, but the Executive is powerless in many cases to prevent the commission of them, even when in possession of ample evidence of an intention on the part of evil-disposed persons to violate our laws.

Your attention is called to this defect in our legislation. It is apparent that the Executive ought to be clothed with adequate power effectually to restrain all persons within our jurisdiction from the commission of acts of this character. They tend to disturb the peace of the country and inevitably involve the Government in perplexing controversies with foreign powers. I recommend a careful revision of all the laws now in force and such additional enactments as may be necessary to vest in the Executive full power to prevent injuries being inflicted upon neighboring nations by the unauthorized and unlawful acts of citizens of the United States or of other persons who may be within our jurisdiction and subject to our control.[32]

✓ ✓ ✓

The President has power, by and with the advice of the Senate, to make treaties with foreign governments. Private rights, subject to judicial investigation, often grow out of public treaties. The interpretation and enforcement of these rights belong exclusively to the judiciary, and in the execution of its power it may hold the treaty, under which the claim arises, unconstitutional for any of the reasons for which laws may be so regarded. Its decision is binding and final upon the parties and their interests.

Then comes the execution of that treaty between the governments that are parties to it. This, on our part, belongs exclusively to the legislative and executive departments. The duty of the former is to pass the laws necessary to its execution, and that of the latter to see to their enforcement, and to do such other acts as he may do, under the Constitution, without a law.[33]

BUCHANAN

The crime of setting on foot or providing the means for a military expedition within the United States to make war against a foreign State with which we are at peace is one of an ag-

gravated and dangerous character, and early engaged the attention of Congress. Whether the Executive Government possesses any or what power under the Constitution, independently
of Congress, to prevent or punish this and similar offences against
the law of nations, was a subject which engaged the attention
of our most eminent statesmen in the time of the administration
of General Washington, and on the occasion of the French Revolution. The act of Congress of the 5th of June, 1794, fortunately
removed all the difficulties on this question which had theretofore
existed. The fifth and seventh sections of this act, which relate
to the present question, are the same in substance with the
sixth and eighth sections of the act of April 20, 1818, and have
now been in force for a period of more than sixty years.

The military expedition rendered criminal by the act, must
have its origin, must "begin," or be "set on foot," in the United
States; but the great object of the law was to save foreign States
with whom we were at peace from the ravages of these lawless
expeditions proceeding from our shores. The seventh section
alone, therefore, which simply defines the crime and its punishment, would have been inadequate to accomplish this purpose
and enforce our international duties. In order to render the law
effectual, it was necessary to prevent "the carrying on" of such
expeditions to their consummation after they had succeeded
in leaving our shores.

This has been done effectually, and in clear and explicit
language, by the authority given to the President under the
eighth section of the act to employ the land and naval forces of
the United States "for the purpose of preventing the carrying on
of any such expedition or enterprise from the territories or
domain of any foreign prince or state, or of any colony, district,
or people with whom the United States are at peace."[34]

✓   ✓   ✓

The Executive government of this country, in its intercourse
with foreign nations, is limited to the employment of diplomacy
alone. When this fails it can proceed no further. It cannot legitimately resort to force without the direct authority of Congress,
except in resisting and repelling hostile attacks. It would have
no authority to enter the territories of Nicaragua, even to prevent the destruction of the transit, and protect the lives and
property of our own citizens on their passage. It is true, that on
a sudden emergency of this character, the President would
direct any armed force in the vicinity to march to their relief;
but in doing this he would act upon his own responsibility.[35]

✦ ✦ ✦

The republics south of the United States on this continent have, unfortunately, been frequently in a state of revolution and civil war ever since they achieved their independence. As one or the other party has prevailed, and obtained possession of the ports open to foreign commerce, they have seized and confiscated American vessels and their cargoes in an arbitrary and lawless manner, and exacted money from American citizens by forced loans, and other violent proceedings, to enable them to carry on hostilities. The Executive Governments of Great Britain, France, and other countries, possessing the war-making power, can promptly employ the necessary means to enforce immediate redress for similar outrages upon their subjects. Not so the Executive Government of the United States.

If the President orders a vessel of war to any of these ports to demand prompt redress for outrages committed, the offending parties are well aware that in case of refusal the commander can do no more than remonstrate. He can resort to no hostile act. The question must then be referred to diplomacy, and in many cases adequate redress can never be obtained. Thus, American citizens are deprived of the same protection under the flag of their country which the subjects of other nations enjoy. The remedy for this state of things can only be supplied by Congress, since the Constitution has confided to that body alone the power to make war. Without the authority of Congress, the Executive cannot lawfully direct any force, however near it may be to the scene of difficulty, to enter the territory of Mexico, Nicaragua or New Granada, for the purpose of defending the persons and property of American citizens, even though they may be violently assailed whilst passing in peaceful transit over the Tehuantepec, Nicaragua or Panama routes. He cannot, without transcending his constitutional power, direct a gun to be fired into a port, or land a seaman or marine to protect the lives of our countrymen on shore, or to obtain redress for a recent outage on their property.[36]

HAYES

The authority of Congress to terminate a treaty with a foreign power by expressing the will of the nation no longer to adhere to it is as free from controversy under our Constitution as is the further proposition that the power of making new treaties or modifying existing treaties is not lodged by the Constitution in Congress, but in the President, by and with the advice and consent of the Senate, as shown by the concurrence of two-thirds of that body. A denunciation of a treaty by any government is confessedly justifiable only upon some reason both of the highest justice and of the highest necessity.[37]

ARTHUR

I send herewith a copy of the circular invitation extended to all the independent countries of North and South America to participate in a general congress to be held in the city of Washington on the 22d of November next for the purpose of considering and discussing the methods of preventing war between the nations of America . . .

Having observed that the authority of the President to convene such a congress has been questioned, I beg leave to state that the Constitution confers upon the President the power, by and with the advice and consent of the Senate, to make treaties, and that this provision confers the power to take all requisite measures to initiate them, and to this end the President may freely confer with one or several commissioners or delegates from other nations. The congress contemplated by the invitation could only effect any valuable results by its conclusions eventually taking the form of a treaty of peace between the States represented; and, besides, the invitation to the States of North and South America is merely a preliminary act, of which constitutionality or the want of it can hardly be affirmed.[38]

CLEVELAND

It is made the constitutional duty of the President to recommend to the consideration of Congress from time to time such measures as he shall judge necessary and expedient. In no matters can the necessity of this be more evident than when the good faith of the United States under the solemn obligation of treaties with foreign powers is concerned.[39]

BENJAMIN HARRISON

The treaty-making power is given to the President (in connection with the Senate) by the second paragraph of Section 2 of the Constitution, in these words:

He shall have power, by and with the advice and consent
of the Senate, to make treaties, provided two-thirds of the
Senators present concur.

It will be noticed that the initiative—the negotiations with
foreign Governments leading up to an agreement—and the framing of the articles of the treaty, are with the President. The
Senate has no part in the matter until the President communi-
cates the treaty to it, and asks its concurrence. It may then, however, either concur or reject, or concur with amendments.[40]

✓ ✓ ✓

In spite then of the provisions of the Constitution lodging the
treaty-making power in the President and the Senate, and declaring that "all treaties made . . . under the authority of the
United States shall be the supreme law of the land," we have
come practically to recognize the fact that legislation is often
necessary to give this part of the "supreme law of the land" any
effect. Indeed, most treaties require appropriations for ex-
penses or indemnities, or the like, and commercial treaties
usually modify our revenue laws. If they do not of their own
force repeal conflicting laws and carry the necessary appropriations, there must be legislation. Usually appropriations to carry
out a treaty have been given freely by the House; but there is
power to withhold them, and so to defeat the treaty. As to
treaties involving our revenue laws, the House—having by the
Constitution the sole power to originate revenue bills—has
claimed the right to act upon a consideration of the wisdom or
unwisdom of the treaty.[41]

THEODORE ROOSEVELT

The decisive action which brought about this beneficent result
[canal rights in Panama] was the exercise by the President of
the powers vested in him, and in him alone, by the Constitution;
the power to recognize foreign Governments by entering into
diplomatic relations with them, and the power to make treaties
which, when ratified by the Senate, become under the Constitution part of the supreme law of the land. Neither in this nor in
any other matter has there been the slightest failure to live up
to the Constitution in letter and in spirit. But the Constitution
must be observed positively as well as negatively. The President's
duty is to serve the country in accordance with the Constitution;

and I should be derelict in my duty if I used a false construction of the Constitution as a shield for weakness and timidity, or as an excuse for governmental impotence.[42]

✶ ✶ ✶

The President is of course responsible for the general policy of the administration in foreign as in domestic affairs, and here and there or now and then he must himself work out some given problem; for example, the Portsmouth peace, the Panama business, the sending of the fleet around the world, the earliest and most important part of the Algeciras business, were all worked out by me personally. But in most things done by the State Department it is the Secretary of State, if he is a man like [Elihu] Root, who does practically all of the work.[43]

TAFT

The first and most important duty connected with foreign relations that the President has is that of initiating and drafting treaties with foreign nations and submitting them to the Senate for the Senate's advice and consent, and a two-thirds vote of those present is required in the Senate lawfully to advise and consent to a treaty.[44]

✶ ✶ ✶

Neither the Senate nor the House, nor both of them together, can compel the President to make a treaty. He has the sole initiative in this regard. Nor is he bound, after he has made a treaty, and the Senate has advised and consented to it, to ratify it and proclaim it, and the treaty does not go into effect until its ratification.[45]

✶ ✶ ✶

The President has a very large authority outside of treaty-making in our foreign relations. He appoints our Ambassadors to other countries, and he receives Ambassadors from them. This gives him necessarily the duty of carrying on foreign negotiations between ourselves and foreign countries. He and he alone is the representative of our nation in dealing with foreign nations. When I say he alone, I mean that it is he to whom the foreign nations look. He has Ambassadors and Ministers and Consuls in other countries, but they only represent him. In receiving foreign Ambassadors and in sending them, he is bound to determine, when there is any dispute, who the lawful government is, to whom he wishes to accredit his Ambassador and from whom he wishes to receive an Ambassador. Therefore in him is necessarily vested the power and duty of recognizing the lawful government of any country.[46]

✦ ✦ ✦

The President carries on the correspondence through the State Department with all foreign countries. He is bound in such correspondence to discuss the proper construction of treaties. He must formulate the foreign policies of our government. He must state our attitude upon questions constantly arising. While strictly he may not bind our government as a treaty would bind it, to a definition of its rights, still in future discussions foreign Secretaries of other countries are wont to look for support of their contentions to the declarations and admissions of our Secretaries of State in other controversies as in a sense binding upon us. There is thus much practical framing of our foreign policies in the executive conduct of our foreign relations.[47]

✦ ✦ ✦

The Supreme Court recognizes the power of the President to decide the question of our foreign relations which it calls political, and holds itself bound by the President's action.[48]

WILSON

I am confident that I am supported by every competent Constitutional authority in the statement that the initiative in directing the relations of our Government with foreign governments is assigned by the Constitution to the Executive and to the Executive only. Only one of the two houses of Congress is associated with the President by the Constitution in an advisory capacity, and the advice of the Senate is provided for only when sought by the Executive in regard to explicit agreements with foreign governments and the appointment of the diplomatic representatives who are to speak for this Government at foreign capitals. The only safe course, I am confident, is to adhere to the prescribed method of the Constitution. We might go very far afield if we departed from it.[49]

COOLIDGE

I know that when I was in Washington I wouldn't have wanted an ex-President poking around Europe. I had enough trouble with amateur diplomats.[50]

HOOVER

One problem has been ever constant, with each succeeding President—that we should maintain and strengthen the will of the Nation and other nations for peace. In this room [Lincoln's study] have been taken those reluctant steps which have led our Nation to war and those willing steps which have again led to peace. Never has there been a President who did not pray that his administration might be one of peace, and that peace should be more assured for his successor. Yet these men have never hesitated when war became the duty of the Nation. And always in these years the thought of our Presidents has been adequate preparedness for defense as one of the assurances of peace. But that preparedness must not exceed the barest necessity for defense or it becomes a threat of aggression against others and thus a cause of fear and animosity of the world. Never have we had a President who was either a pacifist or a militarist.[51]

✶ ✶ ✶

The Executive, under the duty of guarding the interests of the United States, in the protection of future negotiations, and in maintaining relations of amity with other nations, must not allow himself to become guilty of a breach of trust by betrayal of these confidences. He must not affront representatives of other nations, and thus make future dealings with those nations more difficult and less frank. To make public in debate or in the press such confidences would violate the invariable practice of nations. It would close to the United States those avenues of information which are essential for future negotiations and amicable intercourse with the nations of the world.[52]

✶ ✶ ✶

The first responsibility of the President of the United States is to abate war, not to stimulate it. It is not the province of the President of the United States to create hate. Irresponsible talk in explosive times may bring danger. And we need remember that the day will come when we might be of service to humanity in dealing with these same men for peace.[53]

FRANKLIN D. ROOSEVELT

If the American Government is not in a position to make fair offers for fair opportunities, its [foreign] trade will be superseded. If it is not in a position at a given moment rapidly to alter the terms on which it is willing to deal with other countries, it cannot adequately protect its trade against discriminations and against bargains injurious to its interests. Furthermore a promise to which prompt effect cannot be given is not an inducement which can pass current at par in commercial negotiations.

For this reason, any smaller degree of authority in the hands of the Executive would be ineffective. The executive branches of virtually all other important trading countries already possess some such power.[54]

⚹ ⚹ ⚹

The Congress of the United States has given me certain authority to provide safeguards of American neutrality in case of war.

The President of the United States, who, under our Constitution, is vested with primary authority to conduct our international relations, thus has been given new weapons with which to maintain our neutrality.

Nevertheless—and I speak from a long experience—the effective maintenance of American neutrality depends today, as in the past, on the wisdom and determination of whoever at the moment occupy the offices of President and Secretary of State.[55]

TRUMAN

Section 2(d) of the pending bill [S. 1580] wisely provides that the President, or the Secretary of State at the direction of the President, may represent the United States at any meeting of the United Nations regardless of those provisions which call for the appointment of representatives by and with the advice and consent of the Senate.[56]

✓ ✓ ✓

The President, of course, must be prepared to support his Cabinet members when they need backing. This is especially true with regard to the Secretary of State. It is immensely important that these two men—the President and the Secretary of State—understand each other completely and that they know what their respective roles are. The Secretary of State should never at any time come to think that he is the man in the White House, and the President should not try to be the Secretary of State.[57]

✓ ✓ ✓

At this point I thought it necessary to tell [leaders at Potsdam Conference] what my powers as President were with respect to the question of the treaty of peace. When we were discussing matters appropriate for inclusion in the peace treaties, I stated, I wanted all to understand that under the Constitution of the United States a treaty could be concluded only with the consent of the United States Senate. I assured them that when I supported a proposal at the conference I would use my best efforts to support the matter when it came up for consideration in the Senate. This did not preclude, however, my coming back and saying that I considered the political sentiment in the United States was such that I could not press the matter without the danger of injuring our mutual relations. I explained that I was making these remarks not in order to change the basis of any discussion with my colleagues, nor to change the basis upon which the discussions with President Roosevelt had been held, but to make clear what my constitutional powers were. I had to consider these matters, I continued, from the standpoint of the people of the United States, and I wished to be able to be in a position to get the best arrangements approved by the Senate.[58]

✓ ✓ ✓

A President has to know what is going on all around the world in order to be ready to act when action is needed. The President must have all the facts that may affect the foreign policy or the military policy of the United States. Of course he must know what is going on at home, because the attitude of the people of the United States, who, in the final analysis, are the government, must be favorable to any action he takes.[59]

✦ ✦ ✦

But I wanted to make it plain that the President of the United States, and not the second or third echelon in the State Department, is responsible for making foreign policy, and, furthermore, that no one in any department can sabotage the President's policy. The civil servant, the general or admiral, the foreign service officer has no authority to make policy. They act only as servants of the government, and therefore they must remain in line with the government policy that is established by those who have been chosen by the people to set that policy.[60]

✦ ✦ ✦

Of course, I would never deny General MacArthur or anyone else the right to differ with me in opinions. The official position of the United States, however, is defined by decisions and declarations of the President. There can be only one voice in stating the position of this country in the field of foreign relations. This is of fundamental constitutional significance.[61]

✦ ✦ ✦

The President cannot possibly give all the secret information that comes to him to every member of Congress—there are so many of them that secrets would be certain to leak out—and yet he must have their support and co-operation for policies based on this kind of information. Bi-partisanship in foreign policy means simply that the President can repose confidence in the members of the other party and that in turn the leaders of that party have confidence in the President's conduct of foreign affairs.[62]

EISENHOWER

I have thought a great deal about good will tours, and certainly as far as South America is concerned, I have stated many, many times, how terrifically interested I am in that region. I believe we can much improve our relationships with them; but whether or not the President of the United States can find time these days to make one of these trips, with their physical drain and the other features that go with them, I am not so sure. You might make a short one, but I think possibly it would be better to find real emissaries that could go down and spend more time than would be possible for the President.[63]

✓ ✓ ✓

The Bricker amendment, as analyzed for me by the Secretary of State, would, as I understand it, in certain ways restrict the authority that the President must have, if he is to conduct the foreign affairs of this Nation effectively.

Now, I do not mean to say that that is the intent of the amendment. I am perfectly certain that the men that have written the amendment, that are supporting it, are convinced that it would work only to the good of the United States and protect the individual rights of citizens of the United States inside our own country.

I do believe that there are certain features that would work to the disadvantage of our country, particularly in making it impossible for the President to work with the flexibility that he needs in this highly complicated and difficult situation.[64]

The general effect of the Bricker amendment would have been to transfer the treaty-making power to the Congress. It was defeated.

✓ ✓ ✓

Every Senator or Member of Congress, every committee, subcommittee, has a right in their investigative and other processes to give advice to individuals, to indicate the judgment of the speaker as to what he believes our country might do under a given set of circumstances. But the power to negotiate, the responsibility for negotiating with others, rests absolutely and completely in the Executive. And this fact, of course, being so obvious, has universal recognition, including recognition by every Senator that I know.[65]

✓ ✓ ✓

I think there is sufficient power in the Secretary of State, and in the Presidency, to remind all peoples—others, and including our own—that the exclusive power of negotiating such arrangements, anything that is legal, belongs to the Executive, and comes into being when two-thirds of the Senate ratify.[66]

✓ ✓ ✓

To date, the organization of the executive branch for foreign affairs has been deficient in two major respects. First: there has been no clear assignment of central responsibility for foreign policy below the President. Second: a number of programs which implement our foreign policy have been scattered within the executive branch rather than being grouped together for the most efficient and economical administration.[67]

✦ ✦ ✦

Under our form of Government, the President has the duty to conduct foreign affairs. Every American knows this to be our traditional policy which has functioned so well during the lifetime of our Republic.

While I have opposed other amendments which would have had the effect of depriving the President of the capacity necessary to carry on negotiations with foreign governments, I am glad to support the Knowland Amendment for it confirms that this Presidential power cannot be used contrary to the Constitution.

All action of the President, either domestically or in foreign relations, must be within and pursuant to constitutional authority. Consequently I am unalterably opposed to any amendment which could change our traditional treaty making power or which would hamper the President in his constitutional authority to conduct foreign affairs. Today, probably as never before in our history it is essential that our country be able effectively to enter into agreements with other nations.

As President I have taken an oath to defend the Constitution. I therefore oppose any change which will impair the President's traditional authority to conduct foreign affairs. Senator Wiley and others who have joined in the defense of these constitutional powers so important to the integrity and safety of our nation, are entitled to commendation and support for their efforts.

It is my belief that the reassurances contained in the Knowland Amendment meet all legitimate demands that have been made in this field of foreign relations.[68]

The Knowland Amendment would have forbidden incorporating into treaties any provisions that conflicted with provisions of the Constitution.

✦ ✦ ✦

Within a matter of minutes I shall leave the United States on a trip that in some respects is unprecedented for a President of the United States. Other Presidents have left the continental limits of our country for the purpose of discharging their duties as Commander in Chief in time of war, or to participate in conference at the end of a war to provide for the measures that would bring about a peace. But now, for the first time, a President goes to engage in a conference with the heads of other governments in order to prevent wars, in order to see whether in this time of stress and strain we cannot devise measures that will keep from us this terrible scourge that afflicts mankind.

Now, manifestly, there are many difficulties in the way of a President going abroad for a period, particularly while Congress is in session. He has many constitutional duties; he must be here to perform them. . . .[69]

✓ ✓ ✓

Now, let's be perfectly clear: the Constitution holds the President responsible for carrying on the foreign relations of the United States of America; you can't get out of that. And, consequently, knowing that to carry on those foreign affairs you need the approval of Congress, because you need appropriations often, you need organizations set up, you do keep them informed just as a matter of practical workings of a political organization.

On top of that, in such matters as you see a treaty coming up or a resolution, you get them in and confer with them in advance, and try to discover whether there is any better idea than your own.[70]

✓ ✓ ✓

. . . it seems to me imperative that the Tariff Commission's findings and recommendations be subject to the President's approval. In the world of today the tariff policy of the United States can have profound effects not only on our foreign relations generally but upon the security of the entire free world. Some nations of the free world must either export or die, because they must import to live. Their very existence, as well as their defensive strength as free world partners, depends upon trade. For the United States to close its doors, either by high tariffs or import quotas, upon exports from these nations could force them into economic dependence on the Communists and to that extent weaken the strength of the free world.

Moreover, escape clause actions frequently involve questions affecting the national interest, such as the requirements of the domestic economy and the effect of the findings and recommendations of the Tariff Commission on other producers and consumers in the United States, including their effect upon the jobs of those producing for export. The President—who serves the in-

terests of the whole nation—is uniquely qualified to make a rea-
soned judgment as to whether the findings and recommendations of the Commission in such cases are in the national interest.
The Tariff Commission, on the other hand, was not appointed to
make judgments in such matters, involving, as they do, evalua-
tions of the impact of escape clause actions on the whole range
of the American economy.

These problems, and the effect that one course of action or
another would have upon the best interests of the United States,
are peculiarly within the knowledge of the President. In fact
dealing with such problems constitutes a major Constitutional
responsibility of the President, both as President and Commander-in-Chief. The Tariff Commission, on the other hand, has
only a limited responsibility—to find whether or not in its opinion there is injury to a domestic industry as a result of imports
and to make recommendations to the President based upon such
findings. It is essential that the President have authority to weigh
those findings and recommendations along with all of the information the President has in both the domestic and the foreign
field, and to arrive at a decision which will be in the best interests of the United States.

To withdraw from the President his power to make decisions
in escape clause cases and to grant finality to the Tariff Commission's findings and recommendations would in my opinion be
a tragic blunder which could seriously jeopardize the national
interest, the foreign relations, as well as the security of the
United States.[71]

✓ ✓ ✓

And when the Bricker Amendment first came to my attention, it was on this basis, the argument I made: We must make
certain that no treaty is approved by the Senate, or made by
the President, approved by the Senate, if it conflicts with the
Constitution. And I said, "I agree with that. I believe that we
must be completely constitutional." So then, they got the famous
"which" clause and without going into details, it would have
definitely changed our Constitution, and not merely assured us
that the Constitution would not be violated by the President,
by the treaty-making process. So then I went into action and I
began to fight with every tool I could get. I talked, I made
speeches, I wrote letters, and I certainly—I got my own group
working on people in the Congress. It was, to my mind, it would
have been an unjustifiable invasion into the Presidential powers,

and indeed, in this day and time when he may have to make treaties or executive agreements, it's just the kind of thing that we should not allow at all whatsoever.[72]

✶ ✶ ✶

Now, by the Constitution, also, he's responsible for the conduct of our foreign affairs. This is one of his most specific and most urgent duties. At one time, of course, our country was more isolated from the rest of the world than it is now; with the rapid communications, transportation, we are really just a few minutes away from disaster any time that some one would try to initiate really aggressive attack, specifically the Soviets. We, of course, have power that we think will never allow them to do that, but nevertheless, that's his kind of thing, the problem that he has to consider and the decisions he would have to make in emergency.[73]

✶ ✶ ✶

There are a number of ways, of course, in which his power's exerted that I haven't mentioned, but it is clear that since he is the head of the richest and strongest nation in the world, because our nation's position among a free world is so pre-eminent and leading, he has an influence that is world-wide in scope; it is very deep insofar as it touches upon every—the fortunes and the lives of every citizen of our own country. It is truly, I think, the most powerful position in the free world.[74]

KENNEDY

I think that it is most valuable to talk to those with whom we are allied. I also think it is important that we talk to those who are separated from us, because in the final analysis, heavy decisions rest, constitutionally, upon the President of the United States. He must under some conditions make the final judgment himself, and if my judgment may be more lucid, may be based more on reality as a result of this exchange, then I think the trip [to Europe] will be useful.[75]

✶ ✶ ✶

The words of any occupant of this office—particularly his words on foreign policy—are certain to be heard and likely to be acted upon by more than one audience: adversaries, allies, neutrals, the Congress, and other members of the Administration as well as all the diverse individuals and interest groups which compose the American electorate. Each must be taken into account. A boon to one may be a bane to others. No group can later be assured privately that words broadcast to all were meant only for some, or were not intended to mean what they clearly seemed to say.[76]

Chapter VII

THE PRESIDENT AS COMMANDER IN CHIEF

A logical extension of the power of the presidency in foreign affairs is its role as supreme command of the military forces of the United States. The Constitution would appear on the surface to be very specific on this executive function: "The President shall be Commander in Chief of the Army and Navy of the United States, and of the militia of the several States when called into the actual service of the United States."[1] Actually, however, the extent of this command and its application to such attendant problems as direct control over those civil affairs that can affect the strength, supplying, supporting, and effectiveness of the Armed Forces have long been of controversial interest to students of the presidency. It is not without significance that of all the Presidents, Lincoln, Wilson, and Franklin Roosevelt, wartime leaders, have invited the most extreme appraisals, denounced by some and revered by others.

Employment of the full powers of commander in chief has been exercised by only seven Presidents: Madison, in the War of 1812; Polk, in the Mexican War; Lincoln, in the Civil War; McKinley, in the Spanish-American War; Wilson, in the First World War; Franklin Roosevelt, in the Second World War; and Truman, in the Second World War and the Korean War. With the Eisenhower and Kennedy administrations, however, came the age of instant wars, and the war powers became inseparable from the foreign relations conduct of the office.

Madison, whose greatness as a political theorist was never matched by his performance as a President, was the first and least impressive wartime presidential commander in chief; his War of 1812 was a hodgepodge of mismanagement, bad appointments, disastrous reverses, embarrassing retreats, farcical disputes within the administration, and home-front disunity. The United States did not win the war: the British simply lost it. And the ultimate outcome was in spite of rather than because of Madison's employment of the command powers of the presidency.

In the Mexican War, Polk, on the other hand, exhibited a firm grasp of military problems and planning, actively and successfully concerning himself with the major campaigns, even though Congress would not create a new general rank so that he could name his own top field commander: "My situation is most embarrassing. I am held responsible for the war, and I am required to entrust the chief command of the army to a general in whom I have no confidence."[2]

A century later, Truman, when he lost confidence in a top field commander who insisted on making public statements of national policy, took direct action and recalled Douglas MacArthur, who had assumed the dimensions of a folk hero. Actually, Truman showed no lack of respect for MacArthur's military ability; but he reverted firmly to the stand of Washington, Jefferson, and other vigorous exponents of the President's authority in defining and stating the position of the United States. "Of course, I would never deny General MacArthur or anyone else the right to differ with me in opinions. The official position of the United States, however, is defined by decisions and declarations of the President. There can be only one voice in stating the position of this country."[3]

Half a century after Polk and before Truman, McKinley faced a war which he had undertaken only to keep "the war party" happy. Once the war was on, however, he had to run it himself, for he had accumulated the most incompetent war Cabinets ever to sit together. The War Department was headed by Russell A. Alger, one of the least capable men ever to hold that portfolio in war or peace, and the Navy Department by John D. Long, who felt himself to be less the head of the Navy than the people's representative in the Department. McKinley, who did not even have a general staff worth the name, showed no brilliance in conducting a war that he never wanted anyhow. Only the absence of an enemy of any proportions brought it to an early end.

Due primarily to the limited nature of all three of the conflicts over which they presided, Madison, Polk, and McKinley had no occasion to develop fully the wartime command power of the presidency or to touch on all its implications.

Abraham Lincoln, most of whose presidential writings were devoted to the exercise or interpretation of his war powers, had a far different problem, complicated by the facts that, as commander in chief, he was required to head the military forces in operations on an extensive home front and also that, as executor of the laws of the United States, he was charged with putting down an internal insurrection, with enormous civil, constitutional, and political implications, against the authority of the federal government. Inevitably there was an overlapping of these two duties and also, therefore, an intermingling of presidential powers. Moreover, Lincoln was also the ranking leader in an actual theater of war, for the Confederacy had invaded Northern territory. The whole situation furnished a rare occasion for a literal-minded man to be so preoccupied by hairsplitting and rigid adherences to legal points, in the Buchanan manner, that the war would be hopelessly lost. But Lincoln was neither a literal nor a rigid man. His remarkably lucid sense of values convinced him at the outset that a literal observance of the Constitution might cost him the nation and consequently the Constitution iself: "I did understand, however, that my oath to preserve the Constitution to the best of my ability impressed upon me the duty of preserving by every indispensable means, that government—that nation, of which that Constitution was the organic law. Was it possible to lose the nation and yet preserve the Constitution? By general law, life and limb must be protected, yet often a limb must be amputated to save a life; but a life is never wisely given to save a limb. I felt that measures otherwise unconstitutional might become lawful by becoming indispensable to the preservation of the Constitution through the preservation of the nation. Right or wrong, I assumed this ground and now avow it."[4]

Uncongenial as it was, therefore, to the American political temperament, Lincoln assumed a kind of absolute power, a constitutional dictatorship, that no President in war or peace had assumed before or has since. What Lincoln did in effect was to suspend the constitutional limitations on the powers of the presidency and interpret the "Commander in Chief" clause so broadly that it superseded all such limitations: "I conceive that I may in an emergency do things on military grounds which cannot constitutionally be done by the Congress,"[5] and again "as Commander in Chief of the Army and Navy, in time of war I suppose I have a right to take any measure which may best subdue the enemy."[6]

Lincoln did, in fact, take any measures that appeared to him necessary, and some of these were patently, even admittedly, not only extraconstitutional but unconstitutional. Some he first put into effect and then, presenting the Congress with a *fait accompli*, applied for legislative confirmation afterward. Some he did not communicate to Congress at all. Distrustful of the slow and often trivial processes of the Congress, he did not call the houses into special session when the emergency of Fort Sumter and civil war first came. Instead, he acted directly and extraordinarily: he increased the size of the Army and Navy, called for volunteers, paid out unauthorized and unappropriated public funds to unauthorized people, proclaimed a blockade, and suspended the writ of habeas corpus. In some of the most remarkably rational if legally pliable documents in our history, Lincoln justified all these courses to the satisfaction of his wisest contemporaries and to the admiration of posterity. Moreover, still acting as commander in chief, he proclaimed the slaves free in an Emancipation Proclamation that was meant solely as a wartime military measure to expedite the crushing of the Rebellion, with the irony that an essentially confiscatory measure, almost brutal in its treatment of human beings as matériel, was converted by the poetry of history into a great humane document.

The writings of Lincoln, constituting the major rationale he provided for assuming extraordinary powers, are easily the most important documents in all presidential writings, not primarily because of their literary excellence, but because he alone among Presidents practiced one-man rule. He was the best letter writer of the Presidents, and he used the letter as a favorite device for announcing and explaining major policies. It is significant of his trust in solitary power that he put little store by congressional messages, and of his quest for solitary reflection that speeches became less important to him as the war progressed.

That in the employment of his powers he strengthened both the presidency and, sometimes paradoxically, the Constitution is high tribute to the genius of Lincoln. For there is little doubt that, in the pressure of events, the Union would have been lost had Lincoln permitted government by Congress during the war, that the effectiveness of the presidential office in time of grave emergency would never have been established if he had not filled the office with wisdom and rare insight, and that the Constitution itself would have survived only as an interesting but ephemeral document had he not acted beyond its literal limitations in order to preserve it.

Lincoln presided over the republic and conducted a great war in a day of bleeding division—the direct opposite of the usual wartime atmosphere. Both Wilson and Franklin Roosevelt presided over the republic and conducted great wars in climates of national unity possible only in wartime. Consequently neither of the latter two was required to appropriate to himself the kind of power over civil affairs that Lincoln needed. Moreover, since both the World Wars involved military operations outside American continental limits and since there was no immediate threat of direct attack on the home front, Wilson and Roosevelt did not have to *assume* extraordinary powers but could solicit from Congress a carefully weighed scale of *delegated* war powers. In many ways, however, because of the economic intricacies and vast military establishments of modern warfare, the powers, though less dramatic, were far more penetrating and more permeating than those assumed by Lincoln.

Wilson's wartime powers, in general, were derived from Congress, while those of Lincoln were held by him unilaterally to be logical adjuncts of his constitutional role as commander in chief.

Thus, with congressional authorization, Wilson exercised a greater control over the natural resources, industry, commerce, transportation, and communications of the nation than Lincoln did. He was empowered to create and direct vast administrative agencies touching on every aspect of national life. Many of the activities of these agencies and also many of Wilson's direct acts as commander in chief touched sensitively on the status of constitutional provisions in wartime. And again, as in the Civil War, the consensus of judicial and lay minds tended to bolster the theory that certain otherwise inviolate principles of the Constitution had to be compromised in wartime for the greater good —as Lincoln clearly saw—of preserving the nation of which the Constitution is the organic law.

When World War II came and even before, during the lend-lease days, only the legalistic and the querulous were inclined to view with alarm the passing of exceptional powers to the President and his assumption of others as inherent in the office. For the most part, the actual war powers followed the same pattern as those of World War I, with a more far-reaching scope, but one that was no more than proportionate to the greater challenge of events.

Neither Wilson nor Roosevelt wrote broadly of the wartime powers of the President, partly because in the nature of their acquisition they required neither explanation nor justification. But with the new division of the world, after World War II, with the rise of the ultimate weapons, of brinksmanship, of the dialogue of power for menace, the war powers are really constant— an awareness of which heavily preoccupied Truman and Eisenhower. This adds a new and fearful dimension to the American presidency which is bound, as long as conscionable men hold the office, to intrude itself at length into their utterances.

WASHINGTON

The rank of the principal officers of the Army being first settled by me, as follow

First—Gov. Lee of Virginia to be commander in chief if I do not go out myself. . . .[7]

Washington was saying that he saw no limit to the Commander in Chief role of the presidency—even to taking command in the field.

✶ ✶ ✶

As Commander in Chief of the militia, when called into the actual service of the United States, I have visited the places of general rendezvous, to obtain more exact information, and to direct a plan for ulterior movements. Had there been room for a persuasion, that the laws were secure from obstruction; that the civil magistate was able to bring to justice such of the most culpable, as have not embraced the proferred terms of amnesty, and may be deemed fit objects of example; that the friends to peace and good government were not in need of that aid and countenance, which they ought always to receive, and I trust, ever will receive, against the vicious and turbulent; I should have caught with avidity the opportunity of restoring the militia to their families and home. But succeeding intelligence has tended to manifest the necessity of what has been done; it being now confessed by those who were not inclined to exaggerate the ill-conduct of the insurgents, that their malevolence was not pointed merely to a particular law; but that a spirit, inimical to all order, had actuated many of the offenders. If the state of things had afforded reasons for the continuance of my presence with the Army, it would not have been withholden. But every appearance assuring such an issue, as will redound to the reputation and strength of the United States, I have judged it most proper to resume my duties at the seat of government. . . .[8]

JOHN ADAMS

You request to be informed, whether my determination to preserve the order of the three major-generals is final; and whether I mean to appoint another adjutant-general without your concurrence. I presume that before this day you have received information from the Secretary of War, that I some time ago signed the three commissions and dated them on the same day, in hopes, similar to yours, that an amicable adjustment, or acquiescence, might take place among the gentlemen themselves. But, if these hopes should be disappointed and controversies should arise, they will, of course, be submitted to you as Commander-in-chief, and if, after all, any one should be so obstinate as to appeal to me from the judgment of the Commander-in-chief, I was determined to confirm that judgment. Because, whatever construction may be put upon the resolutions of the ancient Congress, which have been applied to this case, and whether they are at all applicable to it or not, there is no doubt to be made that, by the present Constitution of the United States, the President has authority to determine the rank of officers.[9]

MADISON

In the morning, a note, by an express from General Winder was handed me. It was addressed to the Secretary of War. Not doubting the urgency of the occasion [the British march on Washington], I opened and read it, and it went on immediately by the Express to Gen. Armstrong who lodged in the Seven Buildings. Finding by the note that the General requested the speediest counsel, I proceeded to his Head Quarters on the Eastern Branch, trusting for notice to the Secretary of War to follow, to the note from Winder. On my reaching his quarters, we were successively joined by the Secretary of State (who soon with our approbation repaired to Bladensburg) the Secretary of the Navy, and Mr. Rush, the Attorney General. After an hour or so, the Secretary of the Treasury arrived, and quickly after the Secretary of War. The latter had been impatiently expected, and surprize at his delay manifested. Gen. Winder was, at the moment setting off to hurry on the troops to Bladensburg in consequence of certain intelligence that the Enemy had taken that direction. Barney's corps was also ordered thither, leaving the Bridge to be blown up if necessary. On Gen. Armstrong's coming into the room, he was informed of the certain march of the enemy for Bladensburg, and of what had passed before his arrival; and he was asked whether he had any arrangement or advice to offer in the emergency. He said he had not; adding, that as the battle would be between Militia and regular troops, the former would be beaten.

On coming out of the house and mounting our horses, the Secretary of the Treasury, who though in a very languid state of health had turned out to join us, observed to me privately that he was grieved to see the great reserve of the Secretary of War (he lodged in the same house with him), who was taking no part on so critical an occasion; that he found him under the impression, that as the means of defending the District had been committed to Gen. Winder, it might not be delicate to intrude his opinions without the approbation of the President; tho' with that approbation he was ready to give any aid he could. Mr. Campbell said that notwithstanding his just confidence in Gen. Winder, he thought, in the present state of things which called for all the military skill possible, the Military knowledge and experience of the Secretary of War ought to be availed of, and that no considerations of delicacy ought to jeopard the public safety. With these impressions he said, he had thought it his duty to make this communication, and was very anxious, that I should take some proper steps in the case. I told him I could scarcely conceive it possible that Gen. Armstrong could have so misconstrued his functions and duty as Secretary of war; that he could not but know that any proper directions from him would receive any sanction that might be necessary from the Executive; not doubt that any suggestions or advice from him to Gen. Winder would be duly attended to (in this case it had been requested in writing) I told Mr. C. that I would speak to the Secretary of War explicitly on the subject; and accordingly turning my horse to him, expressed to him my concern and surprise at the reserve he shewed at the present crisis, and at the scruples I understood he had at offering his advice or opinions; that I hoped he had not construed the paper of instructions given him some time before, (see the paper of Aug. 13, 1814) so as to restrain him in any respect from the exercise of functions belonging to his office; that at such a juncture it was to be expected that he should omit nothing within the proper agency of Secretary of War, towards the public defence; and that I thought it proper particularly that he should proceed to Bladensburg and give any aid to Gen. Winder that he could; observing that if any difficulty on the score of authority should arise, which was not likely, I should be near at hand to remove it (it was my purpose in case there should be time, to have the members of the Cabinet together in Bladensburg, where it was expected Gen. Winder would be, and in consultation with him to decide on the arrangements suited to the posture of things). He said in reply that he had put no such construction on the paper of instructions as was alluded to; and that as I thought it proper, he would proceed to Bladensburg, and be of any service to Gen. Winder he could. The purport of this conversation I communicated to Mr. Campbell who remained near us. The Secretary of War set off without delay to Bladensburg.

After a short turn to the Marine barracks whither the Secretary of the Navy had gone, I mentioned to Mr. Rush who was with me my purpose of going to Bladensburg and my object in so doing. He readily accompanied me. On approaching the Town, we learned from William Simmons, that Winder was not there, and that the enemy were entering it. We rode up to him [Simmons] instantly. The Secretaries of State and War were with him. I asked the latter whether he had spoken with Gen. Winder on the subject of his arrangements and views. He said he had not. I remarked that tho' there was so little time for it, it was possible he might offer some advice or suggestion that might not be too late, to be turned to account; on which he rode up to the General as I did myself. The unruliness of my horse prevented me from joining in the short conversation that took place. When it was over, I asked Gen. Armstrong whether he had seen occasion to suggest any improvement in any part of the arrangements. He said that he had not; that from his view of them they appeared to be as good as circumstances admitted.

When the Battle had decidedly commenced, I observed to the Secretary of War and Secretary of State that it would be proper to withdraw to a position in the rear, where we could act according to circumstances; leaving military movements now to the military functionaries who were responsible for them. This we did, Mr. Rush soon joining us. When it became manifest that the battle was lost; Mr. Rush accompanying me, I fell down into the road leading to the city and returned to it.

It had been previously settled that in the event of the enemy's taking possession of the city, and the necessity of Executive consultations elsewhere, Fredericktown would be the proper place for the assembling of the Cabinet.[10]

This is the first and only example of presidential action on the field of battle—though Lincoln often visited field headquarters.

✦   ✦   ✦

I am so far from wishing to circumscribe the range of enquiry, on the subject, that I am anxious that every circumstance may be reached that can throw light on it. I am the more anxious, because I understand that a statement furnished by the late Secretary of War, implicates me in two particulars, 1. that I committed to him, the direction of the military operations on the field of battle, which I could not even legally do, 2. that at a critical moment I interposed & prevented it.

On the latter point, I am aware that as you were not on the ground, you can have no direct knowledge & may be without a knowledge of any circumstances indirectly bearing on it. It is a point however which I believe can be disproved by evidence as decisive as can be required to establish the negative.[11]

The Secretary of War had resigned under fire after the British invasion of Washington and sought to transfer responsibility for his failures to the President's inadequacies as Commander in Chief.

✦ ✦ ✦

The only case in which the Executive can enter on a war, undeclared by Congress, is when a state of war has "been actually" produced by the conduct of another power, and then it ought to be made known as soon as possible to the Department charged with the war power. Such a case was the war with Tripoli during the administration of Mr. Jefferson.[12]

JOHN QUINCY ADAMS

. . . the conduct of General Scott was insubordinate and disrespectful to a degree that, were it not for the gallant services which he has rendered to the country, I should some time since have dismissed him from the army; that on the rigorous principle of military subordination it was perhaps my duty so to have done. But it was entirely in the nature of our principles and institutions to temper with kindness and indulgence even the rigidity of military discipline. And I thought it particularly proper so to do in the case of an officer who stood so high in the estimation of his country, and towards whom personally I had no other than friendly feelings.

He had three times successively manifested a disposition of disobedience to lawful commands, and now asked for a furlough till next April, avowedly to make an application in some form to Congress, against the order and decisions of the President. This allegation was itself an insult; for in what manner could Congress control these orders and decisions? Certainly by no other mode than by impeachment of the President, or by an ex post facto law to annul a purely executive act. I should, therefore, on no consideration grant him a furlough. It had occurred to me that in giving him this answer it would be proper to order him peremptorily to his post, and to fix a day when his present leave of absence from it should cease.[13]

VAN BUREN

If resistance is offered to the execution of a judgment or decree —made by the proper court to which jurisdiction of the matter which such judgment or decree seeks to enforce is given by the Constitution—too great to be overcome by the civil power, it is the duty of the President, upon the request of the officers of the court, to order out the military power to sustain that of the judiciary. It would be no answer on his part to such a call to say that the right which the decree or judgment seeks to enforce arises under a law which he deems unconstitutional. That is, under the circumstances, a matter that he has no right to inquire into. The decision of that question has been delegated to a different department, and has by that department been decided differently. The Constitution requires that the judgments of that department, upon subjects committed to it, should be enforced. It makes that enforcement, in extreme cases, the duty of the military. The President is intrusted with the command of that force and, in such a case, his power in regard to it is ministerial only. It is his duty, in such a case, to sustain the judicial power by the aid of the military, and if he failed in its performance he would subject himself to impeachment and removal from office. Not only is the entire power of the government thus pledged to the maintenance of judicial authority, whilst acting in the line of its duties, but there lies no appeal from its judgments or decrees. They are final and obligatory upon the rights and interests of the parties. They can neither be reversed by any other tribunal, nor is it in the power of the remaining departments of the Government united to set them aside or to treat them as a nullity, however contrary to the Constitution they may be.[14]

TYLER

By the fourth section of the fourth article of the Constitution of the United States, it is provided that the United States shall guarantee to every State in this Union a republican form of government, and shall protect each of them against invasion; and on the application of the Legislature, or executive when the Legislature cannot be convened, *against domestic violence*. And by the act of Congress, approved on the 28th of February, 1795, it is declared that, in case of an insurrection in any State *against the government thereof*, it shall be lawful for the President of the

United States, upon application of the Legislature of such State, or of the executive when the Legislature cannot be convened, to call forth such number of the militia of any other State or States as may be applied for, as he may judge sufficient to suppress such insurrection. By the third section of the same act it is provided that, whenever it may be necessary, in the judgment of the President, to use the military force hereby directed to be called forth, the President shall forthwith, by proclamation, command such insurgents to disperse, and retire peaceably to their respective abodes within a reasonable time.

By the act of March 3, 1807, it is provided "that in all cases of insurrection or obstruction to the laws, either of the United States or any individual State or Territory, where it is lawful for the President of the United States to call forth the militia for the purpose of suppressing such insurrection, or of causing the laws to be duly executed, it shall be lawful for him to employ, for the same purposes, such part of the land or naval forces of the United States as shall be judged necessary, having first observed all the prerequisites of the law in that respect."[15]

Thomas Dorr led a revolt against the government of Rhode Island in the cause of free suffrage. He held a people's convention, elected a rump legislature, and led a military attack on the state arsenal. Tyler finally ordered federal troops to intervene.

POLK

By the Constitution the power to "declare war" is vested in Congress, and by the same instrument it is provided that "the President shall be Commander in Chief of the Army and Navy of the United States" and that "he shall take care that the laws be faithfully executed."

When Congress have exerted their power by declaring war against a foreign nation, it is the duty of the President to prosecute it. The Constitution has prescribed no particular mode in which he shall perform this duty. The manner of conducting the war is not defined by the Constitution. The term war used in that instrument has a well-understood meaning among nations. That meaning is derived from the laws of nations, a code which is recognized by all civilized powers as being obligatory in a state of war. The power is derived from the Constitution and the manner of exercising it is regulated by the laws of nations. When Congress have declared war, they in effect make it the duty of the President in prosecuting it, by land and sea, to resort to all the modes and to exercise all the powers and rights which other nations at war possess. He is invested with the same power in this respect as if he were personally present commanding our fleets by sea or our armies by land. He may conduct the war by issuing orders for fighting battles, besieging and capturing cities, conquering and holding the provinces of the enemy, or by capturing his vessels and other property on the high seas. But these are not the only modes of prosecuting war which are recognized by the laws of nations and to which he is authorized to resort. The levy of contributions on the enemy is a right of war well established and universally acknowledged among nations; and one which every belligerent possessing the ability may properly exercise. The most approved writers on public law admit and vindicate this right as consonant with reason, justice, and humanity.[16]

✦ ✦ ✦

Not doubting that our late war with Mexico was just on the part of the United States, I did not hesitate when charged by the Constitution with its prosecution to exercise a power common to all other nations, and Congress was duly informed of the mode and extent to which that power had been and would be exercised at the commencement of their first session thereafter.

Upon the declaration of war against Mexico by Congress the United States were entitled to all the rights which any other nation at war would have possessed. These rights could only be demanded and enforced by the President, whose duty it was, as "Commander in Chief of the Army and Navy of the United States," to execute the law of Congress which declared the war. In the act declaring war Congress provided for raising men and money to enable the President "to prosecute it to a speedy and successful termination." Congress prescribed no mode of conducting it, but left the President to prosecute it according to the laws of nations as his guide. Indeed, it would have been impracticable for Congress to have provided for all the details of a campaign.[17]

✦ ✦ ✦

I have no great confidence in Gen'l [Winfield] Scott as a military commander, and after his very exceptionable letter of May last to the Secretary of War, it is with reluctance that I assign him to this important command. If I had the power I would certainly select some other, but I am compelled to use the officers provided by law, and under all the circumstances feel constrained to assign him to this command. He is the highest in command in the regular army and it is his natural position.[18]

Scott had written to the Secretary of War a most abusive letter criticizing the Mexico campaign.

✦ ✦ ✦

The truth is neither [Zachary] Taylor nor Scott are fit for the command of the army in the great operations in progress and which are contemplated. To add to my embarrassment, & it does greatly do so, Congress does not strengthen the Executive arm. Nearly half the session has passed and they are engaged in debates about slavery and party politics, and have passed none of the essential measures which I have recommended as indispensible to the vigorous & successful prosecution of the war. With a large nominal majority in both Houses, I am practically in a minority. The several cliques & sections of the Democratic party are manifestly more engaged in managing for their respective favourites in the next Presidential election, than they are in supporting the Government in prosecuting the war, or in carrying out any of its great measures. The only corrective is in the hands of the people. I will do my duty to the country and rejoice that with my own voluntary free will & consent I am not to be again a candidate. This determination is irrevocable.[19]

✦ ✦ ✦

I am held responsible for the conduct of the War, & yet Congress refused to give me a commander in whom I have confidence, & I am compelled to employ the officers whom the law has provided, however unfit they may be.[20]

FILLMORE

By the Constitution of the United States the President is constituted Commander in Chief of the Army and Navy, and of the militia of the several states when called into the actual service of the United States. The Constitution declares also that he shall take care that the laws be faithfully executed and that he shall from time to time give to the Congress information of the state of the Union.

Congress has power by the Constitution to provide for calling

forth the militia to execute the laws of the Union, and suitable
and appropriate acts of Congress have been passed as well for
providing for calling forth the militia as for placing other suitable
and efficient means in the hands of the President to enable him
to discharge the constitutional functions of his office.

The second section of the act of the 28th of February, 1795,
declares that whenever the laws of the United States shall be opposed or their execution obstructed in any State by combinations too powerful to be suppressed by the ordinary course of
judicial proceedings or the power vested in the marshals, the
President may call forth the militia, as far as may be necessary,
to suppress such combinations and to cause the laws to be duly
executed.

By the act of March 3, 1807, it is provided that in all cases of
obstruction to the laws either of the United States or any individual State or Territory, where it is lawful for the President to
call forth the militia for the purpose of causing the laws to be
duly executed, it shall be lawful for him to employ for the same
purposes such part of the land or naval force of the United States
as shall be judged necessary.

These several enactments are not in full force, so that if the
laws of the United States are opposed or obstructed in any State
or Territory by combinations too powerful to be suppressed by
the judicial or civil authorities it becomes a case in which it is
the duty of the President either to call out the militia or to employ the military and naval force of the United States, or to do
both if in his judgment the exigency of the occasion shall so require, for the purpose of suppressing such combinations. The
constitutional duty of the President is plain and peremptory and
the authority vested in him by law for its performance clear and
ample.[21]

✦ ✦ ✦

We have had two cabinet meetings, the last this morning, on
the authority and duty of the President to use the Military force
in aid of the civil officer to execute the fugitive slave law, and
have concluded, when necessary, to do it. We were somewhat
embarrassed by the legislation of Congress on the subject, in
1807, and subsequent Acts, which would seem to imply that this
was a power to be conferred by Congress, but after a careful
examination of the subject, I came to the conclusion that it was
an inherent Executive power enforced by the Constitution, when

it made the President commander-in-chief of the Army and Navy, and required him to take care that the laws be faithfully executed.[22]

✦ ✦ ✦

. . . I have to observe that the Constitution declares that "the President shall take care that the laws be faithfully executed," and that "he shall be Commander in Chief of the Army and Navy of the United States, and of the militia of the several States when called into the actual service of the United States," and that "Congress shall have power to provide for calling forth the militia to execute the laws of the Union, suppress insurrections, and repel invasions." From which it appears that the Army and Navy are by the Constitution placed under the control of the Executive; and probably no legislation of Congress could add to or diminish the power thus given but by increasing or diminishing or abolishing altogether the Army and Navy. But not so with the militia. The President can not call the militia into service, even to execute the laws or repel invasions, but by the authority of acts of Congress passed for that purpose. But when the militia are called into service in the manner prescribed by law, then the Constitution itself gives the command to the President. Acting on this principle, Congress, by the act of February 28, 1795, authorized the President to call forth the militia to repel invasion and "suppress insurrections against a State government, and to suppress combinations against the laws of the United States, and cause the laws to be faithfully executed." But the act proceeds to declare that whenever it may be necessary, in the judgment of the President, to use the military force thereby directed to be called forth, the President shall forthwith, by proclamation command such insurgents to disperse and retire peaceably to their respective abodes within a limited time. These words are broad enough to require a proclamation in all cases where militia are called out under that act, whether to repel invasion or suppress an insurrection or to aid in executing the laws. This section has consequently created some doubt whether the militia could be called forth to aid to executing the laws without a previous proclamation. But yet the proclamation seems to be in words directed only against insurgents, and to require them to disperse, thereby implying not only an insurrection, but an organized, or at least an embodied, force. Such a proclamation in aid of the civil authority would often defeat the whole object by giving such notice to persons intended to be arrested that they would be enabled to fly or secrete themselves. The force may be wanted sometimes to make the arrest, and also sometimes to protect the officer after it is made, and to prevent a rescue. I would therefore suggest that this section be modified by declaring that nothing therein contained shall be construed to require any previous proclamation when the militia are called forth, either to repel invasion, to execute the laws, or suppress combinations against them, and that the President may make such call and place such militia under the control of any civil officer of the United States to aid him in executing the laws or suppressing such combinations; and while so employed they shall be paid by and subsisted at the expense of the United States.

Congress, not probably adverting to the difference between the militia and the Regular Army, by the act of March 3, 1807, authorized the President to use the land and naval forces of the United States for the same purposes for which he might call forth the militia, and subject to the same proclamation. But the power of the President under the Constitution, as Commander of the Army and Navy, is general, and his duty to see the laws faithfully executed is general and positive; and the act of 1807 ought not to be construed as evincing any disposition in Congress to limit or restrain this constitutional authority.[23]

BUCHANAN

Congress possess the sole and exclusive power, under the Constitution, "to declare war." They alone can "raise and support armies," and "provide and maintain a navy." But after Congress shall have declared war, and provided the force necessary to carry it on, the President, as commander-in-chief of the army and navy, can alone, employ this force in making war against the enemy. This is the plain language, and history proves that it was the well known intention of the framers of the Constitution.

It will not be denied that the general "power to declare war" is without limitation, and embraces within itself not only what writers on the law of nations term a public or perfect war, but also an imperfect war, and, in short, every species of hostility however confined or limited. Without the authority of Congress the President cannot fire a hostile gun in any case except to repel the attacks of an enemy. It will not be doubted that under this power Congress could, if they thought proper, authorize the President to employ the force at his command to seize a vessel belonging to an American citizen which had been illegally and unjustly captured in a foreign port and restore it to its owner. But can Congress only act after the fact, after the mischief has been done? Have they no power to confer upon the President the authority in advance to furnish instant redress should such a case afterward occur? Must they wait until the mischief has been done, and can they apply the remedy only when it is too late? To confer this authority to meet future cases, under circumstances strictly specified, is as clearly within the war-declaring power as such an authority conferred upon the President by act of Congress after the deed had been done. In the progress of a great nation many exigencies must arise imperatively requiring that Congress should authorize the President to act promptly on certain conditions which may or may not afterward arise.[24]

LINCOLN

. . . These rebels are violating the Constitution to destroy the Union; I will violate the Constitution, if necessary, to save the Union: and I suspect, Chase, that our Constitution is going to have a rough time of it before we get done with this row.[25]

✓ ✓ ✓

Other calls were made for volunteers to serve for three years, unless sooner discharged, and also for large additions to the regular army and navy. These measures, whether strictly legal or not, were ventured upon, under what appeared to be a popular demand and a public necessity; trusting then, as now, that Congress would readily ratify them. It is believed that nothing has been done beyond the constitutional competency of Congress.[26]

Contrary to the command of the Constitution, Lincoln had increased the size of the army without authorization of the Congress.

✓ ✓ ✓

By the act of the 5th of August last, Congress authorized the President to instruct the commanders of suitable vessels to defend themselves against, and to capture, pirates. This authority has been exercised in a single instance only. For the more effectual protection of our extensive and valuable commerce, in the eastern seas especially, it seems to me that it would also be advisable to authorize the commanders of sailing vessels to recapture any prizes which pirates may make of United States vessels and their cargoes, and the consular courts, now established by law in eastern countries, to adjudicate the cases, in the event that this should not be objected to by the local authorities.[27]

✓ ✓ ✓

In this emergency the President felt it his duty to employ with energy the extraordinary powers which the Constitution confides to him in cases of insurrection. He called into the field such military and naval forces, unauthorized by the existing laws, as seemed necessary. He directed measures to prevent the use of the post-office for treasonable correspondence. He subjected passengers to and from foreign countries to new passport regulations, and he instituted a blockade, suspended the writ of *habeas corpus* in various places, and caused persons who were represented to him as being or about to engage in disloyal or treasonable practices to be arrested by special civil as well as military agencies, and detained in military custody, when necessary, to prevent them and deter others from such practices.[28]

✓ ✓ ✓

. . . as commander-in-chief of the army and navy, in time of war I suppose I have a right to take any measure which may best subdue the enemy. . . .[29]

✓ ✓ ✓

That on the first day of January, in the year of our Lord one thousand eight hundred and sixty-three, all persons held as slaves within any State or designated part of a State the people whereof shall then be in rebellion against the United States, shall be then, thenceforward, and forever free; and the Executive Government of the United States, including the military and naval authority thereof, will recognize and maintain the freedom of such persons, and will do no act or acts to repress such persons, or any of them, in any efforts they may make for their actual freedom.

That the Executive will, on the first day of January aforesaid, by proclamation designate the States and parts of States, if any, in which the people thereof, respectively shall then be in rebellion against the United States; and the fact that any State or the people thereof, shall on that day be in good faith represented in the Congress of the United States by members chosen thereto at elections wherein a majority of the qualified voters of such State shall have participated, shall, in the absence of strong countervailing testimony, be deemed conclusive evidence that such State, and the people thereof, are not then in rebellion against the United States.[30]

To the scorn of some abolitionists, Lincoln considered the freeing of the slaves a military measure, for which his authority derived from his powers as Commander in Chief.

✦ ✦ ✦

Whereas it has become necessary to call into service not only volunteers, but also portions of the militia of the States by draft, in order to suppress the insurrection existing in the United States, and disloyal persons are not adequately restrained by the ordinary processes of law from hindering this measure, and from giving aid and comfort in various ways to the insurrection:
Now, therefore, be it ordered—
First. That during the existing insurrection, and as a necessary measure for suppressing the same, all rebels and insurgents, their aiders and abettors within the United States, and all persons discouraging volunteer enlistments, resisting militia drafts, or guilty of any disloyal practice affording aid and comfort to rebels against the authority of the United States, shall be subject to martial law, and liable to trial and punishment by courts martial or military commissions.
Second. That the writ of *habeas corpus* is suspended in respect to all persons arrested, or who are now, or hereafter during the rebellion shall be, imprisoned in any fort, camp, arsenal, military prison or other place of confinement, by any military authority, or by the sentence of any court martial or military commission.[31]

✦ ✦ ✦

And by virtue of the power and for the purpose aforesaid, I do order and declare that all persons held as slaves within said designated States and parts of States are, and henceforward shall be, free; and that the Executive Government of the United States, including the military and naval authorities thereof, will recognize and maintain the freedom of said persons.
And I hereby enjoin upon the people so declared to be free to abstain from all violence, unless in necessary self-defense; and I recommend to them that, in all cases where allowed, they labor faithfully for reasonable wages.
And I further declare and make known that such persons of suitable condition will be received into the armed service of the

United States to garrison forts, positions, stations, and other places, and to man vessels of all sorts in said service.

And upon this act, sincerely believed to be an act of justice, warranted by the Constitution upon military necessity, I invoke the considerate judgment of mankind and the gracious favor of Almighty God.[32]

✓ ✓ ✓

They [secessionists and sympathizers] knew that in times such as they were inaugurating, by the Constitution itself the "habeas corpus" might be suspended; but they also knew they had friends who would make a question as to who was to suspend it; meanwhile their spies and others might remain at large to help on their cause. Or if, as has happened, the Executive should suspend the writ without ruinous waste of time, instances of arresting innocent persons might occur, as are always likely to occur in such cases; and then a clamor could be raised in regard to this, which might be at least of some service to the insurgent cause. It needed no very keen perception to discover this part of the enemy's program, so soon as by open hostilities their machinery was fairly put in motion. Yet, thoroughly imbued with a reverence for the guaranteed rights of individuals, I was slow to adopt the strong measures which by degrees I have been forced to regard as being within the exceptions of the Constitution, and as indispensable to the public safety. Nothing is better known to history than that courts of justice are utterly incompetent to such cases. Civil courts are organized chiefly for trials of individuals, or, at most, a few individuals acting in concert—and this in quiet times, and on charges of crimes well defined in the law. Even in times of peace bands of horse-thieves and robbers frequently grow too numerous and powerful for the ordinary courts of justice. But what comparison, in numbers, have such bands ever borne to the insurgent sympathizers even in many of the loyal States? Again, a jury too frequently has at least one member more ready to hang the panel than to hang the traitor. And yet again, he who dissuades one man from volunteering, or induces one soldier to desert, weakens the Union cause as much as he who kills a Union soldier in battle. Yet this dissuasion or inducement may be so conducted as to be no defined crime of which any civil court would take cognizance.[33]

✦ ✦ ✦

If I be wrong on this question of constitutional power, my error lies in believing that certain proceedings are constitutional when, in cases of rebellion or invasion, the public safety requires them, which would not be constitutional when, in absence of rebellion or invasion, the public safety does not require them: in other words, that the Constitution is not in its application in all respects the same in cases of rebellion or invasion involving the public safety, as it is in times of profound peace and public security. The Constitution itself makes the distinction, and I can no more be persuaded that the government can constitutionally take no strong measures in time of rebellion, because it can be shown that the same could not be lawfully taken in time of peace, than I can be persuaded that a particular drug is not good medicine for a sick man because it can be shown to not be good food for a well one. Nor am I able to appreciate the danger apprehended by the meeting, that the American people will by means of military arrests during the rebellion lose the right of public discussion, the liberty of speech and the press, the law of evidence, trial by jury, and *habeas corpus* throughout the indefinite peaceful future which I trust lies before them, any more than I am able to believe that a man could contract so strong an appetite for emetics during temporary illness as to persist in feeding upon them during the remainder of his healthful life.[34]

✦ ✦ ✦

As it looks to me, Lee's now returning toward Harper's Ferry gives you back the chance that I thought McClellan lost last fall. Quite possibly I was wrong both then and now; but, in the great responsibility resting upon me, I cannot be entirely silent.[35]

✦ ✦ ✦

You ask, in substance, whether I really claim that I may override all the guaranteed rights of individuals, on the plea of conserving the public safety—when I may choose to say the public safety requires it. This question, divested of the phraseology calculated to represent me as struggling for an arbitrary personal prerogative, is either simply a question who shall decide, or an affirmation that nobody shall decide, what the public safety does require in cases of rebellion or invasion.

The Constitution contemplates the question as likely to occur for decision, but it does not expressly declare who is to decide it. By necessary implication, when rebellion or invasion comes, the decision is to be made from time to time; and I think the man whom, for the time, the people have, under the Constitution, made the commander-in-chief of their army and navy, is the man who holds the power and bears the responsibility of making it. If he uses the power justly, the same people will probably justify him; if he abuses it, he is in their hands to be dealt with by all the modes they have reserved to themselves in the Constitution.[36]

✓   ✓   ✓

I do not object to abide a decision of the United States Supreme Court, or of the judges thereof, on the constitutionality of the draft law. In fact, I should be willing to facilitate the obtaining of it, but I cannot consent to lose the time while it is being obtained. We are contending with an enemy, who, as I understand, drives every ablebodied man he can reach into his ranks, very much as a butcher drives bullocks into a slaughter-pen. No time is wasted, no argument is used. This produces an army which will soon turn upon our now victorious soldiers, already in the field, if they shall not be sustained by recruits as they should be. It produces an army with a rapidity not to be matched on our side, if we first waste time to reexperiment with the volunteer system already deemed by Congress, and palpably, in fact, so far exhausted as to be, inadequate, and then more time to obtain a court decision as to whether a law is constitutional which requires a part of those not now in the service to go to the aid of those who are already in it, and still more time to determine with absolute certainty that we get those who are to go in the precisely legal proportion to those who are not to go. My purpose is to be in my action just and constitutional, and yet practical, in performing the important duty with which I am charged, of maintaining the unity and the free principles of our common country.[37]

✓   ✓   ✓

You dislike the emancipation proclamation, and perhaps would have it retracted. You say it is unconstitutional. I think differently. I think the Constitution invests its commander-in-chief with the law of war in time of war. The most that can be said—if so much—is that slaves are property. Is there—has there ever been—any question that by the law of war, property, both of enemies and friends, may be taken when needed? And is it not needed whenever taking it helps us, or hurts the enemy?[38]

✻ ✻ ✻

The original proclamation has no constitutional or legal justification, except as a military measure. The exemptions were made because the military necessity did not apply to the exempted localities. Nor does that necessity apply to them now any more than it did then. If I take the step, must I not do so without the arguments of military necessity, and so without any argument except the one that I think the measure politically expedient and morally right? Would I not thus give up all footing upon Constitution or law? Would I not thus be in the boundless field of absolutism? Could this pass unnoticed or unresisted?[39]

✻ ✻ ✻

In taking the various steps which have led to my present position in relation to the war, the public interest and my private interest have been perfectly parallel, because in no other way could I serve myself so well as by truly serving the Union. The whole field has been open to me where to choose. No place-hunting necessity has been upon me urging me to seek a position of antagonism to some other man, irrespective of whether such position might be favorable or unfavorable to the Union.

Of course I may err in judgment, but my present position in, reference to the rebellion is the result of my best judgment, and, according to that best judgment, it is the only position upon which any executive can or could save the Union. Any substantial departure from it insures the success of the rebellion. An armistice—a cessation of hostilities—is the end of the struggle, and the insurgents would be in peaceable possession of all that has been struggled for. Any different policy in regard to the colored man deprives us of his help, and this is more than we can bear. We cannot spare the hundred and forty or fifty thousand now serving us as soldiers, seamen, and laborers. This is not a question of sentiment or taste, but one of physical force, which may be measured and estimated as horse-power and steam-power are measured and estimated. Keep it, and you can save the Union. Throw it away and the Union goes with it. Nor is it possible for any administration to retain the service of these people with the express or implied understanding that, upon the first convenient occasion, they are to be reenslaved. It cannot be, and it ought not to be.[40]

HAYES

The important provision of the acts of 1792, 1795, and 1807, modified in its terms from time to time to adapt it to the existing emergency, remained in force until, by an act approved by President Lincoln July 29, 1861, it was reenacted substantially in the same language in which it is now found in the Revised Statutes, viz:

> Sec. 5298. Whenever, by reason of unlawful obstructions, combinations, or assemblages of persons, or rebellion against the authority of the Government of the United States, it shall become impracticable, in the judgment of the President, to enforce by the ordinary course of judicial proceedings the laws of the United States within any State or Territory, it shall be lawful for the President to call forth the militia of any or all the States and to employ such parts of the land and naval forces of the United States as he may deem necessary to enforce the faithful execution of the laws of the United States or to suppress such rebellion, in whatever State or Territory thereof the laws of the United States may be forcibly opposed or the execution thereof forcibly obstructed.

This ancient and fundamental law has been in force from the foundation of the Government. It is now proposed to abrogate it on certain days and at certain places. In my judgment no fact has been produced which tends to show that it ought to be repealed or suspended for a single hour at any place in any of the States or Territories of the Union. All the teachings of experience in the course of our history are in favor of sustaining its efficiency unimpaired. On every occasion when the supremacy of the Constitution has been resisted and the perpetuity of our institutions imperiled, the principle of this statute, enacted by the fathers, has enabled the Government of the Union to maintain its authority and to preserve the integrity of the nation.

At the most critical periods of our history my predecessors in the executive office have relied on this great principle. It was on this principle that President Washington suppressed the whisky rebellion in Pennsylvania in 1794.

In 1806, on the same principle, President Jefferson broke up the Burr conspiracy by issuing "orders for the employment of such force, either of the regulars or of the militia, and by such proceedings of the civil authorities, . . . as might enable them to suppress effectually the further progress of the enterprise." And it was under the same authority that President Jackson crushed nullification in South Carolina and that President Lincoln issued his call for troops to save the Union in 1861. On numerous other occasions of less significance, under probably every Administration, and certainly under the present, this power has been usefully exerted to enforce the laws, without objection by any party in the country, and almost without attracting public attention.

The great elementary constitutional principle which was the foundation of the original statute of 1792, and which has been its essence in the various forms it has assumed since its first adoption, is that the Government of the United States possesses under the Constitution, in full measure, the power of self-protection by its own agencies, altogether independent of State authority, and, if need be, against the hostility of State governments. It should remain embodied in our statutes unimpaired, as it has been from the very origin of the Government. It should be regarded as hardly less valuable or less sacred than a provision of the Constitution itself.[41]

BENJAMIN HARRISON

The Constitution declares that "the President shall be Commander-in-Chief of the Army and Navy of the United States, and of the militia of the several States when called into the actual service of the United States." Undoubtedly he might assume the command in person—take the field and conduct military operations—but he has never done so and is not likely to do so. The other duties laid upon him make it practically impossible that he should do so, at least for any length of time. But he does command through others, and his order to any commanding officer is imperative. Mr. Lincoln followed the movements of our armies during the Civil War very closely, and often expressed, with rare good judgment, to the commanding officer, views as to the proper use of his troops; but he did this in a suggestive rather than an imperative form.[42]

✦ ✦ ✦

The President cannot declare war. Congress must do that. But
that the provision of the Constitution making him Commander-
in-Chief was intended to confer upon the President the power
to use military force in executing the laws, and in protecting
the property of the United States and its officers in the discharge of their duties, there can be no doubt. It would not be
appropriate here to discuss the various limitations that Congress
has imposed, or attempted to impose, upon the power of the
President to use the army in enforcing the laws. The people
are very properly jealous of the interference of the military in
civil affairs, and will justify it only in cases of obvious necessity.
This consideration, and the liability to impeachment for any
improper use of his powers, will always make the use of the army,
by the President, to keep the peace, a matter of last resort.[43]

✦ ✦ ✦

A disturbance which is purely local in a state is a state affair.
The president can not send troops or lend any aid unless the
legislature calls upon him for help or the governor, if the legislature is not in session. But when a law of the United States is
resisted, it is the sworn duty of the president to execute it. . . .[44]

✦ ✦ ✦

The civil war called for a president who had faith in time,
for his country as well as himself; who could endure the impatience of others and abide his time.[45]

TAFT

The President is the Commander-in-Chief of the army and navy,
and the militia when called into the service of the United States.
Under this, he can order the army and navy anywhere he will,
if the appropriations furnish the means of transportation. Of
course the instrumentality which this power furnishes, gives the
President an opportunity to do things which involve consequences that it would be quite beyond his power under the
Constitution directly to effect. Under the Constitution, only Congress has the power to declare war, but with the army and the
navy, the President can take action such as to involve the country in war and to leave Congress no option but to declare it
or to recognize its existence.[46]

✦ ✦ ✦

The Constitution provides that the United States shall protect each state against invasion and on the application of the Legislature, or of the Executive when the Legislature cannot be convened, against domestic violence; and an early statute of the United States, still in force, provides that on such an application the President may use the militia of any state or the regular army to suppress such insurrection.[47]

✦ ✦ ✦

There is, however, a far wider exercise of the authority by the Executive in his capacity as Commander-in-Chief. It was exemplified in and after the Spanish War. Before and after the Treaty of Paris was made with Spain, by which there were left in our possession, as owners, the Philippines and Porto Rico, and in our custody, as trustees for the people of Cuba, we acquired responsibilities which were met by occupation of those islands and their government by our army and navy. In the case of Cuba, this continued from 1898 until 1903, when the island was turned over to the Cuban Republic. In the case of Porto Rico this continued from 1898 until the taking effect of the Foraker Act in April, 1900, and in the Philippines from August 13th, 1898, when we took Manila, until March, 1902, when the President was expressly given power to establish a civil government there. During all this interval of Congressional silence, and acquiescence in the action of the President as Commander-in-Chief, he directly, or through his appointed agents, exercised all the executive power and all the legislative power of government in those territories. After suppressing actual disorder, he created a quasi-civil government and appointed an executive, a civil legislature and civil judges, and became the lawgiver of ten millions of people for a period ranging from two years to four. There was nothing new or startling in the principle of this temporary enlargement of his executive functions. Its novelty was in the great volume of power which the circumstances thrust on him and the extent of the responsibilities and the wide discretion which he had to exercise. The validity of such action had been recognized by the Supreme Court in similar cases arising after the Mexican War, when we took over California and New Mexico.[48]

✦ ✦ ✦

The President is made Commander-in-Chief of the army and navy by the Constitution evidently for the purpose of enabling him to defend the country against invasion, to suppress insurrection and to take care that the laws be faithfully executed. If Congress were to attempt to prevent his use of the army for any of these purposes, the action would be void.[49]

✦ ✦ ✦

Under another section of the statute, the President has the power to call upon the army, after proclamation, to resist forcible obstruction of any Federal Laws. In other words, he is to maintain the peace of the United States. I think he would have this power under the Constitution even if Congress had not given him express authority to this end. Again, in the carrying on of war as Commander-in-Chief, it is he who is to determine the movements of the army and of the navy.[50]

WILSON

I have been very much surprised to find several of the public prints stating that the administration had abandoned the position which it so distinctly took, and still holds, that authority to exercise censorship over the press to the extent that that censorship is embodied in the recent action of the House of Representatives is absolutely necessary to the public safety. It, of course, has not been abandoned, because the reasons still exist why such authority is necessary for the protection of the Nation.

I have every confidence that the great majority of the newspapers of the country will observe a patriotic reticence about everything whose publication could be of injury, but in every country there are some persons in a position to do mischief in this field who can not be relied upon and whose interests or desires will lead to actions on their part highly dangerous to the Nation in the midst of a war. I want to say again that it seems to me imperative that powers of this sort should be granted.[51]

✦ ✦ ✦

I have asked the privilege of addressing you in order to report to you that on the twenty-eighth of December last, during the recess of the Congress, acting through the Secretary of War and under the authority conferred upon me by the Act of Congress approved August 29, 1916, I took possession and assumed control of the railway lines of the country and the systems of water transportation under their control. This step seemed to be imperatively necessary in the interest of the public welfare, in the presence of the great tasks of war with which we are now dealing. As our own experience develops difficulties and makes it clear what they are, I have deemed it my duty to remove those difficulties wherever I have the legal power to do so. To assume control of the vast railway systems of the country is, I realize, a very great responsibility, but to fail to do so in the existing circumstances would have been a much greater. I assumed the less responsibility rather than the weightier.

I am sure that I am speaking the mind of all thoughtful Americans when I say that it is our duty as the representatives of the nation to do everything that it is necessary to do to secure the complete mobilization of the whole resources of America by as rapid and effective means as can be found. Transportation supplies all the arteries of mobilization. Unless it be under a single and unified direction, the whole process of the nation's action is embarrassed.[52]

FRANKLIN D. ROOSEVELT

All one has to do is to go back and read those war acts of 1917 which conferred upon the Executive far greater power over human beings and over property than anything that was done in 1933. But the Supreme Court has finally ruled that extraordinary conditions do not create or enlarge constitutional power![53]

*   *   *

I bear an obligation, as President and as Commander-in-Chief of the Army and Navy, which extends to all groups, to all citizens, to the present and to the future. I cannot be true to the office I hold if I do not weigh the claims of all in the scales of equity. I cannot swerve from this moral obligation.[54]

*   *   *

Suppose a nation were to attack the United States or any part thereof, it is undoubtedly the Constitutional duty of the President to defend without the declaring of war.[55]

✓ ✓ ✓

Our patrolling vessels and planes will protect all merchant ships—not only American ships but ships of any flag-engaged in commerce in our defensive waters. They will protect them from submarines; they will protect them from surface raiders.

This situation is not new. The second President of the United States, John Adams, ordered the United States Navy to clean out European privateers and European ships of war which were infesting the Caribbean and South American waters, destroying American commerce.

The third President of the United States, Thomas Jefferson, ordered the United States Navy to end the attacks being made upon American and other ships by the corsairs of the Nations of North Africa.

My obligation as President is historic; it is clear. It is inescapable.

It is no act of war on our part when we decide to protect the seas that are vital to American defense. The aggression is not ours. Ours is solely defense.

But let this warning be clear. From now on, if German or Italian vessels of war enter the waters, the protection of which is necessary for American defense, they do so at their own peril.

The orders which I have given as Commander in Chief of the United States Army and Navy are to carry out that policy—at once.[56]

✓ ✓ ✓

The responsibilities of the President in wartime to protect the Nation are very grave. This total war, with our fighting fronts all over the world, makes the use of executive power far more essential than in any previous war.

If we were invaded, the people of this country would expect the President to use any and all means to repel the invader.

The Revolution and the War Between the States were fought on our own soil but today this war will be won or lost on other continents and remote seas.

I cannot tell what powers may have to be exercised in order to win this war.

The American people can be sure that I will use my powers with a full sense of my responsibility to the Constitution and to my country. The American people can also be sure that I shall not hesitate to use every power vested in me to accomplish the defeat of our enemies in any part of the world where our own safety demands such defeat.

When the war is won, the powers under which I act automatically revert to the people—to whom they belong.[57]

*   *   *

Who are these millions upon whom the life of our country depends? What are they thinking? What are their doubts? What are their hopes? And how is the work progressing?

The Commander in Chief cannot learn all of the answers to these questions in Washington. And that is why I made the trip I did.

It is very easy to say, as some have said, that when the President travels through the country he should go with a blare of trumpets, with crowds on the sidewalks, with batteries of reporters and photographers—talking and posing with all of the politicians of the land.

But having had some experience in this war and in the last war, I can tell you very simply that the kind of trip I took permitted me to concentrate on the work I had to do with expending time, meeting all the demands of publicity. And—I might add—it was a particular pleasure to make a tour of the country without having to give a single thought to politics.[58]

*   *   *

The President is the Commander in Chief and he, too, has his superior officer—the people of the United States.[59]

*   *   *

President Monroe and every American President following him were prepared to use force, if necessary, to assure the independence of other American Nations threatened by aggressors from across the seas.[60]

TRUMAN

The President, as Commander-in-Chief, should not personally have to coordinate the Army and Navy and Air Force. With all the other problems before him, the President cannot be expected to balance either the organization, the training or the practice of the several branches of national defense. He should be able to rely for that coordination upon civilian hands at the Cabinet level.[61]

✓ ✓ ✓

In cases where a difference of opinion might arise between the Military Liaison Committee and the Atomic Energy Commission there is a provision in the law whereby the committee may carry the matter through the Secretary of Defense to the President. The President's decision is final.[62]

✓ ✓ ✓

The President, who is Commander in Chief and who represents the interest of all the people, must be able to act at all times to meet any sudden threat to the nation's security. A wise President will always work with Congress, but when Congress fails to act or is unable to act in a crisis, the President, under the Constitution, must use his powers to safeguard the nation.[63]

EISENHOWER

We do know that there are weapons now in being that give more than ever to the attacker a tremendous advantage, the man who attacks by surprise. The element of surprise, always important in war, has been multiplied by the possibility of creating such widespread destruction quickly. Therefore, any President should be worse than impeached, he should be hanged, I should say, if he didn't do what all America would demand that he do to protect them in an emergency.[64]

✓ ✓ ✓

The President is the Constitutional Commander in Chief of our Armed Forces and is constantly confronted with major questions as to their efficiency, organization, operations and adequacy.[65]

✓ ✓ ✓

Now, there comes a place in the military hierarchy where someone must make a decision, and that decision must stick. The President, constitutionally, is the Commander in Chief, and what he decides to do in these things, in the form and the way that you arm and organize and command your forces, must be carried out.[66]

✓ ✓ ✓

The right of self-preservation is just as instinctive and natural for a nation as it is for the individual. Therefore, if we know we are, at any moment, under a threat of attack, as would be evidenced by missiles or planes coming in our direction, then we have to act just as rapidly as is possible, humanly possible to defend ourselves.

But when you go beyond that point, I don't know exactly what this conversation [between the Secretary of Defense and a House committee] meant, for the simple reason that I'm quite sure the Congress is not thinking of amending the Constitution and putting in the hands of the President the right to declare war. This is a congressional function and it must be observed. But I do point out that when you have got certain circumstances that put your life or could put your life or the Nation's life at stake, then there is no time, and whatever would be necessary the President would then order.[67]

* * *

Your President will also be the Commander in Chief of your Armed Forces. National security will be one of his basic responsibilities and will depend greatly upon his understanding, born of experience. Just wanting to keep out of war will not be enough—as our three major wars in this century have proved. Your President must see to it that your Armed Forces are kept alert and modern, always ready to meet whatever threat may exist in this world.[68]

* * *

When the push of a button may mean obliteration of countless humans, the President of the United States must be forever on guard against any inclination on his part to impetuosity; to arrogance; to headlong action; to expediency; to facile maneuvers; even to the popularity of an action as opposed to the rightness of an action.

He cannot worry about headlines; how the next opinion poll will rate him; how his political future will be affected.

He must worry only about the good—the long-term, abiding, permanent good—of all America.[69]

* * *

Now, the next thing, the President is named by the Constitution as Commander-in-Chief of our Armed Forces. He is in very definite sense responsible for all measures that are taken to defend the United States and provide for securing its rights everywhere in the world.[70]

✓ ✓ ✓

When we've had—been in real emergencies, that is the acute emergencies, a war, almost automatically, the President has to assume powers that otherwise he could never attempt to exercise. Sometimes, these powers are given specifically by the Congress, but often they are not. For example, recognizing that the cold war sometimes heats up to the point almost of a direct crisis, we have the cases of Formosa and the Mideast. In both these cases, I went to the Congress and asked for their specific authority to take certain action under certain conditions. Now, this meant, by and large, that under those conditions, our Armed Forces would be at war if these conditions came about. In other words, Congress gave to the President almost the power of declaring war, but under a given set of conditions. Now, this is the kind of power—as a matter of fact, the President—President Kennedy, today, has that same power. It wasn't given to me individually. It was given as an authority that the President exercises.[71]

KENNEDY

The National Security Council is an advisory body to the President, and in the final analysis, the President of the United States must make the decision. It is his decision. It is not the decision of the National Security Council or any collective decision. That was my view and my statement on Cuba a year ago, and it is my view on Cuba and the policies we followed recently this year.[72]

✓ ✓ ✓

With all of the history of war, and the human race's history unfortunately has been a good deal more war than peace, with nuclear weapons distributed all through the world, and available, and the strong reluctance of any people to accept defeat, I see the possibility in the 1970s of the President of the United States having to face a world in which 15 or 20 or 25 nations may have these weapons. I regard that as the greatest possible danger and hazard.[73]

Chapter VIII

THE BURDENS AND PRIVILEGES
OF THE PRESIDENCY

The President of the United States is both an institution and a man. As the office has evolved, the latter has, in one way or another, accommodated the former. But the infinite variety of capacity, of intelligence, of character, and of temperament represented by the first thirty-four individuals who occupied the office was bound to occasion some abrasions. The demands of the office are heavy and relentless even in quiet times. In times of trouble they are grave in the extreme, frightening in their implications. The "splendid misery," as the presidency has come to be called, came close at times to being a nightmare to the men upon whom it was visited.

Yet, oddly, the men who were most often preoccupied with the burdens of the office, and who dwelt upon them at greatest length, were not always those who worked hardest or of whom the most was asked. Indeed, it is difficult to discern any pattern here, except that the presidency did not entirely escape the chronic complainer. But equally revealing are the nature of the complaints. Lincoln certainly had a heavy sense of the enormous burden of the presidency in wartime, but his occasional articulation of that sense had great dignity and proportion and Grecian greatness. Lesser Presidents were less impressive in their protests, less convincing in their complaints, occasionally trivial and whining.

There is much to be said for those on the Washington scene in the early 1900s who became a little bored by Theodore Roosevelt's joyous chest thumpings. But there is no doubt that he stands light years ahead of those who went before and those who came after as one who delighted in every minute of his tenure. If there had been more like him in temperament, presidential writings might have been more evenly distributed as between the burdens and privileges of the office. As it is, they lean heavily on the side of the burdens.

WASHINGTON

So much is expected, so many untoward circumstances may intervene, in such a new and critical situation, that I feel an insuperable diffidence in my own abilities. I feel, in the execution of the duties of my arduous Office, how much I shall stand in need of the countenance and aid of every friend to myself, of every friend to the Revolution, and of every lover of good Government.[1]

✦ ✦ ✦

At a distance from the theatre of action truth is not always related without embellishment, and sometimes is entirely perverted from a misconception of the causes which produce the effects that are the subjects of censure. 1. This leads me to think that a system which I found it indispensably necessary to adopt upon my first coming to this city, might have undergone severe strictures and have had motives very foreign from those that govern me assigned as causes therefor; I mean, returning no visits; 2. Appointing certain days to receive them generally (not to the exclusion however of visits on any other days under particular circumstances) and 3. at first entertaining no company, and afterwards until I was unable to entertain any at all confining it to official characters. A few days evinced the necessity of the two first in so clear a point of view that, had I not adopted it, I should have been unable to have attended to any sort of business unless I had applied the hours allotted to rest and refreshment to this purpose for by the time I had done breakfast, and thence till dinner, and afterwards till bed time I could not get relieved from the ceremony of one visit before I had to attend to another; in a word, I had no leisure to read or to answer the dispatches that were pouring in upon me from all quarters; and with respect to the third matter I early received information through very respectable channels that the adoption thereof was not less essential (than) that of the other two if the President was to preserve the dignity and respect that was due to the first Magistrate, for that a contrary conduct had involved the late Presidents of Congress in insuperable difficulties, and the office (in this respect) in perfect contempt. for the table was considered as a public one, and every person, who could get introduced, conceived that he had a right to be invited to it. This, although the Table was always crowded (and with mixed company, and the President considered in no better light than as a Maître d'Hôtel) was in its nature impracticable and as many offences given as if no table had been kept.

The citizens of this place were well knowing to this fact, and the principal Members of Congress in both Houses were so well convinced of the impropriety and degrading situation of their President, that it was the general opinion that the President of the United States should neither give or receive invitations. Some from a belief, (independent of the circumstances I have mentioned) that this was fundamentally right in order to acquire respect. But to this I had two objections, both powerful in my mind; first, the novelty of it I knew would be considered as an ostentatious shew [sic] of mimicry of sovereignty; and secondly that so great a seclusion would have stopped the avenues to useful information from the many, and make me more dependent on that of the few; but to hit on a discriminating medium was found more difficult than it appeared to be at first view. for if the Citizens at large were begun upon no line could be drawn, all of decent appearance would expect to be invited, and I should have been plunged at once into the evil I was endeavoring to avoid. Upon the whole, it was thought best to confine my invitations to official characters and strangers of distinction. This line I have hitherto pursued; whether it may be found best to adhere to or depart from it in some measure must be the result of experience and information.

So strongly had the citizens of this place imbibed an idea of the impropriety of my accepting invitations to dinner that I have not received one from any family (though they are remarkable for hospitality, and though I have received every civility and attention possible from them) since I came to the city except dining with the Governor on the day of my arrival, so that, if this should be adduced as an article of impeachment there can be at least one good reason adduced for my not dining out; to wit never having been asked to do so.[2]

✓ ✓ ✓

The duties of my Office, which at all times, especially during the Session of Congress, require an unremitting attention, naturally become more pressing toward the close of it. . . .[3]

✓ ✓ ✓

I suffered every attack that was made upon my Executive conduct . . . to pass unnoticed while I remained in public office, well knowing that if the general tenor of it would not stand the test of investigation, a newspaper vindication would be of little avail.[4]

JOHN ADAMS

I have no idea that I shall be chosen President a second time; though this is not to be talked of. The business of the office is so oppressive that I shall hardly support it two years longer.[5]

✓ ✓ ✓

If I could have my wish, there should never be a show or a feast made for the President while I hold the office.[6]

✓ ✓ ✓

Be not concerned for me. I feel my shoulders relieved from a burden.[7]

✓ ✓ ✓

. . . had I been chosen President again, I am certain I could not have lived another year.[8]

Both Adams and his son, John Quincy Adams, frequently reported intimations of early death. Adams lived to ninety, his son to eighty.

✓ ✓ ✓

And they talked a great deal about "the dignity" of the office of President, which I do not find that any other persons, public or private, regard very much.[9]

JEFFERSON

I am tired of an office where I can do no more good than many others, who would be glad to be employed in it. To myself, personally, it brings nothing but unceasing drudgery and daily loss of friends. Every office becoming vacant, every appointment made, *me donne un ingrat, et cent ennemis*. My only consolation is in the belief that my fellow citizens at large will give me credit for good intentions.[10]

✦ ✦ ✦

Five weeks more will relieve me from a drudgery to which I am no longer equal, and restore me to a scene of tranquility, amidst my family and friends, more congenial to my age and natural inclinations.[11]

JOHN QUINCY ADAMS

I can scarcely conceive a more harassing, wearying, teasing condition of existence. It literally renders life burdensome. What retirement will be I cannot realize, but have formed no favorable anticipation. It cannot be worse than this perpetual motion and crazing cares. The weight grows heavier from day to day.[12]

✦ ✦ ✦

I can never be sure of writing a line that will not some day be published by friend or foe. Nor can I write a sentence susceptible of an odious misconstruction but it will be seized upon and bandied about like a watchword for hatred and derision. This condition of things gives style the cramp.[13]

✦ ✦ ✦

No one knows, and few conceive, the agony of mind that I have suffered from the time that I was made by circumstances, and not by my volition, a candidate for the Presidency till I was dismissed from that station by the failure of my re-election. They were feelings to be suppressed; and they were suppressed.[14]

✦ ✦ ✦

The most plausible and the most popular of all the objections to the Constitution, had been the accumulation of power in the office of the President. His [Washington's] exercise of those powers was watched with a jealous and suspicious eye—trifles lighter than air in his personal deportment and his domestic establishment, were treasured up, and doled out in whispers and surmises, that he was affecting the state, and adopting the forms of a monarchy.[15]

✓ ✓ ✓

It is established by custom that the President of the United States goes not abroad into any private companies; and to this usage I conform. I am, therefore, compelled to take my exercise, if at all, in the morning before breakfast.[16]

✓ ✓ ✓

The four most miserable years of my life were my four years in the Presidency.[17]

JACKSON

I can with truth say mine is a situation of dignified slavery.[18]

✓ ✓ ✓

If I can restore to our institutions their primitive simplicity and purity, can only succeed in banishing those extraneous corrupting influences which tend to fasten monopoly and aristocracy on the constitution and to make the Government an engine of oppression to the people instead of the agent of their will, I may then look back to the honors conferred upon me, with feelings of just pride—with the consciousness that they have not been bestowed altogether in vain.[19]

VAN BUREN

I must not be understood by anything I have here said as undervaluing the honor, dignity, and usefulness of the Presidential office. No American citizen can fail to regard that position as, in every respect, the most exalted as it is the most responsible public trust that can be conferred on man, for the acquisition of which no sacrifices, on the part of one competent to discharge its duties, can be deemed too great which do not include the sacrifice of honor or morality. But the extent to which personal happiness and enjoyment will be promoted by its possession is a question to be solved by the taste and temperament of the incumbent. There are men, and not a few, who derive so much pleasure from the mere possession of great power that any degree of dissatisfaction caused by its exercise is not too dear a price for the coveted indulgence, and the personal adulation which is sure to follow the footsteps of authority while it lasts fills the measure of their satisfaction. Those better regulated minds, however, whose gratification on reaching that high office is mainly derived from the consciousness that their countrymen have deemed them worthy of it and from the hope that they may be able to justify that confidence and to discharge its duties so as to promote the public good, will save themselves from great disappointments by postponing all thoughts of individual enjoyment to the completion of their labors. If those whose sense of duty and whose dispositions are of the character which alone can fit them for that station look to secure much personal gratification while swaying the rod of power they will find in that as in all other human calculations and plans "begun on earth below," that

> The ample proposition that hope makes
> Fails in the promis'd largeness.[20]

*   *   *

At the very head of their potential Presidents' disappointments will stand those inseparable from the distribution of patronage that power so dazzling to the expectant dispenser, apparently so easily performed and so fruitful of reciprocal gratification. Whatever hopes they may indulge that their cases will prove an exception to the general rule they will find, in the end, their own experience truly described by Mr. Jefferson when he said that the two happiest days of his life were those of his entrance upon his office and of his surrender of it. The truth of the matter may be stated in a word: whilst to have been deemed worthy by a majority of the People of the United States to fill the office of Chief Magistrate of the Republic is an honor which ought to satisfy the aspirations of the most ambitious citizen, the period of his actual possession of its powers and performance of its duties is and must, from the nature of things, always be, to a right minded man one of toilsome and anxious probation.[21]

POLK

The idea seems to prevail with many persons that the President is from his position compelled to contribute to every loafer who applies, provided he represents that the sum he wants is to build a church, an academy, or a college. The persons who apply to me in the great majority of cases are wholly unknown to me, and though their applications are very annoying to me, I am compelled to decline a compliance with their wishes. They may censure and slander me, but better this than to be rendered bankrupt without contributing to the public good, or receiving any thanks from the scamps who in a majority of cases apply to me for money.[22]

*   *   *

In truth, though I occupy a very high position, I am the hardest working man in this country.[23]

*   *   *

With me it is emphatically true that the Presidency is "no bed of roses."[24]

*   *   *

No President who performs his duty faithfully and conscientiously can have any leisure. If he entrusts the details and smaller matters to subordinates constant errors will occur. I prefer to supervise the whole operations of the Government myself rather than entrust the public business to subordinates, and this makes my duties very great.[25]

TAYLOR

The appointing power vested in the President imposes delicate and onerous duties.[26]

BUCHANAN

I am now in my 69th year & am heartily tired of my position as President. I shall leave it in the beginning of March, 1861, should a kind Providence prolong my days until that period, with much greater satisfaction than when entering on the duties of the office.[27]

*   *   *

When I parted from President Lincoln, on introducing him to the Executive Mansion, according to custom, I said to him: "If you are as happy, my dear sir, on entering this house as I am in leaving it and returning home, you are the happiest man in this country!" I was then thinking of the comforts and tranquillity of home, as contrasted with the troubles, perplexities, and difficulties inseparable from the Presidential office.[28]

LINCOLN

In God's name! if any one can do better in my place than I have done, or am endeavoring to do, let him try his hand at it, and no one will be better contented than myself.[29]

✦ ✦ ✦

You know better than any man living that from my boyhood up my ambition was to be President. I am President of one part of this divided country at least; but look at me! I wish I had never been born! It is a white elephant on my hands, and hard to manage. With a fire in my front and rear; having to contend with the jealousies of the military commanders, and not receiving that cordial co-operation and support from Congress which could reasonably be expected; with an active and formidable enemy in the field threatening the very life-blood of the government,—my position is anything but a bed of roses.[30]

✦ ✦ ✦

I have enough to look after without giving much of my time to the consideration of the subject of who shall be my successor in office. The position is not an easy one; and the occupant, whoever he may be, for the next four years, will have little leisure to pluck a thorn or plant a rose in his own pathway.[31]

✦ ✦ ✦

I hope, however, that I may never have another four years of such anxiety, tribulation, and abuse. My only ambition is and has been to put down the rebellion and restore peace; after which I want to resign my office, go abroad, take some rest, study foreign governments, see something of foreign life, and in my old age die in peace with the good will of all of God's creatures.[32]

✦ ✦ ✦

I would rather be dead than, as President, thus abused in the house of my friends.[33]

✦ ✦ ✦

It is seventy-two years since the first inauguration of a President under our National Constitution. During that period fifteen different and greatly distinguished citizens have, in succession, administered the executive branch of the government. They have conducted it through many perils, and generally with great success. Yet, with all this scope of precedent, I now enter upon the same task for the brief constitutional term of four years under great and peculiar difficulty. A disruption of the Federal Union, heretofore only menaced, is now formidably attempted.[34]

✓ ✓ ✓

In my position I am environed with difficulties. Yet they are scarcely so great as the difficulties of those who upon the battle-field are endeavoring to purchase with their blood and their lives the future happiness and prosperity of this country.[35]

✓ ✓ ✓

I cannot fly from my thoughts—my solicitude for this great country follows me wherever I go. I do not think it is personal vanity or ambition, though I am not free from these infirmities. . . .[36]

Lincoln was speaking in reply to ex-Governor Alexander W. Randall of Wisconsin, who had suggested that, during the desperately trying summer of 1864, Lincoln "seek seclusion and play the hermit for a fortnight."

✓ ✓ ✓

As a general rule, I abstain from reading the reports of attacks upon myself, wishing not to be provoked by that to which I cannot properly offer an answer.[37]

ANDREW JOHNSON

Notwithstanding a mendacious press; notwithstanding a subsidized gang of hirelings who have not ceased to traduce me, I have discharged all my official duties and fulfilled my pledges. And I say here tonight that if my predecessor [Lincoln] had lived, the vials of wrath would have poured out upon him.[38]

GRANT

No man could hope to perform duties so delicate and responsible as pertain to the Presidential office without sometimes incurring the hostility of those who deem their opinions and wishes treated with insufficient consideration; and he who undertakes to conduct the affairs of a great government as a faithful public servant, if sustained by the approval of his own conscience, may rely with confidence upon the candor and intelligence of a free people whose best interests he has striven to subserve, and can bear with patience the censure of disappointed men.[39]

✓ ✓ ✓

I did not ask for place or position, and was entirely without influence or the acquaintance of persons of influence, but was resolved to perform my part in a struggle threatening the very existence of the nation. I performed a conscientious duty, without asking promotion or command, and without a revengeful feeling toward any section or individual.

Notwithstanding this, throughout the war, and from my candidacy for my present office in 1868 to the close of the last Presidential campaign, I have been the subject of abuse and slander scarcely ever equaled in political history, which to-day I feel that I can afford to disregard in view of your verdict, which I gratefully accept as my vindication.[40]

HAYES

The Boston Post says, "Mr. Hayes will, during the absence of Mrs. Hayes, be acting President!"[41]

A common burden of the presidency is the national pastime of appraising Presidents' wives. Mrs. Hayes was regarded as determined.

✓ ✓ ✓

[James] Parton in an article in the *Magazine of American History* says Washington was in favor of a single Presidential term of seven years. [Parton writes:] "The term of seven years is probably as long as any man can advantageously hold the Presidency. The strain upon the faculties of a good man is too severe to be longer borne and a young country must needs grow faster than an elderly mind."

This is true. The strain is hard to bear. It grows harder as time passes.[42]

✓ ✓ ✓

But as I get rid of the cares and troubles which make the incessant and almost intolerable strain of this place, I find myself valuing more and more friends and relationships which date back.[43]

✓ ✓ ✓

Nobody ever left the Presidency with less regret, less disappointment, fewer heartburnings, or more general content with the result of his term (in his own heart, I mean), than I do.[44]

✓ ✓ ✓

The escape from bondage into freedom is grateful indeed to my feelings. The equanimity of temper which has enabled me to bear without discomposure the vexations and anxieties that every day brought with it during my term of office, no doubt relieved me from a great part of the strain upon the faculties which has broken down so many of my predecessors. But the burden, even with my constitutional cheerfulness, has not been a light one. I am glad to be a *freedman*.[45]

✓ ✓ ✓

Only a few Presidents have had the felicity to see their party stronger at the close of their terms than it was at the beginning. Only a few have left their country more prosperous than they have found it.[46]

✓ ✓ ✓

It is no doubt well to leave the high place now. Those who are in such a place cannot escape the important influence on habit, disposition, and character. In that envied position of honor and distinction they are deferred to, flattered and supported under all circumstances, whether right or wrong by shrewd and designing men and women who surround them. Human nature cannot stand this too long![47]

GARFIELD

Mar. 16—It will cost me some struggle to keep from despising the office seeker. Determined to retire at ten but could not sleep until far past midnight. More sense of annoyance and wrong than I have yet experienced. Vexed with the thought that I am wholly unfit for this sort of work.[48]

✓ ✓ ✓

I do not know that I shall ever become reconciled to this office. I see few signs that I shall. The prospect is,—a long struggle with personal wishes and a painful series of deciding between men. In some way the civil service must be regulated by law, or the president can never devote his time to administration.[49]

⁄ ⁄ ⁄

Once or twice I felt like crying out in the agony of my soul against the greed for office and its consumption of my time. My services ought to be worth more to the government than to be spent thus.[50]

⁄ ⁄ ⁄

My day is frittered away by the personal seeking of people, when it ought to be given to the great problem(s) which concern the whole country. Four years of this kind of intellectual dissipation may cripple me for the remainder of my life. What might not a vigorous thinker do, if he could be allowed to use the opportunities of a Presidential term in vital, useful activity! Some Civil Service Reform will come by necessity after the wearisome years of wasted Presidents have paved the way for it.[51]

⁄ ⁄ ⁄

My God! What is there in this place that a man should ever want to get in it.[52]

ARTHUR

I believe that I am permitted to dine with Cabinet officers, Justices of the Supreme Court, the Vice President, and Mr. George Bancroft [aged historian, Polk's Secretary of the Navy].[53]

CLEVELAND

I have often thought how solemn a thing it is to live and feel the pressure of the duties which life—the mere existence in a social state—imposes; but I have never appreciated the thought in its full solemnity till now. It seems to me that I am as much consecrated to a service, as the religionist who secludes himself from all that is joyous in life and devotes himself to a sacred mission.

I think you know how much of all that has had anything of comfort in my life has grown out of my love for my friends and the hope that I had earned some real unselfish attachments. And if, in carrying my present burden, I must feel that my friends are calling me selfish and doubting my attachment to them and criticising the fact that in the administration of my great trust I am not aiding them, I shall certainly be unhappy, but shall nevertheless struggle on. The end will come; and if on that day I can retire with a sure consciousness that I have done my whole duty according to my lights and my ability, there will be some corner for me where I can rest.[54]

✓ ✓ ✓

The office of President has not, to me personally, a single allurement.[55]

✓ ✓ ✓

Sir, it is a solemn thing to be President of the United States.[56]

✓ ✓ ✓

I am feeling too the punishment of again occupying the office of President without the previous advice and consent of the United States Senate.[57]

✓ ✓ ✓

I believe I shall buy or rent a house near here where I can go and be away from this cursed constant grind.[58]

✓ ✓ ✓

If I am to speak of the President of the United States I desire to mention, as the most pleasant and characteristic feature of our system of government, the nearness of the people to their President and other high officials. A close view afforded our citizens of the acts and conduct of those to whom they have intrusted their interests, serves as a regulator and check upon temptation and pressure in office, and is a constant reminder that diligence and faithfulness are the measure of public duty; and such a relation between President and people ought to leave but little room, in popular judgment and conscience, for unjust and false accusations and for malicious slanders invented for the purpose of undermining the people's trust and confidence in the administration of their government.

No public officer should desire to check the utmost freedom of criticism as to all official acts, but every right-thinking man must concede that the President of the United States should not be put beyond the protection which American love of fair play and decency accords to every American citizen.[59]

✓ ✓ ✓

What I remember most vividly in connection with the great office of President is its responsibilities and the labor and anxiety attending an attempt to do the work which the people had intrusted to me. The impress made upon the mind and heart of one who stands daily face to face with the American people, charged with the protection of their rights and the advancement of their varied interests, can never be effaced, and scarcely gives room for the gratification naturally supposed to attach to high and exalted place. I am led to mention in this connection, as a spur to official labor and as a sign of political health, the watchfulness of the people and their exactions from their chosen representative to whom they have confided their highest trust. If they are exacting and critical, sometimes almost to the point of injustice, this is better than popular heedlessness and indifference concerning the conduct of public servants.[60]

✓ ✓ ✓

I am suffering many perplexities and troubles and this term of the Presidency has cost me so much health and vigor that I have sometimes doubted if I could carry the burden to the end.[61]

✓ ✓ ✓

I do not want the office. It involves a responsibility beyond human strength to a man who brings conscience to the discharge of his duties.[62]

✓ ✓ ✓

I feel that I am in the treadmill again and look forward to the time when another respite shall be due to me and all that must take place between now and then with the gravest concern. If it were not for the full faith I have in the Highest Power that aids honest, faithful endeavor, I should be frightened by all I see before me. But I have not a particle of real fear, though I confess to anxiety, because so much depends upon me. It's a curious state of mind to be in, when all the value of life is measured by its relation to other persons and other things, and when the natural desire to live for the sake of living and enjoying life is nearly gone.[63]

✶ ✶ ✶

You cannot imagine the relief which has come to me with the termination of my official term. There is a good deal yet which seems to result from the Presidency and the kindness of people in a social way which keeps me in remembrance of Washington life, but I feel that I am fast taking the place which I desire to reach—the place of a respectable private citizen.[64]

BENJAMIN HARRISON

. . . and it is a rare piece of good fortune during the early months of an administration if the President gets one wholly uninterrupted hour at his desk each day. His time is so broken into bits that he is often driven to late night work, or to set up a desk in his bedroom, when preparing a message or other paper requiring unbroken attention.[65]

McKINLEY

What an impressive thing it is to assume tremendous responsibilities![66]

✶ ✶ ✶

I have had enough of it [the Presidency], Heaven knows! I have had all the honor there is in the place, and have responsibilities enough to kill any man.[67]

THEODORE ROOSEVELT

It is a dreadful thing to come into the Presidency this way; but it would be a far worse thing to be morbid about it. Here is the task, and I have got to do it to the best of my ability; and that is all there is about it.[68]

✶ ✶ ✶

People want to see the President, and this means that I am wholly unable to make such visits as you and I made when I was governor to the sweatshops in lower New York.[69]

✓ ✓ ✓

I am of course in a perfect whirl of work and have every kind of worry and trouble—but that's what I am here for and down at bottom I enjoy it after all.[70]

✓ ✓ ✓

Well, I have been President for a year and a quarter, and whatever the future may hold I think I may say that during that year and a quarter I have been as successful as I had any right to hope or expect. Of course political life in a position such as this is one long strain on the temper, one long acceptance of the second best, one long experiment of checking one's impulses with an iron hand and learning to subordinate one's own desires to what some hundreds of associates can be forced or cajoled or led into desiring. Every day, almost every hour, I have to decide very big as well as very little questions, and in almost each of them I must determine just how far it is safe to go in forcing others to accept my views and standards and just how far I must subordinate what I deem expedient, and indeed occasionally what I deem morally desirable, to what it is possible under the given conditions to achieve. Hay and Nicolay's *Life of Lincoln* has been to me a great comfort and aid. I have read it and profited by it, and often when dealing with some puzzling affair I find myself thinking what Lincoln would have done. It has been very wearing, but I have thoroughly enjoyed it, for it is fine to feel one's hand guiding great machinery, with at least the purpose, and I hope the effect, of guiding it for the best interests of the nation as a whole.[71]

✓ ✓ ✓

I do but little boxing because it seems rather absurd for a President to appear with a black eye or a swollen nose or a cut lip. Four times I have broken bones in falls with horses.[72]

✓ ✓ ✓

I enjoy being President, and I like to do the work and have my hand on the lever. But it is very worrying and puzzling, and I have to make up my mind to accept every kind of attack and misrepresentation.[73]

✓ ✓ ✓

Any strong man fit to be President would desire a renomination and re-election after his first term.[74]

✓ ✓ ✓

But even a President has feelings. . . .[75]

✓ ✓ ✓

I have finished my career in public life; I have enjoyed it to the full; I have achieved a large proportion of what I set out to achieve; and I am almost ashamed to say that I do not mind in the least retiring to private life. No President has ever enjoyed himself as much as I have enjoyed myself, and for the matter of that I do not know any man of my age who has had as good a time. Of course if I had felt that I could conscientiously keep on in the Presidency I should have dearly liked to have tried again; and I shall miss a very little having my hands on the levers of the great machine; but I am really almost uneasy to find that I do not mind the least bit in the world getting out.[76]

✓ ✓ ✓

. . . no other President ever enjoyed the Presidency as I did.[77]

✓ ✓ ✓

I've had eight years of the Presidency. I know all the honor and pleasure of it and all of its sorrows and dangers. I have nothing more to gain by being President again and I have a great deal to lose. I am *not* going to do it, unless I get a mandate from the American people.[78]

✓ ✓ ✓

A President has a great chance; his position is almost that of a king and a prime minister rolled into one; once he has left office he cannot do very much; and he is a fool if he fails to realize it all and to be profoundly thankful for having had the great chance. No President ever enjoyed himself in the Presidency as much as I did; and no President after leaving the office took as much joy in life as I am taking.[79]

TAFT

I have come to the conclusion that the major part of the work of a President is to increase the gate receipts of expositions and fairs and bring tourists into the town.[80]

❧ ❧ ❧

One trouble is no sooner over in this office than another arises.[81]

❧ ❧ ❧

The assassination of three Presidents led Congress to provide that the Chief of the Secret Service should furnish protection to the President as he moves about either in Washington or in the country at large. While President, I never was conscious of any personal anxiety in large crowds, and I have been in many of them. Yet the record is such that Congress would be quite derelict if it disregarded it. These guards are a great burden to the President. He never can go anywhere that he does not have to inflict upon those whom he wishes to visit the burden of their presence. It is a little difficult for him to avoid the feeling after a while that he is under surveillance rather than under protection.[82]

❧ ❧ ❧

I'll be damned if I am not getting tired of this. It seems to be the profession of a President simply to hear other people talk.[83]

❧ ❧ ❧

I would rather be Chief Justice of the United States, and a quieter life than that which comes at the White House is more in keeping with my temperament, but when taken into consideration that I go into history as a President, and my children and children's children are the better placed on account of that fact, I am inclined to think that to be President well compensates one for all the trials and criticisms he has to bear and undergo.[84]

❧ ❧ ❧

I'm glad to be going—this is the loneliest place in the world.[85]

WILSON

The office of President requires the constitution of an athlete, the patience of a mother, the endurance of an early Christian.[86]

ɪ ɪ ɪ

I cannot choose as an individual what I shall do; I must choose always as a President, ready to guard at every turn and in every way possible, the success of what I have to do for the people. Apparently, the little things count quite as much as the big in this strange business of leading opinion and securing action . . . The President is a superior kind of slave, and must content himself with the reflection that the kind is superior.[87]

ɪ ɪ ɪ

. . . It is not a new feeling on my part, but one which I entertain with a greater intensity than formerly that a man who seeks the Presidency of the United States for anything that it will bring to him is an audacious fool. The responsibilities of the office ought to sober a man even before he approaches it. One of the difficulties of the office seldom appreciated, I dare say, is that it is very difficult to think while so many people are talking in a way that obscures counsel and is entirely off the point.[88]

ɪ ɪ ɪ

I am constantly reminded as I go about, as I do sometimes at the week end, of the personal inconvenience of being President of the United States. If I want to know how many people live in a small town all I have to do is to go there and they at once line up to be counted. I might, in a census-taking year, save the census takers a great deal of trouble by asking them to accompany me and count the people on the spot. Sometimes, when I am most beset, I seriously think of renting a pair of whiskers or of doing something else that will furnish me with an adequate disguise, because I am sorry to find that the cut of my jib is unmistakable and that I must sail under false colors if I am going to sail incognito.[89]

ɪ ɪ ɪ

I have read many biographies of Lincoln; I have sought out with the greatest interest the many intimate stories that are told of him, the narratives of nearby friends, the sketches at close quarters, in which those who had the privilege of being associated with him have tried to depict for us the very man himself "in his habit as he lived;" but I have nowhere found a real intimate of Lincoln's. I nowhere get the impression in any narrative or reminiscence that the writer had in fact penetrated to the heart of his mystery, or that any man could penetrate to the heart of it. That brooding spirit had no real familiars. I get the impression that it never spoke out in complete self-revelation, and that it could not reveal itself completely to anyone. It was a very lonely spirit that looked out from underneath those shaggy brows and comprehended men without fully communing with them, as if, in spite of all its genial efforts at comradeship, it dwelt apart, saw its visions of duty where no man looked on. There is a very holy and very terrible isolation for the conscience of every man who seeks to read the destiny in affairs for others as well as for himself, for a nation as well as for individuals. That privacy no man can intrude upon. That lonely search of the spirit for the right perhaps no man can assist. This strange child of the cabin kept company with invisible things, was born into no intimacy but that of its own silently assembling and deploying thoughts.[90]

✦ ✦ ✦

My work can be properly done only if I devote my whole thought and attention to it and think of nothing but the immediate task in hand.[91]

✦ ✦ ✦

. . . the amount of work a President is supposed to do is preposterous.[92]

✦ ✦ ✦

The responsibilities of the President are great, and I cannot perform them alone. If I can't have the assistance of those in whom I have confidence, what am I to do?[93]

✦ ✦ ✦

I never dreamed such loneliness and desolation of heart possible . . . The very magnitude and fatefulness of the task I have every day to face dominates me and holds steady to my duty. Nothing less great, I imagine, could.[94]

HARDING

I knew that this job would be too much for me.[95]

✦ ✦ ✦

Oftentimes, as I sit here, I don't seem to grasp that I am President.[96]

* * *

If there is anything wrong with the White House job, it is the inability to be a human being.[97]

* * *

I am beginning to find out that this job of being President is one that makes almost inordinate demands upon a man's time.[98]

* * *

This White House is a prison. I can't get away from the men who dog my footsteps. I am in jail.[99]

* * *

In this job I am not worried about my enemies. I can take care of them. It is my friends who are giving me trouble.[100]

* * *

God, what a job![101]

COOLIDGE

The duties of the Presidency are exceedingly heavy. The responsibilities are overwhelming. But it is my opinion that a man of ordinary strength can carry them if he will confine himself very strictly to a performance of the duties that are imposed upon him by the Constitution and the law. If he permits himself to be engaged in all kinds of outside enterprises, in furnishing entertainment and amusement to great numbers of public gatherings, undertaking to be the source of inspiration for every worthy public movement, for all of which he will be earnestly besought with the inference that unless he responds civilization will break down and the sole responsibility will be on him, he will last in office about 90 days.[102]

* * *

It is of course obvious that the President should not burden himself with details. Those should be attended to by his departments and his office staff. He should not do any work that he can have done by others. Such energy as he has should be directed not so much towards doing work as making certain that the work is being well done.[103]

✔ ✔ ✔

... when the events of August, 1923, bestowed upon me the Presidential office, I felt at once that power had been given me to administer it. This was not any feeling of exclusiveness. While I felt qualified to serve, I was also well aware that there were many others who were better qualified. It would be my province to get the benefit of their opinions and advice. It is a great advantage to a President, and a major source of safety to the country, for him to know that he is not a great man. When a man begins to feel that he is the only one who can lead in this republic, he is guilty of treason to the spirit of our institutions.[104]

✔ ✔ ✔

It costs a great deal to be President.[105]

Coolidge was speaking, after the death of his son, of the cost in human terms.

✔ ✔ ✔

In the discharge of the duties of the office there is one rule of action more important than all others. It consists in never doing anything that some one else can do for you.[106]

✔ ✔ ✔

The President gets the best advice he can find, uses the best judgment at his command, and leaves the event in the hands of Providence.[107]

✔ ✔ ✔

The Presidential office differs from everything else. Much of it cannot be described, it can only be felt. After I had considered the reasons for my being a candidate on the one side and on the other, I could not say that any of them moved me with compelling force.[108]

✔ ✔ ✔

I thought I could swing it.[109]

Of the presidency, when Coolidge was asked his first thought on succeeding at Harding's death.

✔ ✔ ✔

... Ten years is too long for one man to be President.[110]

HOOVER

Fishing is the only labor or recreation open to a President in which both the press and the public are prepared to concede privacy.[111]

✦ ✦ ✦

I find that many Presidents have joined the ranks of fishermen only after their inauguration as President, although I can claim over 45 years of apprenticeship—that is, in fishing, not the Presidency.

I have discovered the reason why Presidents take to fishing— the silent sport. Apparently the only opportunity for refreshment of one's soul and clarification of one's thoughts by solitude to Presidents lies through fishing.[112]

✦ ✦ ✦

Many years ago I concluded that a few hair shirts were part of the mental wardrobe of every man. The President differs only from other men in that he has a more extensive wardrobe.[113]

✦ ✦ ✦

Presidents have long since learned that one of the undisclosed articles in the Bill of Rights is that criticism and digging of political graves are reserved exclusively to members of the legislative arm. But presidents have also learned that they have one privilege not extended to members of the legislative arm—they have the option on when to talk and when not to talk.[114]

✦ ✦ ✦

. . . the President has for a few short years the opportunity to speed the orderly march of a glorious people. And the inspiration of that moving host is compensation that comes in larger measure to him than to any other man.[115]

✦ ✦ ✦

There are some valuable privileges attached to being President —among them the duty and right to terminate all interviews, conferences, social parties, and receptions. Therefore, he can go to bed whenever he likes.[116]

✓ ✓ ✓

Another of these useless exhaustions, which had always plagued Presidents, was signing routine papers. No man could read them even on a twenty-four-hour shift. They comprised all military officers' commissions, many appointments of civil servants, Treasury orders, documents relating to the guardianship of individual Indians, pension authorities, etc., all of which the President could only sign on the dotted line and trust to Heaven and his Cabinet officers that they were all right.[117]

✓ ✓ ✓

Getting daily exercise to keep physically fit is always a problem for Presidents. Once the day's work starts there is little chance to walk, to ride, or to take part in a game. Taking walks or rides early in the morning is a lonesome business, and the inevitable secret service guard when the President leaves the White House grounds is not enlivening company.[118]

✓ ✓ ✓

Also, unless the President remains cheerful and optimistic he becomes a depressant.[119]

FRANKLIN D. ROOSEVELT

Last spring, when I went to Washington, there were many people who came forward with the thought, verbally expressed, that the Government should take over all the troubles of the country, that we could, well, as we used to say in the old days, "Let George do it," and I began to think sometimes that my first name was George.[120]

✓ ✓ ✓

Presidential plans for future engagements are, I find to my sorrow, more susceptible to change than the plans of any private citizen.[121]

✓ ✓ ✓

In Washington, as you know, the working day of the Presidency in these days averages about fifteen hours. Even when I go to Hyde Park or to Warm Springs, the White House office, the callers, and the telephones all follow me.[122]

✦ ✦ ✦

Nevertheless, there are times, I think, when the President can speak as an interested citizen.[123]

TRUMAN

I have learned in a very short time that the President of the United States all too often has to act in ways that please others and which are very different from the personal wishes and feelings of the President himself.[124]

✦ ✦ ✦

The presidency of the United States carries with it a responsibility so personal as to be without parallel.

Very few are ever authorized to speak for the President. No one can make decisions for him. No one can know all the processes and stages of his thinking in making important decisions. Even those closest to him, even members of his immediate family, never know all the reasons why he does certain things and why he comes to certain conclusions. To be President of the United States is to be lonely, very lonely at times of great decisions.[125]

✦ ✦ ✦

I felt as if I had lived five lifetimes in my first five days as President.[126]

✦ ✦ ✦

The presidency of the United States in recent times, even in the prewar period, had become a highly complicated and exacting job.[127]

✦ ✦ ✦

There is no exaltation in the office of the President of the United States—sorrow is the proper word.[128]

✦ ✦ ✦

Within the first few months I discovered that being a President is like riding a tiger. A man has to keep on riding or be swallowed.[129]

✓ ✓ ✓

No one who has not had the responsibility can really understand what it is like to be President, not even his closest aides or members of his immediate family. There is no end to the chain of responsibility that binds him, and he is never allowed to forget that he is President.[130]

✓ ✓ ✓

Most Presidents have received more advice than they can possibly use.[131]

✓ ✓ ✓

The President of the United States, of course, cannot spend his time replying to personal attacks and insinuations. If he did, his time would be fully occupied with nothing else.[132]

✓ ✓ ✓

A President can never get away from the urgent and never-ending duties of his office. A political campaign provides no escape. It increases his burdens.[133]

✓ ✓ ✓

I do not know of any easy way to be President. It is more than a full-time job, and the relaxations are few.[134]

✓ ✓ ✓

I had learned that one of the hardest things for the President to do is to find time to take stock. I have always believed that the President's office ought to be open to as many citizens as he can find time to talk to; that is part of the job, to be available to the people, to listen to their troubles, to let them share the rich tradition of the White House. But it raises havoc with one's day, and even though I always got up early, usually was at work ahead of the staff, and would take papers home with me at night to read, there always seemed to be more than I could do.[135]

✓ ✓ ✓

In my opinion eight years as President is enough and sometimes too much for any man to serve in that capacity.[136]

EISENHOWER

I probably long ago used up my time; but you know, there is one thing about being the President, it is hard to tell him to sit down.[137]

✓ ✓ ✓

In many ways the easy course for a President, for the administration, is to adopt a truculent, publicly bold, almost insulting attitude. A President experiences exactly the same resentments, the same anger, the same kind of sense of frustration almost, when things like this occur to other Americans, and his impulse is to lash out.[138]

✓ ✓ ✓

There are in this office thousands of unique opportunities to meet especially interesting people, because the Government up here in Washington has become the center of so many things that, again, you have a very fascinating experience in meeting scientists, leaders in culture, in health, in governmental action, from all over the world.

There are many things about the office and the work, the work with your associates, that are, well, let's say, at least intriguing, even if at times they are very fatiguing. But it is a wonderful experience.[139]

✓ ✓ ✓

Every problem that you take up has inevitably a terrific meaning for many millions of people, so there is no problem that comes up in the Presidency—even some that appear trivial—that is handled as easily as you would handle your own daily living, or even something in the military, or in other activities in which I have been engaged.

I would say that the Presidency is probably the most taxing job, as far as tiring of the mind and spirit; but it also has, as I have said before, its inspirations which tend to counteract each other.[140]

✓ ✓ ✓

Of course, the duties of the President are essentially endless. No daily schedule of appointments can give a full timetable—or even a faint indication—of the President's responsibilities. Entirely aside from the making of important decisions, the formulation of policy through the National Security Council, and the Cabinet, cooperation with the Congress and with the States, there is for the President a continuous burden of study, contemplation and reflection.

Of the subjects demanding this endless study, some deal with foreign affairs, with the position of the United States in the international world, her strength, her aspirations, and the methods by which she may exert her influence in the solution of world problems and in the direction of a just and enduring peace. These—all of them—are a particular Constitutional responsibility of the President.[141]

✱ ✱ ✱

All these matters, among others, are with a President always; in Washington, in a summer White House, on a weekend absence, indeed, even at a ceremonial dinner and in every hour of leisure. The old saying is true, "A President never escapes from his office."[142]

✱ ✱ ✱

The nakedness of the battlefield when the soldier is all alone in the smoke and the clamor and the terror of war is comparable to the loneliness—at times—of the Presidency. These are the times when one man must conscientiously, deliberately, prayerfully, scrutinize every argument, every proposal, every prediction, every alternative, every probable outcome of his action and then —all alone—make his decision.

In that moment he can draw on no brain trust; no pressure group; no warehouse of trick phrases; no facile answers. Even his most trusted associates and friends cannot help him in that moment. He can draw only upon the truths and principles responsible for America's birth and development applying them to the problem immediately before him in the light of a broad experience with men and nations.

He will be face to face with himself, his conscience, his measure of wisdom. And he will have to pray for Divine guidance from Almighty God.[143]

KENNEDY

I know that when things don't go well, they like to blame the President, and that is one of the things Presidents are paid for.[144]

✦ ✦ ✦

No man who enters upon the office to which I have succeeded can fail to recognize how every President of the United States has placed special reliance upon his faith in God.[145]

✦ ✦ ✦

When I ran for the Presidency of the United States, I knew that this country faced serious challenges, but I could not realize—nor could any man realize who does not bear the burdens of this office—how heavy and constant would be those burdens.[146]

✦ ✦ ✦

The Presidency is not a very good place to make new friends. I am going to keep my old friends. But I am responsible for many things under the Constitution, but not for what they write. That is their responsibility. . . .[147]

✦ ✦ ✦

. . . President Eisenhower said to me on January 19—he said that, "No easy matters will ever come to you as President. If they're easy they will be settled at a lower level. The matters that finally come to you as President are always the difficult matters, matters which carry with them large implications." So this contributes to some of the burdens of the office of the Presidency which other Presidents have commented on.[148]

✦ ✦ ✦

The responsibilities placed on the United States are greater than I imagined them to be, and there are greater limitations upon our ability to bring about a favorable result than I had imagined it to be. And I think that's probably true of anyone who becomes President, because there's such a difference between those who advise or speak, or legislate, and between the man who must make—select from the various alternatives proposed and say that this shall be the policy of the United States. It's much easier to make the speeches than it is to finally make the judgments, because unfortunately your advisers are frequently divided. If you take the wrong course, and on occasion I have, the President bears the burden, responsibility, quite rightly. The advisers may move on to new advice.[149]

Chapter IX

THE PRESIDENT AND PARTY POLITICS

There are few areas of presidential activity of which the Presidents have seen fit to write so sparingly as their relations to their political parties. This would have been much to the liking of George Washington, who warned in his Farewell Address that "the common and continued mischiefs of the spirit of Party are sufficient to make it the interest and the duty of a wise People to discourage and restrain it."[1] Notwithstanding, as Washington ruefully conceded in the same message, the rise of parties was inevitable, and the party role thrust upon the Presidents was inescapable. Party leadership became essential to winning office, to keeping office, and to carrying out an administrative and legislative program.

Those Presidents who ignored the party role did so at the cost of their political survival. And yet, not infrequently, it took the greater sense of history to ignore party ties and party demands than to recognize and follow them. The history of the presidency is writ large with names like Polk, Lincoln, Hayes, Arthur, Benjamin Harrison—men whom the events of their time forced to repudiate or sublimate party obligations to the public interest if they were to achieve their purposes.

In general, however, political parties have not evolved, as Washington feared, from factions gone mad. They have been at their best massive machines to get done the necessary political chores not provided for nor even envisioned by the Constitution makers—primarily the nomination of candidates for office but also the enunciation of policies and principles and the linking together of political forces throughout the three levels of local, state, and national government.

The relationship of President to party is absolutely pivotal—

not just before he gets into office but after he gets there. Except for the limited constitutional role of reporting on the state of the Union and recommending legislation, he has no other link with the whole Congress and must function—in the absence of a ministerial, parliamentary system—through his party associations. Political realism requires the President also to participate faithfully and conspicuously in the tribal rites of parties—a situation which leads to such anomalies as Democrats from the great industrial cities celebrating President Jefferson, who had grave distrust of both cities and industrialism, and Republicans, with distinguished guests from the business community, celebrating President Lincoln, who said that in his opinion labor's interest were much to be preferred over capital's.

The writings of the Presidents on their party functions and duties are comparatively lean—inexplicably so, it would seem, from the necessity of effective party relationships to a successful administration. On the other hand, no President sought to conceal the fact that party duties and functions did exist, though to such nonprofessional politicians as Wilson and Eisenhower they did not always seem entirely congenial. Perhaps one reason for the Presidents not going into the matter too deeply is that there is little thát is baffling about it and certainly nothing subtle. The President must control his party or he cannot control his office. It is that simple, and like many extreme simplicities was perhaps thought best left unexplored. It may be significant, too, that when the party system was least healthy, during the period from Jackson to Cleveland, presidential comments on the relation of the office to the party were scarcest.

JOHN ADAMS

The President has, or ought to have, the whole nation before him, and he ought to select the men best qualified and most meritorious for offices at his own responsibility, without being shackled by any check by law, constitution, or institution. Without this unrestrained liberty, he is not a check upon the legislative power nor either branch of it. Indeed, he must be the slave of the party that brought him in. He never can be independent or impartial.[2]

MADISON

The question of re-eligibility in the case of a President of the United States admits of rival views, and is the more delicate because it cannot be decided with equal lights from actual experiment. In general, it may be observed, that the evils most complained of are less connected with that particular question than with the process of electing the Chief Magistrate, and the powers vested in him. Among these, the appointing power is the most operative in relation to the purity of Government and the tranquillity of republican Government, and it is not easy to find a depository for it more free from the dangers of abuse. The powers and patronage of a Chief Magistrate, whether elected for a shorter term and re-eligible for a second, or for a longer, without that capacity, might not, in their effect, be very materially different, though the difference might not be unimportant.

It should not be forgotten that many inconveniences are inseparable from the peculiarity of a federal system of Government, while such a Government is essential to the complete success of republicanism in any form.[3]

MONROE

There have been several candidates, under me, in the adm^n., for the office which I hold, and such the activity & animosity of their respective advocates & friends, towards the rival candidates, that my situation has been peculiarly embarrassing. In the appointment to office, I have been forc'd either to distribute the offices among the friends of the candidates, to guard myself against the imputation of favoritism, or to take my own course, and appoint those whom I knew & confided in, without regard to them. Had I pursued the former, the office in my hands, for two or three years of the latter term, would have sunk to nothing. I therefore adopted the latter, and have steadily pursued it, believing that I had given sufficient proof of respect for, and confidence in each of the members, of the administration, by appointing & continuing him in his place.[4]

✓ ✓ ✓

As a permanent rule I was led to conclude, that it would be better for our country, and contribute more to the success of our excellent system of government, that those who have held the office of Chief Magistrate, should abstain, after their retirement, from becoming partisans in subsequent elections to that office. Instances may occur in the course of time, in the vicissitude of human affairs, in which the opinion of those who have had long experience may be useful. Every government that has existed has been exposed to trying emergencies. All those which were strictly republican have been subverted. Ours will, I trust, experience a different fate. Should an emergency of any kind ever occur, it may be important that there should be among the people some men unconnected with either of the contending parties, and among them, those who have retired from that high office, whose voice might be heard. To render service they must enjoy, in like degree, the confidence of the whole community, in their disinterestedness, & impartiality. If they embark as partisans, on either side, they would have no weight with the other. By remaining neutral it might be otherwise.[5]

✓ ✓ ✓

Whether the present Administration ought to withdraw, in the event that Mr. [John Quincy] Adams should not be re-elected, is a question of great delicacy, as to the numbers, & of interest, by way of example, as to principle. They hold their offices, as others do, as servants of the public, not his. Their appointments do not cease with his. They are responsible, each, for the faithful performance of their duties. He likewise is responsible for them. In this respect there is a difference between our govt. and that of G. Britain; in the latter the Minister alone is responsible. The office of the Chief being hereditary, he is beyond the reach of impeachment. With us, both may be impeached, the Chief and Minister.[6]

JOHN QUINCY ADAMS

By the Constitution of the United States, the President is re-eligible as long as he lives. Washington, Jefferson, and Madison voluntarily retired after one re-election, and Jefferson no doubt intended to make the example a practical exposition of constitutional principle. It was followed by Mr. Monroe, perhaps with not much cordiality, and will be continued as long as a Presidential term of eight years shall wear out the popularity of the person holding the office. One of the consequences of this has been and will be that ex-Presidents will survive for many years the termination of their offices; that as individuals they will take a part in public affairs, and that they will sometimes solicit, and sometimes be elected to, subordinate offices. All the preceding Presidents have held offices of a public nature after the expiration of their Presidential service; none, however, as a member of either House of Congress; and there are many who think it now a derogatory descent. This is a mere prejudice; and had I alleged my former station as a reason for rejecting the suffrages of the people assigning me a seat in the House of Representatives, I should not merely have been chargeable with arrogance, but should have exposed myself to ridicule.[7]

✦ ✦ ✦

This election of a chief magistrate for the whole Union will never be settled to the satisfaction of the people. The theory of frequent elections is, that power cannot be long trusted to the same hands, even of the wisest and best. The two parts can be reconciled to each other only by the inconsistency and corruptibility of human nature in its best estate; and never, never will any great people be satisfied with the result of their own elections of an Executive head.[8]

✦ ✦ ✦

The excitement of the Presidential election [of 1836] is here as we have found it all along on the road. The remarkable character of this election is, that all the candidates are at most third-rate men whose pretensions rest neither upon high attainments nor upon eminent services, but upon intrigue and political speculation. The Presidency has fallen into a joint-stock company.[9]

✦ ✦ ✦

In all governments of which the chief magistrate is elective, the organizations, the character and the movements of parties will depend in great degree upon the anticipation to the succession. Among the citizens most distinguished for their talents and services, it is to be expected there will always be several ambitious of attaining the summit of honour and power, around whom others of considerable influence will rally, and whose conflicting pretensions will be supported by partizans more or less numerous and pressed forward for the popular suffrages with degrees of zeal and address not always proportioned to their merit. The prospect of succession to the presidency must in the ordinary course of events be confined to the vice-president, the heads of the executive departments, and a very small number of citizens of great eminence in the several states of the Union. The election of the second and third Presidents of the United States had fallen upon incumbents of the vice-presidency; but those persons, even when elected to the vice-presidency, had been voted for as candidates for the presidency. An amendment to the Constitution then prescribed that the office should be voted for distinctly, and since that time the Vice-President's office had been an insuperable barrier to that of President.[10]

JACKSON

I consider it one of the most urgent of my duties to bring to your attention the propriety of amending that part of our Constitution which relates to the election of President and Vice-President. Our system of government was by its framers deemed an experiment, and they therefore consistently provided a mode of remedying its defects.

To the people belongs the right of electing their Chief Magistrate; it was never designed that their choice should in any case be defeated, either by the intervention of electoral colleges or by the agency confided, under certain contingencies, to the House of Representatives. Experience proves that in proportion as agents to execute the will of the people are multiplied there is danger of their wishes being frustrated. Some may be unfaithful; all are liable to err. So far, therefore, as the people can with convenience speak, it is safer for them to express their own will.

The number of aspirants to the Presidency and the diversity of the interests which may influence their claims leave little reason to expect a choice in the first instance, and in that event the election must devolve on the House of Representatives, where it is obvious the will of the people may not be always ascertained, or, if ascertained, may not be regarded. From the mode of voting by States the choice is to be made by 24 votes, and it may often occur that one of these will be controlled by an individual Representative. Honors and offices are at the disposal of the successful candidate. Repeated ballotings may make it apparent that a single individual holds the cast in his hand. May he not be tempted to name his reward? But even without corruption, supposing the probity of the Representative to be proof against the powerful motives by which it may be assailed, the will of the people is still constantly liable to be misrepresented. One may err from ignorance of the wishes of his constituents; another from a conviction that it is his duty to be governed by his own judgment of the fitness of the candidates; finally, although all were inflexibly honest, all accurately informed of the wishes of their constituents, yet under the present mode of election a minority may often elect a President, and when this happens it may reasonably be expected that efforts will be made on the part of the majority to rectify this injurious operation of their institutions. But although no evil of this character should result from such a perversion of the first principle of our system— *that the majority is to govern*—it must be very certain that a President elected by a minority can not enjoy the confidence necessary to the successful discharge of his duties.

In this as in all other matters of public concern policy requires that as few impediments as possible should exist to the free operation of the public will. Let us, then, endeavor so to amend our system that the office of Chief Magistrate may not be conferred upon any citizen but in pursuance of a fair expression of the will of the majority.

I would therefore recommend such an amendment of the Constitution as may remove all intermediate agency in the election of the President and Vice-President. The mode may be so regulated as to preserve to each State its present relative weight in the election, and a failure in the first attempt may be provided for by confining the second to a choice between the two highest candidates. In connection with such an amendment it would seem advisable to limit the service of the Chief Magistrate to a single term of either four or six years. If, however, it should not be adopted, it is worthy of consideration whether a provision disqualifying for office the Representatives in Congress on whom such an election may have devolved would not be proper.[11]

✝   ✝   ✝

A provision which does not secure to the people a direct choice of their Chief Magistrate, but has a tendency to defeat their will, presented to my mind such an inconsistency with the general spirit of our institutions that I was induced to suggest for your consideration the substitute which appeared to me at the same time the most likely to correct the evil and to meet the views of our constituents. The most mature reflection since has added strength to the belief that the best interests of our country require the speedy adoption of some plan calculated to effect this end. A contingency which sometimes places it in the power of a single member of the House of Representatives to decide an election of so high and solemn a character is unjust to the people, and becomes when it occurs a source of embarrassment to the individuals thus brought into power and a cause of distrust of the representative body. Liable as the Confederacy is, from its great extent, to parties founded upon sectional interests, and to a corresponding multiplication of candidates for the Presidency, the tendency of the constitutional reference to the House of Representatives is to devolve the election upon that body in almost every instance, and, whatever choice may then be made among the candidates thus presented to them, to swell the influence of particular interests to a degree inconsistent with the general good. The consequences of this feature of the Constitution appear far more threatening to the peace and integrity of the Union than any which I can conceive as likely to result from the simple legislative action of the Federal Government.[12]

The process by which presidential electors become universally chosen by direct popular vote, rather than by state legislatures, was brought about in Jackson's time not by Constitutional or statutory reform but by the sheer force of public opinion. There was no change in federal law.

✦   ✦   ✦

It was a leading object with the framers of the Constitution to keep as separate as possible the action of the legislative and executive branches of the Government. To secure this object nothing is more essential than to preserve the former from all temptations of private interest, and therefore so to direct the patronage of the latter as not to permit such temptations to be offered. Experience abundantly demonstrates that every precaution in this respect is a valuable safeguard of liberty, and one which my reflections upon the tendencies of our system incline me to think should be made still stronger. It was for this reason that, in connection with an amendment of the Constitution removing all intermediate agency in the choice of the President, I recommended some restrictions upon the re-eligibility of that officer and upon the tenure of offices generally. The reason still exists, and I renew the recommendation with an increased confidence that its adoption will strengthen those checks by which the Constitution designed to secure the independence of each department of the Government and promote the healthful and equitable administration of all the trusts which it has created. The agent most likely to contravene this design of the Constitution is the Chief Magistrate. In order, particularly, that his appointment may as far as possible be placed beyond the reach of any improper influences; in order that he may approach the solemn responsibilities of the highest office in the gift of a free people uncommitted to any other course than the strict line of constitutional duty, and that the securities for this independence may be rendered as strong as the nature of power and the weakness of its possessor will admit, I can not too earnestly invite your attention to the propriety of promoting such an amendment of the Constitution as will render him ineligible after one term of service.[13]

FILLMORE

Now, I remember when it was proposed to abolish the present electoral system altogether and leave the election of President to the senior members of the United States Senate. Of course, no one would have known beforehand who was to be elected, and his political color would not be known until afterwards, thus saving the country endless excitement and preventing that interruption to business and commercial interests that sometimes occurs. Although the citizens repelled the idea, because every man believed to have in himself the right by birth of an expression of opinion on this subject, there was considerably more wisdom in the proposition than was generally seen.

I would, however, prefer that the spirit of the Constitution be adhered to. Washington and Lincoln lived in exceptional times, and I would rather see a precedent of only one term established. That term I would make six years instead of four, as now, which would enable the successful candidate to entirely master the duties of the office, and would extend by one-half the periods between which these interruptions occur to the country.

But I would go further in the way of revising the Constitution. With the view of preventing this trafficing while in office, in order to provide for the days that are to follow an exit from the White House, I would pension the outgoing President by permitting him to draw an annual amount equal to the half of his salary while in office, this to continue as long as he lives.

It is a national disgrace that our Presidents, after having occupied the highest position in the country, should be cast adrift, and, perhaps, be compelled to keep a corner grocery for subsistence. We make a bargain with our Supreme Court Judges, and agree that after the expiration of twenty years' service in the Appellate Court, if they shall be seventy years of age, we will give them a pension. The Lord High Chancellor of England, when he goes out of office, receives a handsome pension to compensate him for the loss of his profession, which he cannot follow afterwards. But we elect a man to the Presidency, expect him to be honest, to give up a lucrative profession, perhaps, and after we have done with him we let him go into seclusion and perhaps poverty.[14]

HAYES

The President of the United States of necessity owes his election to office to the suffrage and zealous labors of a political party, the members of which cherish with ardor and regard as of essential importance the principles of their party organization; but he should strive to be always mindful of the fact that he serves his party best who serves the country best.

In furtherance of the reform we seek, and in other important aspects of change of great importance, I recommend an amendment to the Constitution prescribing a term of six years for the Presidential office and forbidding a reelection.[15]

✓ ✓ ✓

It is to be remarked that a non-partisan President or Administration will of course be feebly supported, if at all, in Congress or by the press. The party men do not like it among the Republicans, and Democrats find no interest in heartily supporting an Administration they did not elect.[16]

✓ ✓ ✓

Let me emphasize in my last message the idea that, the Constitution should be so amended as to lengthen the term of the President to six years, and so as to render him ineligible for a second term.[17]

CLEVELAND

Do you remember that I opposed a second term on the ground that, human nature being what it is, the President would work for his reelection instead of for the country's good?[18]

✦ ✦ ✦

I wonder if I am to be called on to wade up to my ears in the political disturbances of all the States. I like my "friends", but if I am to be charged with the care of them in every locality and against all attacks, I shall certainly find no time to do anything else.[19]

✦ ✦ ✦

Gentlemen, I will not go into the White House pledged to you or to anyone else. I will make no secret promises. I'll be damned if I will.[20]

THEODORE ROOSEVELT

I don't know anything about seven years. But this I do know— I am going to be President for three years, and I am going to do my utmost to give the country a good President during that period. I am going to be full President, and I would rather be full President for three years than half a President for seven years. Now, mind you, I am no second Grover Cleveland. I admire certain of his qualities, but I have no intention of doing with the Republican party what he did with the Democratic party. I intend to work with my party and to make it strong by making it worthy of popular support.[21]

✦ ✦ ✦

I want to make a good President and to keep the administration upright and efficient; to follow policies external and internal which shall be for the real and ultimate benefit of our people as a whole; and all party considerations will be absolutely secondary.[22]

✦ ✦ ✦

While I have a right to have my choice, my chief business is not to nominate the President but to try to do my own work as

President for the next eighteen months, and this is a big enough
job by itself.[23]

✓ ✓ ✓

I have thoroughly enjoyed the job. I never felt more vigorous,
so far as the work of the office is concerned, and if I had followed my own desires I should have been only too delighted to
stay as President. I had said that I would not accept another
term, and I believe the people think that my word is good, and I
should be mighty sorry to have them think anything else. However, for the very reason that I believe in being a strong President and making the most of the office and using it without regard to the little, feeble, snarling men who yell about executive
usurpation, I also believe that it is not a good thing that any one
man should hold it too long.[24]

✓ ✓ ✓

If I had said that I did not believe in a third consecutive term,
it would have been accepted by all my enemies and a large number of my friends as an actual announcement of candidacy after
one term had expired and would have had a thoroughly un-
healthy effect. What I said was that I was loyal to the substance
and not to the form of the tradition. Of course, the objection to a
third term is merely that a President can perpetuate himself in
office. When he is out of office, it is simply preposterous that the
fact that he has been in office is of any consequence, for the
whole immense machinery of patronage is in the hands of someone else.[25]

✓ ✓ ✓

The Presidency is a great office, and the power of the President can be effectively used to secure a renomination, especially
if the President has the support of certain great political and
financial interests. It is for this reason, and this reason alone, that
the wholesome principle of continuing in office, so long as he is
willing to serve, an incumbent who has proved capable, is not
applicable to the Presidency. Therefore, the American people
have wisely established a custom against allowing any man to
hold that office for more than two consecutive terms. But every
shred of power which a President exercises while in office vanishes absolutely when he has once left office. An ex-President
stands precisely in the position of any other private citizen, and

has not one particle more power to secure a nomination or election than if he had never held the office at all—indeed, he probably has less because of the very fact that he has held the office. Therefore the reasoning on which the anti-third term custom is based has no application whatever to an ex-President, and no application whatever to anything except consecutive terms.[26]

TAFT

I am afraid I am a constant disappointment to my party. The fact of the matter is, the longer I am President the less of a party man I seem to become.

. . . it seems to me to be impossible to be a strict party man and serve the whole country impartially.[27]

*   *   *

I am strongly inclined to the view that it would have been a wiser provision, as it was at one time voted in the Convention, to make the term of the President six or seven years, and render him ineligible thereafter. Such a change would give to the Executive greater courage and independence in the discharge of his duties.[28]

*   *   *

The President so fully represents his party, which secures political power by its promises to the people, and the whole government is so identified in the minds of the people with his personality that they are inclined to make him responsible for all the sins of omission and of commission of society at large. This would be ludicrous if it did not have sometimes serious results. The President cannot make clouds to rain and cannot make the corn to grow, he cannot make business good, although when these things occur, political parties do claim some credit for the good things that have happened in this way. He has no power over state legislation, which covers a very wide field and which comes in many respects much closer to the happiness of the people than the Federal government.[29]

WILSON

When I think of the number of men who are looking to me as the representative of a party, with the hope for all varieties of salvage from the things they are struggling in the midst of, it makes me tremble. It makes me tremble not only with a sense of inadequacy and weakness, but as if I were shaken by the very things that are shaking them and, if I seem circumspect, it is because I am so diligently trying not to make any colossal blunders. If you just calculate the number of blunders a fellow can make in twenty-four hours if he is not careful and if he does not listen more than he talks, you would see something of the feeling that I have.[30]

✓ ✓ ✓

My job I now know can be done best only if I devote my whole thought and attention to it and think of nothing but the duties of the hour. I am not at liberty and shall not be, so far as I can now see, to turn away from those duties to undertake any kind of political canvass.[31]

COOLIDGE

Under our system the President is not only the head of the government, but is also the head of his party.[32]

✓ ✓ ✓

It is the business of the President as party leader to do the best he can to see that the declared party platform purposes are translated into legislative and administrative action.[33]

✓ ✓ ✓

I can conceive a situation in which a President might be warranted in exercising the influence of his office in selecting his successor. That condition did not exist in the last primary. The party had plenty of material, which was available, and the candidate really should be the choice of the people themselves. This is especially so now that so many of the states have laws for the direct expression of the choice of the voters.

A President in office can do very much about the nomination

of his successor, because of his influence with the convention, but the feeling that he had forced a choice would place the nominee under a heavy handicap.[34]

HOOVER

It was new in American life for a President to endeavor to estop conscientious opposition from members of his own party by opposing their reelection.[35]

✓ ✓ ✓

The President and the Vice President are elected as the chosen leaders of a political party with declared mandates, principles, solutions of issues, and promises to the people.[36]

✓ ✓ ✓

The Congress, in one or both Houses, is often controlled by an opposition political party, and thus by those who are, in practice, mostly opposed to the mandates or promises upon which the President and Vice President are elected by the people.[37]

FRANKLIN D. ROOSEVELT

It is true that we Americans have found party organizations to be useful, and indeed necessary, in the crystallization of opinion and in the demarcation of issues. It is true that I have received many honors at the hands of one of our great parties. It is nevertheless true that in the grave questions that confront the United States at this hour, I, as President of the United States, must and will consider our common problems first, foremost and preeminently from the American point of view.[38]

✓ ✓ ✓

In these recent years the average American seldom thinks of Jefferson and Jackson as Democrats or of Lincoln and Theodore Roosevelt as Republicans; he labels each one of them according to his attitude toward the fundamental problems that confronted him as President, when he was active in the affairs of government.[39]

✦ ✦ ✦

To carry out my responsibility as President, it is clear that if there is to be success in our Government there ought to be cooperation between members of my own party and myself—cooperation, in other words, within the majority party, between one branch of Government, the Legislative branch, and the head of the other branch, the Executive. That is one of the essentials of a party form of government.[40]

✦ ✦ ✦

I believe it to be my sworn duty, as President, to take all steps necessary to insure the continuance of liberalism in our government. I believe, at the same time, that it is my duty as the head of the Democratic party to see to it that my party remains the truly liberal party in the political life of America.[41]

✦ ✦ ✦

. . . no call of Party alone would prevail upon me to accept re-election to the Presidency.[42]

TRUMAN

Under our party system, political responsibility must rest with the President and with the majority in the Congress.[43]

✦ ✦ ✦

In the first place, the President became the leader of a political party. The party under his leadership had to be dominant enough to put him in office, and while often many members regretted it afterward, the majority of the party wanted to do it again.[44]

✦ ✦ ✦

When the President is sitting in the White House, the National Convention of his party has never gone against his recommendations in the choice of a candidate or in the formation of a platform on which that convention is to operate.[45]

✦ ✦ ✦

The President is traditionally the leader of his party.[46]

EISENHOWER

I am trying to be President of all the United States. Arguments are going to come up—these partisan arguments; when they come within the membership of your own party, they are of course saddening, because it looks like someone is doubting your efforts to be President of all the United States.[47]

✦ ✦ ✦

Most Americans would agree with me that it is not appropriate for the President of the United States to indulge incessantly in partisan political activities—every day on every possible occasion. Many of the most critical problems before our country are in no sense partisan issues. They involve all Americans; and in meeting them the President must strive to serve all our citizens. For these problems threaten freedom itself. They summon and demand unadulterated patriotism.

Yet all Americans also have the deep conviction that representative government requires a healthy two-party system. In this sense, the responsibility of the President as party leader is recognized an an inescapable duty, essential to democracy itself.[48]

✦ ✦ ✦

Under this form of Government, a special duty of the Executive is to devise and present to the Congress broad programs affecting the welfare of America and her citizens both at home and abroad. So long as the Republicans are in power, these programs must conform to certain basic beliefs that distinguish us as a party.[49]

✦ ✦ ✦

I don't consider it my function to interfere in the local and State elections. After all, there are certain responsibilities placed upon the President of the United States. There are certain attitudes I think that he is expected normally to observe. I hope to do that.

Now, my own contention is this: the only worthwhile political program, particularly for the party in power, is to present at each new election, to the people of the United States, an accomplishment, a worthwhile progress that earns approbation. I can see no other way of approaching this thing, and I don't see how the

President could interfere or attempt to interfere appropriately in the local political struggles—city, county, State, or anything of that kind.[50]

✓ ✓ ✓

I have got certain conceptions of what the President of the United States can logically and properly do.

Those things I shall do, but behind it all, I believe in party responsibility. I believe in it, and when we talk and give merely lip service to a two-party system in the United States, and then say there is no party responsibility, we are just guilty of self-contradiction.[51]

✓ ✓ ✓

The party that has been given responsibility for the Federal Government through the elections to the National Legislature and to the Presidency has its head in the Presidency. The individual occupying the President's post cannot escape, of course, party responsibility, which does not mean by any manner of means that he approves of everything that goes on within the party, and he does his best in the party councils and wherever he thinks it would be effective to keep things going ahead that have an effect on the public mind.

The important thing, however, is a legislative program, things that have some permanent value and effect within the country. He gets the advice that is available to him to devise a program and to push it through. The long-term effects of his incumbency are going to be reflected in that way, in my opinion.[52]

✓ ✓ ✓

From the moment that any man is first elected President of the United States, there is continuous public interest in the question as to whether or not he will seek re-election. In most instances, Presidents in good health have sought, or at least have made themselves available for, a second term.[53]

✓ ✓ ✓

By and large, the United States ought to be able to choose for its President anybody that it wants, regardless of the number of terms he has served.

That is what I believe. Now, some people have said "You let him get enough power and this will lead toward a one-party government." That, I don't believe. I have got the utmost faith in the long-term common sense of the American people.

Therefore, I don't think there should be any inhibitions other than those that were in the 35-year age limit and so on. I think that was enough, myself.[54]

This was in opposition to the Twenty-second Amendment, limiting the President to two terms.

✦ ✦ ✦

He [the President] is the leader not of the, you might say, hierarchy of control in any political party. What he is is the leader who translates the platform into a legislative program in collaboration with his own executive department and with the legislative leaders.

And after that, once that program is established, I think it is his duty to use whatever means he deems most effective in order to get that program as large as he can translated into law.[55]

✦ ✦ ✦

It used to be that the succession went from the President, the Vice President, and the Secretary of State, and through the Cabinet. Now, it goes right after the Vice President to the Speaker of the House. Now, this means that if you have elected to the Executive Department a man of one party, and in the Congress you have a majority of the other party, you immediately change the political complexion of the Executive Department, if both the President and the Vice President die or are disabled. You'd go now from the Democrats to the Republicans, or vice versa. Now, this, I think, is wrong. I think that the people who have elected the President should have, for their President, for those four years, a man of that same political complexion, and I would go back to the old one. But I never brought it up as a matter of legislation for the simple reason that I had, by the time I had studied these things and was ready to make things, I had an opposition Congress, and I knew they were not going to make that change, so that's that. But I think that is a logical way to handle the thing.[56]

KENNEDY

The President is the Commander-in-Chief and he is the head of state, and he has responsibilities as a legislative leader. But one of these responsibilities—and I think all of our Presidents, our great Presidents, in both of our political parties have recognized it—is also to be head of a political party, because a political party, as Woodrow Wilson so often pointed out, is the means by which the people are served, the means by which those programs of benefit to our country are written into the statutes.[57]

Chapter X

THE PRESIDENT AS REFORMER

Genuine reform motives have been surprisingly scarce in the presidency—a fact which may on the surface appear more disturbing than it really is in a democratic society. Reformers are apt to be fanatics who see life wholly in terms of the evil they seek to correct, and the American presidency requires far broader vision and far more broadly diffused efforts than those the true reformer usually is willing to adopt or is capable of adopting. Moreover, reforms imposed from above are seldom lasting and are seldom accomplished without disruptions that frequently undermine fundamental institutions. Finally, there is within the unilateral competence of the President neither method nor machinery for the imposition of reforms.

The one great moral issue in the history of the United States was, of course, slavery and its residue, denial or abridgement of civil rights. The case against slavery was as old as the Republic. It had, for decades, preoccupied the politics, the literature, the pulpit, the press, and the lecture halls of the nation. Yet no President either won office on promises to abolish it or, having won office, sought to abolish it. "Wrong as we think slavery is, we can yet afford to let it alone where it is, because that much is due to the necessity arising from its actual presence in the nation," said Lincoln in the Cooper Institute speech often credited with winning him the nomination and election in 1860. Yet Lincoln was deeply aware of the unqualified evil and injustice of slavery, and he was brilliantly articulate on the subject in the debates on the extension of slavery. But he always separated his views of his capacities as President from his personal convictions—a discrimination, made by him again and again, which would probably be beyond the powers of a reformer to recognize. And for a hundred years after Lincoln, no President spoke militantly against depriving Negroes of civil rights until 1963.

There is some moral content in the civil service reforms sought by Hayes and such of his successors as Garfield and Arthur; but it was in the main a political question, except when open and brazen corruption was rife, as it was in the post-Civil War era. Hayes, therefore, stands out among the Presidents as reformers, not only because he affirmed the reformer role amid circumstances which, however ugly, represented the ruling political mores of his time, but also because he was willing to sacrifice the continuance of his political career to bring about those reforms. Garfield's few months in office were terminated by a bullet fired by a disappointed office seeker—an event which in itself was a product of the cynical spoils system and which aroused wide but short-lived public indignation.

Arthur, who served all but six months of Garfield's term, was one of the surprises in the history of the presidency that contributed toward the myth that the man rises to the office. It is true that some men whose previous careers gave little reason to expect much of them as Presidents conducted themselves with merit and even distinction in the office. But they were all men whose qualities of intelligence and character equipped them with sound and workable concepts of the office, and those who had weak concepts or none at all failed. In the case of Arthur, he had himself been removed from the collectorship of the port of New York, the only public office he ever held, by President Hayes as an episode in Hayes' reform program. He had gone to the 1880 Republican convention pledged to recalling Grant for a third term, after the reform administration of Hayes, and was himself nominated for the vice presidency only as a political sop to the old spoilsman ("stalwart") element when Garfield won the presidential nomination. But Arthur was a man of great personal integrity and high standards of political conduct within the limits of machine politics. He had the perception to distinguish between the demands made of a President and those of a political wheel horse, and though without any direct mandate from the people he set his sights high and refused to become the tool of his old political associates. His administration was a reform administration; for his pains, he was deprived of a nomination for a term of his own.

The major area of reforms stemming from presidential action has been the economic life of the nation, but there is perhaps less here than meets the eye, except, to an extent, in the first administration of Wilson. Jackson's battle to wrest public funds from private control by Nicholas Biddle's Bank of the United States was less impelled by profound moral convictions than immediate political conflict. Cleveland's economic reforms were sturdy enough but fell short of any consistent moral convictions about the nature of the new industrialism. Tariff reforms, generally, were politico-economic revisionist moves—not reform in the sense of moral correction. Theodore Roosevelt inveighed against the malefactors of great wealth; but it was never clear what really bothered him, and many of his malefactors of great wealth had a more serious social consciousness than he had and were steadily contributing to the growth of the institutions that gave character and drive to the American experience.

Wilson was of a different stripe—the only true Calvinist to sit in the White House and something of an anomaly in the Democratic party. There was in him a genuine zest for reform, and it related less to political considerations than those of other "reform" Presidents. Wilson was a missionary, first to Princeton University, then successively to the State of New Jersey, to the United States, and to the world. The very idea of a "covenant" as the formal charter of the League of Nations is significant. Wilson deeply believed that democracy, ideally, was a voluntary compact to move to higher, better levels. Yet, with him as with most others, utterances on the subject of the President as reformer do not occur. And with those others who were reforming influences to one extent or another, he saw reform as such more as a by-product of a serious recognition and responsible execution of presidential duties than as, in itself, a function of the presidency.

JACKSON

The recent demonstration of public sentiment inscribes on the list of Executive duties, in characters too legible to be overlooked, the task of *reform*, which will require particularly the correction of those abuses that have brought the patronage of the Federal Government into conflict with the freedom of elections, and the counteraction of those causes which have disturbed the rightful course of appointment and have placed or continued power in unfaithful or incompetent hands.[1]

*   *   *

The President has felt it his duty to exert the power with which the confidence of his countrymen has clothed him in attempting to purge the Government of all sinister influences which have been incorporated with its administration.[2]

LINCOLN

I would save the Union. I would save it the shortest way under the Constitution. The sooner the national authority can be restored, the nearer the Union will be the Union as it was. If there be those who would not save the Union unless they could at the same time save slavery, I do not agree with them. If there be those who would not save the Union unless they could at the same time destroy slavery, I do not agree with them. My paramount object in this struggle is to save the Union, and is not either to save or to destroy slavery. If I could save the Union without freeing any slave, I would do it; and if I could save it by freeing all the slaves, I would do it; and if I could save it by freeing some and leaving others alone, I would also do that. What I do about slavery and the colored race, I do because I believe it helps to save the Union; and what I forbear, I forbear because I do not believe it would help to save the Union. I shall do less whenever I shall believe what I am doing hurts the cause, and I shall do more whenever I shall believe doing more will help the cause. I shall try to correct errors when shown to be errors, and I shall adopt new views so fast as they shall appear to be true views.

I have here stated my purpose according to my view of official duty; and I intend no modification of my oft-expressed personal wish that all men everywhere could be free.[3]

✓ ✓ ✓

I do not want to issue a document that the whole world will see must necessarily be inoperative, like the Pope's bull against the comet. Would my word free the slaves, when I cannot even enforce the Constitution in the rebel States? Is there a single court, or magistrate, or individual that would be influenced by it there?[4]

✓ ✓ ✓

I am naturally antislavery. If slavery is not wrong, nothing is wrong. I cannot remember when I did not so think and feel, and yet I have never understood that the presidency conferred upon me an unrestricted right to act officially upon this judgment and feeling. It was in the oath I took that I would, to the best of my ability, preserve, protect, and defend the Constitution of the United States. I could not take the office without taking the oath. Nor was it my view that I might take an oath to get power, and break the oath in using the power. I understood, too, that in ordinary civil administration this oath even forbade me to practically indulge my primary abstract judgment on the moral question of slavery. I had publicly declared this many times, and in many ways. And I aver that, to this day, I have done no official act in mere deference to my abstract judgment and feeling on slavery. I did understand, however, that my oath to preserve the Constitution to the best of my ability imposed upon me the duty of preserving, by every indispensable means, that government—that nation, of which that Constitution was the organic law. Was it possible to lose the nation and yet preserve the Constitution? By general law, life and limb must be protected, yet often a limb must be amputated to save a life; but a life is never wisely given to save a limb. I felt that measures otherwise unconstitutional might become lawful by becoming indispensable to the preservation of the Constitution through the preservation of the nation. Right or wrong, I assumed this ground, and now avow it. I could not feel that, to the best of my ability, I had even tried to preserve the Constitution, if, to save slavery or any minor matter, I should permit the wreck of government, country, and Constitution all together. When, early in the war, General Fremont attempted military emancipation, I forbade it, because I did not then think it an indispensable necessity. When, a little later, General Cameron, the Secretary of War, suggested the arming of the blacks, I objected because I did not yet think it an indispensable necessity. When, still later, General Hunter attempted military emancipation, I again forbade it, because I did not yet think the indispensable necessity had come. When in March and May and July, 1862, I made earnest and successive appeals to the border States to favor compensated emancipation, I believed the indispensable necessity for military emancipation and arming the blacks would come unless averted by that measure. They declined the proposition, and I was, in my best judgment, driven to the alternative of either surrendering the Union, and with it the Constitution, or of laying strong hand upon the colored element. I chose the latter. In choosing it, I hoped for greater gain than loss; but of this, I was not entirely confident. More than a year of trial now shows no loss by it in our foreign relations, none in our home popular sentiment, none in our white military force—no loss by it anyhow or anywhere. On the contrary it shows a gain of quite a hundred and thirty thousand soldiers, seamen, and laborers. These are palpable facts, about which, as facts, there can be no caviling. We have the men; and we could not have had them without the measure.

And now let any Union man who complains of the measure test himself by writing down in one line that he is for subduing the rebellion by force of arms; and in the next, that he is for taking these hundred and thirty thousand men from the Union side, and placing them where they would be but for the measure he condemns. If he cannot face his case so stated, it is only because he cannot face the truth.

I add a word which was not in the verbal conversation. In telling this tale I attempt no compliment to my own sagacity. I claim not to have controlled events, but confess plainly that events have controlled me.[5]

HAYES

Convinced that the people of New York and of the country generally wish the New York custom-house to be administered solely with a view to the public interest, it is my purpose to do all in my power to introduce into this great office the reforms which the country desires.

With my information of the facts in the case, and with a deep sense of the responsible obligation imposed upon me by the Constitution "to take care that the laws be faithfully executed," I regard it as my plain duty to suspend the officers in question and to make the nominations now before the Senate, in order that this important office may be honestly and efficiently administered.[6]

* * *

The most serious obstacle, however, to an improvement of the civil service, and especially to a reform in the method of appointment and removal, has been found to be the practice, under what is known as the spoils system, by which the appointing power has been so largely encroached upon by members of Congress. The first step in the reform of the civil service must be a complete divorce between Congress and the Executive in the matter of appointments. The corrupting doctrine that "to the victors belong the spoils" is inseparable from Congressional patronage as the established rule and practice of parties in power. It comes to be understood by applicants for office and by the people generally that Representatives and Senators are entitled to disburse the patronage of their respective districts and States. It is not necessary to recite at length the evils resulting from this invasion of the Executive functions. The true principles of Government on the subject of appointments to office, as stated in the national conventions of the leading parties of the country, have again and again been approved by the American people, and have not been called in question in any quarter. These authentic expressions of public opinion upon this all-important subject are the statement of principles that belong to the constitutional structure of the Government.

Under the Constitution the President and heads of Departments are to make nominations for office. The Senate is to advise and consent to appointments, and the House of Representatives is to accuse and prosecute faithless officers. The best interest of the public service demands that these distinctions be respected; that Senators and Representatives, who may be judges and accusers, should not dictate appointments to office.

To this end the cooperation of the legislative department of the Government is required alike by the necessities of the case and by public opinion. Members of Congress will not be relieved from the demands made upon them with reference to appointments to office until by legislative enactment the pernicious practice is condemned and forbidden.

It is therefore recommended that an act be passed defining the relations of members of Congress with respect to appointment to office by the President; and I also recommend that the provisions of section 1767 and of the sections following of the Revised Statutes, comprising the tenure-of-office act of March 2, 1867, be repealed.[7]

✔ ✔ ✔

The points of civil service reform which I must call attention to are:—

1. *To separate office-holding from political management* . . .

2. To restore the legitimate and constitutional exercise of the appointing power to the Executive Department of the Government, subject to confirmation by the Senate in the case of important offices . . . It is generally conceded that Senators and Representatives ought not to seek to dictate appointments and only a small minority in practice now undertake even to influence appointments. But there is irritation and misunderstanding on the subject. It is exceedingly desirable that Members of Congress should be relieved from the pressure, [the] demands, of their constituents for places in the public service. This cannot be done by executive action alone.[8]

✔ ✔ ✔

In the *Nation* of the 8th there are criticisms of my course on the reform of the civil service. Agreeing generally with the *Nation* on this subject, I would like to make it clear to all such friends of the reform, that public opinion and Congress must be right on the question before we can have a thorough and complete reform. The President has neither time nor authority, neither means nor men, to gather the information required to make appointments and removals. In my last message I may frankly admit my own shortcomings (albeit they are not what the *Nation* supposes), enlarge on the importance of the reform, and urge that my successors shall have, what I have not had, a board of well paid, able men, to supply the information required to ascertain [the] qualifications of applicants for office, and to furnish ways to examine as to the conduct and qualifications of the incumbents.[9]

✓ ✓ ✓

If a decided majority in each house is opposed to reform, it cannot be established. It can only be made radical, thorough, and complete by the support of a majority in both the House and Senate. The first great step in the reform is to abolish congressional patronage; to restore to the Executive the appointing power which has been usurped by Congress, and especially by the Senate.[10]

GARFIELD

I love to deal with doctrines and events, but my day is frittered away with the personal seeking of people. Some Civil Service Reform will come by necessity after the wearisome years of wasted Presidents have paved the way for it.[11]

CLEVELAND

Don't you suppose that if I did exactly what you Civil Service Reform people want, in every particular, and should fail in the great, important measures of policy, and let the country go to the dogs on the currency, you people would be the first to say the President had no tact?[12]

✓ ✓ ✓

If a President yields to the demands of the spoilsmen, he can never satisfy them. As between satisfying them and seeing this great Government well administrated, there ought to be no choice- and civil-service reform above all things is a relief to the Executive and a good thing in itself.[13]

THEODORE ROOSEVELT

Unfortunately, the strength of my public position before the country is also its weakness. I am genuinely independent of the big monied men in all matters where I think the interests of the public are concerned, and probably I am the first President of recent times of whom this could be truthfully said. I think it right and desirable that this should be true of the President. But where I do not grant any favors to these big monied men which

I do not think the country requires that they should have, it is out of the question for me to expect them to grant favors to me in return. I treat them precisely as I treat other citizens; that is, I consider their interests so far as my duty requires and so far as I think the needs of the country warrant. In return, they will support me, in so far as they are actuated purely by public spirit, simply accordingly as they think I am or am not doing well; and so far as they are actuated solely by their private interests they will support me only on points where they think it is to their interest to do so.[14]

* * *

One of the things one must learn, unfortunately, as President or Governor or any like position, is not to jeopardize one's power for doing the good that is possible by efforts to correct evils over which one has no control and with which one is only himself *generally* concerned; save in wholly exceptional instances.[15]

* * *

Four years ago Booker Washington and I discussed what ought to be done by a President to the South. We agreed that in the Gulf and South Atlantic states, where, unlike what is the case in Tennessee and North Carolina, there is no real Republican party organization which has any particular effect at the polls, the thing to do would be freely to recognize Democrats; to try to appoint men of the highest character—Republicans where they were available, Democrats where they were not; and to appoint a very few colored men of high character—just enough to make it evident that they were not being entirely proscribed. This is precisely the plan I have followed, and in the abstract every reputable southerner agrees that it is the right plan, while every reputable and intelligent southerner agrees that it has actually been put into practice in his district. And yet it has not prevented such coarse and malignant mendacity from the political and newspaper leaders of the South as to create a corresponding bitterness in the North—a bitterness which I am doing all in my power to allay, or at least to prevent from finding expression.[16]

*   *   *

It is one of the chief duties—and it is the highest privilege—of a President of the United States to be the active leader and exponent of policies which will help the people to obtain such legislative and administrative reforms as are required to meet any reasonable popular demand which makes for the common good.[17]

Chapter XI

LIMITATIONS OF THE PRESIDENCY

All Presidents have been conscious of the limitations of the office. Virtually all have mentioned some of these limitations in their writings. Most have, however, worked around them, when they have been constitutional limitations, and have accepted them philosophically, when they have been human limitations. Some, however, have read into the office more limitations than most students of the presidency would believe were there. In times of stress, such essentially negative views have led to desperation on the part of the uncomfortable occupant of the office, and in relaxed times to a certain vacuity.

Herbert Hoover, for example, had such a confined notion of the powers of the presidency that he was, at one critical point, seriously convinced that the President of the United States had no alternative to sitting impotently by while the nation skidded to economic ruin, though he labored long, hard and with thorough conscientiousness within the rigid limitations of the office as he saw them.

The least of the adequate Presidents, Calvin Coolidge, simply gave up and thought the office relatively meaningless: "I suppose I am the most powerful man in the world, but great power doesn't mean much except great limitations."[1] If Jefferson and Polk had shared that persuasion, the United States would have remained a thin strip of colonies along the Atlantic seaboard. Presiding over one of the most amoral periods in America's economic history, Coolidge had an ice-bound concept not only of the presidency but of the whole Federal Government: "It does not at all follow because abuses exist that it is the concern of the Federal Government to attempt their reform."[2] It never occurred to Coolidge to ask why, other than to correct and prevent abuses, governments were institued among men at all. And he lived to see the abuses that he had in mind result in the most desperate plight of the nation since the dark day of Fort Sumter.

Coolidge did, however, have one string on his lute, which he plucked from time to time with a brittle snap: economy. A custodial view of public office almost always expresses itself in saving money, but with Coolidge, it was not just a political ploy: "Economy is idealism in its most practical form."[3] He meant it.

This stood in favorable contrast to the three total failures in the presidency: Buchanan, too flaccid and irresolute to face the problems of slavery and secession; Grant, too confused and imperceptive to see the corruption that invaded his own office; and Harding, too weak and undiscriminating even to form an adequate administration. What these three men lacked was the remotest sense of what the presidency was all about, although, as Polk's Secretary of State, Buchanan certainly had adequate opportunity to gain one. They seemed to move only under the spell of what they apparently thought to be its limitations, to become mired in its imagined impotence. Whether as individuals they could ever have got anything constructive done remains a completely academic question since, as Presidents, none of them showed any signs of knowing how it should have been attempted. The only rewarding aspect they present to the democracy now is their relatively low number—less than one in eleven of American Presidents—and the brevity of their combined tenure—fourteen years, or less than a twelfth of the span of our national history.

As for the rest, the limitations of the office, when they were conceded, were no great stumbling blocks and usually accepted with grace, though occasionally with a sharp protest.

WASHINGTON

For as the Constitution of the United States, and the laws made under it, must mark the line of my official conduct, I could not justify my taking a single step in any matter, which appeared to me to require their agency, without its being first obtained. . . .[4]

JOHN ADAMS

No! the real fault is, that the president has not influence enough, and is not independent enough. Parties will not allow him to act himself. For twelve years one party prevailed, and that party would not allow their presidents to be impartial. The other party has now prevailed eight years, and they have not permitted their president, in many instances, to act his own judgment. The power of removal was never abused in the first twelve years, except, perhaps, in two instances, and those removals were made at the earnest and repeated solicitations of all the members of the house, and one of the members of the senate, from New Hampshire, much against the inclination of the president. Representations of misconduct in office were made to the president, and probably credited by those members of congress; but there is now reason to suspect, that they were dictated by too much of a party spirit.

In short, presidents must break asunder their leading strings, and the people must support them in it. They must unite the two parties, instead of inflaming their divisions. They must look out for merit, wherever they can find it; and talent and integrity must be a recommendation to office, wherever they are seen, though differing in sentiments from the president, and in an opposite party to that whose little predominance brought him into power.[5]

◄ ◄ ◄

The President has no control over the opinions of judges. They are as independent as he is. Their judgments in courts must be executed.[6]

JEFFERSON

No one would more willingly than myself pay the just tribute due to the services of Capt. Barry, by writing a letter of condolence to his widow, as you suggest. But when one undertakes to administer justice, it must be with an even hand, & by rule; what is done for one, must be done for every one in equal degree. To what a train of attentions would this draw a President? How difficult would it be to draw the line between that degree of merit entitled to such a testimonial of it, & that not so entitled? If drawn in a particular case differently from what the friends of the deceased would judge right, what offence would it give, & of the most tender kind? How much offence would be given by accidental inattentions, or want of information? The first step into such an undertaking ought to be well weighed.[7]

✓ ✓ ✓

If a member of the Executive or Legislature does wrong, the day is never far distant when the people will remove him.[8]

✓ ✓ ✓

But when a person charged with an offence is placed in the possession of the judiciary authority, the laws commit to that solely the whole direction of the case; and any interference with it on the part of the Executive would be an encroachment on their independence, and open to just censure. And still more censurable would this be in a case originating, as yours does, not with the Executive, but an independent authority. I am persuaded therefore, that on reconsideration, you will be sensible that, in declining to interpose in the present case, I do but obey the vigorous prescriptions of duty.[9]

✓ ✓ ✓

Be this as it may, every one must act according to the dictates of his own reason, & mine tells me that civil powers alone have been given to the President of the US. and no authority to direct the religious exercises of his constituents.[10]

✓ ✓ ✓

I am for responsibilities at short periods, seeing neither reason nor safety in making public functionaries independent of the nation for life, or even for long terms of years. On this principle

I prefer the Presidential term of four years, to that of seven
years, which I myself had at first suggested, annexing to it,
however, ineligibility forever after; and I wish it were now
annexed to the 2d quadrennial election of President.[11]

MADISON

Having examined and considered the bill entitled "An act providing for the trial of causes pending in the respective district
courts of the United States, in case of the absence or disability
of the judges thereof," which bill was presented to me on the
25th of March past, I now return the same to the House of
Representatives, in which it originated, with the following objections: . . .

Because, by referring to the President of the United States
questions of disability in the district judges and of the unreason-
ableness of delaying the suits or causes pending the district
courts, and leaving it with him in such causes to require the
justices of the Supreme Court to perform additional services,
the bill introduces an unsuitable relation of members of the
judiciary department to a discretionary authority of the executive department.[12]

MONROE

If the Chief Magistrate has any power of restraint while in office,
it must cease after his retirement.[13]

JOHN QUINCY ADAMS

Called from my nursery and garden by a visit from Mr. Quincy,
President of Harvard University . . . He told me also that as
President Jackson is about visiting Boston, the Corporation of
the university had thought it necessary to invite him to visit
the colleges; that he (Mr. Quincy) should address him in a
Latin discourse, and confer upon him the degree of Doctor of
Laws; and he intimated that I should receive an invitation to be
present at these ceremonies.

I said that the personal relations in which President Jackson
had chosen to place himself with me were such that I could
hold no intercourse of a friendly character with him. I could
therefore not accept an invitation to attend upon this occasion.
And, independent of that, as myself an affectionate child of

our Alma Mater, I would not be present to witness her disgrace
in conferring her highest literary honors upon a barbarian who
could not write a sentence of grammar and hardly could spell
his own name. Mr. Quincy said he was sensible how utterly
unworthy of literary honors Jackson was, but the Corporation
thought it was necessary to follow the precedent, and treat him
precisely as Mr. Monroe, his predecessor, had been treated.
As the people of the United States had seen fit to make him
their President, the Corporation thought the honors which they
conferred upon him were compliments due to the station, by
whomsoever it was occupied. Mr. Quincy said it was thought
also that the omission to show the same respect to President
Jackson which had been shown to Mr. Monroe would be imputed to party spirit—which they were anxious to avoid . . . I
adhered to my determination to stay at home.[14]

*Adams stayed home, but Jackson got the degree. The President of
Harvard: "As the people have twice decided that this man knows
law enough to be their ruler, it is not for Harvard College to
maintain that they are mistaken." This somewhat graceless citation
is in Josiah Quincy, Figures of the Past, 361.*

✦ ✦ ✦

I paid a visit this morning to Mr. Tyler, who styles himself
President of the United States, and not Vice-President acting as
President, which would be the correct style. But it is a construction in direct violation both of the grammar and context of
the Constitution, which confers upon the Vice-President, on the
decease of the President, not the office, but the powers and duties of the said office. There is a dogmatical article in the *National Intelligencer* asserting this false construction; which is not
worth contesting, but which to a strict constructionist would warrant more than a doubt whether the Vice-President has the right
to occupy the President's house, or to claim his salary, without
an Act of Congress. He moved into the house two days ago,
and received me in the old southeast Cabinet chamber.[15]

JACKSON

Whilst I concur with the synod in the efficacy of prayer, and in
the hope that our country may be preserved from the attack of
Pestilence and "that the judgments now abroad in the earth may
be sanctified to the good of nations," I am constrained to decline

the appointment of any period or mode as proper for the public manifestation of this reliance. I could not do otherwise without transcending those limits which are prescribed by the Constitution for the President and without feeling that I might in some degree disturb the security which religion now enjoys in this country in its complete seperation from the political concerns of the General Government.[16]

VAN BUREN

Recent experience on the southern boundary of the United States and the events now daily occurring on our northern frontier have abundantly shown that the existing laws are insufficient to guard against hostile invasion from the United States of the territory of friendly and neighboring nations.

The laws in force provide sufficient penalties for the punishment of such offenses after they have been committed, and provided the parties can be found, but the Executive is powerless in many cases to prevent the commission of them, even when in possession of ample evidence of an intention on the part of evil-disposed persons to violate our laws.

Your attention is called to this defect in our legislation. It is apparent that the Executive ought to be clothed with adequate power effectually to restrain all persons within our jurisdiction from the commission of acts of this character. They tend to disturb the peace of the country and inevitably involve the Government in perplexing controversies with foreign powers. I recommend a careful revision of all the laws now in force and such additional enactments as may be necessary to vest in the Executive full power to prevent injuries being inflicted upon neighboring nations by the unauthorized and unlawful acts of citizens of the United States or of other persons who may be within our jurisdiction and subject to our control.[17]

✦ ✦ ✦

When the Constitution makers of France strove to reconcile the first Napoleon to an abridgment of his immediate power by proposing to confer upon him authority to direct what should be done after his decease he promptly refused the offer for the reason that a dead man was nothing in respect to power whatever or whoever he may have been when alive. The same may be said of a President whom a few short months will dispossess of his station in obediance to the decree of the People.[18]

WILLIAM H. HARRISON

I am not insensible of the great difficulty that exists in drawing a proper plan for the safe-keeping and disbursement of the public revenues, and I know the importance which has been attached by men of great abilities and patriotism to the divorce, as it is called, of the Treasury from the banking institutions. It is not the divorce which is complained of, but the unhallowed union of the Treasury with the executive department, which has created such extensive alarm. To this danger to our republican institutions and that created by the influence given to the executive through the instrumentality of the Federal officers I propose to apply all the remedies which may be at my command. It was certainly a great error in the framers of the Constitution not to have made the officer at the head of the Treasury Department entirely independent of the Executive. He should at least have been removable only upon the demand of the popular branch of the legislature.[19]

*   *   *

I have determined never to remove a Secretary of the Treasury without communicating all the circumstances attending such removal to both Houses of Congress.

The influence of the Executive in controlling the freedom of the elective franchise through the medium of the public officers can be effectually checked by renewing the prohibition published by Mr. Jefferson forbidding their interference in elections further than giving their own votes, and their own independence secured by an assurance of perfect immunity in exercising this sacred privilege of freemen under the dictates of their own unbiased judgments. Never with my consent shall an officer of the people, compensated for his services out of their pockets, become the pliant instrument of Executive will.[20]

*   *   *

There is no part of the means placed in the hands of the Executive which might be used with greater effect for unhallowed purposes than the control of the public press. The maxim which our ancestors derived from the mother country that "the freedom of the press is the great bulwark of civil and religious liberty" is one of the most precious legacies which they have left us. We have learned, too, from our own as well as the experience of other countries, that golden shackles, by whomsoever or by whatever pretense imposed, are as fatal to it as the iron bonds of despotism. The presses in the necessary employment of the Government should never be used "to clear the guilty or to varnish crime." A decent and manly examination of the acts of the Government should be not only tolerated, but encouraged.[21]

TYLER

In view of the fact, well avouched by history, that the tendency of all human institutions is to concentrate power in the hands of a single man, and that their ultimate downfall has proceeded from this cause, I deem it of the most essential importance that a complete separation should take place between the sword and the purse. No matter where or how the public moneys shall be deposited, so long as the President can exert the power of appointing and removing at his pleasure the agents selected for their custody the Commander in Chief of the Army and Navy is in fact the treasurer. A permanent and radical change should therefore be decreed.[22]

✦ ✦ ✦

I must be permitted to disclaim entirely and unqualifiedly the right on the part of the Executive to make any real or supposed defects existing in any State constitution or form of government the pretext for a failure to enforce the laws or the guaranties of the Constitution of the United States in reference to any such State. I utterly repudiate the idea, in terms as emphatic as I can employ, that those laws are not to be enforced or those guaranties complied with because *the President* may believe that the right of suffrage or any other great popular right is either too restricted or too broadly enlarged. I also with equal strength resist the idea that it falls within the Executive competency to decide in controversies of the nature of that which existed in Rhode Island on which side is the majority of the people or as to the extent of the rights of a mere numerical majority. For the Executive to assume such a power would be to assume a power of the most dangerous character. Under such assumptions the States of this Union would have no security for peace or tranquility, but might be converted into the mere instruments of Executive will. Actuated by selfish purposes, he might become the great agitator, fomenting assaults upon the State constitutions and declaring the majority of to-day to be the minority of to-morrow, and the

minority, in its turn, the majority, before whose decrees the established order of things in the State should be subverted. Revolution, civil commotion, and bloodshed would be the inevitable
consequences. The provision in the Constitution intended for the
security of the States would thus be turned into the instrument
of their destruction. The President would become, in fact, the
great *constitution maker* for the States, and all power would be
vested in his hands.[23]

POLK

Gov. Thomas applied to the President to order a nolle prosequi,
in the case of an indictment pending against him in the Circuit
Court of the U. States for the District of Columbia, in which Col.
Benton was prosecutor. Gov. Thomas made a lengthy statement
of the facts & circumstances of the case, and assigned the reasons
why he thought the President should interpose and stop the prosecution. The President promptly declined to do so. He informed
Gov. Thomas that he did not consider that he possessed any such
power; that the Judiciary & the Executive were independent and
coordinate Departments, and that he had never known such a
power exerted by the Executive of any State, and that he had
never heard of it having been exercised by the President of the
U. States. Gov. Thomas insisted that the power existed and had
been often exercised by the Governor of Maryland. The President replied that the practice in Maryland might be an exception
to the General rule; & inquired of Gov. Thomas what power he
would have to enforce such an order, if he were to issue it? The
Judges of the Court in this District would not be bound to obey
him, and if they disobeyed him he would have no power to impose obedience; that according to the law as he understood it,
the Court was the exclusive judge of the propriety of permitting
or ordering a nolle prosequi in any case pending before them,
and without the assent of the Court it could not be done. Gov.
Thomas said if the President would entertain the question, he
would make a written application and produce authorities to establish the existence of the power. The President replied that it
was unnecessary to do so, as his mind was made up on the subject; that he had never examined the merits of the case, and
must leave the decision of the case exclusively to the Court, without any interference on his part. Gov. Thomas made a long statement of the facts, and dwelt on the hardship of the case, alledg-
ing that in this criminal proceeding he could not command the

attendance of witnesses residing out of this District, and under
the issue joined could not give in evidence facts material to his
defence, and therefore it was, that he appealed to the President
to exert the power which, he insisted, he possessed, to arrest the
proceedings. The President made no reply except to reiterate his
decision.[24]

FILLMORE

The duty of the Executive extends only to the execution of laws
and the maintenance of treaties already in force and the protection of all the people of the United States in the enjoyment of
the rights which those treaties and laws guarantee.

It is exceedingly desirable that no occasion should arise for the
exercise of the powers thus vested in the President by the Constitution and the laws. With whatever mildness those powers
might be executed, or however clear the case of necessity, yet
consequences might, nevertheless, follow of which no human
sagacity can foresee either the evils or the end.[25]

PIERCE

But it is not the duty of the President of the United States to
volunteer interposition by force to preserve the purity of elections either in a State or Territory. To do so would be subversive
of public freedom. And whether a law be wise or unwise, just
or unjust, is not a question for him to judge. If it be constitutional
—that is, if it be the law of the land—it is his duty to cause it to
be executed, or to sustain the authorities of any State or Territory
in executing it in opposition to all insurrectionary movements.[26]

✦ ✦ ✦

In those parts of the United States where, by reason of the in-
flamed state of the public mind, false rumors and misrep-
resentations have the greatest currency it has been assumed that
it was the duty of the Executive not only to suppress insurrectionary movements in Kansas, but also to see to the regularity
of local elections. It needs little argument to show that the President has no such power. All government in the United States rests
substantially upon popular election. The freedom of elections is
liable to be impaired by the intrusion of unlawful votes or the
exclusion of lawful ones, by improper influences, by violence, or
by fraud. But the people of the United States are themselves the

all-sufficient guardians of their own rights, and to suppose that they will not remedy in due season any such incidents of civil freedom is to suppose them to have ceased to be capable of self-government. The President of the United States has not power to interpose in elections, to see to their freedom, to canvass their votes, or to pass upon their legality in the Territories any more than in the States. If he had such power the Government might be republican in form, but it would be a monarchy in fact; and if he had undertaken to exercise it in the case of Kansas he would have been justly subject to the charge of usurpation and of violation of the dearest rights of the people of the United States.[27]

BUCHANAN

Wisely limited and restrained as is his power under our Constitution and laws, he alone can accomplish but little for good or for evil on such a momentous question.[28]

*   *   *

From the very nature of his office, and its high responsibilities, he must necessarily be conservative. The stern duty of administering the vast and complicated concerns of this government affords in itself a guarantee that he will not attempt any violation of a clear constitutional right.

After all, he is no more than the chief executive officer of the government. His province is not to make but to execute the laws. . . .[29]

*   *   *

What, in the meantime, is the responsibility and true position of the Executive? He is bound by solemn oath, before God and the country, "to take care that the laws be faithfully executed," and from this obligation he cannot be absolved by any human power. But what if the performance of this duty, in whole or in part, has been rendered impracticable by events over which he could have exercised no control? Such, at the present moment, is the case throughout the State of South Carolina, so far as the laws of the United States to secure the administration of justice by means of the federal judiciary are concerned. All the federal officers within its limits, through whose agency alone these laws can be carried into execution, have already resigned. We no longer have a district judge, a district attorney, or a marshal in

South Carolina. In fact, the whole machinery of the federal government necessary for the distribution of remedial justice among the people has been demolished, and it would be difficult, if not impossible, to replace it.

The only acts of Congress on the Statute book bearing upon this subject are those of the 28th February, 1795, and 3d March, 1807. These authorize the President, after he shall have ascertained that the marshal, with his *posse comitatus,* is unable to execute civil or criminal process in any particular case, to call forth the militia and employ the army and navy to aid him in performing this service, having first by proclamation commanded the insurgents "to disperse and retire peaceably to their respective abodes within a limited time." This duty cannot by possibility be performed in a State where no judicial authority exists to issue process, and where there is no marshal to execute it, and where, even if there were such an officer, the entire population would constitute one solid combination to resist him.[30]

✓ ✓ ✓

Apart from the execution of the laws, so far as this may be practicable, the Executive has no authority to decide what shall be the relations between the federal government and South Carolina. He has been invested with no such discretion. He possesses no power to change the relations heretofore existing between them, much less to acknowledge the independence of that State. This would be to invest a mere executive officer with the power of recognizing the dissolution of the Confederacy among our thirty-three sovereign States. It bears no resemblance to the recognition of a foreign *de facto* government, involving no such responsibility. Any attempt to do this would, on his part, be a naked act of usurpation.[31]

✓ ✓ ✓

Congress, and Congress alone, under the war-making power, can exercise the discretion of agreeing to abstain "from any and all acts calculated to produce a collision of arms" between this and any other Government. It would therefore be a usurpation for the Executive to attempt to restrain their hands by an agreement in regard to matters over which he has no constitutional control. If he were thus to act they might pass laws which he should be bound to obey, though in conflict with his agreement.[32]

✓ ✓ ✓

If two years after a Presidential term has expired the Senate can go back & try, condemn, & execute the former incumbent, who would accept the office?[33]

LINCOLN

By the Constitution and laws, the President is charged with no duty in the conduct of a presidential election in any State; nor do I, in this case, perceive any military reason for his interference in the matter. . . .

. . . Except it be to give protection against violence, I decline to interfere in any way with any presidential election.[34]

✓ ✓ ✓

They can at any moment have peace simply by laying down their arms and submitting to the national authority under the Constitution. After so much the government could not, if it would, maintain war against them. The loyal people would not sustain or allow it. If questions should remain, we would adjust them by the peaceful means of legislation, conference, courts, and votes, operating only in constitutional and lawful channels. Some certain, and other possible, questions are, and would be, beyond the executive power to adjust; as, for instance, the admission of members into Congress, and whatever might require the appropriation of money. The executive power itself would be greatly diminished by the cessation of actual war. Pardons and remissions of forfeitures, however, would still be within executive control.[35]

✓ ✓ ✓

What is the Presidency to me if I have no country.[36]

✓ ✓ ✓

The Constitution reads:
"The United States shall guarantee to every State in this Union a republican form of government."
Does that authorize the Executive, upon his own volition, upon his mere *ipse dixit*, to take charge of a State Government in person or by his agent, some man selected from the army? No, sir, it authorizes no such thing; and the interference with the State

of Louisiana to-day, by the President taking charge of that Government, is palpable violation of the Constitution of the United States.[37]

GRANT

It was my fortune, or misfortune, to be called to the office of Chief Executive without any previous political training. From the age of 17 I had never even witnessed the excitement attending a Presidential campaign but twice antecedent to my own candidacy, and at but one of them was I eligible as a voter.

Under such circumstances it is but reasonable to suppose that errors of judgment must have occurred. Even had they not, differences of opinion between the Executive, bound by an oath to the strict performance of his duties, and writers and debaters must have arisen. It is not necessarily evidence of blunder on the part of the Executive because there are these differences of views. Mistakes have been made, as all can see and I admit, but it seems to me oftener in the selections made of the assistants appointed to aid in carrying out the various duties of administering the Government—in nearly every case selected without a personal acquaintance with the appointee, but upon recommendations of the representatives chosen directly by the people. It is impossible, where so many trusts are to be allotted, that the right parties should be chosen in every instance. History shows that no Administration from the time of Washington to the present has been free from these mistakes. But I leave comparisons to history, claiming only that I have acted in every instance from a conscientious desire to do what was right, constitutional, within the law, and for the very best interests of the whole people. Failures have been errors of judgment, not of intent.[38]

HAYES

It is not the duty of the President of the United States to use the military power of the Nation to decide contested elections in the States. He will maintain the authority of the United States and keep the peace between the contending parties. But local self-government means the determination by each State for itself of all questions as to its own local affairs.[39]

ARTHUR

. . . when a lawfully constituted court-martial has duly declared its findings and its sentence and the same have been duly approved neither the President nor the Congress has any power to set them aside.[40]

CLEVELAND

It has always seemed to me that, beyond the greatness of the office and the supreme importance of its duties and responsibilities, the most impressive thing connected with the Presidency is the fact that after its honor has been relinquished, and after its labor and responsibility are past, we simply see that a citizen whom the people had selected from their ranks to do their bidding for a time and to be their agent in the discharge of public duty, has laid aside the honor and the work of the highest office in the world and has returned again to the people, to resume at their side the ordinary duties which pertain to everyday citizenship.[41]

✤ ✤ ✤

But it must be admitted that our people are by no means united in their ideas concerning the place which our ex-Presidents ought to occupy, or the disposition which should be made of them. Of course the subject would be relieved of all uncertainty and embarrassment if every President would die at the end of his term. This does not seem, however, to meet the view of those who under such an arrangement would be called on to do the dying; and so some of them continue to live, and thus perpetuate the perplexity of those who burden themselves with plans for their utilization or disposition.[42]

✤ ✤ ✤

I frequently think what a glorious boon omniscience would be to one charged with the Chief Magistracy of our nation.[43]

THEODORE ROOSEVELT

I suppose few Presidents can form the slightest idea whether their policies have met with approval or not—certainly I cannot.

But as far as I can see these policies have been right, and I hope that time will justify them. If it does not, why, I must abide the fall of the dice, and that is all there is about it.[44]

✓ ✓ ✓

There is one point of inferiority in our system to yours which has been very little touched on, and that is the way in which the Presidential office tends to put a premium upon a man's keeping out of trouble rather than upon his accomplishing results. If a man has a very decided character, has a strongly accentuated career, it is normally the case of course that he makes ardent friends and bitter enemies; and unfortunately human nature is such that more enemies will leave their party because of enmity to its head than friends will come in from the opposite party because they think well of that same head. In consequence, the dark horse, the neutral-tinted individual, is very apt to win against the man of pronounced views and active life. The electorate is very apt to vote with its back to the future![45]

✓ ✓ ✓

But of course a President can't go on the stump and can't indulge in personalities, and so I have to sit still and abide the result.[46]

✓ ✓ ✓

If it were not for the certainty of fools misunderstanding the terminology, and failing to see that a short-term elective King has nothing whatever in common with a hereditary King, I could best express to a foreigner the President's power by putting it in that form. Of course a constitutional King reigns all his life and does not govern at all, while the President never reigns, but governs most actively for 4 or 8 years; and our President, in the actual exercise of his power, resembles the Prime Minister far more than he does a functionary like the French President. But his power is even greater, and therefore it is natural that the people should desire to hedge it about with certain restrictions, and above all to make it certain that it can only be of limited duration.[47]

✓ ✓ ✓

After eight years in the Presidency, not only is it unwise for other reasons to re-elect a man, but is inadvisable because it is

almost certain that someone can be found with the same prin-
cipals, who, from the mere fact that he is someone else, can better succeed in putting those principles into practice.[48]

✓ ✓ ✓

The President of the United States ought to have no title; and
if he did have a title it ought to be a bigger one [than "Excellency"]. Whenever an important prince comes here he is apt
to bring a shoal of "excellencies" in his train. Just as I should
object to having the simple dignity of the White House changed
for such attractions as might lie in a second-rate palace, so I feel
that the President of a great democratic republic should have no
title but President. He could not have a title that would not be
either too much or too little. Let him be called the President,
and nothing more.[49]

✓ ✓ ✓

Any President on retiring ought to be proud and grateful to
serve as President of Harvard.[50]

*But in 1909, when with Eliot's resignation the presidency of Harvard
fell vacant two months after the end of Roosevelt's term, the latter
was not among the twenty-four mentioned by the Harvard Corporation as among those advocated for the job—though he was mentioned by many outside the Corporation, which thereby stood by its
tradition of electing no one prominently mentioned for the post.*

✓ ✓ ✓

I think you are right in regretting that I went into this na-
ture-faker fight. This is another way of saying that a President
ought not to go into anything outside of his work as President;
that he ought not to do as Gladstone did and take an interest in
outside studies of any kind. But it is rather a hard proposition to
live up to. For instance, in *The Outlook* I reviewed Robinson's
poems because I felt that he merited more consideration than he
had received and that my position as President gave the chance
to call attention to him. In the same way, I wrote an article on
the Irish sagas because it seems to me that intelligent laymen
should take a greater interest in them. So in the same way I have
written articles on hunting and outdoor life. (I do not know
whether in what I have said on race suicide and on various labor
and social questions I ought to be held as going outside of my
proper position or not; but you must remember that, as President

Pritchett says, the by-products of the Presidency are important, and I am mighty glad to have had the chance to say my say on certain big moral matters.) But I will not write in praise if I do not write, where necessary, in blame. Most certainly the President never should condemn any man unless the offense is flagrant and unless the facts are absolutely undoubted.[51]

✓ ✓ ✓

To put a good man with a good character who has not been "prominently identified with officeholding" into the Presidency, is just the kind of inanity of which you speak. He has got to learn all of these things during his first months of years of the Presidency, instead of knowing them already.[52]

✓ ✓ ✓

Not only law but wise custom and propriety demand that the President shall be addrest only as "Mr. President" or as "The President." It is wholly improper to permit the use of a silly title like "Excellency" (and incidentally if titles were to be allowed at all, this title is entirely unworthy of the position of the President). Any title is silly when given the President.[53]

✓ ✓ ✓

I am the only man in the United States who can speak of the presidency without the thrill that always comes to the man who has never been in the White House. To go to the White House simply for the sake of being President doesn't interest me in the least. There are so many things that I haven't yet done and that I want so much to do. I want to take some time now, in the next few years, to do some of those things. I have done something in geography and something in ornithology, and something in other lines. I want to put myself in position where I can be rightfully recognized as a scientist in one or two of these lines.

Most men in this country think of the presidency as the supreme thing, and that is natural and all right. But I've had that, and another term could not add anything to what I have had there. Of course, if there were a big job of work to be done, which the people of the country wanted me to handle, that would be a different thing. But then it would be going back in order to do a particular thing, and one that I had not done before. It would not be going back simply for the sake of being President again. There is a far greater probability that another term in the White House, unless under the exceptional conditions I spoke about, would detract from my record, than there is that it would add to the record.[54]

✦ ✦ ✦

The Presidency is a great office, and the power of the President can be effectively used to secure a renomination, especially if the President has the support of certain great political and financial interests. It is for this reason, and this reason alone, that the wholesome principle of continuing in office, so long as he is willing to serve, an incumbent who has proved capable, is not applicable to the Presidency. Therefore, the American people have wisely established a custom against allowing any man to hold that office for more than two consecutive terms. But every shred of power which a President exercises while in office vanishes absolutely when he has once left office. An ex-President stands precisely in the position of any other private citizen, and has not one particle more power to secure a nomination or election than if he had never held the office at all—indeed, he probably has less because of the very fact that he has held the office. Therefore the reasoning on which the anti-third term custom is based has no application whatever to anything except consecutive terms. As a barrier of precaution against more than two consecutive terms the custom embodies a valuable principle. Applied in any other way it becomes a mere formula, and like all formulas a potential source of mischievous confusion.[55]

TAFT

One cannot always be sure of the truth of what one hears if he happens to be the President of the United States.[56]

✦ ✦ ✦

The constitutional functions of the President seem very broad, and they are. When many speak of his great power, they have in mind that what the President does, goes, like kissing, by favor. I beg of you to believe that the Presidency offers but few opportunities for showing power of this sort. The responsibility of the office is so heavy, the earnest desire that every man who fills the place has to deserve the approval of his countrymen by doing the thing that is best for the country is so strong, and the fear of just popular criticism is so controlling, that it is difficult for one who has borne the burden of the office for four years to remember more than a few favors that he was able to confer.[57]

* * *

The truth is that great as his powers are, when a President comes to exercise them, he is much more concerned with the limitations upon them than he is affected, like little Jack Horner, by a personal joy over the big personal things he can do.[58]

* * *

The true view of the Executive functions is, as I conceive it, that the President can exercise no power which cannot be fairly and reasonably traced to some specific grant of power or justly implied and included within such express grant as proper and necessary to its exercise. Such specific grant must be either in the Federal Constitution or in an act of Congress passed in pursuance thereof. There is no undefined residuum of power which he can exercise because it seems to him to be in the public interest, and there is nothing in the Neagle case and its definition of a law of the United States, or in other precedents, warranting such an inference. The grants of Executive power are necessarily in general terms in order not to embarrass the Executive within the field of action plainly marked for him, but his jurisdiction must be justified and vindicated by affirmative constitutional or statutory provision, or it does not exist.[59]

WILSON

If you pick up the Federalist, some parts of it read like a treatise on astronomy instead of a treatise on government. They speak of the centrifugal and the centripital forces, and locate the President somewhere in a rotating system. The whole thing is a calculation of power and an adjustment of parts.[60]

COOLIDGE

I suppose I am the most powerful man in the world, but great power does not mean much except great limitations. I cannot have any freedom even to go and come. I am only in the clutch of forces that are greater than I am.[61]

* * *

It is an advantage to a President to know that he is not a great man.[62]

✦   ✦   ✦

I had some experiences of that kind, of course, in other executive positions, but I was not prepared for so much of it and with so much persistent under-cover pressure. It seemed strange to me that a President, if he is to avoid mistakes, has to suspect and resist almost every suggestion from callers until he can look into it most searchingly—and then usually ignore it.[63]

✦   ✦   ✦

A President on his way out is never given much consideration. That's politics.[64]

HOOVER

I had felt deeply that no President should undermine the independence of legislative and judicial branches by seeking to discredit them. The constitutional division of powers is the bastion of our liberties and was not designed as a battleground to display the prowess of Presidents. They just have to work with the material that God—and the voters—have given them.[65]

✦   ✦   ✦

Fishing seems to be the sole avenue left to Presidents through which they may escape to their own thoughts and may live in their own imaginings and find relief from the pneumatic hammer of constant personal contacts, and refreshment of mind in the babble of rippling brooks.

Moreover, it is a constant reminder of the democracy of life, of humility and of human frailty—for all men are equal before fishes. And it is desirable that the President of the United States should be periodically reminded of this fundamental fact—that the forces of nature discriminate for no man.[66]

✦   ✦   ✦

A revered President, long since dead, once told me that there was no solution to this relation of the White House to the press; that there never would be a President who could satisfy the press until he was twenty years dead.[67]

ꜰ ꜰ ꜰ

I will not go into the doctor's definition of an exhibitionist; suffice it to say they comprise those who have an abnormal desire to preen in public. One well-defined form is represented by those who visit the White House to say a hurried few words to the President and on leaving hand out a long statement to the reporters at the door on subjects that have never been or are little discussed with the President, but with the firm confidence that the implication of their visit will put them on page one, column one.[68]

ꜰ ꜰ ꜰ

The Executive is bound to recommend appropriations adequate to provide for the functions and activities of the Government as now established by law. This is mandatory, and the opportunity for administrative savings is limited.[69]

ꜰ ꜰ ꜰ

Of course there is no constitutional nor statutory authority to Presidents to stop booms.
. . . The only way I can see that a President could even tilt with a boom would be to turn himself personally into a blue sky law and go on the stump analyzing balance sheets and stock market prices and proving to the people that their investments were overvalued. I have little taste for this proposal that the White House should be turned into a stock tipster's office.[70]

FRANKLIN D. ROOSEVELT

In a spirit of cooperation I have as Executive noted the representations of the British Government with respect to the payment of the June fifteenth installment [incomplete payment on debt to U.S.], inasmuch as the payment made is accompanied by a clear acknowledgment of the debt itself. In view of those representations and of the payment I have no personal hesitation in saying that I do not characterize the resultant situation as a default.

Beyond this the law and the Constitution do not permit me to go. The American public understands clearly that the settlement under which these debts are now being paid was made under the authority of Congress and that Congress alone has the right to alter the amount and method of payment of this debt.[71]

✦ ✦ ✦

In 1919 a law was finally passed providing that the President "may" appoint additional district and circuit judges, but only upon a finding that the incumbent judge over seventy "is unable to discharge efficiently all the duties of his office by reason of mental or physical disability of permanent character." The discretionary and indefinite nature of this legislation has rendered it ineffective. No President should be asked to determine the ability or disability of any particular judge.[72]

✦ ✦ ✦

. . . I described the American form of Government as a three horse team provided by the Constitution to the American people so that their field might be plowed. The three horses are, of course, the three branches of government—the Congress, the Executive and the Courts. Two of the horses are pulling in unison today; the third is not. Those who have intimated that the President of the United States is trying to drive that team, overlook the simple fact that the President, as Chief Executive, is himself one of the three horses.[73]

✦ ✦ ✦

The President of the United States does not sue for libel and the Department of Justice does not proceed for libel.[74]

✦ ✦ ✦

Any person is constitutionally entitled to criticize and call to account the highest and the lowest in the land—save only in one exception. For be it noted that the Constitution of the United States itself protects Senators and Representatives and provides that "for any speech or debate in either House they shall not be questioned in any other place." And that immunity is most carefully not extended to either the Chief Justice of the United States or the President.[75]

✦ ✦ ✦

You see, unfortunately, in spite of what some people say, the President of the United States is more or less bound by the law.[76]

TRUMAN

The existing statute governing the succession to the office of President was enacted in 1886. Under it, in the event of the death of the elected President and Vice President, members of the Cabinet successively fill the office.

Each of these Cabinet members is appointed by the President with the advice and consent of the Senate. In effect, therefore, by reason of the tragic death of the late President, it now lies within my power to nominate the person who would be my immediate successor in the event of my own death or inability to act.

I do not believe that in a democracy this power should rest with the Chief Executive.

In so far as possible, the office of the President should be filled by an elective officer. There is no officer in our system of government, besides the President and Vice President, who has been elected by all the voters of the country.[77]

✦ ✦ ✦

I have said it time and again, and I will keep on saying it, that I would rather have a Medal of Honor than be President of the United States.[78]

EISENHOWER

No President can delegate his constitutional duties. How can he do it? He has to sign the papers. He has to sign them, and he is responsible for them.[79]

KENNEDY

I don't have the power to cut off the [Federal] aid [to states] in a general way, as was proposed by the Civil Rights Commission [in the case of Mississippi], and I think it would probably be unwise to give the President of the United States that kind of power, because it could start in one state and for one reason or another it might be moved to another state which was not measuring up as the President would like to see it measure up in one way or another.[80]

Addendum

A NOTE ON KENNEDY AS PRESIDENT AND WRITER

One of the most distinctive personalities to leave their imprints on the presidential office, John F. Kennedy did so in what was, comparatively, an extremely short time. His administration, lasting scarcely thirty-four months, was—second to Harding's —the shortest of the twentieth century and—next to those of William Henry Harrison, Garfield, Taylor, Harding, and Fillmore—the sixth shortest in the nation's history. But Kennedy brought to the office exceptional gifts of mind and personality, style and grace, a broad and inclusive concept of the reach and significance of presidential action, so that his figure stands out among modern Presidents—although more for the temperament and interests it represented than for the two major achievements of historic importance while he held office, the handling of the second Cuba crisis and the nuclear test ban.

More than any President since John Quincy Adams, Kennedy was cast in the mold of the eighteenth-century "whole man"— alert, curious, widely read, in league with the arts, socially graceful, unlimited in his interests, savoring fully all that life offered, delighting in action of the mind as well as of the body. And, like the men of the Age of Reason, he had both a deep appreciation of the values of classical Greece and a tendency to return to them as a source of inspiration, carefully avoiding the bland evangelical mumbo jumbo offered by some of his predecessors as the finest flowering of the human mind. He said, quite extemporaneously only shortly before his death, that to him happiness consisted, as the Greeks maintained, in "the full use of your powers along lines of excellence."[1] And not in so many days had it happened that great minds, for their own stimulative sake, were invited to the White House that it was a great national event when Kennedy gave a dinner to honor forty-nine Nobel Prizewinners—scientists, artists, philosophers.

His admirations lay where his spirit felt at home: he called his guests "the most extraordinary collection . . . of human knowledge that has ever been gathered at the White House with the possible exception of when Thomas Jefferson dined alone."[2]

Yet Kennedy was not an intellectual, as often the journals of his time, and sometimes his opponents, maintained. Intellectuals are absorbed in theories for their own sake. They delight in fine analysis and the careful construction of theses, hypotheses, and antitheses. Action is not characteristic of them; and particularly does acting on intuition go against their grain. Among Democratic aspirants to the Presidency since Wilson, Adlai Stevenson came much closer to intellectualism than did Kennedy, who inherited not a little of the capacity to act on political instinct that marked the career of his maternal grandfather, John F. Fitzgerald, a popular mayor of Boston. But if he was himself a man of action rather than an intellectual, Kennedy had a great awareness of the uses of intellectualism, and he liked intellectuals around him. He was more cerebral than intellectual in his own processes and in his own approach to affairs. He had brains, knowledge, an incredible command of facts. At the same time, he was pragmatic, intensely practical, an activist. He used ideas as tools and knowledge as a weapon. But he was not a creature of the study. No life, short as it was, illustrated more vividly Holmes's conclusion that repose is not the lot of man and that life is action.

The absorbing interest that Kennedy had in courage was really a variation of the familiar theme of Carlyle's "hero" concept of history—history as the record of the action of great men rather than as the repercussion of great ideas. Kennedy's widow, Jacqueline, thought that there were deep roots for this in that at a very early age, before intellectually competent to cope with the great ideas of history, his Gaelic spirit was stirred by the acts of great men—the heroes of the ages. She told a sympathetic and sharp-sighted reporter, Theodore H. White, that she "realized history made Jack what he was. You must think of him as this little boy, sick so much of the time, reading in bed, reading history, reading the Knights of the Round Table, reading

Marlborough. For Jack, history was full of heroes. . . . Jack had this hero idea of history, the idealistic view."[3]

Even in maturity, Kennedy clung to an essentially romantic view of the role of the hero. When, a United States Senator, he was immobilized by a long convalescence from a critical surgical operation, he occupied himself with writing *Profiles in Courage,* which could well have been subtitled, "The Hero as a Force in American History." And it is not insignificant that the actions of his heroes were largely sacrificial and their causes, however just, often losing ones. Courage was, if not a religion, the basic ethic of life for Kennedy: "A man does what he must—in spite of personal consequences, in spite of obstacles and dangers and pressures—and that is the basis for all human morality."[4]

Courage was not, however, merely an obsession, or of lip-service importance, or a romantic interest of Kennedy. His personal heroism—he was a man of enormous physical courage, revealed not only in the heroic nature of his war record but in the extraordinary forbearance with which he endured almost constant physical pain—was well known to all those around him. Courage was, actually, the major theory of history that he had, though until his Presidency it was phrased more often in narrative terms of episodes in the lives of departed men than as a great constant in the steady struggle of humankind to improve its lot on this planet. And he was ready to translate the role of the hero from the memorable past to the uncertain present. "A nation reveals itself not only by the men it produces but also by the men it honors, the men it remembers,"[5] he said at Amherst College, four weeks before he died. And he understood better than most literary critics that the mainspring in Robert Frost's long and tragedy-ridden life was no more his lyric gift than his indomitable courage. He saw the presidency, indeed, primarily as an opportunity to master events, not to serve them, as he made known somewhat abrasively to those who contested the idea or practice of presidential mastery. He used the presidency coolly, sure of his facts and determined in his purpose, to control events. "Let us resolve," he told a convocation at the University of Maine, "to be the masters, not the victims, of our history, controlling our own destiny without giving way to blind suspicions and emotions."[6] To characterize the complex political achievement and the unique political character of the long-time Speaker of the House, Sam Rayburn, many a Congressional orator went on interminably without knowing exactly where he came out. To Kennedy there was but one key to the Rayburn genius: "He has the courage of ten men."[7]

Among the Presidents as writers, Kennedy belonged with the relatively few who delighted in the written word, who appreciated literary craftsmanship, and who practiced it. As Henry R. Luce was quick to recognize, *Why England Slept*, the book-length inquiry that Kennedy wrote into Britain's drift toward impotence during the 1930s, was an extraordinary achievement for so young a man as Kennedy at twenty-three then was. Its style was straightforward, its syllogisms disciplined, its details consistently relevant. But it was more. As Luce also seemed to recognize ("If John Kennedy is characteristic of the younger generation—and I believe he is—many of us would be happy to have the destinies of this Republic handed over to his generation at once,"[8] he wrote, as Wendell Willkie contended with Franklin D. Roosevelt for the presidency in 1940), Kennedy's early book revealed an impressive ability to distil from the raw data of history meanings applicable to new situations. It revealed, too, the kind of conscience required of a President who, in Wilson's words, "seeks to read the destiny in affairs for others as well as for himself, for a nation as well as for individuals."[9] There was also, of course, a striking practicality about *Why England Slept*. Far from just an intellectual exercise, it came close to being a political tract importuning the American people to avoid the mistakes of England—not by way of implied moral but in outright appeal: "We should profit by the lesson of England and make our democracy work."[10] The same purposiveness, the same practical, political uses of words, underlay *Profiles in Courage:* "The stories of past courage . . . can teach, they can offer hope, they can provide inspiration."[11]

Kennedy thus came to the presidency not only with a respect for the power of words but a professional skill in using them. On the other hand, he was not among the spellbinders of the House or of the Senate—perhaps because, unlike many from whom torrents of verbiage flowed, he respected words too much to use them pointlessly, indiscriminately, sloppily, or lavishly. He used them with sharply defined purpose, judiciously, carefully, economically. "Words can do more than convey policy," he wrote at the end of his first year in the White House. "They can also convey and create a mood, an attitude, an atmosphere—or an awakening."[12]

Less eloquent but more precise than Churchill, Kennedy in the presidency used words with much the same sense of public purpose that Churchill did and the same talent for the vast proposition. In Naples, at the North Atlantic Treaty Organization's headquarters, in the summer of 1963, he took just two sentences to make a historic summary of the United States's position with regard to Europe—unmatched for its clarity, for its strength, for its forthrightness: "I came to Europe to reassert as clearly and persuasively as I could that the American commitment to the freedom of Europe is reliable—not merely because of goodwill, although that is strong; not merely because of a shared heritage, though that is deep and wide; and not at all because we seek to dominate, because we do not. I came to make it clear that this commitment rests upon the inescapable requirement of intelligent self-interest—it is a commitment whose wisdom is confirmed by its absence when two World Wars began and by its presence in eighteen years of well-defended peace."[13] Similarly, he was able, a year earlier, to summarize the entire nature of the American economic dynamic in a single memorable sentence: "As President, my interest is in an economy which will be strong enough to absorb the potential of a rapidly expanding population, steady enough to avert the wide swings which bring grief to so many of our people, and noninflationary enough to persuade investors that this country holds a steady promise of growth and stability."[14] Finally, of peace, he could ask with simple inclusiveness, "And is not peace, in the last analysis, basically a matter of human rights—the right to live out our lives without fear of devastation—the right to breathe air as nature provided it—the right of future generations to a healthy existence?"[15]

If Kennedy's speeches had strong motives associated with his presidential responsibilities, they also had a quality of variety and delight and relaxation about them, digressing pleasantly to make a philosophic point, a comment on the nature of the human experience, its sadness or its folly. He seemed peculiarly at home in addressing college and university groups, almost as though on such occasions he did not need to speak as President but only reflectively as a member of the fellowship of educated men. Thus, at the University of North Carolina, "Peace and freedom do not come cheap, and we are destined—all of us here today—to live out most if not all of our lives in uncertainty and challenge and peril."[16] At Vanderbilt University, "Liberty without learning is always in peril and learning without liberty is always in vain."[17] And at Amherst College, of Frost, "He brought an unsparing instinct for reality to bear on the platitudes and pieties of society. His sense of the human tragedy fortified him against self-deception and easy consolation. 'I have been,' he wrote, 'one acquainted with the night.' And because he knew the midnight as well as the high noon, because he understood the ordeal as well as the triumph of the human spirit, he gave his age strength with which to overcome despair."[18]

Kennedy, alone among the Presidents, had a concern about the arts, including letters, because—as Richard H. Rovere has pointed out[19]—he felt that there was inherent in the presidency a responsibility for the whole fabric of American life and not only for diplomatic, political, economic, and military action. His own art was the art of writing and, as to all men of letters who admire the Greeks and are always going home to them, writing to him meant, in its highest form, poetry—whether its manner happened to be verse, drama, or something else. He had no trouble reconciling this with the quest for power, which was the very heart of his respect for the presidential office. He noted that "it's hardly an accident that Robert Frost coupled poetry and power. For he saw poetry as the means of saving power from itself. When power leads man toward arrogance, poetry reminds him of his limitations. When power narrows the areas of man's concern, poetry reminds him of the richness and diversity of his existence. When power corrupts, poetry cleanses."[20]

He delighted, too, in quoting from wise men back over the centuries, with a casual familiarity and a relevance that avoided any sententiousness. In his address to the Irish Parliament, without once seeming to drag the citation in, he quoted no less than nine literary and historical figures—Franklin, Robert E. Lee, Charles Parnell, William Butler Yeats, Henry Grattan, John Boyle O'Reilly, George Bernard Shaw, an unnamed orator, and an unnamed poet. In the last six months of his life, one can list among those to whose thought and expression he turned in his speeches, Bismarck, Wilson, Aristotle, Jefferson, John Adams, Bishop Holland N. McTyeire of the Methodist Church, Archibald MacLeish, Frost, Marshal Louis Hubert Lyautey of France, Joseph Henry, Thucydides, Tocqueville, Malthus, Milton, Shelley, Archimedes, Masefield, Goethe, the Old and New Testaments, and the Hungarian patriot, Louis Kossuth. He seemed to derive more than words from these men, ranging chronologically back to classical times and geographically to the Attic peninsula; he seemed to draw strength from them.

Despite his consummate skill with words and his vast reading, Kennedy never confused words with action. He was as careful to differentiate mere rhetoric from learning as he was the right word from the wrong one. In a speech that he was to deliver at Dallas on the day that he died, he offered a highly relevant historic note on the relationship between great words and great deeds. "Above all, words alone are not enough. The United States is a peaceful nation. And where our strength and determination are clear, our words need merely to convey conviction, not belligerence. If we are strong, our strength will speak for itself. If we are weak, words will be no help. I realize that this nation often tends to identify turning points in world affairs with the major addresses which precede them. But it was not the Monroe Doctrine that kept all Europe away from this hemisphere—it was the strength of the British fleet and the width of the Atlantic Ocean. It was not General Marshall's speech at Harvard which kept communism out of Western Europe—it was the strength and stability made possible by our military and economic assistance."[21]

Fully aware as he was of the power of the presidency, through utterances, to shape and mobilize public opinion— though he had not a fraction of the personal talent to wield it that Franklin Roosevelt, for example, had—it was far more the presidency as a source of action—the seat of decisions—that interested him. "The American presidency," he wrote in a foreword to some lectures by his special counsel, Theodore C. Sorensen, "is a formidable, exposed, and somewhat mysterious institution. It is formidable because it represents the point of ultimate decision in the American political system. It is exposed because decision cannot take place in a vacuum: the presidency is the center of play of pressure, interest, and idea in the nation; and the presidential office is the vortex into which all the elements of national decision are irresistibly drawn. And it is mysterious because the essence of ultimate decision remains impenetrable to the observer—often, indeed, to the decider himself."[22]

The usages of power may have turned out to be more complex than he thought (*cf.* the last excerpt on page 374), but he knew from the beginning that his own quest for the presidency was a drive for action. A hardheaded politician and at the same time a man of a historical turn of mind, with a probing interest in the nature of political power, he had, during the campaign of 1960, a disarmingly blunt answer to why he sought the presidency: "Because that's where the power is."[23] He was no less direct with his Boston neighbors on the eve of his election: "I run for the presidency of the United States because it is the center of action. . . ."[24] He was for both the assertion and the challenging of power, not only as a definition of political life, but as the satisfaction of personal life. "The men who create power make an indispensable contribution to the nation's great-

ness," he said. "But the men who question power make a contribution just as indispensable. . . ."[25]

The realities of presidential powers, however, as he himself
was quick to note, were not so susceptible of exuberant expression. "The President . . . is rightly described as a man of extraordinary powers. Yet it is also true that he must wield these
powers under extraordinary limitations—and it is these limitations
which so often give the problem of choice its complexities and
even poignancy. Lincoln, Franklin Roosevelt once remarked,
'was a sad man because he couldn't get it all at once. And nobody can.' Every President must endure a gap between what
he would like and what is possible."[26]

Kennedy endured a greater gap than most, and he left some
of his followers exasperated because he did not fight the Congress more ruthlessly or go over its head more forcibly to the
people. But he took the long view, and he knew that he was
dealing in beginnings—not in culminations—the beginning of
"a new world of law, where the strong are just, and the weak
secure and the peace preserved."[27] And he added, "All this
will not be finished in the first hundred days. Nor will it be
finished in the first thousand days, nor in the life of this administration, nor even perhaps in our lifetime on this planet.
But let us begin."[28]

"The life of this administration" was short, one thousand and
thirty-six days—and the task was not finished. Even the dimensions of the effort will not be truly measurable for years to
come. Meanwhile, the last word may well rest with a young
physician who was first to attend him after he was shot: "I
thought to myself he's a much bigger man than his pictures."[29]

NOTES AND SOURCES

In the notes, James D. Richardson (ed.), *Messages and Papers of the Presidents, 1798–1897*, 10 vols., 1895–1899, is referred to as "Richardson." The collected writings of individual Presidents are, when not otherwise specified, the following editions: for Washington, John C. Fitzpatrick (ed.), *Writings of George Washington*, 39 vols., 1931–1944; for John Adams, Charles Francis Adams, *The Life and Works of John Adams*, 10 vols., 1850–1856; for Jefferson, Paul L. Ford (ed.), *The Writings of Thomas Jefferson*, 10 vols., 1892–1899; for Madison, G. Hunt (ed.), *Writings of James Madison*, 9 vols., 1900–1910; for Monroe, S. M. Hamilton (ed.), *The Writings of James Monroe*, 7 vols., 1896–1903; for John Quincy Adams, Charles Francis Adams (ed.), *The Memoirs of John Quincy Adams*, 12 vols., 1874–1877; for Buchanan, J. B. Moore (ed.), *The Works of James Buchanan*, 12 vols., 1908–1911; for Lincoln, J. G. Nicolay and J. Hay (eds.), *Complete Works of Abraham Lincoln*, 12 vols., 1905; for Theodore Roosevelt, H. Hagedorn (ed.), *The Works of Theodore Roosevelt*, 20 vols., 1920, and E. E. Morison *et al.* (eds.), *The Letters of Theodore Roosevelt*, 8 vols., 1951–1954; for Wilson, R. S. Baker and W. E. Dodd (eds.), *The Public Papers of Woodrow Wilson*, 6 vols., 1925–1927; for Franklin D. Roosevelt, S. I. Rosenman (ed.), *The Public Papers and Addresses of Franklin D. Roosevelt*, 13 vols., 1936–1950; and for Truman, Eisenhower, and Kennedy, the definitive editions of *Public Papers of the Presidents of the United States* under the name of each, published by the United States Government Printing Office.

INTRODUCTION: THE PRESIDENTS AS WRITERS

1. See Madison, *Writings*, VI, 111 n., and H. C. Lodge (ed.), *Works of Alexander Hamilton*, X, 165.
2. *Writings*, XXXV, 48 f. See also V. H. Paltsits, *Washington's Farewell Address* (1935).
3. *Memoirs*, I, 36.
4. *Working with Roosevelt*, xiii.
5. *Ibid.*, 11. The Rosenman book is the best exposition of the construction of presidential speeches.
6. Inaugural Address, March 4, 1921, *Inaugural Addresses of the Presidents* (1961 ed.), 209.

7. *Ibid.*
8. *Ibid.,* 212
9. *Writings,* I, 19.
10. *Ibid.,* II, 287.
11. To John Quincy Adams, October 4, 1790.
12. To John Quincy Adams, 1784, n.d.
13. To J. Brazier, August 24, 1819, S. K. Padover, *Complete Jefferson,* 1087.
14. December 7, 1826, Allan Nevins (ed.), *Diary of John Quincy Adams,* 368.
15. *Ibid.,* March 20, 1827, 373.
16. *Ibid.,* November 13, 1831, 425.
17. Third Annual Message, December 19, 1859, *Works,* X, 339.
18. *Patriotic Gore,* 117.
19. *Herndon's Lincoln,* III, 479.
20. *Works,* I, 291.
21. *Ibid.,* VI, 185.
22. *Ibid.,* VI, 110.
23. *Ibid.,* XI, 46.
24. *Ibid.,* IX, 102.
25. See communications to Stanton in *Works.*
26. To Horace Greeley, August 22, 1862, *Works,* VIII, 16.
27. *The Forum,* December, 1896.
28. Speech at Des Moines, September 6, 1919. A. B. Tourtellot (ed.), *Woodrow Wilson: Selections for Today,* 1.
29. Speech at St. Louis, September 5, 1919. *Ibid.,* 238.
30. *The Adams Papers,* I, xiv.
31. Letter to Joseph Pulitzer, *St. Louis Post-Dispatch,* August 10, 1928.
32. *Autobiography,* 13.
33. *Diary,* July 26, 1881, IV, 40.
34. To Washington, May 17, 1789, *Works,* VIII, 492.

CHAPTER I — THE PRESIDENT AS NATIONAL LEADER

1. Protest to the Senate, April 15, 1834, Richardson, III, 85.
2. Fourth Annual Message, Dec. 5, 1848, Richardson, IV, 665.
3. Special Message to Congress, July 4, 1861, *Works,* VI, 309.
4. Speech at Lancaster, September 28, 1866, N. Y. *Herald.*
5. *Presidential Problems,* 11.
6. *Autobiography,* 282.
7. *Ibid.,* 388.
8. To G. O. Trevelyan, June 19, 1908, *Letters,* VI, 1087.

9. Quoted in C. E. Stevens, *Sources of the Constitution*, 169 f.
10. Horace Greeley, *The American Conflict*, I, 106.
11. *National Intelligencer*, March 5, 1835.
12. *Presidential Problems*, 10.
13. To James Madison, May 5, 1789, *Writings*, XXX, 310–311.
14. To Adams, *et al.*, May 10, 1789, *Ibid.*, 319 ff.
15. To James Madison, May 12, 1789, *Ibid.*, 322 f.
16. To John Hancock, October 26, 1789, *Ibid.*, 453.
17. To Catherine M. Graham, January 9, 1790, *Ibid.*, 496.
18. To Alexander Hamilton, July 2, 1794, *Writings*, XXXIII, 422.
19. Review of Propositions to Amend the Constitution, 1808, *Works*, VI, 539.
20. To *Boston Patriot*, 1809, *Works*, IX, 270.
21. To the Secretary of State, April 23, 1800, *Ibid.*, 50.
22. To *Boston Patriot*, 1809, *Ibid.*, 302.
23. Inaugural Address, March 4, 1825, Richardson, II, 294.
24. *Jubilee of the Constitution*, 115.
25. Proclamation, December 10, 1832, Richardson, II, 648.
26. To R. Y. Hayne, February 8, 1831, *Correspondence*, IV, 241.
27. To the Secretary of War, 1831, n.d. *Ibid.*, 220.
28. *Inquiry into the Origin and Course of Political Parties*, 290.
29. *Ibid.*, 334.
30. *Ibid.*, 335.
31. Inaugural Address, March 4, 1841, Richardson, IV, 10 f.
32. Inaugural Address, April 9, 1841, *Ibid.*, 37.
33. Protest to House of Representatives, August 30, 1842, *Ibid.*, 192.
34. To Norwalk Democratic Association, September 2, 1844, *Letters*, II, 96.
35. *Diary*, December 23, 1848, IV, 253.
36. First Annual Message, December 2, 1852, Richardson, V, 80.
37. Inaugural Address, March 4, 1853, Richardson, V, 201.
38. Fourth Annual Message, December 2, 1856, Richardson, V, 397.
39. Special Message to the House, March 28, 1860, *Works*, X, 400.
40. *Ibid.*, 401.
41. *Mr. Buchanan's Administration*, *Works*, XII, 141.
42. Reply to delegation, March 5, 1861, *Works*, XI, 118.
43. Memorandum, August 25, 1864, *Works*, X, 203.
44. To Leonard Swett, n.d. *Herndon's Lincoln*, III, 533.
45. To Horace Maynard, n.d. *Ibid.*, III, 508.
46. Third Annual Message, December 3, 1867, Richardson, VI, 568.
47. Veto Message to Senate, February 19, 1866, *Ibid.*, 404.
48. *Diary*, March 1, 1878, III, 463.

49. *Diary,* July 26, 1881, IV, 40.
50. Inaugural Address, March 4, 1885, Richardson, VIII, 301.
51. At Clinton N.Y., Centennial, July 13, 1887, G. F. Parker (ed.), *Writings and Speeches of Grover Cleveland,* 116.
52. At Philadelphia, September 17, 1887, *Ibid.,* 121.
53. At Milwaukee Merchants' Association, October 7, 1887, *Ibid.,* 145.
54. *Ibid.,* 146.
55. On accepting renomination, September 8, 1888, *Ibid.,* 16.
56. Concerning a fourth renomination, March 9, 1892, *Ibid.,* 549.
57. R. W. Gilder, *Grover Cleveland, A Record of Friendship,* 30.
58. At Harvard College, November 9, 1886, Parker, *op. cit.,* 115.
59. *Presidential Problems,* 10.
60. *Ibid.,* 76.
61. Allan Nevins, *Grover Cleveland, A Study in Courage,* 377.
62. Inaugural Address, March 4, 1889, Richardson, IX, 5.
63. First Annual Message, December 3, 1889, Richardson, IX, 56.
64. *This Country of Ours,* 69.
65. *Ibid.,* 72.
66. *Ibid.,* 183.
67. C. S. Olcott, *Life of William McKinley,* II, 296.
68. To W. H. Taft, June 9, 1903, *Letters,* III, 485.
69. To G. B. Cortelyou, July 13, 1903, *Ibid.,* 513.
70. To H. C. Lodge, September 30, 1903, *Ibid.,* 608
71. To G. O. Trevelyan, May 28, 1904, *Letters,* IV, 807.
72. To J. B. Worrall, August 1, 1904, *Ibid.,* 876.
73. To newspaper correspondents, September, 1901, D. S. Barry, *Forty Years in Washington,* 267.
74. To Southern Congressmen, September 21, 1901, *Works,* XXIII, 179.
75. To Richard Olney, September 23, 1901, *Ibid.,* 175f.
76. To L. C. Davis, 1903 n.d., *Ibid.,* 293.
77. To G. O. Trevelyan, October 1, 1911, *Works,* XXIV, 230.
78. At Dallas, April 5, 1905, *Presidential Addresses and State Papers,* III, 320.
79. To G. O. Trevelyan, June 19, 1908, *Works,* XXIV, 107ff.
80. To J. J. Juserand, August 3, 1908, *Letters,* VI, 1148.
81. On return from Africa, June 18, 1910, *Works,* XIX, 5.
82. *An Autobiography,* 388.
83. *Ibid.,* 395.
84. To M Poindexter, May 22, 1918, *Letters,* VIII, 1320.
85. *Ibid.,* 1322.
86. *Works,* XXI, 325.

87. *Our Chief Magistrate and His Powers*, 53.
88. *Ibid.*, 156.
89. Speech at Buckingham Palace, December 27, 1918, *International Ideals*, 22.
90. To his daughter, n.d., A. Walworth, *Woodrow Wilson, American Prophet*, I, 310.
91. *St. Louis Post-Dispatch*, August 10, 1928.
92. *The Autobiography of Calvin Coolidge*, 184.
93. *Ibid.*, 198.
94. *Ibid.*, 229.
95. *Ibid.*, 233.
96. Address to Gridiron, April 13, 1929, *Papers*, I, 27.
97. *Ibid.*, December 14, 1929, *Ibid.*, 189.
98. To W. O. Thompson, December 30, 1929, *Ibid.*, 198.
99. Address to Gridiron, April 26, 1930, *Ibid.*, 269.
100. At Detroit, October 22, 1932, *Papers*, II, 383.
101. At Elko, Nevada, November 7, 1932, *Ibid.*, 479.
102. *Memoirs*, II, 216.
103. *Address upon the American Road*, 255.
104. Address to Bankers' Convention, October 24, 1934, *Papers, 1934*, 436.
105. Fireside chat, April 28, 1935, *Papers, 1935*, 133.
106. Radio address, August 24, 1935, *Ibid.*, 337.
107. At San Diego, October 2, 1935, *Ibid.*, 409.
108. At New York, October 31, 1936, *Papers, 1936*, 570.
109. Radio speech, November 2, 1936, *Ibid.*, 580.
110. *Ibid.*, 581.
111. At Cheyenne, September 24, 1937, *Papers, 1937*, 379.
112. At Boise, September 27, 1937, *Ibid.*, 386.
113. Fireside chat, October 12, 1937, *Ibid.*, 430.
114. At Denton, Md., September 5, 1938, *Papers, 1938*, 520.
115. At Philadelphia, October 23, 1940, *Papers, 1940*, 488.
116. To labor and management group, November 4, 1941, *Papers, 1941*, 491.
117. Press conference, November 11, 1946, *Papers, 1946*, 478.
118. *Memoirs*, I, 36.
119. *Ibid.*
120. *Ibid.*, 47.
121. *Ibid.*, 54.
122. *Ibid.*, 64.
123. *Memoirs*, II, 24.
124. *Ibid.*, 103.
125. *Ibid.*, 196.

126. *Ibid.*, 414.
127. *Ibid.*, 415.
128. *Ibid.*, 473.
129. *Ibid.*
130. *Ibid.*, 493.
131. Press conference, October 21, 1953, *Papers, 1953*, 701.
132. *Ibid.*, September 27, 1956, *Papers, 1956*, 811.
133. Broadcast address, May 14, 1957, *Papers, 1957*, 341.
134. Press conference, April 30, 1958, *Papers, 1958*, 354.
135. *Ibid.*, 356.
136. Press conference, September 7, 1960, *Papers, 1960–61*, 680.
137. At Philadelphia, October 28, 1960, *Ibid.*, 817.
138. C.B.S. Reports, October 12, 1961.
139. Press conference, February 8, 1961, *Papers, 1961*, 69.
140. Address to newspaper editors, April 20, 1961, *Ibid.*, 304.
141. Special Message to Congress, April 27, 1961, *Ibid.*, 334.
142. Broadcast address, June 6, 1961, *Ibid.*, 443.
143. J. W. Gardner (ed.), *To Turn the Tide*, xiii.

CHAPTER II — THE PRESIDENT AS ADMINISTRATOR

1. Findings summarized in *The Hoover Commission Report* (McGraw-Hill, n.d.).
2. To the Secretary of War, October 17, 1796, *Writings*, XXXV, 245.
3. To G. Walker, January 26, 1797, *Ibid.*, 375.
4. To J. Trumbull, July 21, 1797, *Writings*, XXXVII, 214.
5. To U. Forrest, May 13, 1799, *Works*, VIII, 645.
6. To Attorney General, March 29, 1799, *Ibid.*, 629.
7. To Secretary of the Treasury, October 20, 1797, *Ibid.*, 555.
8. To E. Livingston, November 1, 1801, *Writings*, VIII, 57 f.
9. To U. S. District Attorney, June 12, 1807, *Writings*, IX, 55.
10. To W. Short, June 12, 1807, *Ibid.*, 69 f.
11. To D. Le Tracy, January 26, 1811, *Ibid.*, 306 ff.
12. To War Department, August 13, 1814, *Letters*, III, 417.
13. To T. Jefferson, March 12, 1815, *Letters*, II, 604.
14. To J. A. G. Davis, 1833 n.d., *Letters*, IV, 248.
15. To E. Coles, August 29, 1834, *Ibid.*, 355.
16. Inaugural Address, March 4, 1817, Richardson, II, 9.
17. Message to the House, May 4, 1822, *Ibid.*, 151.
18. *The People, the Sovereigns*, 46.
19. Special Message to Congress, January 16, 1833, Richardson, II, 611 ff.

20. To Cabinet, September 18, 1833, Richardson, III, 5.
21. *Ibid.*, 9.
22. *Ibid.*, 10.
23. *Ibid.*, 11.
24. *Ibid.*, 18.
25. Protest to the Senate, April 15, 1834, Richardson, III, 82.
26. *Ibid.*, 84.
27. *Ibid.*, 90.
28. *Inquiry into the Origin and Course of Political Parties,* 333.
29. Inaugural Address, March 4, 1841, Richardson, IV, 14.
30. Message to the House, February 9, 1842, *Ibid.*, 99.
31. *Ibid.*, January 31, 1843. Richardson IV, 222.
32. *Ibid.*, 224.
33. To committee of Democratic Convention, May 30, 1844, *Letters,* II, 319.
34. Message to the Senate, August 1, 1854. Richardson, V, 246.
35. Special Message to Congress, January 24, 1856, *Ibid.*, 359.
36. *Ibid.*, 358.
37. *Mr. Buchanan's Administration, Works,* XII, 102.
38. W. H. Lamon, *Recollections of Abraham Lincoln,* 213.
39. Inaugural Address, March 4, 1861, *Works,* VI, 175.
40. Reply to Seward, April 1, 1861, *Ibid.*, 237.
41. Special Message to Congress, July 4, 1861, *Ibid.*, 322.
42. Response to Serenade, October 19, 1864, *Works,* X, 243.
43. First Annual Message, December 4, 1865, Richardson, VI, 365.
44. To Senate, March 2, 1867, *Ibid.*, 497.
45. Veto Message to the House, July 19, 1867, *Ibid.*, 543.
46. To Senate, December 12, 1867, *Ibid.*, 589.
47. *Ibid.*, 592.
48. Special Message to Congress, February 25, 1873, Richardson, VII, 213.
49. Sixth Annual Message, December 7, 1874, *Ibid.*, 298.
50. Special Message to Senate, January 13, 1875, *Ibid.*, 313.
51. Veto Message, June 23, 1879, Richardson, VII, 543.
52. *Diary,* March 24, 1879, III, 535.
53. First Annual Message, December 6, 1881, Richardson, VIII, 65.
54. Second Annual Message, December 4, 1882, *Ibid.*, 147.
55. Third Annual Message, December 4, 1883, *Ibid.*, 187.
56. *Presidential Problems,* 14.
57. *Ibid.*, 16.
58. To W. F. Vilas, April 4, 1885, Allan Nevins, *Grover Cleveland, A Study in Courage,* 256.
59. Press conference, January 4, 1886, *Ibid.*, 270.

60. *This Country of Ours,* 70.
61. *Ibid.,* 98.
62. *Ibid.,* 105.
63. *Ibid.,* 118.
64. *Ibid.,* 120.
65. *Ibid.,* 146.
66. *Ibid.,* 159.
67. *An Autobiography,* 379.
68. To W. M. Crane, October 22, 1902, *Letters,* III, 362.
69. To L. Abbott, September 5, 1903, *Ibid.,* 592.
70. To J. Sparks, January 4, 1908, *Letters,* VI, 895.
71. To de Constant, September 1, 1903, J. B. Bishop, *Theodore Roosevelt and His Time,* I, 252.
72. To G. O. Trevelyan, June 19, 1908, *Letters,* VI, 1087.
73. To Editor, *Review of Reviews,* January 1, 1909.
74. *An Autobiography,* 395.
75. *Ibid.,* 397.
76. *Ibid.,* 504.
77. *The Chief Magistrate and His Powers,* 40.
78. *Ibid.,* 78.
79. *Ibid.,* 79.
80. *Ibid.,* 83.
81. *Ibid.,* 85.
82. *Ibid.,* 118.
83. *Ibid.,* 121.
84. *Life and Letters,* IV, 189.
85. *The Autobiography of Calvin Coolidge,* 196.
86. *Ibid.,* 197.
87. *Ibid.,* 211.
88. To Frank W. Stearns, C. M. Fuess, *Calvin Coolidge, the Man from Vermont,* 323.
89. Press statement, September 24, 1929, *Papers,* I, 102.
90. First Annual Message, December 3, 1929, *Ibid.,* 163.
91. To Dr. W. O. Thompson, December 20, 1929, *Ibid.,* 197.
92. Press statement, July 28, 1932, *Papers,* II, 245.
93. *Memoirs,* II, 276.
94. *Ibid.,* III, 354.
95. *The Challenge to Liberty,* 76.
96. *Addresses upon the American Road,* 225.
97. *Ibid.,* 238.
98. *Ibid.,* II.
99. Executive order, June 16, 1933, *Papers, 1933,* 248.
100. To a congressional delegation, April 13, 1934, *Papers, 1934,* 182.

101. Message on reorganizing the Executive Branch, January 12, 1937, *Papers, 1937*, 670.
102. *Ibid.*, 673.
103. Political address, March 4, 1937, *Papers, 1937*, 115.
104. Fireside chat, October 12, 1937, *Ibid.*, 434.
105. Press conference, April 8, 1938, *Papers, 1938*, 203.
106. Message to Congress, April 25, 1939, *Papers, 1939*, 247.
107. Press conference, December 20, 1940, *Papers, 1940*, 623.
108. Press conference, December 21, 1940, H. Finer, *The Presidency, Crisis and Regeneration*, 182.
109. Special Message to Congress, September 6, 1945, *Papers, 1945*, 277.
110. *Memoirs*, I, 228.
111. *Ibid.*, 329.
112. *Ibid.*, 330.
113. *Ibid.*, 545.
114. *Memoirs*, II, 165.
115. *Ibid.*, 198.
116. *Ibid.*, 305.
117. *Ibid.*, 454.
118. *Ibid.*, 508.
119. Press conference, March 3, 1954. *Papers, 1954*, 289.
120. At Chestertown, Md., June 7, 1954, *Ibid.*, 542.
121. Broadcast address, September 24, 1957, *Papers, 1957*, 692.
122. Press conference, August 20, 1958, *Papers, 1958*, 627.
123. Press conference, October 1, 1958, *Ibid.*, 717.
124. Press conference, February 18, 1959, *Papers, 1959*, 192.
125. Press conference, August 12, 1959, *Ibid.*, 575.
126. C.B.S. Reports, October 12, 1961.
127. *Ibid.*, November 23, 1961.
128. Special Message to Congress, April 13, 1961, *Papers, 1961*, 268.
129. Interview for B.B.C., April 19, 1961, *Ibid.*, 287.

CHAPTER III — THE APPOINTIVE AND REMOVAL POWER

1. To S. Vaughan, March 21, 1783, *Writings*, XXX, 240.
2. To E. Rutledge, May 5, 1789, *Ibid.*, 309.
3. To J. Bowdoin, May 9, 1789, *Ibid.*, 313 f.
4. To G. Plater, May 14, 1789, *Ibid.*, 324.
5. To Bushrod Washington, July 27, 1789, *Ibid.*, 366.
6. To Senate Committee, August 8, 1789, *Ibid.*, 374.
7. To B. Bidwell, August 27, 1800, *Works*, IX, 79.
8. To J. Marshall, September 9, 1800, *Ibid.*, 82.
9. To J. McHenry, June 19, 1799, *Works*, VIII, 659.

10. *Ibid.*, April 16, 1799, *Works*, VIII, 632.
11. *Statesman and Friend*, 56 f.
12. To George Jefferson, March 27, 1801, *Writings*, VIII, 38.
13. To the Attorney General, August 26, 1801, *Ibid.*, 83.
14. To the Secretary of the Treasury, n.d., *Ibid.*, 211.
15. To Thomas McKean, February, 19, 1803, *Ibid.*, 217 f.
16. To William Duane, July 24, 1803, *Ibid.*, 255 f.
17. To U. Tracy, January 1806, *Ibid.*, 412 f.
18. To Thomas Jefferson, December 10, 1820, *Letters*, III, 196.
19. To E. Coles, August 29, 1834, *Letters*, IV, 356.
20. *Ibid.*, October 15, 1834, *Letters*, IV, 368.
21. *Ibid.*, 369.
22. To the House, April 6, 1822, Richardson, II, 132.
23. To James Madison, May 10, 1822, *Writings*, VI, 285.
24. *Diary*, February 27, 1828, *Memoirs*, VII, 424 f.
25. *Diary*, March 7, 1828, *Ibid.*, 465.
26. *Diary*, February 17, 1830, *Memoirs*, VIII, 189.
27. *Jubilee of the Constitution*, 79.
28. First Annual Message, December 8, 1829, Richardson, II 448.
29. To M. Van Buren, March 31, 1829, *Correspondence*, IV, 19.
30. To J. Coffee, May 20, 1829, *Ibid.*, 39.
31. To R. Y. Hayne, February 8, 1831, *Ibid.*, 1831.
32. Protest to the Senate, April 15, 1834, Richardson, III, 79.
33. *Ibid.*, 79 ff.
34. *Ibid.*, 85.
35. *Autobiography*, 742.
36. *Inquiry into the Origin and Course of Political Parties*, 290.
37. Inaugural Address, March 4, 1841, Richardson, IV, 12.
38. Inaugural Address, April 9, 1841, *Ibid.*, 38.
39. To the House, March 23, 1842, *Ibid.*, 105.
40. *Diary*, December 10, 1846, II, 278 f.
41. *Diary*, January 7, 1847, II, 314.
42. *Diary*, January 8, 1848, IV, 62 f.
43. *Diary*, October 18, 1848, IV, 160 f.
44. First Annual Message, December 2, 1850, Richardson, V, 80.
45. To Secretary of the Navy, September 24, 1852, *Papers*, I, 367 f.
46. *Papers*, II, 136 f.
47. Message to House, June 22, 1860, *Works*, X, 438.
48. To the Cabinet, July 14, 1864, *Works*, X, 158.
49. To Senate, March 2, 1867, Richardson, VI, 493.
50. *Ibid.*
51. *Ibid.*, 495.
52. Veto Message, July 19, 1867, Richardson, VI, 543.

53. Third Annual Message, December 3, 1867, *Ibid.*, 569.
54. To Senate, February 22, 1868, *Ibid.*, 622.
55. *Ibid.*, 626.
56. Answer to impeachment charges, March 23, 1868, Richardson, VI, 730.
57. Second Annual Message, December 5, 1870, Richardson, VII, 109.
58. First Annual Message, December 3, 1877, *Ibid.*, 465 f.
59. *Diary*, May 19, 1881, IV, 19.
60. To R. U. Johnson, September 5, 1881, *Diary*, IV, 34.
61. Second Annual Message, December 4, 1882, Richardson, VIII, 145.
62. H. L. Stoddard, *It Costs to Be President*, 127.
63. Allan Nevins, *Grover Cleveland, A Study in Courage*, 235.
64. *Ibid.*, 248.
65. To Senate, March 1, 1886, Richardson, VIII, 379.
66. *Presidential Problems*, 19.
67. *This Country of Ours*, 103.
68. *Ibid.*, 104.
69. *Ibid.*, 107.
70. *Ibid.*, 111.
71. *Ibid.*, 179.
72. Inaugural Address, March 4, 1889, Richardson, IX, 11.
73. To A. P. Gardner, October 28, 1904, *Letters*, IV, 1002.
74. To W. A. Smith, April 24, 1908, *Letters*, VI, 1017.
75. To J. W. Stewart, May 7, 1908, *Ibid.*, 1025.
76. *Autobiography*, 390.
77. A. Butt, *Taft and Roosevelt*, 41.
78. *Our Chief Magistrate and His Powers*, 55.
79. *Ibid.*, 56.
80. *Ibid.*, 59.
81. *Ibid.*, 70.
82. *Ibid.*, 72.
83. To Senate, February 11, 1924. C. B. Slemp, *The Mind of the President*, 87.
84. *Memoirs*, II, 217.
85. *Ibid.*, 218.
86. *Ibid.*, 269.
87. To F. E. Britten, September 26, 1929, *Papers*, I, 105.
88. Press statement, January 10, 1931, *Ibid.*, 486.
89. To Judge Roberts, February 7, 1939, *Papers, 1939*, 127.
90. *Ibid.*, 129.
91. *Ibid.*, 131.

CHAPTER IV — THE PRESIDENCY AND THE CONGRESS

1. Inaugural Address, March 4, 1841, Richardson, IV, 11.
2. To Whitelaw Reid, March 30, 1881, R. Cortissoz, *Life of Whitelaw Reid*, II, 62.
3. *Autobiography*, 282.
4. To A. Mitchell Palmer, Appendix to H. J. Ford, *Woodrow Wilson, The Man and His Work*.
5. First Special Message, April 8, 1913, *Selected Literary and Political Papers*, 25.
6. To Senate Committee, August 10, 1789, *Writings*, XXX, 377 ff.
7. To J. Trumbull, March 3, 1797, *Writings*, XXXV, 411 f.
8. Review of propositions to amend the Constitution, 1808, *Works*, VI, 533.
9. *Ibid.*, 534.
10. To *Boston Patriot*, 1809, *Works*, IX, 288.
11. To Thomas Jefferson, November 14, 1813, L. J. Cappon, *Adams-Jefferson Letters*, II, 400.
12. To R. Rush, May 11, 1821, *Works*, X, 397.
13. Special Message to Senate, July 6, 1813, Richardson, I, 531.
14. To James Monroe, December 27, 1817, *Writings*, VIII, 406.
15. To H. Clay, June, 1833, *Letters*, IV, 299.
16. *Letters*, IV, 350 (unaddressed, n.d.).
17. *The People, the Sovereigns*, 48 ff.
18. *Ibid.*, 50 ff.
19. *Diary*, January 2, 1826, *Memoirs*, VII, 100.
20. *Diary*, January 3, 1826, *Ibid.*
21. *Congressional Globe*, August 16, 1842.
22. *Jubilee of the Constitution*, 70 f.
23. Second Annual Message, December 6, 1830, Richardson, II, 512.
24. Special Message to Senate, December 12, 1833, Richardson, III, 36.
25. *Ibid.*, March 11, 1834, Richardson, III, 42.
26. Protest to Senate, April 15, 1834, *Ibid.*, 69.
27. *Ibid.*, 71.
28. *Ibid.*, 71.
29. *Ibid.*, 73.
30. *Ibid.*, 86.
31. To Senate, February 10, 1835, Richardson, III, 132.
32. Seventh Annual Message, December 7, 1835, *Ibid.*, 167.
33. To Congress, January 15, 1836, *Ibid.*, 190.

34. *Inquiry into the Origin and Course of Political Parties*, 336.
35. *Ibid.*, 340.
36. Inaugural Address, March 4, 1841, Richardson, IV, 9.
37. *Ibid.*, 9.
38. *Ibid.*, 10.
39. *Ibid.*, 13.
40. *Ibid.*, 14.
41. Veto Message, September 9, 1841, Richardson, IV, 68.
42. Message to Congress, June 25, 1842, *Ibid.*, 159.
43. To Fourth of July Committee, July 2, 1842, *Letters*, II, 171.
44. To House, August 9, 1842, Richardson, IV, 183.
45. Third Annual Message, December n.d., 1843, *Ibid.*, 265.
46. Fourth Annual Message, December 5, 1848, Richardson, IV, 662 f.
47. *Ibid.*, 664 ff.
48. *Ibid.*, 667 f.
49. *Ibid.*, 669 f.
50. First Annual Message, December 4, 1849, Richardson, V, 23.
51. Veto Message, February 17, 1855, *Ibid.*, 307 ff.
52. First Annual Message, December 8, 1857, *Works*, X, 162.
53. Message to Congress, June 12, 1858, *Ibid.*, 222.
54. Message to House, March 28, 1960, *Ibid.*, 400.
55. *Ibid.*, 440.
56. W. A. Lamon, *Recollections of Abraham Lincoln*, 184.
57. Veto Message, January 5, 1867, Richardson, VI, 479.
58. *Ibid.*
59. To Cabinet, November 30, 1867, S. S. Jones, *Life of Andrew Jackson*, 246.
60. To Congress, June 13, 1870, Richardson, VII, 66.
61. Second Annual Message, December 5, 1870, *Ibid.*, 130.
62. Fifth Annual Message, December 1, 1873, *Ibid.*, 242.
63. Special Message to House, May 4, 1876, *Ibid.*, 361.
64. Veto Message, April 29, 1879, Richardson, VII, 530 ff.
65. *Diary*, February 26, 1878, III, 461.
66. *Diary*, March 18, 1879, III, 529.
67. *Diary*, March 21, 1879, III, 531.
68. *Diary*, March 24, 1879, III, 534.
69. *Diary*, March 27, 1879, III, 536.
70. *Ibid.*, 538.
71. *Diary*, March 28, 1879, III, 540.
72. *Diary*, March 29, 1879, III, 540 f.
73. *Diary*, March 30, 1879, III, 541.
74. *Diary*, April 2, 1879, III, 543.

75. *Diary,* April 6, 1879, III, 546.
76. *Diary,* May 16, 1879, III, 552.
77. To A. Snead, April 27, 1881, *Diary,* IV, 10.
78. To Whitelaw Reid, March 30, 1881, T. C. Smith, *James Garfield, Life and Letters,* II, 1115.
79. Second Annual Message, December 4, 1882, Richardson, VIII, 138.
80. First Annual Message, December 8, 1885, *Ibid.,* 324.
81. Message to Congress, April 22, 1886, *Ibid.,* 395.
82. R. W. Gilder, *Grover Cleveland, A Record of Friendship,* 8.
83. Allan Nevins, *Grover Cleveland, A Study in Courage,* 708.
84. *This Country of Ours,* 94.
85. *Ibid.,* 126.
86. *Ibid.,* 129.
87. *Ibid.,* 131.
88. *Ibid.,* 132.
89. *Ibid.,* 132.
90. *Ibid.,* 152.
91. Inaugural Address, March 4, 1897, *Inaugural Addresses of the Presidents* (1952 ed.), 165.
92. To C. A. S. Rice, February 27, 1905, *Letters,* IV, 1130.
93. To H. C. Lodge, July 18, 1905, *Ibid.,* 1279.
94. To J. St. L. Strachey, February 12, 1906, *Letters,* V, 151.
95. To A. H. Lee, April 8, 1907, *Ibid.,* 644.
96. To Theodore Roosevelt, Jr., January 31, 1909, *Letters,* VI, 1498.
97. *An Autobiography,* 397 f.
98. *Our Chief Magistrate and His Powers,* 4.
99. *Ibid.,* 11.
100. *Ibid.,* 12.
101. *Ibid.,* 14.
102. *Ibid.,* 15.
103. *Ibid.,* 18.
104. *Ibid.,* 19.
105. *Ibid.,* 23.
106. *Ibid.,* 24.
107. *Ibid.,* 25.
108. *Ibid.,* 27.
109. *Ibid.,* 37.
110. *Ibid.,* 73.
111. *Ibid.,* 125.
112. *Ibid.,* 126.

113. *Ibid.*, 129.
114. Address to Gridiron, December 4, 1929, *Papers*, I, 188.
115. *Memoirs*, II, 216.
116. *Challenge to Liberty*, 127.
117. *Addresses upon the American Road*, 227.
118. *Ibid.*, 203.
119. *Memoirs*, II, 325.
120. *Further Addresses upon the American Road*, 26.
121. Inaugural Address, March 4, 1933, *Papers, 1933*, 15.
122. Fireside chat, May 7, 1933, *Ibid.*, 161.
123. To Congress, June 16, 1933, *Ibid.*, 256.
124. Press conference, December 29, 1933, *Ibid.*, 552.
125. At Dallas, June 12, 1936, *Papers, 1936*, 215.
126. *On Our Way*, 22.
127. Annual Message, January 6, 1937, *Papers, 1937*, 634.
128. Letter to Senator Alben Barkley, July 15, 1937.
129. *The New York Times*, January 6, 1938.
130. *Ibid.*
131. *Ibid.*
132. Introduction to *Papers, 1938*, xxviii.
133. Statement on proposed tariffs, March 29, 1939, *Papers, 1939*, 177.
134. Annual Message, January 3, 1940, *Papers, 1940*, 5.
135. Message to Congress, May 16, 1940, *Ibid.*, 204.
136. *Ibid.*, April 11, 1943, *Papers, 1943*, 159.
137. Memorandum, December 22, 1945, *Papers, 1945*, 583.
138. Annual Message, January 21, 1946, *Papers, 1946*, 37.
139. Special Message to Congress, May 24, 1945, *Papers, 1945*, 71.
140. *Memoirs*, II, 453.
141. *Ibid.*, 454.
142. *Ibid.*, 479.
143. *Ibid.*, 479.
144. *Ibid.*, 480.
145. To Secretary of Defense, May 17, 1954, *Papers, 1954*, 483.
146. Political address, October 8, 1954, *Ibid.*, 898.
147. Special Message to Congress, July 13, 1955, *Papers, 1955*, 689.
148. Press conference, May 22, 1957, *Papers, 1957*, 401.
149. *Ibid.*, July 31, 1957, *Papers, 1957*, 577.
150. To Senator L. Johnson, January 22, 1958, *Papers, 1958*, 117.
151. Press conference, January 21, 1959, *Papers, 1959*, 129.
152. *Ibid.*, July 15, 1959, *Papers, 1959*, 523.
153. *Ibid.*, July 22, 1959, *Papers, 1959*, 545.

154. Message to Congress, January 16, 1961, *Papers, 1960–61,* 1026.
155. Broadcast address, January 17, 1961, *Ibid.,* 1036.
156. C.B.S. Reports, October 12, 1961.
157. *Ibid.,* November 23, 1961.
158. *Ibid.,* February 15, 1962.
159. Press conference, June 28, 1962, Transcript.
160. Annual Message, January 30, 1961, *Papers, 1961,* 19.
161. Broadcast interview, C.B.S., December 17, 1962.
162. *Ibid.*
163. Press conference, May 8, 1963, *The New York Times,* May 9, 1963.

Chapter V — The Presidency and the Judiciary

1. To Abigail Adams, September 11, 1804, L. J. Cappon, *Adams-Jefferson Letters,* I, 279.
2. To G. Hay, June 2, 1807, *Writings,* IX, 53.
3. *Ibid.,* June 20, 1807, *Writings,* X, 103 f.
4. *Writings,* X, 160 f.
5. To Governor Snyder, April 13, 1809, *Letters,* II, 438.
6. To T. Jefferson, June 4, 1810, *Ibid.,* 479.
7. Veto Message, July 10, 1832, Richardson, II, 582.
8. *An Inquiry into the Origin and Course of Political Parties,* 342.
9. *This Country of Ours,* 312.
10. Message to Congress, February 5, 1937, *Papers, 1937,* 51.
11. Fireside chat, March 9, 1937, *Ibid.,* 129.
12. *Ibid.*
13. Press conference, January 21, 1959, *Papers, 1959,* 123.

Chapter VI — The Presidency and Foreign Relations

1. Article II, Section 2.
2. 14th Congress, 1st Session.
3. To the King of France, October 9, 1789, *Writings,* XXX, 431 f.
4. To Gouverneur Morris, October 13, 1789, *Writings,* XXX, 440.
5. Robert E. Sherwood, *Roosevelt and Hopkins,* 232.
6. To Gouverneur Morris, October 13, 1789, *Writings,* XXX, 439 ff.
7. *Autobiography,* 551 f.
8. *Memoirs,* IV, 205 f.
9. To the House of Representatives, March 30, 1796, *Writings,* XXXV, 5.
10. *Writings,* XXX, 162.

11. M. A. DeWolf Howe, *Life and Letters of George Bancroft,* II, 49.
12. Address at Washington, May 27, 1916, A. B. Tourtellot (ed.), *Woodrow Wilson: Selections for Today,* 124.
13. *Ibid.,* 125.
14. Address, May 27, 1916, Tourtellot, *op. cit.,* 124.
15. To Comte de Moustier, May 25, 1789, *Writings,* XXX, 334 f.
16. To Congress, August 7, 1789, *Ibid.,* 373 f.
17. To the King of France, October 9, 1789, *Ibid.,* 431.
18. *Diaries,* March 19, 1790, IV, 105.
19. *Ibid.,* April 27, 1790, IV, 122.
20. To House, March 30, 1796, *Writings,* XXXV, 2 ff.
21. To Alexander Hamilton, June 26, 1796, *Ibid.,* 102 f.
22. To Lancaster inhabitants, May 8, 1798, *Works,* IX, 190.
23. To T. Pickering, August 6, 1799, *Ibid.,* 1.
24. To W. S. Smith, February 22, 1815, P. Smith, *John Adams,* II, 1110.
25. To James Madison, July 15, 1801, *Writings,* VIII, 73.
26. To Governor Sullivan, October 18, 1807, *Writings,* X, 203.
27. To M. Carey, November 11, 1816, *Ibid.,* 67.
28. To E. Coles, October 15, 1834, *Letters,* IV, 370.
29. *Jubilee of the Constitution,* 80.
30. To Congress, December 21, 1836, Richardson, III, 267.
31. Inaugural Address, March 4, 1837, *Ibid.,* 319.
32. Special Message to Congress, January 5, 1838, *Ibid.,* 399.
33. *Inquiry into the Origin and Course of Political Parties,* 343.
34. Message to Senate, January 7, 1858, *Works,* X, 172.
35. Second Annual Message, December 6, 1858, *Ibid.,* 259.
36. Message to Congress, February 18, 1859, *Ibid.,* 297.
37. Veto Message, March 1, 1879, Richardson, VII, 518.
38. Message to Congress, April 18, 1882, Richardson, VIII, 97.
39. Message to Congress, March 1, 1886, *Ibid.,* 383.
40. *This Country of Ours,* 134.
41. *Ibid.,* 139.
42. Letter accepting nomination, September 12, 1904, *Presidential Addresses and State Papers,* III, 51.
43. To Andrew Carnegie, February 26, 1909, *Letters,* VI, 1538.
44. *Our Chief Magistrate and His Powers,* 105.
45. *Ibid.,* 106.
46. *Ibid.,* 112.
47. *Ibid.,* 113.
48. *Ibid.,* 117.

49. To Senator Fall, December 8, 1919, *The New York Times,* December 9, 1919.
50. To Raymond Clapper, 1932, C. M. Fuess, *Calvin Coolidge — The Man From Vermont,* 458.
51. Radio address, September 18, 1929, *Papers,* I, 101.
52. Message to Senate, July 11, 1930, *Ibid.,* 357.
53. *Addresses upon the American Road,* 221.
54. Message to Congress, March 2, 1934, *Papers, 1934,* 14.
55. At Chappaqua, N.Y., August 14, 1936, *Papers, 1936,* 290.
56. Special Message to Senate, December 19, 1945, *Papers, 1945,* 561.
57. *Memoirs,* I, 330.
58. *Ibid.,* 388.
59. *Memoirs,* II, 55.
60. *Ibid.,* 165.
61. *Ibid.,* 355.
62. *Ibid.,* 430.
63. Press conference, March 19, 1953, *Papers, 1953,* 105.
64. *Ibid.,* March 26, 1953, *Papers, 1953,* 132.
65. *Ibid.,* April 2, 1953, *Papers, 1953,* 148.
66. *Ibid.,* 149.
67. Special Message, June 1, 1953, *Papers, 1953,* 343.
68. Statement, July 22, 1953, *Ibid.,* 510.
69. Broadcast address, July 15, 1955, *Papers, 1955,* 701.
70. Press conference, March 21, 1956, *Papers, 1956,* 333.
71. Letter to Ways and Means Committee, June 10, 1958, *Papers, 1958,* 462.
72. C.B.S. Reports, November 23, 1961.
73. *Ibid.*
74. *Ibid.*
75. In Paris, June 2, 1961, *Papers, 1961,* 433.
76. Introduction to *To Turn the Tide* J. W. Gardner (ed.), xiii.

CHAPTER VII — THE PRESIDENT AS COMMANDER IN CHIEF

1. Article II, Section 2.
2. *Diary,* February 27, 1847, II, 394.
3. *Memoirs,* II, 355.
4. To A. G. Hodges, April 4, 1864, *Works,* X, 66.
5. J. G. Nicolay and J. Hay, *Abraham Lincoln: A History,* 120 f.
6. Reply to a committee, September 13, 1862, *Works,* VIII, 31.
7. *Diaries,* October 6–12, 1794, IV, 217.
8. Sixth Annual Message, November 19, 1794, *Writings,* XXXIV, 32.

9. To George Washington, October 9, 1798, *Works*, VIII, 600.
10. Memorandum, August 24, 1814, *Writings*, VIII, 294.
11. To G. W. Campbell, November 2, 1814, *Ibid.*, 317.
12. To James Monroe, November 16, 1827, *Letters*, III, 600.
13. *Diary*, June 24, 1828, Allan Nevins (ed.), 380.
14. *Inquiry into Origin and Course of Political Parties*, 337.
15. To the Governor of Rhode Island, April 11, 1842, *Letters*, II, 194.
16. Special Message to House, January 2, 1849, Richardson, IV, 674.
17. *Ibid.*, 675.
18. *Diary*, November 18, 1846, II, 243 f.
19. *Diary*, January 4, 1847, II, 328.
20. *Diary*, January 25, 1847, II, 355 f.
21. Message to Congress, August 6, 1850, Richardson, V, 68.
22. To Daniel Webster, October 28, 1850, *Papers*, I, 335.
23. To Senate, February 19, 1851, Richardson, V, 104.
24. Third Annual Message, December 19, 1859, *Works*, X, 360.
25. W. H. Lamon, *Recollections of Abraham Lincoln*, 221.
26. Message to Congress, July 4, 1861, *Works*, VI, 308.
27. Annual Message, December 3, 1861, *Works*, VII, 33.
28. Amnesty, February 14, 1862, *Ibid.*, 102.
29. Reply to Church Committee, September 13, 1862, *Works*, VIII, 31.
30. Preliminary Emancipation Proclamation, September 22, 1862, *Ibid.*, 37.
31. Proclamation, September 24, 1862, *Ibid.*, 41.
32. Final Emancipation Proclamation, January 1, 1863, *Ibid.*, 163.
33. To E. Corning *et al.*, June 12, 1863, *Ibid.*, 302.
34. *Ibid.*, 309.
35. To General Hooker, June 16, 1863, *Works*, VIII, 321.
36. To M. Birchard *et al.*, June 29, 1863, *Works*, IX, 3.
37. To Governor Seymour, August 7, 1863, *Ibid.*, 60.
38. To J. C. Conkling, August 26, 1863, *Ibid.*, 98.
39. To Secretary of Treasury, September 2, 1863, *Ibid.*, 108.
40. To I. M. Schermerhorn (unfinished draft), *Works*, X, 221.
41. Veto message, May 12, 1789, Richardson, VII, 534 f.
42. *This Country of Ours*, 124.
43. *Ibid.*, 125.
44. *Views of an ex-President*, 432.
45. *Ibid.*, 477.
46. *Our Chief Magistrate and His Powers*, 94.
47. *Ibid.*, 97.
48. *Ibid.*, 98.

49. *Ibid.,* 128.
50. *Ibid.,* 129.
51. To Congressman Webb, May 22, 1917, *Congressional Record,* LV, 3144.
52. Address to Congress, January 4, 1918, *Papers* ("War and Peace"), I, 150.
53. Press conference, May 31, 1935, *Papers, 1935,* 206.
54. Veto message, May 22, 1935, *Ibid.,* 192.
55. Press conference, March 7, 1939, *Papers, 1939,* 157.
56. Fireside chat, September 11, 1941, *Papers, 1941,* 391.
57. Message to Congress, September 7, 1942, *Papers, 1942,* 369.
58. Fireside chat, October 12, 1942, *Papers, 1942,* 411.
59. To R. E. Hannigan, July 11, 1944, *Papers, 1944,* 197.
60. Address at New York, October 21, 1944, *Ibid.,* 343.
61. Special Message to Congress, December 19, 1945, *Papers, 1945,* 556.
62. *Memoirs,* II, 295.
63. *Ibid.,* 478.
64. Press conference, March 17, 1954, *Papers, 1954,* 325.
65. Broadcast address, February 29, 1956, *Papers, 1956,* 275.
66. Press conference, May 23, 1956, *Ibid.,* 514.
67. *Ibid.,* March 4, 1859, *Papers, 1959,* 228.
68. Political address, October 28, 1960, *Papers, 1960–61,* 817.
69. *Ibid.,* November 4, 1860, *Papers, 1960–61,* 851.
70. C.B.S. Reports, November 23, 1961.
71. *Ibid.*
72. *Ibid.,* December 12, 1962, Transcript.
73. *Ibid.,* March 21, 1963, Transcript.

CHAPTER VIII — THE BURDENS AND PRIVILEGES OF THE PRESIDENCY

1. To E. Rutledge, May 5, 1789, *Writings,* XXX, 309.
2. To D. Stuart, July 26, 1789, *Ibid.,* 360 ff.
3. To Thomas Paine, May 6, 1792, *Writings,* XXII, 39.
4. To W. Gordon, October 15, 1797, *Writings,* XXXVI, 50.
5. To Abigail Adams, February 22, 1799, *Works,* I, 544 f.
6. *Ibid.,* March 11, 1799, C. F. Adams (ed.), *Letters of John Adams to His Wife,* II, 249.
7. On defeat for re-election, 1800, Page Smith, *John Adams,* II, 1055.
8. To *Boston Patriot,* 1809, *Works,* IX, 281.
9. To Thomas Jefferson, April 19, 1817, *Works,* X, 253.

10. To J. Dickinson, January n.d., 1807, *Writings*, IX, 10.
11. To James Monroe, January 28, 1809, *Ibid.*, 244.
12. *Diary*, March 5, 1827, Allan Nevins (ed.), 371.
13. *Ibid.*, March 18, 1827, 372.
14. *Ibid.*, November 4, 1830, 406.
15. *Jubilee of the Constitution*, 87 f.
16. *Diary*, December, 1825, *Memoirs*, VII, 97.
17. Charles Francis Adams in Rutherford B. Hayes, *Diary*, IV, 40.
18. To R. J. Chester, November 30, 1829, *Correspondence*, IV, 96.
19. To T. A. Howard, August 20, 1833, *Correspondence*, V, 165.
20. *Autobiography*, 447.
21. *Ibid.*, 448.
22. *Diary*, July 16, 1846, II, 28 f.
23. *Diary*, January 28, 1847, II, 360.
24. *Diary*, September 4, 1847, III, 162.
25. *Diary*, December 29, 1848, IV, 261.
26. Inaugural Address, March 4, 1849, Richardson, V, 6.
27. To Mrs. J. K. Polk, September 19, 1859, *Works*, X, 332.
28. At Wheatland, Penn., March 6, 1861, *Works*, XI, 161.
29. W. H. Lamon, *Recollections of Abraham Lincoln*, 182.
30. *Ibid.*, 182.
31. *Ibid.*, 190.
32. *Ibid.*, 208.
33. *Ibid.*, 261.
34. First Inaugural Address, March 4, 1861, *Works*, VI, 173.
35. Reply to Serenade, September 24, 1862, *Works*, VIII, 44.
36. Interview with J. T. Mills, August 15, 1864, *Works*, X, 189.
37. Last address, April 14, 1865, *Works*, XI, 85.
38. At Cleveland, September 3, 1866, *Trial*, I, 326.
39. Second Annual Message, December 5, 1870, *Ibid.*, 131.
40. Second Inaugural Address, March 4, 1873, Richardson, VII, 223.
41. To Mrs. Hayes, March 27, 1878, *Diary*, III, 472.
42. *Diary*, July 26, 1879, III, 569.
43. *Diary*, July 18, 1880, III, 613.
44. To G. M. Bryan, January 1, 1881, *Diary*, III, 632.
45. To W. H. Smith, March 29, 1881, *Diary*, IV, 5.
46. *Diary*, December 10, 1891, V, 38.
47. H. L. Stoddard, *It Costs to Be President*, 127.
48. Journal, March 16, 1881, T. C. Smith, *Life and Letters*, II, 1147.
49. Journal, March 26, 1881, *Ibid.*, 1150.
50. Journal, June 8, 1881, *Ibid.*, 1151.
51. Journal, June 13, 1881, *Ibid.*, 1151.

52. R. McElroy, *Grover Cleveland*, I, 117.
53. G. F. Howe, *Chester A. Arthur*, 243.
54. To W. E. Bissell, June 25, 1885, R. McElroy, *op. cit.*, I, 135.
55. *Ibid.*, 485.
56. *Ibid.*, 508.
57. *Ibid.*, 544.
58. *Ibid.*, 774.
59. At Harvard College, November 9, 1886, G. F. Parker (ed.), *Writings and Speeches*, 115.
60. At Sandwich, Mass., July 25, 1891, *Ibid.*, 546.
61. R. W. Gilder, *Grover Cleveland, A Record of Friendship*, 149.
62. H. L. Stoddard, *It Costs to Be President*, 215.
63. R. McElroy, *op. cit.*, I, 143.
64. A. Nevins, *op. cit.*, 448.
65. *This Country of Ours*, 167.
66. To Cleveland, March 4, 1897, C. S. Olcott, *Life of William McKinley*, II, 367.
67. M. Leech, *In the Days of McKinley*, 463.
68. To H. C. Lodge, September 23, 1901, *Letters*, III, 150.
69. To Jacob Riis, November 12, 1902, *Ibid.*, 377.
70. To Kermit Roosevelt, December 4, 1902, *Ibid.*, 389.
71. To Maria L. Storer, December 8, 1902, *Ibid.*, 391.
72. To P. De Coubertin, June 15, 1903, *Ibid.*, 491.
73. To Kermit Roosevelt, October 2, 1903, *Works*, XXI, 501.
74. To L. C. Davis, October 5, 1903, *Letters*, III, 619.
75. To J. W. Wadsworth, Jr., June 29, 1904, *Letters*, IV, 850.
76. To E. S. Martin, November 6, 1908, *Works*, XXIV, 144.
77. To G. O. Trevelyan, September 10, 1909, *Letters*, VII, 29.
78. To H. K. Smith, 1911, *Works*, XIX, xiv.
79. To Lady Delamere, March 7, 1911, Lord Charnwood, *Theodore Roosevelt*, 223.
80. A. Butt, *Taft and Roosevelt*, I, 109.
81. *Ibid.*, 253.
82. *Our Chief Magistrate and His Power*, 51.
83. A. Butt, *op. cit.*, II, 220.
84. *Ibid.*, I, 294.
85. To Woodrow Wilson, March 4, 1913, A. Walworth, *Woodrow Wilson, American Prophet*, I, 283.
86. H. Finer, *The Presidency, Crisis and Regeneration*, 145.
87. A. Walworth, *op. cit.*, I, 310.
88. To the Gridiron, February 26, 1916, A. B. Hart (ed.), *Selected Addresses*, 107.

89. To National Press Club, May 15, 1916, *Selected Literary and Political Addresses*, 159.

90. At Lincoln's Birthplace, September 4, 1916, A. B. Tourtellot (ed.), *Woodrow Wilson: Selections for Today*, 17.

91. To New Jersey Democrats, March 20, 1918, *Congressional Record*, LVI, 5491.

92. *Life and Letters*, IV, 176.

93. H. Finer, *op. cit.*, 191.

94. *Life and Letters*, IV, 460.

95. K. Schriftgiesser, *This Was Normalcy*, 140.

96. To David Lawrence, S. H. Adams, *Incredible Era*, 224.

97. At National Press Club, Mark Sullivan, *Our Times*, VI, 242.

98. *The New York Times*, March 12, 1923.

99. W. A. White, *Masks in a Pageant*, 431.

100. *Ibid.*, 432.

101. *Ibid.*, 423.

102. *St. Louis Post-Dispatch*, August 10, 1928.

103. *Ibid.*

104. *The Autobiography of Calvin Coolidge*, 172.

105. *Ibid.*, 192.

106. *Ibid.*, 196.

107. *Ibid.*, 215.

108. *Ibid.*, 246.

109. C. M. Fuess, *Calvin Coolidge, The Man from Vermont*, 311.

110. To Hubert Work, August, 1927, *Ibid.*, 398.

111. To the Gridiron, April 13, 1929, *Papers*, I, 29.

112. At Madison Courthouse, Virginia, August 17, 1929, *Papers*, I, 88.

113. To the Gridiron, December 14, 1929, *Papers*, I, 187.

114. *Ibid.*

115. To Dr. W. O. Thompson, December 30, 1929, *Papers*, I, 197.

116. *Memoirs*, II, 325.

117. *Ibid.*, 326.

118. *Ibid.*, 327.

119. *Memoirs*, III, 104.

120. At Hyde Park, September 29, 1933, *Papers*, *1933*, 368.

121. To the Holland Society, January 17, 1935, *Papers*, *1935*, 41.

122. Political address, March 29, 1941, *Papers*, *1941*, 82.

123. Message to Congress, January 25, 1944, *Papers*, *1944*, 60.

124. To F. C. Walker, May 2, 1945, *Papers*, *1945*, 33.

125. *Memoirs*, I, ix.

126. *Ibid.*, 53.

127. *Ibid.*, 199.
128. *Ibid.*, 504.
129. *Memoirs*, II, 1.
130. *Ibid.*
131. *Ibid.*, 10.
132. *Ibid.*, 154.
133. *Ibid.*, 212.
134. *Ibid.*, 361.
135. *Ibid.*
136. *Ibid.*, 488.
137. To Governors' Conference, August 4, 1953, *Papers, 1953,* 542.
138. Press conference, December 2, 1954, *Papers, 1954,* 1075.
139. *Ibid.*, May 31, 1955, *Papers, 1955,* 553.
140. *Ibid.*, January 8, 1956, *Papers, 1956,* 34.
141. Broadcast address, February 29, 1956, *Ibid.*, 275.
142. *Ibid.*
143. Political address, November 4, 1960, *Papers, 1960–61,* 851.
144. Press conference, June 15, 1962, Transcript.
145. To Christian Leadership meeting, February 9, 1961, *Papers, 1961,* 76.
146. Broadcast address, July 25, 1961, *Ibid.*, 539.
147. Press conference, December 12, 1962, Transcript.
148. Broadcast interview, C.B.S., December 17, 1962.
149. *Ibid.*

CHAPTER IX — THE PRESIDENT AND PARTY POLITICS

1. *Writings*, XXXV, 227.
2. To J. Quincy, February 18, 1811, *Works*, IX, 634.
3. To R. Lee, February 22, 1830, *Letters*, IV, 66.
4. To Thomas Jefferson, March 22, 1824, *Writings*, VII, 11.
5. To F. Brooke, February 21, 1828, *Ibid.*, 54.
6. To W. Wirt, October 24, 1828, *Ibid.*, 181.
7. *Diary*, November 7, 1830, *Memoirs*, VIII, 245 f.
8. *Diary*, May 4, 1841, *Memoirs*, IX, 468.
9. *Diary*, November 11, 1836, Allan Nevins (ed.), 471.
10. *Parties in the United States*, 124.
11. First Annual Message, December 8, 1829, Richardson, II, 447.
12. Second Annual Message, December 6, 1830, *Ibid.*, 518.
13. *Ibid.*, 519.
14. *Papers*, II, 139 f.
15. Inaugural Address, March 4, 1887, Richardson, VII, 49.
16. *Diary*, March 12, 1878, III, 466.

17. *Diary*, June 5, 1880, III, 600.
18. Allan Nevins, *Grover Cleveland, A Study in Courage*, 377.
19. R. W. Gilder, *Grover Cleveland, A Record of Friendship*, 113.
20. Allan Nevins, *op. cit.*, 497.
21. To J. B. Bishop, September 20, 1901, *Works*, XXIII, 174.
22. To R. Olney, September 23, 1901, *Letters*, III, 149.
23. To W. A. White, July 30, 1907, *Letters*, V, 736.
24. To W. W. Sewall, June 25, 1908, W. W. Sewall, *Bill Seward's Story of T.R.*, 113.
25. To J. Strachey, March 26, 1912, *Letters*, VII, 532.
26. *An Autobiography*, 423.
27. A. Butt, *Taft and Roosevelt*, II, 645.
28. *Our Chief Magistrate and His Powers*, 4.
29. *Ibid.*, 52.
30. To National Press Club, March 20, 1914.
31. *Papers*, VII, 166.
32. *The Autobiography of Calvin Coolidge*, 230.
33. *Ibid.*, 231.
34. *Ibid.*, 245.
35. *Memoirs*, III, 379.
36. To Senate Subcommittee, January 20, 1958.
37. *Ibid.*
38. Political address, January 8, 1936, *Papers, 1936*, 39.
39. *Ibid.*, 38.
40. At Barnesville, Georgia, August 11, 1938, *Papers*, 469.
41. Introduction to *Papers, 1938*, xxviii.
42. Political address, July 19, 1940, *Papers*, 294.
43. Political address, March 23, 1946, *Papers, 1946*, 167.
44. *Mr. Citizen*, 221.
45. *Memoirs*, II, 186.
46. *Ibid.*
47. Press conference, March 26, 1953, *Papers, 1953*, 138.
48. At Mt. Rushmore, S.D., June 11, 1953, *Ibid.*, 399.
49. *Ibid.*, 407.
50. Press conference, July 8, 1953, *Papers, 1953*, 474.
51. *Ibid.*, October 28, 1953, *Papers, 1953*, 725.
52. *Ibid.*, August 4, 1954, *Papers, 1954*, 679.
53. Political address, February 29, 1956, *Papers, 1956*, 274.
54. Press conference, October 5, 1956, *Ibid.*, 862.
55. *Ibid.*, June 8, 1957, *Papers, 1957*, 435.
56. C.B.S. Reports, October 12, 1961.
57. Political address, November 2, 1961, *Papers, 1961*, 695.

CHAPTER X — THE PRESIDENT AS REFORMER

1. First Inaugural Address, March 4, 1829, Richardson, II, 438.
2. To Cabinet, September 18, 1833, *Correspondence*, V, 194.
3. To Horace Greeley, August 22, 1862, *Works*, VIII, 15.
4. Reply to committee seeking an emancipation proclamation, September 13, 1862, *Works*, VIII, 30.
5. To A. G. Hodges, April 4, 1864, *Works*, X, 1864.
6. Special Message to Senate, January 31, 1879, Richardson, VII, 512.
7. Fourth Annual Message, December 6, 1880, *Ibid.*, 605.
8. *Diary*, March 30, 1878, III, 473.
9. *Diary*, July 11, 1880, III, 609.
10. *Diary*, July 13, 1880, III, 612.
11. H. L. Stoddard, *It Costs to Be President*, 127.
12. R. W. Gilder, *Grover Cleveland, A Record of Friendship*, 110.
13. *Ibid.*, 204.
14. To H. C. Lodge, September 27, 1902, *Letters*, III, 332.
15. To Bishop Talbot, October 29, 1902, *Ibid.*, 371.
16. To James Ford Rhodes, December 15, 1904, *Letters*, IV, 1072.
17. *Outlook*, April 20, 1912, 852.

CHAPTER XI — LIMITATIONS OF THE PRESIDENCY

1. Letter to his father, January 1, 1926, *Autobiography*, 373.
2. McClure Syndicate, n.d.
3. Inaugural Address, March 4, 1925, *Inaugural Addresses of the Presidents* (1961 ed.), 220.
4. To E. Randolph, February 11, 1790, *Writings*, XXXI, 9.
5. Review of Propositions to Amend the Constitution, 1808, *Works*, VI, 539.
6. *Works*, IX, 44.
7. To Dr. B. Rush, October 4, 1803, *Writings*, VIII, 264.
8. To W. B. Giles, April 20, 1807, *Writings*, IX, 45 f.
9. To Jonathan Dayton, August 17, 1807, *Writings*, IX, 126.
10. To Rev. S. Miller, January 23, 1808, *Ibid.*, 175 f.
11. To J. Martin, September 20, 1813, *Ibid.*, 420.
12. Veto Message, April 3, 1812, Richardson, I, 511.
13. To S. Southard, February 8, 1831, *Writings*, VII, 220.
14. *Diary*, June 18, 1833, Allan Nevins (ed.), 439.
15. *Ibid.*, April 16, 1841, 522.

16. To Reformed Church, June 12, 1832, *Correspondence,* IV, 447.
17. Special Message to Congress, January 5, 1838, Richardson, III, 399.
18. Autobiography, 284.
19. Inaugural Address, March 4, 1841, Richardson, IV, 12.
20. *Ibid.,* 13.
21. *Ibid.*
22. Inaugural Address, April 9, 1841, Richardson, IV, 37.
23. Message to House, April 9, 1844, *Ibid.,* 284.
24. *Diary,* October 7, 1845, I, 51 f.
25. Message to Congress, August 6, 1850, Richardson, V, 72.
26. Special Message, January 24, 1856, *Ibid.,* 358.
27. Fourth Annual Message, December 2, 1856, *Ibid.,* 406.
28. Fourth Annual Message, December 3, 1860, *Works,* XI, 9.
29. *Ibid.,* 9.
30. *Ibid.,* 17.
31. *Ibid.,* 18.
32. Message to Congress, January 28, 1861, *Works,* IX, 117.
33. To Dr. Blake, December 16, 1862, *Ibid.,* 324.
34. To W. B. Campbell, *et al.,* October 22, 1864, *Works,* X, 249.
35. Fourth Annual Message, December 6, 1864, *Ibid.,* 308.
36. H. L. Stoddard, *It Costs to Be President,* 13.
37. J. S. Jones, *Life of Andrew Johnson,* 362.
38. Eighth Annual Message, December 5, 1876, Richardson, VII, 399.
39. *Diary,* March 23, 1877, III, 429.
40. Veto Message, July 2, 1884, Richardson, VIII, 222.
41. At Sandwich, Mass., July 25, 1891, G. F. Parker, *Writings and Speeches of Grover Cleveland,* 547.
42. *Ibid.*
43. R. W. Gilder, *Grover Cleveland, A Record of Friendship,* 159.
44. To C. R. Robinson, September 23, 1903, *Letters,* III, 605.
45. To G. O. Trevelyan, May 28, 1904, *Letters,* IV, 806.
46. To Kermit Roosevelt, October 26, 1904, *Ibid.,* 993.
47. To G. O. Trevelyan, November 24, 1904, *Ibid.,* 1045.
48. *Ibid.,* 1046.
49. To G. O. Trevelyan, May 13, 1905, *Letters,* IV, 1173.
50. To E. D. Brandegee, March 7, 1906, *Letters,* V, 172.
51. To L. F. Abbott, July 8, 1907, *Ibid.,* 707.
52. To Nicholas Murray Butler, September 24, 1907, *Ibid.,* 807.
53. To Department of State, December 2, 1908, *Letters,* VI, 1405.
54. Oscar K. Davis, *Released for Publication,* 200 f.

55. *An Autobiography*, 423.
56. A. Butt, *Taft and Roosevelt*, II, 435.
57. *Our Chief Magistrate and His Powers*, 48.
58. *Ibid.*, 49.
59. *Ibid.*, 139.
60. At Suffrage Convention, September 8, 1916, A. B. Hart (ed.), *Selected Addresses of Woodrow Wilson*, 155.
61. To his father, January 1, 1926, C. M. Fuess, *Calvin Coolidge, The Man from Vermont*, 373.
62. H. L. Stoddard, *It Costs to Be President*, 133.
63. *Ibid.*, 125.
64. *Ibid.*, 145.
65. *Memoirs*, III, 104.
66. Address at Madison Courthouse, Va., August 17, 1929, *Papers*, I, 88.
67. At the Gridiron, December 12, 1931, *Papers*, II, 86.
68. *Ibid.*, 87.
69. Message to Congress, April 4, 1932, *Papers*, II, 153.
70. Political speech, November 4, 1932, *Ibid.*, 434.
71. Statement, June 14, 1933, *Papers, 1933*, 243.
72. Message to Congress, February 5, 1937, *Papers, 1937*, 54.
73. Fireside chat, March 9, 1937, *Ibid.*, 123.
74. Press conference, May 18, 1937, *Ibid.*, 203.
75. Address to Congress, March 4, 1939, *Papers, 1939*, 152.
76. To Brazil, November 7, 1939, *Ibid.*, 568.
77. Special Message, December 6, 1945, *Papers, 1945*, 129.
78. On presenting medal, March 27, 1946, *Papers, 1946*, 170.
79. Press conference, May 4, 1956, *Papers, 1956*, 462.
80. To newspaper editors, April 19, 1963, *The New York Times*, April 20, 1963.

ADDENDUM: A NOTE ON KENNEDY AS PRESIDENT AND WRITER

1. Cited in *Life*, LV, 22, 4.
2. Cited in *Newsweek*, LXII, 23, 52.
3. "For President Kennedy—An Epilogue," *Life*, LV, 23, 158.
4. *Profiles in Courage*, 246.
5. At Dedication of Robert Frost Library, *The New York Times*, October 27, 1963.
6. At Orono, Maine, *Christian Science Monitor*, October 23, 1963.
7. Cited in *Life*, John F. Kennedy Memorial Edition, no date, no pagination.

8. John F. Kennedy, *Why England Slept* (1940 edition), xiv.
9. Address at Hodgenville, Kentucky, September 4, 1916, A. B. Tourtellot (ed.), *Woodrow Wilson: Selections for Today*, 17.
10. *Why England Slept*, 231.
11. *Profiles in Courage*, 246.
12. John W. Gardner (ed.), *To Turn the Tide*, i.
13. At Naples, Italy, *The New York Times*, July 9, 1963.
14. Before the United States Chamber of Commerce, *The New York Times*, May 1, 1962.
15. At the American University, in Washington, *The New York Times*, June 11, 1963.
16. At Chapel Hill, October 12, 1961, Cited in J. W. Gardner (ed.), *To Turn the Tide*, 167.
17. At Nashville, *The New York Times*, May 19, 1963.
18. At Amherst, *The New York Times*, October 27, 1963.
19. In *The New Yorker*, XXXIX, 49.
20. At Amherst, *The New York Times*, October 27, 1963.
21. Text prepared for Dallas, *The New York Times*, November 24, 1963.
22. Theodore C. Sorensen, *Decision-Making in the White House*, xi.
23. Cited in *Time*, LXXXII, 22, 29.
24. Cited in *Life*, LV, 22, 32E.
25. At Amherst, *The New York Times*, October 27, 1963.
26. Sorensen, *op. cit.*, xii.
27. Inaugural, January 20, 1961, *Inaugural Addresses of the Presidents* (1961 edition), 269.
28. *Ibid.*
29. Reported in *Newsweek*, XLII, 23, 22.

A BIBLIOGRAPHY OF PRESIDENTIAL WRITINGS

The only compilation of the public writings of the Presidents is James D. Richardson (ed.), *Messages and Papers of the Presidents, 1798–1897*, 10 vols., 1895–1899, ending with the second Cleveland administration. The appendix has some of the messages of the first year of the McKinley administration. The Richardson collection is not inclusive, but for some Presidents it is the only extensive published source. In 1957 the National Historical Publications Commission recommended that the U. S. Government publish, for each year, a volume containing the public papers of the Presidents. Eight volumes covering the Eisenhower terms have appeared, as have the first two for the Truman years and the first for the Kennedy years. The publication for any years prior to the Truman administration may be authorized by the Administrative Committee of the Federal Register. The need in the case of such Presidents as Coolidge, Harding, and Taft, whose public papers are assembled in no publication, is clear.

The bibliography below contains listings of published writings of presidential and post-presidential years only and not the writings of the Presidents before their accession to the office. The unpublished papers are not, in most cases, segregated by presidential and pre-presidential years, but only collections known to include presidential years have been included. The entries are arranged by Presidents in the order of their succession.

I. George Washington (1732–1799; President, 1789–1797)
PAPERS:
The Library of Congress has some 800 volumes of letters, diaries, official papers, and other manuscripts. The Henry E. Huntington Library (San Marino, California) has 450 letters. The Connecticut State Library has the extensive Trumbull correspondence. Other collections are in the Chicago Historical Society (150 pieces), the U. S. Naval Academy (15 pieces), Maryland Historical Society (62 pieces), Boston Public Library (5 vols.), Harvard College Library (88 pieces), William L. Clements Library (Ann Arbor) with 147 items, Detroit Public Library (part of the diary), Minnesota Historical Society (123 pieces), Princeton University Library, New Jersey State Library (32 items), Long Island Historical Society (123 pieces), Cornell University Library (80 pieces),

Morristown National Historical Park (95 pieces), Columbia University Library (57 pieces, including parts of the diary), New York Historical Society (215 pieces), New York Public Library, Pierpont Morgan Library (New York, N.Y.) (114 items), Duke University Libraries (99 pieces), Historical Society of Pennsylvania, Virginia Historical Society (225 pieces), Virginia State Library, and William and Mary College (205 pieces). The Washington home, Mount Vernon, has family papers and diaries of the later years.

PUBLISHED WRITINGS:

The definitive edition, not including the diaries, is John C. Fitzpatrick (ed.), *Writings of George Washington*, 39 vols., 1931–1944. The diaries are published separately as John C. Fitzpatrick (ed.), *The Diaries of George Washington*, 4 vols., 1925. Other editions are Jared C. Sparks (ed.), *The Writings of George Washington*, 12 vols., 1834–1837; and Worthington C. Ford (ed.), *The Writings of George Washington*, 14 vols., 1889–1893.

The greater part of Washington's writings on the presidency deal with the establishment of executive procedures, customs, and usages, but they also are highly important for the extent to which, by forceful example, they staked out the dimensions of the office and its relationship to the Congress.

II. John Adams (1735–1826; President, 1797–1801)

PAPERS:

The Adams papers are largely in the Massachusetts Historical Society, which has the diaries, the autobiography, and various manuscripts. There are four boxes of papers dated from 1776 to 1813. The Boston Public Library has some papers and some books with annotations by Adams. The post-presidential papers in the Harvard College Library are chiefly retrospective comments on the Revolution. There are scattered papers in the Columbia University Library, the Duke University Hospital Library, Princeton University Library, the Pierpont Morgan Library, and the Historical Society of Pennsylvania.

PUBLISHED WRITINGS:

The most complete collection will be Lyman H. Butterfield (ed.), *The Adams Papers*, of which six volumes have thus far (1963) been published. Meanwhile, with the limitations noted by Mr. Butterfield in his introduction to the above, the best published collection remains Charles Francis Adams, *The Life and Works of John Adams,* 10 vols., 1850–1856. This should be supplemented by L. J. Cappon (ed.), *The Adams-Jefferson Letters,* 2 vols., 1959; *Correspondence between the Hon. J. Adams and the late William Cunningham,* 1823; Charles Francis Adams (ed.), *Letters of John Adams Addressed to His Wife,* 2 vols., 1841, sometimes erroneously thought to be identical with *Familiar Letters of John Adams and His Wife Abigail,* 1876, which has no presidential letters; and Worthington C. Ford (ed.), *Statesman and Friend,* 1927, which is correspondence between Adams and Dr. Benjamin Waterhouse.

III. Thomas Jefferson (1743–1826; President, 1801–1809)
PAPERS:
   The Library of Congress has 236 volumes of the correspondence, and the Massachusetts Historical Society has 77 volumes of papers and some of his record books. The University of Virginia has 2500 items, Colonial Williamsburg 600 pieces, and William and Mary College 265 pieces. The Virginia Historical Society has 100 items, and there are some assorted papers in the Virginia State Library. Other collections are the Henry E. Huntington Library (800 pieces), the Historical Society of Delaware (14 items), the William L. Clements Library (91 pieces), the Missouri Historical Society (130 items), Princeton University Library, Columbia University Library (21 items), New York Historical Society (130 items), New York Public Library, Pierpont Morgan Library (245 pieces), Duke University Libraries (33 pieces), American Philosophic Society (Philadelphia), Historical Society of Pennsylvania, and the University of Texas (68 items).

PUBLISHED WRITINGS:
   A definitive edition, Julian P. Boyd (ed.), *The Papers of Thomas Jefferson,* is in progress, and sixteen volumes had been published by 1963. Standard but far less inclusive collections are Paul L. Ford (ed.), *The Writings of Thomas Jefferson,* 10 vols., 1892–1899; and A. A. Lipscomb and A. E. Bergh (eds.), *The Writings of Thomas Jefferson,* 20 vols., 1903. Supplementary, but less complete is H. A. Washington (ed.), *The Writings of Thomas Jefferson,* 9 vols., 1853–1854. Other important collections are L. J. Cappon, *op. cit.; The Jefferson Papers: Private Correspondence of Thomas Jefferson, 1770–1826* (Collections of the Massachusetts Historical Society, Seventh Series, Vol. I), 1900; Worthington C. Ford (ed.), *Thomas Jefferson Correspondence,*

1916; G. Chinard (ed.), *The Letters of Lafayette and Jefferson,* 1929; Worthington C. Ford (ed.), *Thomas Jefferson and James Thomson Callender,* 1897; Dumas Malone (ed.), *Correspondence between Thomas Jefferson and Pierre Samuel du Pont,* 1930; and *Glimpses of the Past,* 1930, correspondence (in the Missouri Historical Society) during the years 1788–1826.

IV. James Madison (1751–1836; President, 1809–1817)

PAPERS:

There are 114 boxes and 10 volumes of papers in the Library of Congress. The University of Virginia has 165 items, the New York Historical Society 134 pieces, and the Henry E. Huntington Library 104 pieces. There are smaller collections at the Virginia State Library, William and Mary College, the Virginia Historical Society, the Historical Society of Pennsylvania, the Pierpont Morgan Library, William L. Clements Library, and Princeton University Library. The New York Public Library has a collection of 390 items.

PUBLISHED WRITINGS:

There is no satisfactory collection, the best being G. Hunt (ed.), *Writings of James Madison,* 9 vols., 1900–1910; earlier collections are H. D. Gilpin (ed.), *The Papers of James Madison,* 3 vols., 1840, and *Letters and Other Writings of James Madison,* 4 vols., 1865. At the University of Chicago a definitive edition of the Madison papers is in progress.

V. James Monroe (1758–1831; President 1817–1825)

PAPERS:

Chief repositories are the Library of Congress with 40 volumes and five boxes, New York Public Library with 1300 items, and the James Monroe Memorial Foundation (Fredericksburg, Virginia) with an extensive and varied collection. There are also materials at William and Mary College (111 pieces), the University of Virginia (160 pieces), the New York Historical Society (50 items), the Pierpont Morgan Library (30 items), University of Pennsylvania Library (30 items), the Virginia Historical Society (35 items), and the Virginia State Library.

PUBLISHED WRITINGS:

The most complete collection is S. M. Hamilton (ed.), *The Writings of James Monroe,* 7 vols., 1898–1903. Supplementary are those in the *Proceedings of the Massachusetts Historical*

Society, Vol. XLII, 1909, and in the *Bulletin* of the New York Public Library, 1900, 1902. *The People, the Sovereigns*, S. L. Gouverneur (ed.), 1867, is Monroe's consideration, in post-presidential years, of American political institutions as compared to their classical democratic counterparts.

VI. John Quincy Adams (1767–1848; President, 1825–1829)

PAPERS:

Most are in the Massachusetts Historical Society (some 15,000 diary pages and 6300 letters). The Library of Congress has several boxes, and scattered items are in the New York Historical Society, the New York Public Library, and the Pierpont Morgan Library.

PUBLISHED WRITINGS:

Lyman Butterfield, *op. cit.* (*vide* John Adams), will include the writings of John Quincy Adams. Charles Francis Adams (ed.), *The Memoirs of John Quincy Adams*, 12 vols., 1874–1877, is the standard collection, to be supplemented by *Correspondence between John Quincy Adams and Several Citizens of Massachusetts*, 1829. *Eulogy on James Monroe*, 1831; *Eulogy on James Madison*, 1836; *Letters to His Constituents*, 1837; *Speech on Rights of Petition*, 1838; and *Jubilee of the Constitution*, 1839 —especially the last—are important. There are some occasional papers on Masonic or literary subjects unrelated to the presidency.

VII. Andrew Jackson (1767–1845; President, 1829–1837)

PAPERS:

The Library of Congress has a collection of over 340 volumes and boxes. The Tennessee State Library has 1500 items, and the Tennessee Historical Society and the Jackson home, The Hermitage, have additional materials. Other collections are the Chicago Historical Society (450 items), New York Public Library (250 items), Pierpont Morgan Library (72 pieces), Duke University Libraries (50 items), Missouri Historical Society (40 items), Princeton University Library, and New York Historical Society.

PUBLISHED WRITINGS:

The largest collection is J. S. Bassett (ed.), *Correspondence of Andrew Jackson*, 5 vols., 1926–1931. Some letters are in *American History Magazine*, 1899, 1900, 1904, and the *Bulletin* of the New York Public Library.

VIII. Martin Van Buren (1782–1862; President, 1837–1841)

PAPERS:

The Library of Congress has 73 volumes and containers, and the New York State Library has a collection of letters. There are smaller collections in the Columbia County Historical Society (Kinderhook, N.Y.), the Pierpont Morgan Library and the Massachusetts Historical Society.

PUBLISHED WRITINGS:

The *Autobiography*, John C. Fitzpatrick (ed.) (Annual Report of the American Historical Association, Vol. II), 1918, was written in 1854 but ends with the year 1832. The correspondence with George Bancroft is in the *Proceedings of the Massachusetts Historical Society*, Vol. XLII, 1909. His *Inquiry into the Origin and Course of Political Parties in the United States* was published posthumously, 1867.

IX. William Henry Harrison (1773–1841; President, March 4–April 4, 1841)

PAPERS:

Most are in the Library of Congress and Indiana State Library, but significant presidential writings are limited to his inaugural address.

PUBLISHED WRITINGS:

L. Esary (ed.), *Messages and Letters of William Henry Harrison*, 2 vols. (Indiana Historical Society Collection), 1922.

X. John Tyler (1790–1862; President, 1841–1845)

PAPERS:

There are eight volumes in the Library of Congress, and a smaller collection in the Duke University Libraries. The University of Virginia Library, William and Mary College, and the Pierpont Morgan Library have collections ranging up to 130 pieces.

PUBLISHED WRITINGS:

L. G. Tyler (ed.), *The Letters and Times of the Tylers*, 3 vols., 1884–1896. Volume II concerns John Tyler.

XI. James Knox Polk (1795–1849; President, 1845–1849)

PAPERS:

The Library of Congress has 188 volumes and boxes. The diary, running to 25 volumes of up to 200 pages each, is in the Chicago Historical Society. Scattered correspondence and papers are in the William L. Clements Library and the Tennessee Historical Society.

PUBLISHED WRITINGS:

The major source is M. M. Quaife (ed.), *The Diary of James K. Polk*, 4 vols., 1910. The Polk-Johnson letters are in the *Tennessee Historical Magazine*, 1915; and the Polk-Donelson letters in the same, 1917.

XII. Zachary Taylor (1784–1850; President, 1849–1850)

PAPERS:

One volume and two boxes are in the Library of Congress. The Kentucky Historical Society (Frankfort), the University of Kentucky Library and the University of North Carolina Library have assorted papers, mostly pre-presidential.

PUBLISHED WRITINGS:

These are limited to some military letters.

XIII. Millard Fillmore (1800–1874; President, 1850–1853)

PAPERS:

The Buffalo Historical Society has all but a few that are in the Library of Congress.

PUBLISHED WRITINGS:

F. H. Severance (ed.), *Millard Fillmore Papers*, 2 vols. (Buffalo Historical Society Publications, Vols. X, XI) 1907.

XIV. Franklin Pierce (1804–1869; President, 1853–1857)

PAPERS:

The largest collection, 1500 items, is in the New Hampshire Historical Society. The Library of Congress has a few additional pieces. But the papers relating to the period of the presidency have, for the most part, disappeared.

PUBLISHED WRITINGS:

"Some Pierce Papers" appeared in *American Historical Review*, Vol. X, 1904–1905.

XV. James Buchanan (1791–1868; President, 1857–1861)

PAPERS:

The Library of Congress has 11 volumes and boxes, and the

Historical Society of Pennsylvania has 25,000 items. There is a considerable collection in the Lancaster County (Penn.) Historical Society. Smaller collections are in Franklin and Marshall College Library, Dickinson College Library, the Rutherford B. Hayes Library (Fremont, Ohio), the Pierpont Morgan Library, the New York Historical Society, and the Princeton University Library.

PUBLISHED WRITINGS:

J. B. Moore (ed.), *The Works of James Buchanan*, 12 vols., 1908–1911, republished in 1960.

XVI. Abraham Lincoln (1809–1865; President, 1861–1865)

PAPERS:

The major collection, over 100 volumes and boxes, is in the Library of Congress. The Illinois Historical Society has over 6000 items, and the Brown University Library 1678 pieces. There are four boxes of material at the University of Chicago. Other collections are at the Chicago Historical Society (50 items), Indiana University Library (215 items), Boston University Libraries (60 items), Harvard College Library (40 items), New York Historical Society (4 volumes and boxes), New York Public Library (4 boxes), Minnesota Historical Society (11 items), Missouri Historical Society (41 items), the Pierpont Morgan Library (36 items), the Rutherford B. Hayes Library (Fremont, Ohio), and Lincoln Memorial University (Harrogate, Tennessee).

PUBLISHED WRITINGS:

Partial collections and selected writings are available in scores of editions. The inclusive collections are J. G. Nicolay and J. Hay (eds.), *Complete Works of Abraham Lincoln*, 12 vols., 1905; and R. P. Basler (ed.), *Collected Works of Abraham Lincoln*, 8 vols., 1953. The papers that had been sealed until 1947 are in David C. Mearns (ed.), *The Lincoln Papers*, 2 vols., 1948. G. A. Tracy (ed.), *Uncollected Letters*, 1917, and P. M. Angle (ed.), *New Letters*, 1930, has other material. A useful though not inclusive bibliography is Paul M. Angle, *A Shelf of Lincoln Books*, 1946.

Lincoln's writings on the presidency relate primarily to his conduct of the office during time of a war of insurrection and with the extraordinary powers forced upon the office by exceptional events.

XVII. Andrew Johnson (1808–1875; President, 1865–1869)
PAPERS:
The Library of Congress has 275 volumes and boxes. The Rutherford B. Hayes Library has 158 items, and the Duke University Libraries have 42 items.

PUBLISHED WRITINGS:
The only collection is F. Moore (ed.), *Speeches of Andrew Johnson*, 1865, but *Proceedings in the Trial of Andrew Johnson* (U. S. Government document), 1868, contains all speeches related to the congressional charges and other materials.

XVIII. Ulysses S. Grant (1822–1885; President, 1869–1877)
PAPERS:
The Library of Congress has over 100 volumes and boxes. The Henry E. Huntington Library has 345 items, and the Rutherford B. Hayes Library 255 items. Smaller collections are at the Chicago Historical Society (125 pieces), Illinois State Historical Library (200 pieces), Chicago Public Library (10 pieces), Illinois Historical Society (27 letters), the New York Historical Society (35 items), and the Pierpont Morgan Library (11 pieces).

PUBLISHED WRITINGS:
For the presidential years, writings are limited to J. G. Cramer (ed.), *Letters of Ulysses S. Grant to His Father and His Youngest Sister*, 1912, and J. G. Wilson (ed.), *General Grant's Letters to a Friend, 1861–1880*, 1897.

XIX. Rutherford B. Hayes (1822–1893; President, 1877–1881)
PAPERS:
Some 300 volumes and 75,000 items are in the Rutherford B. Hayes Library in Fremont, Ohio, Hayes's home. Western Reserve University Library has 8 boxes, and the Library of Congress has 5 boxes.

PUBLISHED WRITINGS:
C. R. Williams (ed.), *Diary and Letters of Rutherford B. Hayes*, 5 vols., 1922–1926, is fairly inclusive. His "Notes of Four Cabinet Meetings" is in *American Historical Review*, XXI (1932).

XX. James A. Garfield (1831–1881; President, March 4–Sept. 19, 1881)

PAPERS:

There are 343 volumes and boxes, most pre-presidential, in the Library of Congress. The Ohio Historical Society has one box, and the Rutherford B. Hayes Library has 30 items.

PUBLISHED WRITINGS:

The standard collection is B. A. Hinsdale (ed.), *The Works of Jas. Abram Garfield*, 2 vols., 1882–1883, but there is much additional material in T. C. Smith, *The Life and Letters of James A. Garfield*, 2 vols., 1925. Supplementary is M. L. Hinsdale (ed.), *Garfield-Hinsdale Letters*, 1949.

XXI. Chester A. Arthur (1830–1886; President, 1881–1885)

PAPERS:

The Library of Congress has five boxes; the New York Historical Society eight volumes of letters and a box of other papers. The Rutherford B. Hayes Library has 16 items.

PUBLISHED WRITINGS:

There are none.

XXII. Grover Cleveland (1837–1908; President, 1885–1889 and 1893–1897)

PAPERS:

The major collections are at the Library of Congress with 407 volumes and 109 boxes and the Detroit Public Library with 1250 items largely relating to the second administration. The Buffalo Historical Society has 75 items, New York Historical Society 30 items, and Pierpont Morgan Library 14 pieces. Princeton University Library also has a varied collection.

PUBLISHED WRITINGS:

Presidential Problems, 1904, treats the presidency in relation to specific problems in his administrations. Collections are George F. Parker (ed.), *Writings and Speeches of Grover Cleveland*, 1892, and Allan Nevins (ed.), *Letters of Grover Cleveland*, 1933.

XXIII. Benjamin Harrison (1833–1901; President, 1889–1893)
PAPERS:
The Library of Congress has 290 volumes and 193 boxes. Indiana State Library has a box of papers, and the Rutherford B. Hayes Library 42 items.

PUBLISHED WRITINGS:
This Country of Ours, 1897, is a comprehensive survey of political institutions in the United States. *Views of an Ex-President*, 1901, is a collection of post-presidential speeches. The *Correspondence of Benjamin Harrison and James G. Blaine*, 1940, is the only collection of letters.

XXIV. William McKinley (1843–1901; President, 1897–1901)
PAPERS:
There is a collection of 417 volumes and boxes in the Library of Congress, and other sizable collections are at the Western Reserve Historical Society and the Western Reserve University Library (2 volumes of letters). A few papers are at the Rutherford B. Hayes Library.

PUBLISHED WRITINGS:
None have appeared.

XXV. Theodore Roosevelt (1858–1919; President, 1901–1909)
PAPERS:
The Library of Congress has well over 1000 volumes and boxes. There is another large collection at the Harvard College Library. The Pierpont Morgan Library has the manuscript of his autobiography and some letters. William L. Clements Library has 290 items, the University of Southern California Library 60 items, Bowdoin College Library 15 items, Duke University Libraries 43 pieces, and Yale University Library assorted letters.

PUBLISHED WRITINGS:
The standard collection is H. Hagedorn (ed.), *The Works of Theodore Roosevelt*, 20 vols., 1920. The standard correspondence is E. E. Morison, J. M. Blum, and J. J. Buckley (eds.), *The Letters of Theodore Roosevelt*, 8 vols., 1951. The *Autobiography* was published in 1913. Supplementary are J. B. Bishop (ed.), *Theodore Roosevelt and His Time Shown in*

His Own Letters, 2 vols., 1920; *Presidential Addresses*, 8 vols., 1910; *Selections from the Correspondence of Theodore Roosevelt and Henry Cabot Lodge*, 2 vols., 1925; *Letters from Theodore Roosevelt to Anna Roosevelt Cowles, 1870–1918*, 1924; and *Theodore Roosevelt's Letters to His Children*, 1919.

Roosevelt's extensive comments on the presidency constitute a vigorous exposition of the activist theory.

XXVI. William Howard Taft (1857–1930; President, 1909–1913)

PAPERS:

There are 1300 boxes at the Library of Congress. Other collections are at the Yale University Library, Princeton University Library, Western Reserve University Library, and the Ohio Historical Society.

PUBLISHED WRITINGS: .

The Presidency, 1916, and *Our Chief Magistrate and His Powers*, 1916, are substantially the same work. The first title is a collection of lectures delivered at the University of Virginia in January, 1915, and the second the same lectures in somewhat expanded form delivered at Columbia University. Additional material is in *Presidential Addresses and State Papers*, 1910; *Popular Government*, 1913; *The Anti-Trust Act and the Supreme Court*, 1914; and *Ethics in Service*, 1915.

XXVII. Woodrow Wilson (1856–1924; President, 1913–1921)

PAPERS:

The Library of Congress has 1325 boxes. Yale University Library has the Wilson-House correspondence. Harvard College Library has the letters to Walter Hines Page. There are major materials at Princeton University Library and 1150 items at Columbia University Library. The University of Virginia Library has 248 pieces, the Historical Society of Wisconsin 30 items, the Maryland Historical Society 12 items, and the Woodrow Wilson Foundation has some materials.

PUBLISHED WRITINGS:

The standard collections are R. S. Baker and W. E. Dodd (eds.), *The Public Papers of Woodrow Wilson*, 6 vols., 1925–1927; and R. S. Baker, *Woodrow Wilson: Life and Letters*, 5 vols., 1927–1935. Other collections are *Selected Literary and Political Papers and Addresses*, 3 vols., 1925–1927; A. R. Leonard (ed.), *War Addresses of Woodrow Wilson*,

1918; R. S. Baker, *Woodrow Wilson and World Settlement,* 3 vols., 1922; and A. B. Tourtellot (ed.), *Woodrow Wilson: Selections for Today,* 1946. A definitive collection is now in progress, edited by Arthur S. Link.

Wilson wrote much more extensively about the presidency, as a political scientist and historian, before he held the office. His parliamentary concept of the office underwent considerable change as his experience in the presidency grew. His *The President of the United States,* though published in 1916, was written four years before his election.

XXVIII. Warren G. Harding (1865–1923; President, 1921–1923)

PAPERS:

There are four boxes in the Library of Congress, two boxes in the Ohio Historical Society and an undisclosed amount in the Harding Memorial Association, Marion, Ohio.

PUBLISHED WRITINGS:

These are limited to an unimportant collection, *Speeches and Addresses of Warren G. Harding . . . Delivered during the Course of His Tour from Washington, D.C., to Alaska . . . June 20 to August 2, 1923,* published as a memorial in 1923.

XXIX. Calvin Coolidge (1872–1933; President, 1923–1929)

PAPERS:

The Library of Congress has 347 boxes, and the Forbes Library, Northampton, Massachusetts, 79 volumes and boxes. Smaller collections are at Amherst College Library, the State Library of Massachusetts, and Tulane University Library.

PUBLISHED WRITINGS:

There are two collections of speeches of presidential years, *The Price of Freedom,* 1924, and *Foundations of the Republic,* 1926. More revealing is the *Autobiography of Calvin Coolidge,* 1931. There is a series of over 300 slender news syndicate columns, of some 200 words each, by Coolidge, written from April 1930 to April 1931, some of which touch upon the presidency, and there are also occasional popular magazine pieces.

XXX. Herbert Hoover (1874–   ; President, 1929–1933)

PAPERS:

The chief repository is the Hoover Institution on War, Revolution, and Peace at Stanford University. There are small collections at the University of Southern California, Yale University Library, Harvard College Library, and Princeton University Library.

PUBLISHED WRITINGS:

Standard collection for the presidential years is W. S. Myers (ed.), *State Papers of Herbert Hoover*, 3 vols., 1934. The last two volumes of *Memoirs*, 3 vols., 1951–1952, cover the presidency. Post-presidential materials are in *Addresses on the American Road*, 8 vols., 1933–1960; and *The Challenge to Liberty*, 1934. Recollection of Hoover's World War I career are *The Ordeal of Woodrow Wilson*, 1958; and *An American Epic*, 3 vols., 1959–1961.

XXXI. Franklin D. Roosevelt (1882–1945; President, 1933–1945)

PAPERS:

There is a great and expanding collection in the Franklin D. Roosevelt Library at Hyde Park, New York. The Library of Congress had one volume and two boxes, and the Duke University Libraries have 26 items.

PUBLISHED WRITINGS:

Definitive for the presidential years is S. I. Rosenman (ed.), *The Public Papers and Addresses of Franklin D. Roosevelt*, 13 vols., 1938–1950. Some correspondence is in Elliott Roosevelt (ed.), *F.D.R.: His Personal Letters*, 1947–1950. *Looking Forward*, 1933, and *On Our Way*, 1934, are current topical reports. There has been a wide range of collections of selected writings.

XXXII. Harry S Truman (1884–   ; President, 1945–1953)

PAPERS:

The central collection is at the Truman Library, Independence, Missouri. There are a few papers in the Library of Congress.

PUBLISHED WRITINGS:

The *Memoirs* consist of *Year of Decisions*, 1955, and *Years of Trial and Hope*, 1956. *Mr. Citizen*, 1960, contains further comment. *Public Papers of the Presidents of the United States—Harry S Truman* will eventually consist of eight volumes of which the first two, for 1945 and 1946, have been published (1963).

XXXIII. Dwight D. Eisenhower (1890–   ; President, 1953–1961)
PAPERS:

The papers will be housed at the Eisenhower Museum in Abilene, Kansas.

PUBLISHED WRITINGS:

Inclusive for the presidential writings are *Public Papers of the Presidents of the United States—Dwight D. Eisenhower,* 8 vols., 1960–1961. The memoirs of the presidential years are in process (1963).

XXXIV. John F. Kennedy (1917–1963; President, 1961–1963)
PAPERS:

The papers of Kennedy, as well as others relating to his administration, will be housed in a memorial library at Harvard University.

PUBLISHED WRITINGS:

Writings for the first presidential year are in *Public Papers of the Presidents of the United States—John F. Kennedy, 1961,* published in 1962. Selections appeared in John W. Gardner (ed.), *To Turn the Tide,* 1962, also covering the first presidential year. There is a brief but significant foreword by Kennedy to Theodore C. Sorenson, *Decision-Making in the White House,* 1963.

INDEX

INDEX BY AUTHOR

This index consists of all references to Presidents as authors. For general references to Presidents and for references to other persons, see the index by subject.

Adams, John, 4–5, 10
  on administration, 78–79
    Cabinet, 78
    plural executive, 79
    seat of government, 78
  on appointments and removals, 138–40
    letters of recommendation, 139
    party politics and, 376–77
    provisional appointments, 139
    reasons for dismissal, 139–40
    signature as act of appointment, 139
  on burdens and privileges, 348
  on Commander in Chief, 315–16
  on Congress, 192–93
    Senate and executive business, 193
  on foreign relations, 288–89
  on judiciary, 408
  on limitations of presidency, 408
  on national leadership, 15, 32–34
    electors chosen by people, 34
    Government Printer, 33–34
    independence of presidency, 32
  on party politics, 376–77, 408
Adams, John Quincy, 1, 5–6, 10
  on administration, access to President, 146–47
  on appointments and removals, 145–48
    law limiting tenure, 145–46
    power of removal, 147–48
  on burdens and privileges, 349–50
    social relations, 350
  on Commander in Chief, insubordination, 319
  on Congress, 200–1
  diary of, 6
  on foreign relations
    direct negotiations by President, 290
    recognition, 278
  on limitations of presidency, 410–11

  on national leadership, 34–35
    presidential succession and, 38, 379–80
  on party politics, 378–80
  poetry of, 6
Arthur, Chester A., viii
  on administration, 108–9
    illness of President, 108–9
  on appointments and removals, 165–66
  on burdens and privileges, 357
  on Commander in Chief, court-martial findings, 421
  on Congress, appropriation bills, 238–39
  on foreign relations, congresses of peace, 295
  on limitations of presidency, 421

Buchanan, James, viii, 7
  on administration, 417
    fugitive slave laws, 100
  on appointments and removals, 158
  on burdens and privileges, 352
  on Commander in Chief, prompt action by President, 326–27
  on Congress, 222–24
    censure of President, 224
    "riders" on appropriations bills, 223
    time to consider bills, 222–23
    veto power, 223
  on foreign relations, 292–94
    military expeditions from U.S., 292–93
    President and resort to force, 293–94
  on limitations of presidency, 417–19
    secession and, 7, 42, 417–18
  on national leadership
    in dangerous emergencies, 42
    impeachment, 41

Cleveland, Grover, 2, 11
  on administration, 110–11
  on appointments and removals,
    166–72
    civil service, 403
    office-seeking, 166
    suspension and removal, 166–72
  on burdens and privileges, 357–60
  on Congress, 239–40
    independence of executive and
      legislative, 111
    state of the Union message,
      239, 240
  on foreign relations, 295
  on limitations of presidency, 421
  on national leadership, 20, 26, 44–
    49
    presidential oath, 44–45
  on party politics, 385
    dignity of presidency, 45
    local politics, 385
    popular participation, 47
  on reform, 403
Coolidge, Calvin, viii, 10
  on administration, 120–21
    economy, 407
    influence of President, 121
    presidency as place of last re-
      sort, 120–21
    unofficial advisers, 121
  on appointments and removals,
    60–61, 177
  autobiography, 11
  on burdens and privileges, 366–
    67
  on Congress, 60–61
  on foreign relations, 299
  on limitations of presidency, 406,
    426–27
  on national leadership, 59–61
    unconstitutional laws, 61
    weight of words of President,
      60
  on party politics, 388–89
    nomination of successor, 388–89
  on reform, 406

Eisenhower, Dwight D.:
  on administration, 130–33
    advisors, 131, 132
    confidential information, 131
    delegation of duties, 430
    endless responsibilities, 372–73,
      374
    execution of laws, 133
    President's office, 130
    staff organization, 132
    stewardship of President, 130
  on burdens and privileges, 372–73
  on Commander in Chief, 342–45
    authority of Congress for spe-
      cific actions, 344
    enforcement of laws, 132–33
    surprise attack, 342
  on Congress, 257–62
    administration of appropria-
      tions, 258
    Congress controlled by opposite
      party, 259, 260, 261–62
    furnishing of information, 257–
      58, 259–60, 262
    veto power, 260–61
  on foreign relations, 302–7
    Bricker amendment, 303, 306–
      7
    deficient management, 303–4
    good will tours, 302
    Knowland amendment, 304
    Tariff Commission, 305–6
  on judiciary, 271
  on limitations of presidency, 430
  on national leadership, 68–71
    inconsequential detail, 70
    visitors, 71
  on party politics, 68–69, 391–93
    local elections, 391–92
  on press conferences, 69–70

Fillmore, Millard:
  on appointments and removals,
    157–58
    recess appointments, 157–58
  on Commander in Chief,
    enforcement of laws, 323–26
  on limitations of presidency, 416
  on national leadership, 40
  on party politics, 383–84

Garfield, James A.:
  on appointments and removals,
    356–57, 403
  on burdens and privileges, 356–57
  on Congress, 186, 238
  on reform, 403

Grant, Ulysses S., viii
  on administration:
    President and States, 105–7
    seat of government, 229–31
  on appointments and removals, 164, 169, 420
  on burdens and privileges, 354–55
  on Congress, 228–31
    charges of corruption, 228
    extra sessions, 228
    filibustering, 228
    furnishing of information, 229–31
    partial veto, 228
  on foreign relations, 228
  on limitations of presidency, 420

Harding, Warren G., 3–4
  on burdens and privileges, 365–66
  on foreign relations, 3
Harrison, Benjamin, 11–12
  on administration, 111–14
    Cabinet, 112
    execution of laws, 112, 113
    plural executive, 50, 111
    power to pardon, 113
    President's living quarters, 114
    violence in States, 113
  on appointments and removals, 173–75
    advice of Congressmen of President's party, 173–74
    burden of appointive power, 174–75
    removal power, 173
  on burdens and privileges, 360
  on Commander in Chief, 335–36
    command in person, 335
    execution of laws, 336
  on Congress, 240–42
    assumption of powers not granted, 50
    impeachment, 242
    "riders," 241
    State of the Union message, 240
    veto power, 240–42
  on foreign relations:
    appropriations for treaties, 296
    responsibility of President, 295–96
  on judiciary, political questions, 270

  on national leadership, 49–50
    presidential oath, 49
Harrison, William Henry, 2
  on administration:
    supervision of territories, 95
    Treasury, 213, 413
  on appointments and removals, 152–53
  on Congress, 211–13
    President not part of legislative power, 211–12
    President not source of proposed legislation, 213
    revenue bills, 213
    veto power, 37–38, 185, 212–13
  on judiciary, declaring laws unconstitutional, 212
  on limitations of presidency, 413–14
  on national leadership, 3, 23, 37–38
Hayes, Rutherford B.:
  on administration, 107–8
  on appointments and removals, 164–65
    civil service, 401–3
    supervision of officers, 400–1
  on burdens and privileges, 355–56
  on Commander in Chief:
    contested elections, 420
    enforcement of law, 334–35
  on Congress, 232–38
    appropriations bills, 232–34
    "riders" on appropriations bills, 234–38
    veto power, 234–35, 238
  diaries of, 12–13
  on foreign relations, termination of treaties, 294–95
  on limitations of presidency, 420
  on national leadership, 22, 44
    honesty of Presidents, 15, 44
  on party politics, 384
  on reform, 400–3
Hoover, Herbert:
  on administration, 121–23
    Cabinet, 251
    growth of power of President, 122–23
    plural executive, 123
    Prohibition laws, 122
    signing papers, 369
    Tariff Commission, 121–22

on appointments and removals,
178–79
influence of senators, 178
removal of officers, 178–79
on burdens and privileges, 368–69
fishing, 368, 427
on Congress, 250–51
devil - and - deep - blue - sea
trap, 250
veto power, 250
on foreign relations, 299–300
breaches of trust, 299
peace, 299–300
on national leadership, 61–63
President as link in chain of
destiny, 62
on judiciary, appointments, 178
on limitations of presidency, 427–
28
on party politics, 389
on press, 61
on Wilson as President, viii

Jackson, Andrew, 6–7
on administration, 84–95
Bank of the U.S. and federal
deposits, 87–95
power of Secretaries, 90–95
on appointments and removals,
148–52
friends in office, 148
power of Senate, 149–50
reasons for appointment, 149
removal from office, 149, 150–
52
on burdens and privileges, 350
on Congress, 201–10
denunciations by Senate, 203–
8
Senate's refusal to confirm, 203
submission of information, 97,
202, 208–9
veto power, 201–2
on foreign relations, 210
recognition, 291
on judiciary, 268–69
on limitation of presidency, 411–
12
on national leadership, 19, 22
nullification, 35–36, 84–87
President represents people, 35,
36

on party politics, 380–83
on reform, 398
Jefferson, Thomas, 5
on administration, 79–81
Cabinet, 79
plural executive, 79–81
on appointments and removals,
140–42
appointments of relatives, 140
information on recommendations, 140–41, 142
on burdens and privileges, 348–49
on Congress, furnishing of information, 140–41, 142
on foreign relations, 280, 289
on judiciary, 265–68
commands of courts, 266–67
constitutionality of laws, 265–
66, 267–68
on limitations of presidency, 409–
10
term of office, x
Johnson, Andrew, viii, 2
on administration, 102–5
Cabinet, 104–5
frugality in expenditures, 102
military rule of South, 103–4
separation of powers, 102
on appointments and removals,
159–64
removal power, 104, 159–64
vacancy from removal, 162–63
on burdens of presidency, 354
on Congress, 225–28
impeachment, 225–27
unconstitutional laws, 43
veto power, 225
on national leadership, 43–44

Kennedy, John F.:
on administration, 133–34
advisors, 263
judicial function in administration, 133–34
regulatory agencies, 133
on burdens and privileges, 373–74
on Commander in Chief, 344
on Congress, 262–63
on foreign relations, 307–8
on limitations of presidency, 374,
430

on national leadership, 72
irreproachable standards, 72
on party politics, 393–94

Lincoln, Abraham, 1, 7–9
on administration, 100–2
after Civil War, 101
Cabinet, 101
if beaten in election, 42, 101–2
on appointments and removals, 158
on burdens and privileges, 353–54
on Commander in Chief, 327–34
constitutional rights of individuals, 329–32
emancipation, 328–30, 332–33
extent of powers, 312, 328
privateers, 327–28
on Congress, 224
on limitations of presidency, 419–20
on national leadership, 42–43
violation of Constitution, x, 19, 311, 312, 327
poetry of, 8
on slavery, 9, 328–30, 332–33, 395, 398–400

McKinley, William, 2
on burdens and privileges, 360
on Congress, 242
on national leadership, 50
Madison, James, vii–viii, 5
on administration, 81–83
Cabinet, 81–82
custody of money, 83
regulation of commerce, 82–83
on appointments and removals, 142–44
claim of Senate to removal power, 143
law limiting tenure, 142
recess appointments, 143–44
spoils of victory, 142–43
on Commander in Chief, 316–19
President on field of battle, 316–19
undeclared war, 319
on Congress, 193–97
expiring Congresses, 194
recess appointments, 195–97
time to consider bills, 194–95
on foreign relations, 290

recess appointments, 143–44, 195–97
on judiciary, 268, 410
on limitations of presidency, 410
on party politics, 377
Monroe, James, 3, 5
on administration, 83–84
disbursement of money, 83–84
plural executive, 84
on appointments and removals, 144–45
on Congress, impeachment, 198–200
on foreign relations, appointments, 145
on limitations of presidency, 410
on party politics, 377–78
ex-Presidents, 378

Pierce, Franklin:
on administration, 98–100
territories, 99–100, 416–17
on Congress, veto power, 221–22
on foreign relations, Cuban invasion, 98–99
on limitations of presidency, 416–17
on national leadership, 41
Polk, James K., viii, 7
on appointments and removals, 155–57
office-seekers, 157
petty local feeling, 155–56
President's power, 156
on burdens and privileges, 351–52
on Commander in Chief, 321–32
naming of generals, 310, 322–23
on Congress, 216–21
veto power, 216–21
diary of, 6, 12–13
on judiciary, stopping prosecutions, 415–16
on limitations of presidency, 415–16
on national leadership, 39
President represents whole people, 19

Roosevelt, Franklin Delano, 2–3, 10
on administration, 123–27
delegation of power, 127

ineffective management, 124–25

messages to President, 125

NIRA, 123–24

power of spending money, 126

on appointments and removals, 179–80

on burdens of presidency, 369–70

on Commander in Chief, 339–41

on Congress, 251–55
emergency powers, 251–52
expenditures, 253
item veto, 254–55
"riders," 254–55
State of the Union message, 253–54, 270
tariffs, 255

on foreign relations:
foreign trade, 300
keeping out of war, 65
neutrality, 300
war debts, 428–29

on judiciary, 270–71
disability of judges, 429

on limitations of presidency, 428–29
libel, 429

on national leadership, 63–65
labor disputes, 63–64

on party politics, 63, 389–90

Roosevelt, Theodore:
on administration, 114–18
incredible amount of work, 117
presidential succession, 52, 114, 360

on appointments and removals, 175–76
influence of senators, 175, 176

on burdens and privileges, 360–62, 386, 424–25

on Congress, 117, 188, 243–44, 253
recommendation of legislation, 243
Senate as obstructionist, 243–44

on foreign relations:
executive agreement, 277–78
importance of Secretary of State, 297
Panama Canal, 296–97

on limitations of presidency, 421–25
title of "President," 423, 424

on national leadership, 21–22, 51–57
criticism of President, 56
fair play, 51
national support of President, 57
political expediency, 116
President vs. King, 53, 422
religion, 51
"stewardship theory," 20, 55–56, 118

on party politics, 385–87
nomination of successor, 385–86
re-election, 52–53, 361, 385

on reform, 403–5
in South, 404

Taft, William Howard, 11–12
on administration, 118–20
legislative powers conferred by Congress, 118
pardon, 119–20
President and permanent governmental structure, 119

on appointment and removals, 176–77, 249
civil service rules, 177
issuance of commissions, 118
patronage as club, 176
political under-secretaries, 177
removal of officers, 176–77

on burdens and privileges, 362–63

on Commander in Chief, 336–38
civil government, 337
enforcement of laws, 337, 338
involving nation in war, 336

on Congress, 244–50
furnishing of information, 249–50
"riders" on appropriations bills, 248
State of the Union message, 248–49
veto power, 245–48

on foreign relations, 297–98
recognition, 297–98
treaties, 119, 297

on limitations of presidency, 425–26

on national leadership, 57–59, 426
presidential domination, 58–59

on party politics, 387

Taylor, Zachary:
  on appointments and removals, 352
  on burdens and privileges, 352
  on Congress, veto power, 221
Truman, Harry S., viii
  on administration, 127–30
    advisors, 128–29, 130
    Cabinet, 128
    career officials, 129
    delegation of authority, 128
    executive reorganization, 127
    transfer of government to successor, 130
  on burdens and privileges, 370–71
  on Commander in Chief:
    crisis power, 342
    coordination of military, 341–42
    recall of MacArthur, 302, 310
  on Congress, 256–57
    budget, 256
    furnishing information, 256–57
    veto power, 256, 257
  on foreign relations, 300–2
    bi-partisanship, 302
    Secretary of State, 301
    UN representation, 300
  on limitations of presidency, 430
  on national leadership, 11, 65–68
    ceremonial and informal functions, 66, 67
    economic responsibilities, 68
    popularity, 67
    reliability of information, 68
    Vice-President, 66
  on party politics, 390
    nomination of successor, 390
    political campaigns, 371
  on writings of Presidents, 2, 66
Tyler, John:
  on administration, 96–98
    presidential succession, 38–39, 96, 98, 411
  on appointments and removals, 153–55
    information about applications, 154–55
    patronage, 153–54
  on Commander in Chief, enforcement of laws, 320–21
  on Congress, 213–16
    furnishing of information, 96–98, 154–55

revenue power, 215–16
    veto power, 213–16
  on limitations of presidency, 414–15

Van Buren, Martin:
  on administration, 95
  on appointments and removals, 152, 351
    removal of officers, 152
  on burdens of presidency, 350–51
  on Commander in Chief, enforcement of laws, 320
  on Congress, 210–11
    veto power, 210–11
  on foreign relations, 291–92
    hostile action from neighboring nations, 291–92, 412
  on judiciary:
    private rights and treaties, 292
    unconstitutional laws, 269
  on limitations of presidency, 412
  on national leadership, 36–37
    presidential succession, 36

Washington, George, 1–2
  on administration, 77–78
    Cabinet, 77
    seat of government, 78
  on appointments and removals, 137–38
    best made by written messages, 138
  on burdens and privileges, 346–48
    social relations, 29–30, 346–47
  on Commander in Chief, field command, 314–15
  on Congress, 190–92
    furnishing of information, 280, 286–87
    time to consider bills, 192
  diaries of, 4
  Farewell Address, 1–2, 375
  on foreign relations, 283–88
    consultation with Senate, 190–91, 284, 285
    oral communications, 284
    reception of emissaries, 285
    special emissaries, 287–88
  on limitations of presidency, 408
  on national leadership, 29–32
  on party politics, 375
  poetry of, 4

Wilson, Woodrow, vii–viii, 1, 9–10
on administration, 120
on burdens and privileges, 363–65
President as "superior kind of slave," 59, 264
on Commander in Chief:
censorship, 338
control of railways, 338–39
on Congress, President as prime minister, 189
on education, 9
on foreign relations:
League of Nations, 10, 190
President's authority, 298
U.S. and world, 282, 283
on immigrants, 9–10
on limitations of presidency, 426
on national leadership, vii, xi, 59
on party politics, 388

INDEX BY SUBJECT

Adams, John, 6, 31
    as Commander in Chief, 340
    foreign relations and, 282
    judiciary and, 270
    national leadership and, 25
    See also the index by author
Adams, John Quincy, 6, 275
    Monroe Doctrine and, 1
    national leadership and, 25
    See also the index by author
Administrative responsibilities of
    President, 73–77
    See also Cabinet; Laws—President
        as executor of; Seat of gov-
        ernment; the index by author
Alger, Russell A., 310
Amnesties, Taft on, 119
Appointive and removal powers, ix,
    135–37
    appointments to Supreme Court,
        265
    choice of military officers, xi, 310
    See also the index by author
Arthur, Chester A.:
    background of, 26, 396–97
    national leadership of, 25, 26, 27–
        28
    See also the index by author
Atchison, Senator, 156
Autobiographies of Presidents, viii,
    10–12

Bancroft, George, 357
    Johnson and, 2
    on Polk, 281
Bank of the United States, 18, 397
    Jackson on, 87–95
Barkley, Alben, 254
Blount, J. H., 275
Boxer Indemnity Protocol, 277
Bricker Amendment, 273–74, 276
    Eisenhower on, 303, 306–7
Buchanan, James:
    Civil War and, viii, 7, 42, 417–
        18
    Congress and, 186
        uses patronage to influence Con-
            gressmen, 41

as national leader, 16, 23
    See also the index by author
Bullock, Seth, 51
Burdens and privileges of presi-
    dency, 345–46
    See also the index by author
Burroughs, John, 51
Butler, Nicholas Murray, 51
Butterfield, Lyman, on the Adamses,
    10

Cabinet:
    J. Adams and, 78
        Secretary of the Treasury, 79
    Coolidge and, 121
    B. Harrison and, 112
    Hoover and, 251
    Jackson and:
        friends in Cabinet, 148
        furnishing of information, 97,
            202
        power of secretaries, 90–95
    Jefferson and, 79
    Johnson and, 104–5
    Lincoln and, 101
    Madison and, 81–82
    Taft and, political under-secre-
        taries, 177
    Truman and, 128, 301
    Tyler and, furnishing of informa-
        tion, 96–98
    Washington and, 77, 283–84
Civil Rights Commission, 430
Civil service:
    Cleveland and, 403
    Garfield and, 357, 403
    B. Harrison and, 174
    Hayes and, 396, 401–3
    Taft and, 177
Civil War:
    Buchanan and, viii, 7, 42, 417–18
    See also Lincoln, Abraham, in
        both indexes
Cleveland, Grover:
    Congress and, 20, 186–87
    foreign relations and, 275, 282
    national leadership and, 20, 26
    reform and, 397
    See also the index by author

Commerce, regulation of
  Jefferson and, 82–83
  Madison and, 82–83
Commander in Chief, President as,
    309–14
  active leadership of forces by
    President, xi, 309–10
  Constitution and, x–xi, 309
  See also Military and naval
    affairs; the index by author
Congress and presidency, ix, 181–90
  activist concept of, 187–90
  Constitution on, 181
  foreign relations and, 182–85, 190,
    272–76, 279–80
  legislation proposed by President,
    18, 76
  State of the Union message, 182,
    189
  Whig theory of congressional
    leadership, ix, 3, 20, 23, 181,
    185–88
  See also the index by author
Conkling, James, 9
Constitution:
  on functions of presidency, x–xi,
    16, 73, 181, 272, 309
  J. Q. Adams and, 34
  Coolidge and, 60
  Huges' comments on, ix
  unconstitutional laws:
    Coolidge and, 61
    Jackson and, 268–69
    Jefferson and, 265–66, 267–68
    Johnson and, 43
    Van Buren and, 269
  violation of:
    Lincoln and, x, 17, 18, 311,
      327, 328, 331–32
    Alfred E. Smith and, 19
  See also Presidential oath
Coolidge, Calvin:
  national leadership of, 23, 27, 28
  press conferences of, 14
  See also the index by author
Crawford, William Harris, 145–46
Cuba:
  Kennedy and, 344
  Pierce and, 98–99

Debates between presidential candi-
    dates, xi
Democracy, J. Q. Adams on, 35

Diaries of Presidents, 12–13
  J. Adams, 4
  J. Q. Adams, 6
  Hayes, 12–13
  Polk, 6, 12–13
Dickerson, Mahlon, 145
Dorr, Thomas, 321

Economic life, President and:
  Coolidge and, 407
  reform and, 397
  T. Roosevelt and, 21
  Truman and, 68
  See also Financial policy and
    President; Labor; Tariff
    Commission
Education, Wilson on, 9
Eisenhower, Dwight D.:
  Bricker amendment and, 273–74,
    276, 303, 306–7
  national leadership of, 23, 24
  press conferences of, 14
  See also the index by author
Elections, local:
  Eisenhower and, 391–92
  Hayes and, 108, 420
  Lincoln and, 419
  Pierce and, 416–17
  See also States—President and in-
    ternal affairs of
Elections of Presidents:
  campaigns for:
    debates, xi
    F. D. Roosevelt and, 65
    T. Roosevelt and, 422
    Truman and, 371
  electors in:
    J. Adams and, 34
    Fillmore and, 383
    Jackson and, 35, 380–82
  popular participation in nomina-
    tions, Cleveland and, 47
  re-election:
    J. Adams and, 348
    Eisenhower and, 392
    Lincoln and, 101–2
    Madison and, 377
    F. D. Roosevelt, 390
    T. Roosevelt and, 52–53, 361,
      385
  See also Term of presidency
Emancipation Proclamation, 312,
    328–30, 332–33, 399–400

Executive agreements, 182, 276–78
Ex-Presidents:
  J. Q. Adams and, 378–79
  Cleveland and, 421
  Fillmore and, 383–84
  Monroe and, 378
  Van Buren and, 412

Fairfax, Sally, 4
Fillmore, Millard:
  as national leader, 23, 27
  See also the index by author
Financial policy and President:
  J. Adams and, power of Secretary
    of Treasury, 79
  Arthur and, appropriations bills,
    238–39
  Buchanan and, "riders" on ap-
    propriations bills, 223
  Eisenhower and:
    administration of appropria-
      tions, 258
    item veto on appropriations
      bills, 261
  B. Harrison and:
    appropriations for treaties, 296
    "riders" on appropriations bills,
      241
  W. H. Harrison and:
    independence of Treasury, 413
    prime responsibility of Con-
      gress, 213
  Hayes and:
    appropriations bills, 232–34
    "riders" on appropriations bills,
      234–38
  Hoover and:
    principle of control of the purse,
      250
    tariffs, 121–22
  Jackson and, Bank of the U.S.
    and federal deposits, 18, 83,
    87–95, 397
  Johnson and, frugality in expend-
    itures, 102
  Monroe and, 83–84
  F. D. Roosevelt and:
    legislative function, 253
    power of spending money, 126
    "riders" on appropriations bills,
      254–55
    tariffs, 255

Taft and, "riders" on appropriations bills, 248
Truman and, budget, 256
Tyler and:
  revenue power, 215–16
  separation of sword and purse,
    414
Fishing, Hoover on, 368, 427
Fitch, Stephen, 146
Foreign relations, 272–83
  centralized in presidency, 272–74,
    280–83
  executive agreements, 182, 276–
    78
  House of Representatives and,
    279–80
  joint resolutions, 182–85, 190
  neutrality, 278–79
  private emissaries of President,
    274–75
  recognition, 278
  treaty-making power of Senate,
    182–85, 190, 279
  See also the index by author
French Directory, Jefferson on, 79–
  81
Fugitive slave laws:
  Buchanan and, 100
  Fillmore and, 324–25

Garfield, James A.:
  assassination of, 135, 396
  See also the index by author
Glass, Carter, 179
Government Printer, J. Adams and,
  33–34
Governors of States, President's re-
  lations with, 31
Grant, Ulysses S.:
  Congress and, 186
  judiciary and, 270
  national leadership and, 23
  See also the index by author
Greeley, Horace, 9

Habeas corpus suspended by Lin-
  coln, 329–31
Hamilton, Alexander, 31, 193
  Washington's Farewell Address
    and, 1
Hancock, John, Washington and, 31
Harding, Warren G.:
  Congress and, 187

national leadership and, 23
press conferences of, 14
See also the index by author
Harrison, Benjamin:
Congress and, 186–87
judiciary and, 270
national leadership and, 23, 24
See also the index by author
Harrison, William Henry:
Congress and, 23, 185
national leadership and, 3, 23
Webster and, 2
See also the index by author
Harvard University:
Jackson and, 410–11
T. Roosevelt and, 423
Hawaii, annexation of, 277
Hay, John, McKinley and, 2
Hayes, Rutherford B.:
appointments and removals and, 135
Congress and, 186
national leadership and, 22, 25
See also the index by author
Herndon, William, on Lincoln's writing, 8
Honesty of Presidents:
Hayes on, 15, 44
Hoover on, 63
Hoover, Herbert:
Depression and, 7, 428
Hoover Commission, 76–77, 276
national leadership and, 16, 23, 27
See also the index by author
Hopkins, Harry, 275, 276
House, Col. Edward M., 276
House of Representatives:
foreign affairs and, 182–85, 190, 279–80
See also Congress; Financial policy and President
Hughes, Charles Evans, on Constitution, ix

Illness of President, Arthur on, 108–9
Immigrants, Wilson on, 9–10
Impeachment of President:
Buchanan and, 41
B. Harrison and, 242
Johnson and, 136–37, 225–27
Monroe and, 198–200

Implied powers of presidency, xi.
See also National leadership of President
International trade:
Harding on, 3
F. D. Roosevelt on, 300

Jackson, Andrew:
Bancroft and, 2
as Commander in Chief, 335
Congress and, 22
financial policy and, 18, 83, 397
foreign relations and, 275
judiciary and, 22, 270
national leadership of, 18–19, 22
nullification and, 2, 18, 335
receives Harvard degree, 410–11
See also the index by author
Jay, John, 31
Jay's treaty, 279–80
Jefferson, Thomas:
appointments and removals and, 148, 153
as Commander in Chief, 319, 340
judiciary and, 23, 270
Louisiana Purchase of, 60, 281
national leadership of, 17, 18
regulation of commerce and, 82–83
See also the index by author
Johnson, Andrew:
impeachment of, 136–37
national leadership of, 27, 28
See also the index by author
Joint resolutions, 182–85
Journalism. *See* Press
Judiciary and the President, 22–23, 264–65
appointments to Supreme Court, 265
clashes between President and judiciary, 264–65
foreign relations and, 273
Supreme Court supports active Presidents, 264, 278
See also the index by author

Kansas, Pierce and, 99–100, 416–17
Kennedy, John F.:
press conferences of, 14
See also the index by author
Knowland amendment, Eisenhower on, 304

Labor, President's role in disputes:
Cleveland and, 26
B. Harrison and, 113
F. D. Roosevelt and, 63–64
T. Roosevelt and, 20, 22, 114–15
Laws:
President as executor of, 73, 74
Buchanan and, 100, 417–18
Cleveland and, 110–11
Eisenhower and, 131, 132–33
Fillmore and, 40, 323–26, 416
Grant and, 106–7
B. Harrison and, 112, 113, 336
Hayes and, 107, 334–35
Hoover and, 122
Jackson and, 85–86
Jefferson and, 79
Johnson and, 103–5
Lincoln and, x, 17, 18, 100
Pierce and, 99–100
Taft and, 118–19, 337, 338
Truman and, 129
Van Buren and, 269, 320
unconstitutional:
Coolidge and, 61
Jackson and, 268–69
Jefferson and, 265–66, 267–68
Johnson and, 43
Van Buren and, 269
See also Constitution; Nullification
Leadership. See National leadership of President
League of Nations, 184
Harding and, 3
Wilson and, 10, 190
Libel and the President, F. D. Roosevelt on, 429
Limitations of presidency, 406–7
See also the index by author
Lincoln, Abraham:
as Commander in Chief, 311–14
foreign relations and, 282
judiciary and, 270
national leadership and, x, 16–19
Wilson on, 364–65
Little Rock crisis, Eisenhower and, 132–33
Livingston, Edward, Nullification Proclamation and, 2
Long, John D., 310

Louisiana, 1872 electoral dispute in, 105
Louisiana Purchase, 60, 281

MacArthur, Gen. Douglas, recall of, 302, 310
McKinley, William:
as Commander in Chief, 310–11
Congress and, 187
foreign relations and, 282, 283
executive agreements, 277
national leadership and, 23
See also the index by author
Madison, James:
as Commander in Chief, xi, 309–10
foreign relations and, 275, 282, 283
national leadership and, 25
Washington's Farewell Address and, 1
Manifest destiny, 22
Marshall, John, 22
Mexican War, Polk and, xi, 310, 321–23
Military and naval affairs:
appointment of officers, xi
command by President in field, xi, 309–10
military rule of South, 103–4
See also Commander in Chief, President as
Money. See Financial policy and President
Monroe, James, 288
national leadership and, 25
See also the index by author
Monroe Doctrine, 1, 282
Morris, Gouverneur, 275
Muir, John, 51

National Industrial Recovery Act, F. D. Roosevelt and, 123–24
National leadership of President, vii, 16–29
doctrines of, ix–xi, 16–18, 56
states' rights, 23
"stewardship theory," 20–21, 55–56, 118, 130
Whig, ix, 20, 23, 181, 185–88
expansion of powers of President, 17–23, 24–25

Presidents who succeeded as Vice-Presidents, 27–28
weak Presidents, 25–27
See also the index by author
National Security Council:
Eisenhower and, 131
Kennedy and, 344
Negroes, 396
Grant and, 106
See also Slavery
Neutrality of United States, 278–79
F. D. Roosevelt on, 300
Nullification, Jackson and, 2, 18, 35–36, 84–87, 335

Oath of President, x
Cleveland and, 44–45
B. Harrison and, 49
Lincoln and, x
Van Buren and, 36
Olney, Richard, Cleveland and, 2
Ordeal of Woodrow Wilson (Hoover), viii

Panama Canal, 21
T. Roosevelt on 296–97
Pardons and reprieves, President's power to grant, x
B. Harrison and, 113
Taft and, 119–20
Party politics and presidency, 375–76
See also Elections of Presidents; Term of presidency; *the index by author*
People, the Sovereign, The (Monroe), 5
Pierce, Franklin:
Congress and, 3, 186
national leadership and, 23, 27
See also the index by author
"Planned Economy," Hoover on, 122
Polk, James K.:
appointments and removals and, 135
as Commander in Chief, xi, 310
election of, 183
foreign affairs and, 281–82
national leadership of, 17, 22
See also the index by author
Popularity of President, Truman on, 67

Presidential oath, x
Cleveland and, 44–45
B. Harrison and, 49
Lincoln and, x
Van Buren and, 36
Presidential succession:
J. Q. Adams and, 379–80
Coolidge and, 367
Eisenhower and, 393
national leadership of Vice-Presidents who became Presidents, 27–28
T. Roosevelt and, 52, 114, 360
Truman and, 430
Tyler and, 38–39, 96, 98, 411
Van Buren and, 36
See also Illness of President; Transfer of government to successor
President's quarters:
Coolidge and, 10
Eisenhower and, 130
B. Harrison and, 114
Press:
Eisenhower and, 14, 69–70
W. H. Harrison and, 413–14
Hoover and, 61, 427
press conferences, 13–14, 69–70
Truman and, 66, 67
Prohibition laws, 122

Randall, Alexander W., 354
Reconstruction acts, Johnson and, 43
Recognition of foreign governments, 278
Jackson and, 291
Taft and, 297–98
Re-election of President:
J. Adams and, 348
Eisenhower and, 392
Lincoln and, 101–2
Madison and, 377
F. D. Roosevelt and, 390
T. Roosevelt and, 52–53, 361, 385
Reform, Presidents and, 395–97
See also the index by author
Religion:
Jackson and, 411–12
Jefferson and, 409
T. Roosevelt and, 51
Removal power. *See* Appointive and removal powers

Reorganization of executive agencies:
Hoover Commission, 76–77, 276
Truman and, 127
Reprieves. *See* Pardons and reprieves
Roosevelt, Franklin Delano:
foreign relations and, 183
executive agreements, 278
special emissaries, 274–76
Hoover on, 122–23
judiciary and, 22–23
national leadership and, 16, 22–23
historic significance, 25
influence of Wilson, 24–25
press conferences of, 13–14
See also the index by author
Roosevelt, Theodore:
foreign relations and, 282
national leadership and, 17, 20–22, 28
reform and, 397
Taft and, 11–12
See also the index by author
Root, Elihu, 275, 297
Rosenman, Samuel I., on F. D. Roosevelt's writing, 2–3

Scott, Lieut. Gen. Winfield, 319, 322–23
Seat of government:
J. Adam and, 78
Washington's comment, 78
Eisenhower and, 70
Grant and, 229–31
Washington and, 78
See also Travel by Presidents
Secret Service:
Hoover and, 369
Taft and, 363
Senate. *See* Appointive and removal powers; Congress
Seward, William Henry:
Johnson's writing and, 2
Lincoln and, 8, 9, 101
Slavery:
Buchanan and, 100
Fillmore and, 323–26
Lincoln and, 9, 312, 328–30, 332–33, 395, 398–400
See also Negroes
Smith, Alfred E., on putting Constitution "on the shelf," 19

Smith, Robert, 5
Social relations of Presidents:
J. Q. Adams and, 350
Arthur and, 357
Coolidge and, 366
Eisenhower and, 372
Hoover and, 368
Kennedy and, 374
Washington and, 29–30, 346–47
Spanish-American War, 310–11
Taft and, 337
Sports:
Hoover and, 368, 369, 427
T. Roosevelt and, 361
Stanton, Edwin, removed by Johnson, 104, 136
State of the Union message:
Cleveland and, 239, 240
B. Harrison and, 240
F. D. Roosevelt and, 253–54, 270
Taft and, 248–49
Wilson and, 182, 198
States:
attempted treaties by, 273
Governors of, President's relationship to, 31
President and internal affairs of
Fillmore and, 323–26
Grant and, 105–7
B. Harrison and, 113, 336
Kennedy and, 430
Lincoln and, 419–20
Pierce and, 416–17
T. Roosevelt and, 115
Taft and, 337
Tyler and, 320–21, 414–15
See also Elections, local
states' rights, Pierce and, 23
Stevens, Thaddeus, on President as servant of people, 20
"Stewardship theory" of President:
Eisenhower and, 130
T. Roosevelt and, 20–21, 55–56, 118
Strikes and labor disputes, President's role in:
Cleveland and, 26
B. Harrison and, 113
F. D. Roosevelt and, 63–64
T. Roosevelt and, 20, 22, 114–15
Supreme Court. *See* Judiciary and the President

Taft, William Howard:
Congress and, 187
national leadership and, 23, 24, 27
T. Roosevelt and, 11–12
See also the index by author
Tariffs:
Eisenhower and, 305–6
Hoover and, 121–22
F. D. Roosevelt and, 255
Taylor, Myron, 275
Taylor, Zachary, 323
Congress and, 186
national leadership and, 23
See also the index by author
Tennessee Valley Authority, 21
Term of presidency:
length of:
Fillmore and, 383
B. Harrison and, 50
Hayes and, 384
Jefferson and, 409–10
Taft and, 387
number of terms:
J. Q. Adams and, 34–35, 378–79
Cleveland and, 385
Eisenhower and, 392–93
Fillmore and, 383
B. Harrison and, 50
Hayes and, 384
Jackson and, 382–83
Jefferson and, x, 409–10
T. Roosevelt and, 54–55, 386–87, 422–23, 425
Taft and, 387
See also Elections of Presidents
Territories, supervision by President of:
W. H. Harrison and, 95
Pierce and, 99–100, 416–17
Texas, annexation of, 19, 183, 281
Transfer of government to successor:
Lincoln and, 42, 101–2
Truman and, 130
Travel by Presidents:
Coolidge and, 59
Eisenhower and, 70
good will tours, 302
to peace conferences, 304–5
Kennedy and, 307
F. D. Roosevelt and, 64, 124, 341
T. Roosevelt and, 51

Washington and, 30
See also Seat of government
Treasury:
federal deposits and Jackson, 83, 87–95
President and Secretary of J. Adams and, 79
W. H. Harrison and, 413
Jackson and, 90–95, 152
Treaties:
Cleveland and, 295
Eisenhower and:
Bricker amendment, 273–74, 276, 303, 306–7
Knowland amendment, 304
executive agreements, 182, 276–78
Grant and, 228
B. Harrison and, 295–96
Hayes and, 294–95
Jefferson and, 289
Madison and, 290
as "supreme law of the land," 273
Taft and, 119, 297
treaty-making power of Senate, 182–85, 190, 279–80
Truman and, 301
Van Buren and, 292
Washington and, 284
Tripoli, war with, 319, 340
Truman, Harry S:
foreign relations and, 279, 282
national leadership and, 11, 17, 28
press conferences of, 14
See also the index by author
Tyler, John:
annexes Texas, 19, 183, 281
Congress and, 185–86
foreign relations and, 281
first uses joint resolution, 183
national leadership and, 19, 27
See also the index by author

United Nations, 184
Truman and, 300

Van Buren, Martin:
national leadership and, 25
See also the index by author
Veto power:
Buchanan and, 223

Eisenhower and, 260
  item veto, 261
Grant proposes partial veto, 228
B. Harrison and, 240–42
W. H. Harrison, 37–38, 185
Hayes and, 234, 238
  and "riders" on appropriations
    bills, 234–38
Hoover and, 250
Jackson and, 201–2
Johnson and, 225
Pierce and, 3, 221–22
Polk and, 216–21
F. D. Roosevelt and, 254–55
Taft and, 245–48
Taylor and, 221
Truman and, 256, 257
Tyler and, 213–16
Whigs propose abolition of, 186
Vice-Presidents:
  relationship of President to, 66
  See also Illness of President; Pres-
    idential succession
Vinson, Fred, 279

War. See Commander in Chief;
  Foreign relations
War of 1812, Madison and, xi, 309–
  10, 316–19
Washington, Booker T., 404
Washington, George:
  appointive and removal power
    and, 140, 148
  as architect of presidency, 17
  Congress and, 181
  foreign relations and, 274–75
    consultation with Senate, 279
  Jay's treaty, 279–80

neutrality, 278–79
  recognition, 278
  special emissaries, 275
  national leadership and, 17
  See also the index by author
Webster, Daniel, W. H. Harrison
  and, 2, 185
Wheeler, Benjamin Ide, 51
Whigs:
  doctrine of presidency of, ix, 3,
    20, 23, 181, 185–88
  propose abolition of veto power,
    186
White, Stewart, 51
Wilson, Edmund, on Lincoln, 8
Wilson, Woodrow:
  as Commander in Chief, 313–14
  Congress and, 181–82, 188–90
    League of Nations, 190
    State of the Union message,
      182, 189
  foreign relations and, special
    emissaries, 274–76
  national leadership and, vii, xi, 17
  as prototype of F. D. Roose-
    velt's leadership, 24–25
  party politics and, 376, 394
  reform and, 397
  See also the index by author
Writers, Presidents as, vii–viii, 1–15
  autobiographies, viii, 10–12
  diaries, 12–13
  J. Adams, 4
  J. Q. Adams, 6
  Hayes, 12–13
  Polk, 6, 12–13
  literary assistance, 1–3
  Truman on, 2, 68